The NEW
Where's That

An index of poems for children
Arranged by subject,
with a bibliography of
books of poetry

Helen Morris
Formerly Principal Lecturer in English
Homerton College, Cambridge

Basil Blackwell

First published 1985
Reprinted 1986, 1988

First published in paperback 1990

Typeset in 9 and 10pt Baskerville by
Katerprint Co. Ltd, Oxford.

Printed in Great Britain by
T.J. Press (Padstow) Ltd, Padstow, Cornwall

British Library Cataloguing in Publication Data

Morris, Helen, *1909–*
    The new where's that poem.
    1. English poetry — Indexes
    I. Title
    016.821′008′09282   Z2015.P7

    ISBN 0-631-17814 7Pbk

Contents

Foreword

The first *Where's that Poem?* was produced because I was so often asked by my students 'Do you remember that poem about . . . Samson, or sardines, or Satan, or scarecrows? And where can I find it?' I began to list poems and keep references, and in 1967 the lists became a book which I believe has proved useful to teachers of poetry. New anthologies appear in increasing numbers and the first edition had to be revised and enlarged in 1974. Now over half the anthologies in that edition are out of print, and there are many new books of poetry available. Many contain poetry by people of other lands, and by members of the ethnic minorities in Britain; when it clarified the meaning of the poem I have added the nationality, or sometimes the dates, of the writer.

The poems have been chosen, as before, with children of approximately seven to fifteen in mind. Children of five and six are usually best suited by nursery rhymes and jingles, of which there are several admirable collections (particularly, for the teacher, *Ox Dic* and *Ox NR* and for the children *Fab NV*, *Puf NR* and *Puf Y*, see page 221). However many of the poems listed can be read to and with even the youngest children in the infant school. The secondary teacher of upper forms will naturally use the widest selection of adult poetry to suit various classes. But how arbitrary and how artificial these divisions are! Much really great poetry can be appreciated (admittedly at very different levels) both by small children and by adults: parts of *The Ancient Mariner*, Robert Frost's *Stopping by Woods on a Snowy Evening* and some of Blake's songs illustrate this point.

To classify poems as suitable for a particular age group is to make two mistakes: it is to expect a poem to speak exclusively to children at a certain stage of development, and to assume that children of a certain age are all at the same stage of poetic education and appreciation. The appreciation of poetry has to be learnt, as much as the appreciation of music or art. Though some poems, like some tunes and paintings, may at first hearing or sight be obvious enough to appeal to the uneducated, yet it is the teacher's business to foster real enjoyment and appreciation of more difficult poetry by a sensitive choice of poems for each class – and if possible for each individual child. When poetry has been established as worth reading, because interesting or even exciting, then pupils should browse in as many different books as possible, find a poem that says something particularly relevant, and copy it into a personal anthology, or read it aloud to teacher or to the class. For those who dismiss poetry as 'soppy', there are many really tough ballads, traditional and modern, and it is often useful to sing them with a guitar and impromptu percussion.

Since grouping by age seems impracticable, the poems have been grouped under subject-headings, with ample cross-reference. Carols, ballads and nursery rhymes are not listed as such, but many appear under subject-headings.

Some songs by Shakespeare are here, and children often enjoy snatches from the plays; very few of the latter have been included, from lack of space, but every teacher must have favourite Shakespearean passages, a few lines to quote at the appropriate moment, which pupils may remember, and later grow to comprehend.

Reference is given to a wide variety of sources – pages 222–252 list 237 titles comprising 291 volumes. It is to be hoped that teachers will procure as many different books of poetry as possible, to give children the opportunity to browse widely. In the list of books, each is identified by a symbol, a group of letters giving some indication of its title if it is an anthology, or of its author if it is by a single poet. These symbols are explained on page 221 and arranged alphabetically on pages 222–252 for convenient reference and identification. I hope the few words of comment on each book may assist the teacher who is building up a collection of books of poetry, to decide whether any particular book is worth closer inspection.

This index is by no means comprehensive, but highly selective and personal. No poem is included that I would not, in particular circumstances, be happy to offer to a class. No one person can choose poems for another to teach with any *certainty* of success – though many poems are widely popular with a majority of teachers and pupils. No teacher should ever give a class a poem unless he himself, or she herself, receives genuine pleasure from it. Enjoyment and boredom are both infectious.

In laying great emphasis upon the *enjoyment* of poetry I find myself in good company. Sir Philip Sidney wrote that the end of poesie is 'to teach and delight'; Dr Johnson declared that 'the end of poetry is to instruct by pleasing'; Robert Frost said that a poem 'begins in delight and ends in wisdom'. I hope that this book may help teachers to find poems which will both delight and enlighten their classes.

Helen Morris
Cambridge 1984

The Grouping of Poems

The poems are grouped according to their subjects, but certain *kinds* of poems will be found under the following headings: COUNTING RHYMES, COUNTING-OUT RHYMES, CUMULATIVE RHYMES, FABLES, LIMERICKS, NONSENSE, ORIENTAL POEMS (BRIEF), PAINTING: POEMS FOR PICTURE-MAKING, PARODY, QUESTION AND ANSWER, RIDDLES, TALES (CAUTIONARY) and TALES (TALL).

Sometimes a group of poems on the same subject is divided into two sections, (L & D) for 'Lyric and Descriptive' and (N) for 'Narrative', so that the teacher looking for a few vivid lines will not find a long story, and vice versa.

The poems are arranged alphabetically, by title, under each heading. The articles 'A', 'An' and 'The' have been ignored. When only part of a poem is given, the title is preceded by either 'from' or 'part'.

Explanation of the letters and numbers following each poem will be found on page 221

The Index

1

The Donibristle Moss Moran Disaster (J. Ferguson)
On the 26th of August, our fatal moss gave way
Iron III 45; Oral 371

The Explosion (Philip Larkin)
On the day of the explosion
Bat S 50; Fab Mod 358; Mus 75; Rat 144

The Gresford Disaster (anon)
You've heard of the Gresford disaster
Deli 23; Fab P V 225; Nar 139; Peng B 347; Theme VI 46; Voi II 142

The Last Shift (Wilfrid Gibson)
You're surely early home, lad?
Your shift's not over?
Tel 75

The Miner's Dream or *Don't go down in the Mine* (J. R. Lincoln)
A miner was leaving his home for his work
Brit 66

Trimdon Grange Explosion 1882 (Thomas Armstrong)
Let's not think of tomorrow
Bal 154

ACCIDENTS: RAILWAY

The Tay Bridge Disaster (William McGonagall)
Beautiful Railway Bridge of the Silv'ry Tay!
Rail 20

The Wreck on the C. & O. (anon)
Along came the F. F. V., the fastest on the line
Rail 40

ACCIDENTS: ROAD

At Any Rate (James Michie)
'He's dead,' they shouted as he left his motorbike
DP IV 138; RR 77

Auto Wreck (Karl Shapiro)
Its quick soft silver bell beating, beating
Flock 131; Rat 54

Beat that Light! (Ogden Nash)
I think the horses must be laughing
Conf 77

The Catch (Kit Wright)
You'll receive a/Vauxhall Viva
Wri H 46

The Diverting History of John Gilpin (William Cowper)
John Gilpin was a citizen
Bat L 28; DP III 88; Nar 157; Plea 171; Puf V 66; Touch I 61

Driving Home (Dannie Abse)
Opposing car beams wash my face
RR 192; Tel 65

Fifteen (William Stafford)
South of the bridge on Seventeenth
Bite III 26; Imp 73; Voi II 89

Highway: Michigan (Theodore Roethke)
Here from the fields edge we survey
Mov 86

Interruption to a Journey (Norman MacCaig)
The hare we had run over
Drag 60; J Vo IV 6; Rat 214; Theme VII 59

The Lagos-Ibadan Road before Shagamu (John Pepper Clark)
A bus groaned uphill. Trapped
Att 55; Ima 127; RAP 58

Meditation on the A30 (John Betjeman)
A man on his own in a car
Conf 79; Mov 84; Rat 283

A Motorbike (Ted Hughes)
We had a motorbike all through the war
Gang 16; Hug SP 213

Solitude (T. Transtromer, trans Robert Bly)
Right here I was nearly killed one night in February
Rat 397

To the Station (J. B. Boothroyd)
'Bye/dear/no, I
Conf 78

Travelling through the Dark (William Stafford)
Travelling through the dark I found a deer
Flock 225; Theme I 48; Voi II 65

Unholy Marriage (David Holbrook)
Her mother bore her, father cared
DP III 14

ACROBATS

Acrobats (Ted Hughes)
Among ropes and dark heights
Theme VI 65

Blondin (Walter de la Mare)
With clinging dainty catlike tread
RR 27

The Equilibrist (James Kirkup)
The taut path of air
Tel 14

Tightrope Walker (Vernon Scannell)
High on the thrilling strand he dances
Theme VI 64

Trapezists (Louis MacNeice)
Intricacy of engines
Tel 15

ADAM AND EVE

Adam lay Ybounden (anon)
Adam lay ybounden
Puf V 255; RR 153

Ancient History (Siegfried Sassoon)
Adam, a brown old vulture in the rain
Sun 51

Eve (Ralph Hodgson)
Eve with her basket was
My V 46

Eve (Christina Rossetti)
While I sit at the door
FM 181

In the Cool of the Evening (James Stephens)
I thought I heard Him calling! Did you hear
By 245

ADVERTISING

Advertisement (anon)
The codfish lays a million eggs
Fab UV 203

Advertising (A. S. J. Tessimond)
You without gleam or glint or fire
DP III 34; RR 20

Attack on the Ad-Man (A. S. J. Tessimond)
This trumpeter of nothingness, employed
Conf 101

Breakfast with Gerard Manley Hopkins (Anthony Brode)
Serious over my cereals I broke one breakfast my fast
Ox LV 315

The Catch (Kit Wright)
You'll receive a/Vauxhall Viva
Wri H 46

Essential Beauty (Philip Larkin)
In frames as large as rooms that face all ways
Gold IV 36

The Great Merchant . . . Cries his Wares 1563 (Thomas Newberry)
What lack you, sir? What seek you? What will you buy?
Ox CV 14

Mad Ad (Roger McGough)
A Madison Avenue whizzkid
Deli 31

My Brother gets Letters (Michael Rosen)
My brother gets letters – not many, but some
Ros W 17

AEROPLANES

See also Air Travel, Flying, Gliding, Helicopters, Parachuting, Wars: 1914–18 and 1939–45 (Air)

Flight to Australia (Cecil Day Lewis)
Sing we the two lieutenants, Parer and McIntosh
TCN 40

The Landscape near an Aerodrome (Stephen Spender)
More beautiful and soft than any moth
Mov 101

AFTER-LIFE

After We've Gone (Fran Landesman)
Who will live in our house
Four 123; Strict 143

An Old Jamaican Woman thinks about the Hereafter (A. L. Hendriks)
What would I do forever in a big place, who
Bite II 73; NS 83; Rhy 88

Fare Well (Walter de la Mare)
When I lie where shades of
darkness
Ten 51

Guest (D. J. Enright)
Is the kitchen tap still dripping?
Mus 71

Is my Team Ploughing?
(A. E. Housman)
Is my team ploughing
EGV 280; Ima 136; Theme II 19

AGE

See Old Age, Old and Young

AGINCOURT

Agincourt (Michael Drayton)
Fair stood the wind for France
*By 18; EGV 24; Fab CV 237; Fab PR
28; Iron II 7; PW 52*

Before Agincourt (William
Shakespeare)
Now entertain conjecture of a time
Henry V IV Prol 1; Rat 312
O! that we now had here
Henry V IV iii 16; ND 162; PW 66
This day is called the feast of
Crispian
*Henry V IV iii 40; DP IV 53;
EGV 41; Ev 214; Fab PR 33;
Rain 108*

AIR RAIDS

See also Wars: Spanish Civil,
1914–18 (Air), 1939–45 (Air and
Blitz)

Suddenly the air cracks (Gabriel
Imomotime Okara)
Suddenly the air cracks
AP 51

AIR TRAVEL

Honeymoon Flight (Seamus
Heaney)
Below, the patchwork earth, dark
hems of hedge
Seven 109

London-Tokyo (James Kirkup)
There is no other creature like
Touch IV 53

747 (London-Chicago) (Robert
Conquest)
After the horrors of Heathrow
Mus 59; Ox Con 87

ALBATROSS

Albatross (Eleanor Farjeon)
Hush . . . hush . . . hush . . .
Far M 16

ALIENATION

Parting of Ways (Khadambi
Asal-ache, Kenya)
Leaving behind the family's hut
Ima 43

ALL-IN WRESTLING

All-in Wrestlers (James Kirkup)
These two great men battling like
lovers
DP 11 48; Tel 21; Voi III 144

ALPHABET RHYMES

A was an Apple-pie (anon)
A was an apple-pie
*Fab UV 135; Ox Dic 47; Ox NR 108;
Puf NR 12; Trad 12*

A was an Archer (anon)
A was an archer and shot an arrow
Trad 16

A was an Archer (anon)
A was an Archer who shot at a frog
*Fab NV 43; Fab UV 137; Merry
232; Ox CV 43; Ox Dic 48; Ox NR
106; Rhyme I 1; Word 104*

A was once an Apple-Pie (Edward
Lear)
A was once an apple-pie
Fab NV 186; Ox CV 192

An ABC (anon)
In Adam's fall/We sinned all
Fab PV 309

The ABC (Spike Milligan)
'Twas midnight in the schoolroom
CBC 60; Like 101

ABC of Names (anon)
A is Ann, with milk from the cow
Fab NV 96

Pigs, Platypuses, Polar Bears,
Ponies, Porcupines, Rabbits,
Rams, Rats, Rhinoceroses, Sheep,
Skunks, Sloths, Squirrels, Stags,
Tigers, Vicunas, Weasels, Wolves,
Wombats, Yaks, Zebras

Animals' Houses (James Reeves)
Of animals' houses
Puf Q 75; Ree C 19

Auguries of Innocence (William
Blake)
To see a World in a Grain of Sand
*Bat R 28; Choice 48; DP IV 13; EGV
114; Fab CV 63; Fab PR 62; FM 90;
Iron III 66; My V 180; Puf V 60; Rat
47; RR 174*
(part) *TD 14*
A Robin Redbreast in a cage
ND 58; WAS 124
A dog starved at his master's gate
Sun 26

Beasts and Birds (Adelaide
O'Keefe)
The dog will come when he is
called
Ox CV 125; Puf V 37

The Bells of Heaven (Ralph
Hodgson)
'Twould ring the bells of heaven
*Bric 41; By 223; DP I 11; Poems 29;
Rhyme IV 116; Touch I 84*

Better be Kind to them Now
(D. J. Enright)
A squirrel is digging up the bulbs
Enr R 19; Round 12; Sort 56

The Big Three (D. J. Enright)
Late one night I returned home
Enr R 23

Covering the Subject (Richard
Armour)
The turtle, clam and crab as well
CTV 39; Imp 33

Daydreams (Norma L. Davies,
Australia)
The possum lies curled
SAS 162

The Exile (Frances Bellerby)
The fool said to the animals
Sun 26

The Human Attitude (Geoffrey
Dearmer)
When I catch myself agape
Bite III 31

The Intruder (James Reeves)
Two-boots in the forest walks
Full 94; Once 60; Puf Q 86; Ree C 72

Paltry-looking People
(D. H. Lawrence)
And think how the nightingale,
who is so shy
Choice 201

Rattlesnake (trad American)
Rattlesnake, O rattlesnake
J Vo II 44

Solutions (Edmund Blunden)
The swallow flew like lightning
over the green
RR 184

from *Song of Myself* (Walt
Whitman)
I think I could turn and live with
animals
Ev 68; FM 162; PW 231; Theme I 52

Tit for Tat (Walter de la Mare)
Have you been catching of fish,
Tom Noddy?
de la M Col 104

from *The Vision of Piers Plowman*
(William Langland, trans
Ronald Tamplin)
Birds I saw in bushes made nests
Sun 29

ANIMALS: FANTASTIC

*See also Dou T, Nas C throughout,
Bel CV 91–131, Fab NV 74–90;
FV 8–34, Ree C 118–142, Wes N
21–8 & 59–70*
See also Dragons, Griffins,
Monsters, Pegasus, Sea
Monsters, Unicorns,
Werewolves

An Animal Alphabet (Edward
Lear)
The Absolutely Abstemious Ass
Rat 32

The Centaurs (James Stephens)
Playing upon a hill three centaurs
were
AM 81

The Common Cormorant (anon)
The common cormorant or shag
*CBC 143; Fab CV 88; Fab Non 292;
Fab NV 82; FV 20; If 27; In O I 29;
My V 158; Ox PC 66; Plea 47; R Eig
66; Touch I 118; Trad 109*

Crafty Creatures (Max Fatchen)
The flea is small
Fat W 32–5

The Derby Ram (trad)
As I was going to Derby, sir
*Come 194; Fab Non 45; Fab NV 70;
Fab PV 81; Gold I 43; Iron I 2; Merry
173; Non 176; Ox Dic 145; Ox NR
205; Rain 54; Rhyme II 16; R Ten 54;
Voi I 37*

The Doze (James Reeves)
Through Dangly Woods the
aimless Doze
AM 13; Ree C 124

Fur and Feathers (A. B. Paterson)
The Emus formed a football team
Pat A 26

The Hippocrump (James Reeves)
Along the valley of the Ump
*Hap 45; Ree C 121;
(part) Full 20*

Moon-Whales (Ted Hughes)
They plough through the
moon-stuff
Hug M 16

from *A Moral Alphabet* (Hilaire
Belloc)
The dreaful Dinotherium he
Ox LV 194

The Phoenix (Edward Lowbury)
Fire to the phoenix was
Low G 19

'Quack!' said the billy-goat
(Charles Causley)
'Quack!' said the billy-goat
Hap II 49

The Roc (Edward Lowbury)
Scattered like flotsam on the
erupting sea
Low G 18

Some Natural History (Don
Marquis)
the patagonian/penguin
Rhyme IV 94; Tam 79

Welsh Incident (Robert Graves)
But that was nothing to what
things came out
*EGV 345; ND 212; P Tale 185; RR
178; Str 27; Theme II 51; Voi II 11*

The Wendigo (Ogden Nash)
The Wendigo
AM 29; Fab NV 80; Nas C 36

ANTELOPES

Kob Antelope (Yoruba, trans Ulli
Beier)
A creature to pet and spoil
*Afr II 14; Oral 161; Rat 202; Rhy 79;
Tam 78*

APES AND MONKEYS

See also Baboons, Gorillas

At Woodward's Gardens (Robert
Frost)
A boy, presuming on his intellect
Gold IV 2

The Prayer of the Monkey
(Carmen Bernos de Gasztold)
Dear God/why have You made me
so ugly?
Full 28

The Ship of Rio (Walter de la
Mare)
There was a ship of Rio
*de la M Col 110; Fab NV 242; Plea
147; P Life III 19*

The Signifying Monkey (trad
American)
The Monkey and the Lion
J Vo II 39

Sonnet on a Monkey (Marjory
Fleming aged 8)
O lovely O most charming pug
Bat A 36; By 155; Voi I 97

APOLOGIES

Laurie and Dorrie (Kit Wright)
The first thing that you'll notice if
Wri H 66

This is Just to Say (William
Carlos Williams)
I have eaten/the plums
*Al I 31; BE 18; Bits p; Flock 232;
Hap II 54; Prel IV 24; Tap 13; Word
13*

APPLES

After Apple-Picking (Robert
Frost)
My long two-pointed ladder's
sticking through a tree
*Choice 279; Say 150; Ten 79; Touch
V 33*

The Apple-Raid (Vernon Scannell)
Darkness came early, though not yet cold
Poems 86; Sca A 23

Apples (Laurie Lee)
Behold the apples' rounded worlds
Drag 50; Round 43; Tap 11; Time 113

Apple Song (Brian Jones)
I am an apple
Jon S 23

The Apple's Song (Edwin Morgan)
Tap me with your finger
Strict 40

If I were an apple (anon)
If I were an apple
Come 45

APRIL

Abroad Thoughts (Edward Blishen)
Oh not to be in England
Ox LV 297

April Birthday (Ted Hughes)
When your birthday brings the world under your window
Duck 27; Hug S 20

April Day: Binsey (Michael Hamburger)
Now the year's let loose; it skips like a feckless child
Dawn 96; TD 119

April Rise (Laurie Lee)
If ever I saw blessing in the air
Drag 42; Ev 17; Flock 13; Liv 46; Mod 48; ND 8; Out 33; Time 111

Home Thoughts from Abroad (Robert Browning)
O to be in England
BB 31; By 173; EGV 222; Fab PR 162; ND 7; P Life IV 71; Puf V 177; Rain 82; Root 48; Scene 64

Two Tramps in Mud-Time (Robert Frost)
Out of the mud two strangers came
Gold III 46

ARITHMETIC

See Mathematics, Numbers

THE ARK

See Noah

ARMADA

The Armada (Lord Macaulay)
Attend all ye who list to hear our noble England's praise
Fab CV 243; Fab PR 122

The Armada (John Wilson 1588–1677)
Our little fleet in July first
Ox CV 24

A Ballade of the Armada (Austin Dobson)
King Philip had vaunted his claims
Fab PR 198

A Joyful New Ballad (Edward White 1588)
O noble *England* fall downe upon thy knee
Bal 10

Some Years of Late (anon)
Some years of late, in eighty-eight
DP II 57; Fab CV 241; Fab PV 185

ARMADILLOS

Armadillo (Mary Innes)
An armadillo as a pet
Inn B 'A'

ARTHUR, KING

from *Morte d'Arthur* (Thomas Malory)
Then the king got his spear in both hands
Flock 246

from *The Passing of Arthur* (Alfred, Lord Tennyson)
So all day along the noise of battle roll'd
P Tale 95
And answer made King Arthur, breathing hard
ND 203
Then quickly rose Sir Bedivere, and ran
Puf M 137

ASPENS

See Poplars

ASSES

See Donkeys

AT SEA

Huzza! Hodgson, we are Going (Lord Byron)
Huzza! Hodgson, we are going
Sea 114

She is far from the Land (Thomas Hood)
Cables entangling her
Sea 111

AUDEN, W.H.

Letter from Jericho (Charles Causley)
Auden, today in Jericho
Cau C 209

AUGUST

August Weather (Katharine Tynan)
Dead heat and windless air
Fan 54

Day-Dreams (William Canton)
Broad August burns in milky skies
BB 20

AUSTRALIA

See also Aus, Pat A, SAS throughout
See also Bandicoots, Bushrangers, Dingoes, Drovers, Shearers, Swagmen, Transportation, Wombats

Australian Windmill Song (Max Fatchen)
By the clay-red creek on the dry summer day
Fat S 60

The Banks of the Condamine (anon)
O hark the dogs are barking, love
Fab Bal 231; Fab PV 212; Peng B 306; SAS 94

A Bush Christening (A. B. 'Banjo' Paterson)
On the outer Barcoo where the churches are few
Aus 49; Bat S 40

A Bushman's Song (A. B. 'Banjo' Paterson)
I'm travelling down the Castlereagh and I'm a station hand
Iron II 26

The Dying Stockman (anon)
A strapping young stockman lay dying
Bk Bal 117; Imp 57

For Australia (Joseph Abela, Malta)
I came with a mind/ready to learn
Root 53

The Great South Land (Rex Ingamells)
Cook shortened sail
Aus 26

Hare in Summer (Flexmore Hudson)
In the little strip of shade
Aus 69

HMS Glory at Sydney (Charles Causley)
Now it seems an old forgotten fable
Cau C 20

The Stockman's Last Bed (anon)
Whether Stockman or not, for a moment give ear
J Vo III 95

The Tantanoola Tiger (Max Harris)
There in the bracken was the ominous spoor mark
Theme II 52

This Land (Ian Mudie)
Give me a harsh land to wring music from
Burn 30

West of Alice (W. E. Harney)
We are travelling west of Alice Springs and Sam is at the wheel
Mov 80; SAS 98

AUTOMOBILES

See Motor Cars

AUTUMN

See also Hug S 43–58
See also October

Autumn (John Clare)
I love the fitful gust that shakes
Come 85; Rhyme III 57; Say 51;
TD 129; Touch III 106

from *Autumn* (Vernon Scannell)
It is the football season once more
Flock 264; Mod 170

Autumn (T. E. Hulme)
A touch of cold in the autumn
night
ADT 103; Bric 54; Deli 123; Fab
Mod 87; My V 10; PW 297; TD 132;
Touch I 27

Autumn Nature Notes (Ted
Hughes)
The laburnum top is silent, quite
still
Hug S 45

Autumn Song (Ted Hughes)
There came a day that caught the
summer
Hug S 55; Sec 90; TD 133

A Day in Autumn (R. S. Thomas)
It will not always be like this
Choice 309; TD 22; Touch III 107

The Dry Season (Kwesi Brew)
The year is withering; the wind
Att 75; RAP 35

Late Autumn (Andrew Young)
The boy called to his team
Out 48; Ten 168

Leaves (Ted Hughes)
Who's killed the leaves?
Hug S 43; Ox Con 237; Third 66

Something told the Wild Geese
(Rachel Field)
Something told the wild geese
CTV 27; My V 114; Once 51; Out 60;
Rhyme IV 13; R Nine 91; TD 130;
WAS 109

Song (Richard Watson Dixon)
The feathers of the willow
BB 56; Bk S 53; Fab CV 55; Ox PC
134; This W 61

To Autumn (John Keats)
Season of mists and mellow
fruitfulness
Bat R 100; BB 52; By 140; Choice 66;
DP IV 33; EGV 163; Gold IV 45; Iron
IV 117; Like 174; Plea 128; Prel IV 4;
PW 211; Rat 434; Rhyme IV 10; RR
87; Say 132; Scene 112; Touch III 105;
(part) F Feet 142

When the Frost is on the Punkin
(James Whitcomb Riley)
When the frost is on the punkin
and the fodder's in the shock
EGV 269; Out 50

BABEL

The Tower of Babel (Nathaniel
Crouch)
After the dreadful Flood was past
Sun 58

BABIES

The Baby in the Train
(J. Ashby-Sterry)
Let babies travel – leave me lonely
P Rail 84

Baby running Barefoot
(D. H. Lawrence)
When the white feet of the baby
beat across the grass
Touch V 117

Baby Song (Thom Gunn)
From the private ease of Mother's
womb
Rat 56

Bringing up Babies (Roy Fuller)
If babies could only speak they'd
tell mother or nurse
Ful S 9; R Six 32; Sort 74; Young 36

By the Firelight (L. A. G. Strong)
If my baby have a squint
Dawn 25

Child Crying (Anthony Thwaite)
My daughter cries, and I
PC 18

Early Morning Feed (Peter
Redgrove)
The father darts out on the stairs
Sun 228; Touch V 192

Infant Joy (William Blake)
I have no name
By 112; PC 15; This W 52; Trad 125

Johnnie Crack and Flossie Snail
(Dylan Thomas)
Johnnie Crack and Flossie Snail
Bric 26; Dawn 18; J Vo I 21; R Eig 62

Morning Song (Sylvia Plath)
Love set you going like a fat gold
watch
Touch V 116

BABOONS

Silly Old Baboon (Spike Milligan)
There was a baboon
FV 13; Like 77; Third 103

BADGERS

The Badger (John Clare)
The badger grunting on his woodland track
FM 129; Rat 57; Voi I 102
(part) When Midnight comes a host of dogs and men
DP IV 10; Ev 70; PW 207; Theme I 61

The Badgers (Eden Phillpotts)
Brocks snuffle from the holt within
DP II 14

Coming Down through Somerset (Ted Hughes)
I flash-glimpsed in the headlights – the high moment
Hug SP 196

The Six Badgers (Robert Graves)
As I was a-hoeing, a-hoeing my lands
Fab NV 22; J Vo II 59; Merry 141; R Eig 41; Say 24

BAKING

Baking Day (Rosemary Joseph)
Thursday was baking day in our house
Gold III 25; Many 35; Mod 137; PT V 10; Theme IV 44

I Love The (Marc Matthews, Caribbean)
Friday night/smell
Stuf 60

BALAAM

Balaam (Charles Causley)
King Balak sat on his gaudy throne
Cau C 189; Cau N 15

BALACLAVA

The Charge of the Light Brigade (Alfred, Lord Tennyson)
Half a league, half a league
CTV 82; EGV 209; Fab PR 192; Like 43; ND 177; Rain 105

BALDNESS

On His Baldness (Po Chü-I, trans Arthur Waley)
At dawn I sighed to see my hairs fall
Pluc 81

BALLOONS

from *Les Ballons* (Oscar Wilde)
Against these turbid turquoise skies
Fan 78

Balloons (Sylvia Plath)
Since Christmas they have lived with us
Mod 93; Prel II 31; Touch IV 56
(part) Your small/Brother is making
BE 27

The Balloon Seller (Elizabeth Fleming)
I'd like to peddle toy balloons
PT V 19

The Orange Balloon (Stanley Cook)
Big balloons carrying people in baskets beneath them
Four 28

BANDICOOTS

Benjamin Bandicoot (A. B. Paterson, Australia)
If you walk in the bush at night
Pat A 29

BANDS

The Ceremonial Band (James Reeves)
The old king of Dorchester
Once 136; PT IV 11; Ree C 68

Old King Cole's Band (anon)
Old King Cole was a merry old soul
Merry 57; Puf NR 120; Puf SB 132; Rhyme II 2

Street Bands (Marian Lines)
The Old Retainers
Lin T 32

BANJOS

The Song of the Banjo (Rudyard Kipling)
You couldn't pack a Broadwood half a mile
Fab CV 37

BANNOCKBURN

Scots Wha Hae (Robert Burns)
Scots wha hae wi' Wallace bled
Fab CV 143

BAPTISM

from *The Vision of Piers Plowman* (Langland, trans Ronald Tamplin)
You can't dress
Sun 227

BARBERS

Alex at the Barber's (John Fuller)
He is having his hair cut. Towels are tucked
Hap 42; Out Sc 19; Theme VI 53

The Barber (C. J. Dennis)
I'd like to be a barber, and learn to shave and clip
Puf Y 40

Haircut (Allan Ahlberg)
I hate having may hair cut
Ahl P 89

BARLEY

John Barleycorn (?Robert Burns)
There were three kings into the east [west]
Bk Bal 182; DP I 85; Fab Bal 156; Fab CV 197; Iron II 70; Merry 326; ND 131; Rain 22; Rat 222; Touch I 59; Voi I 70

The Ripe and Bearded Barley (anon)
Come out, 'tis now September
DT 86; Fab PV 46

BATHING

After a Bath (Aileen Fisher)
After my bath
ADT 112; Here 13

from *Anthony Washes* (E. V. Rieu)
Anthony washed his face today
Croc 17

Down at the Swimming Pool (Gerda Mayer)
Down at the swimming pool
May K 15

East Anglian Bathe (John Betjeman)
Oh when the early morning at the seaside
Prel II 39; Ten 35; Theme V 36

First Dip (John Walsh)
Wave after wavelet goes
Bric 5; R Ten 42; Word 151; World 91

The Indignant Male (A. B. Ross)
The way they scrub
Hi 46

In the Bathroom (Roy Fuller)
What is that blood-stained thing
Ful P 18; Sec 37

Old Mrs Lazibones (Gerda Mayer)
Old Mrs Lazibones
May K 10

Pater's Bathe (Edward A. Parry)
You can take a tub with a rub and a scrub in a two-foot tank of tin
Ox CV 309

Sunday Dip (John Clare)
The morning road is thronged with merry boys
Out Sc 28

Why is it? (Max Fatchen)
Why is it/that
Fat S 54; Third 14

BATS

Bat (D. H. Lawrence)
At evening, sitting on this terrace
Gold III 30; PW 300; Theme I 46; Touch I 74

The Bat (Ogden Nash)
Myself, I rather like the bat
Nas C 123

The Bat (Ruth Pitter)
Lightless, unholy, eldritch thing
Dawn 67; FM 265

The Bat (Theodore Roethke)
By day the bat is cousin to the mouse

Bric 39; Fan 16; Flock 209; Gold I 57; J Vo III 13; My V 125; Poems 35; PT VI 30; R Eig III; Theme II 33; Zoo 68

Bats (Randall Jarrell)
A bat is born
Drum 32; Mod 152; R Eig 19; Rhy 107; Voi I 99

Bats (George MacBeth)
have no accidents. They loop
Drag 26

How to Address a Bat (trad)
Arymouse, Arymouse, fly over my head
Drum 33

Man and Bat (D. H. Lawrence)
When I went into my room, at mid-morning
Rat 262

Noah and the Bat (George MacBeth)
bat/flies next like a broken
Say 30

BATTLES

See Sea Battles
See Agincourt, Balaclava, Bannockburn, Blenheim, Culloden, El Alamein, Hohenlinden, Otterbourne, Waterloo

BEACHCOMBING

Beachcomber (George Mackay Brown)
Monday I found a boot
Ox Con 123; Sea 63

BEACHES

See also Seaside
The Beach (William Hart Smith)
The beach is a quarter of golden fruit
Al III 24; Aus 82; SAS 39; Say 16

Dover Beach (Matthew Arnold)
The sea is calm tonight
EGV 235; Flock 53; ND 45; Plea 212 (part) GV V 12

The Fringe of the Sea
(A. L. Hendriks)
We do not like to awaken
Blue 10

July Day Spectacular (Norman MacCaig)
I sit in the third row of
Seven 183

Stone Speech (Charles Tomlinson)
Crowding this beach
Sea 50

BEARS

See also Polar Bears
The Bear (Frederick Brown)
His sullen shaggy-rimmed eyes followed my every move
Deli 48; Full 30

The Bear (Robert Frost)
The bear puts both arms round the tree above her
Bat A 60

Black Bear (Ted Hughes)
The bear's black bulk
Hug U 18; Sec 70

Furry Bear (A. A. Milne)
If I were a bear
F. Feet 189; Mil NS 46; Zoo 28

The Grizzly Bear (Ted Hughes)
I see a bear
Hug U 30

The Lady and the Bear (Theodore Roethke)
A Lady came to a Bear by a Stream
My R 30; Voi I 95

My Mother saw a Dancing Bear (Charles Causley)
My Mother saw a dancing bear
Bric 40; Cau C 241; Cau F 94; Poems II 73; PT IV 20; Sort 65

Navaho Song of a Bear (trad)
There is danger where I move my feet
Drum 66

Song to a Dead Bear (Athabascan Indian)
We apologise for depriving you of your life
Dis 3

BECKET, ARCHBISHOP

from *Murder in the Cathedral*
(T. S. Eliot)

Bar the door. Bar the door.
Sun 186

BEDTIME

Bed in Summer (Robert Louis Stevenson)
In winter I get up at night
Ox CV 293; P Life I 67; Puf V 137; Rain 121; Rhyme II 22; Ste CG 2

Bedtime (Eleanor Farjeon)
Five minutes, five minutes more, please
ADT 113; Puf Y 46

The Dark (Roy Fuller)
I feared the darkness as a boy
Ful P 44; Poems 30

Hard Cheese (Justin St John)
The grownups are all safe
J Vo III 68; Liv 8; PT III 18

Hark! (Walter de la Mare)
My little Charles is afraid of the dark
de la M Col 250

I Like to Stay Up (Grace Nichols)
I like to stay up
Stuf 72

In the Daytime (Michael Rosen)
In the daytime I am Rob Roy and a tiger
Poems 30; Ros M 67

The Longest Journey in the World (Michael Rosen)
Last one into bed
Drum 116; Ros Y; Sec 24

BEECHES

The Beech (Andrew Young)
Strength leaves the hand I lay on this beech-bole
Touch II 177

BEES

Against Idleness and Mischief (Isaac Watts)
How doth the little busy bee
CTV 73; EGV 89; Merry 275; Ox CV 49

The Arrival of the Bee Box (Sylvia Plath)
I ordered this, this clean wood box
Fab Mod 411; Say 154

Bee (George Barker)
I buzz, I buzz, I buzz
Bar A 'B'; Zoo 23

Bees (related by Percy Mumilla, Australia, to Roland Robinson)
From the hollow trees in their native home
Imp 34

The Bees' Song (Walter de la Mare)
Thousandz of thornz there be
de la M Col 134; Rhyme II 30

from *The Georgics IV* (Virgil, trans C. Day Lewis)
Next I come to the manna, the heavenly gift of honey
Flock 113
(trans John Dryden)
Now, when thou hast decreed to seize their stores
Fab UV 42

from *Henry V* (William Shakespeare)
For so work the honey bees
Henry V I ii 187; F Feet 79

from *The Land* (V. Sackville-West)
. . . In February, if the days be clear
F Feet 77

The New City (T. H. Parker)
Thousands upon thousands
PT VI 13

Robbing the Tree Hive (Ernest G. Moll)
They leaned a good stout rail against the tree
SAS 48

Two Children (Small) (Spike Milligan)
Two children (small), one Four, one Five
Mil SV 23

BEETLES

Beetle (Hugh Finn)
A beetle caught my eye one day
Word 44

I knew a Black Beetle (Christopher Morley)

I knew a black beetle that lived
down a drain
Fab NV 172; Young 19

Rendez-vous with a Beetle
(E. V. Rieu)
Meet me in Usk
P Life III 73; Puf Q 114

BEING BLACK

*See also AP, Att, Blue, Ima, NS,
RAP, Root* throughout
See also Race Relations

Blackness (Glyne Walrond,
Caribbean)
Blackness is me
Stuf 10

Dream of a Black Mother
(Kalungano, trans Philippa
Rumsey)
Black mother
GV III 12

Dream Variation (Langston
Hughes)
To fling my arms wide
Al III 45; My R 16

The Little Black Boy (William
Blake)
My mother bore me in the
southern wild
*Gold I 37; Iron I 22; Merry 291;
Ox CV 85; Prel I 42; PW 153*

The Negro (Langston Hughes)
I am a Negro
Gold I 36

Nikki-Rosa (Nikki Giovanni)
childhood remembrances are
always a drag
Tam 96

Signature (Shabban Robert)
I am an honest African
Afr I 69

BELFAST

*Identification in Belfast: IRA
Bombing* (Robert Lowell)
The British Army now carries two
rifles
Ox Con 99

Kill the Children (James
Simmons)
On Hallowe'en in Ship Street
Strict 57

BELL-BIRDS

The Bell-Bird (William Sharp,
Australia)
The stillness of the Austral noon
FM 225

BELLS

Bells (James Reeves)
Hard as crystal
Ree C 41

from *The Bells* (Edgar Allen
Poe)
Hear the sledges with the bells
Ev 34; Puf V 29

The Bells of Aberdovey (Duncan
Young)
Gaily ringing o'er the dales
Puf SB 60

The Bells of London (trad)
Gay go up and gay go down *or*
Oranges and lemons
*Come 26; Fab NV 116; Merry 60; My
V 165; Ox Dic 337; Ox NR 68; Plea
15; Puf NR 46; Puf SB 96; Puf V 178;
Trad 45; Young 47*

The Bells of Shropshire (trad)
A nut and a kernel
Puf NR 47

Ring Out, Wild Bells (Alfred,
Lord Tennyson)
Ring out, wild bells, to the wild sky
*DP I 20; EGV 208; Fab PR 160; GV
IV 44; Rain 73*
(part) *Bk S 76*

School Bell (Eleanor Farjeon)
Nine o'clock bell!
ADT 34; TD 76

BELSHAZZAR

Vision of Belshazzar (Lord
Byron)
The King was on his throne
Puf M 177

BENBOW, ADMIRAL

The Death of Admiral Benbow
(anon)
Come all you sailors bold and draw
near
*Bal 40; Fab PV 239; Iron III 19;
Merry 260; Ox PC 44; Peng B 255;
Rhyme III 35*

BEOWULF

from *Beowulf's Fight with
Grendel's Mother* (Anglo-Saxon,
trans Michael Alexander)
After these words the
Weather-Geat Prince
Oral 408

BEREAVEMENT

The Identification (Roger
McGough)
So you think it's Stephen?
NV 102

The Voice (Thomas Hardy)
Woman much missed, how you call
to me, call to me
Choice 136

The Walk (Thomas Hardy)
You did not walk with me
Choice 143

BERMUDAS

Bermudas (Andrew Marvell)
Where the remote Bermudas ride
Rat 73

BETTING

Off to Epsom Races (anon)
When I was young and in my
prime about 24 years old
Brit 151

Prosser's Betting Shop (Dennis
O'Neill)
There's a shop around the corner
which I visit every day
Brit 150

BICYCLING

The Cyclist (Louis MacNeice)
Freewheeling down the escarpment
past the unpassing horse
Mov 66

Esmé on her Brother's Bicycle
(Russell Hoban)
One foot on, one foot pushing,
Esmé starting off beside
Deli 69; Drum 127; Hob P 14; Mov 67

The Poor Wake Up Quickly
(D. J. Enright)
Surprised at night/The trishaw
driver
Mov 74

BILBERRIES

Bilberries (John Fuller)
Late in the season: reason then not
to wait
Ful C 22

BIRCHES

Birches (Robert Frost)
When I see birches bend to left and
right
*Choice 281; DP IV 28; Gold II 33;
Hap 55; Rat 78; Tam 25; Ten 81;
Touch V 155; (part) Out Sc 80*

BIRDS

See also Bir, Hea P throughout
See also Albatrosses, Bell-Birds,
Birds of Paradise, Blackbirds,
Bullfinches, Chickens,
Cockatoos, Cocks, Corbies,
Cormorants, Cranes, Crows,
Cuckoos, Dodos, Ducks,
Eagles, Egrets, Geese,
Goldfinches, Hawks, Herons,
Hoopoes, Humming-Birds,
Jackdaws, Jays, Kestrels,
Kingfishers, Larks, Loons,
Magpies, Mallard, Missel
Thrushes, Nightingales,
Ostriches, Owls, Parrots,
Pelicans, Penguins, Pheasants,
Phoenixes, Pigeons, Quails,
Ravens, Robins, Rooks,
Seabirds, Seagulls, Siskins,
Skylarks (see Larks), Sparrows,
Starlings, Swallows, Swans,
Swifts, Terns, Thrushes,
Toucans, Turkeys, Turtle
Doves, Vultures, Wagtails,
Woodpeckers, Wood Swallows,
Wrens

Answer to a Child's Question
(Samuel Taylor Coleridge)
Do you ask what the birds say? The
sparrow, the dove
*Bat A 74; Ox CV 111; Ox PC 68; Plea
118; Puf V 53; Rain 15; This W 42;
WAS 69*

Autumn Birds (John Clare)
The wild duck startles like a
sudden thought
Ev 25

The bird (George MacBeth)
When I got home
DP II 11

Bird and Boy (Leslie Norris)
So you want to fly. Why?
Drum 36

A Bird came down the Walk
(Emily Dickinson)
A bird came down the walk
Bir 82; FM 188; Hap 35; Iron IV 71;
ND 72; Theme I 40; Touch III 117;
Voi I 75

The Birds (Margaret
Stanley-Wrench)
A lark's song is the whitening seed
of harvests
F Feet 61

The Caged Bird in Springtime
(James Kirkup)
What can it be?
Drag 30; Zoo 72

Cherry Tree (Ivy Eastwick)
The chaffinch flies fast
Come 94; WAS 85

Field-Glasses (Andrew Young)
Though buds still speak in hints
Ev 43; Prel IV 5; Rat 152; Ten 163;
Theme I 39

Forgive my Guilt (Robert
P. Tristam Coffin)
Not always sure what things called
sins may be
Bite III 28

How to Paint the Portrait of a Bird
(J. Prevert, trans Paul Dehn)
First paint a cage
Drum 152; Flock 96; Hap 23; My V
138; Round 62. Trans L. Ferlinghetti
Touch III 43

from *The Manciple's Tale*
(Geoffrey Chaucer)
Tak any brid, and put it in a cage
Bat A 60

Proud Songsters (Thomas Hardy)
The thrushes sing as the sun is
going
Flock 90

Saint Francis and the Birds
(Seamus Heaney)
When Francis preached love to the
birds
Flock 89; WAS 124

Stupidity Street (Ralph Hodgson)
I saw with open eyes
Deli 22; DP II 10

What Bird so Sings (John Lyly)
What bird so sings, yet so does
wail?
Ox PC 67

BIRDNESTING

In Glencullen (J. M. Synge)
Thrush, linnet, stare and wren
DP II 11

Rhyme (Christina Rossetti)
Hear what the mournful linnets say
F Feet 43; Rhyme II 29; WAS 57

The Robin and the Wren (anon)
The robin and the redbreast
Puf V 40

Wild Duck's Nest (John Clare)
As boys were playing in their
school's dislike
Prel II 19

BIRDS' NESTS

Birds' Nests (Millicent Seager)
'Caw', said the rook
Come 144

Birds' Nests (anon)
The skylark's nest among the grass
EV 92; Rhyme III 50

Birds' Nests (Edward Thomas)
The summer nests uncovered by
autumn wind
Gold II 34

The Nest (Andrew Young)
Four blue stones in this thrush's
nest
Bits b

The Pettichap's Nest (John Clare)
Well: in my many walks I've rarely
found
Iron I 56; Touch I 105

The Raven's Nest (John Clare)
Upon the collar of a huge old oak
Voi II 36

The Thrushes' Nest (John Clare)
Within a thick and spreading
hawthorn bush
Bir 23; By 153; Ev 90; F Feet 42;
Flock 12; My V 118; Ox PC 67; This
W 117

BIRDS OF PARADISE

Bird of Paradise (Robert Graves)
At sunset, only to his true love
BB 48

BIRTH

At Birth (Anthony Thwaite)
Come from a distant country
RR 190

Deliverance (Walter de la Mare)
Starch-capped, implacable,
through the slow dark night
RR 190

BIRTHDAYS

Between Birthdays (Ogden Nash)
My birthdays take so long to start
Nas C 19

Monday's Child (trad)
Monday's child is fair of face
Croc 108; CTV 79; Fab CV 93;
Fab NV 226; Ox Dic 309; Ox NR 1;
P Life I 17; Rain 10; TD 70; Trad 32;
Young 44

BISON

The Bison (Hilaire Belloc)
The Bison is vain and (I write it
with pain)
Bat A 14; Fab Non 252; FV 8

BLACKBIRDS

Blackbird (John Drinkwater)
He comes on chosen evenings
DP II 9; F feet 53; Theme VII 16

The Blackbird (Humbert Wolfe)
In the far corner
F Feet 51; Like 70; Puf Y 95; R Eig
94; Zoo 64; (part) *Bits y*

A Blackbird Singing
(R. S. Thomas)
It seems wrong that out of this bird
Choice 310

Dead and Gone (Anthony
Thwaite)
This blackbird stared at us six feet
away
Prel I 21

Dead Blackbird (Phoebe
Hesketh)
The blackbird used to come each
day
Hes S 21

I watched a Blackbird (Thomas
Hardy)
I watched a blackbird on a
budding sycamore
Bat A 46; Bir 42; WAS 56

Thirteen Ways of Looking at a
Blackbird (Wallace Stevens)
Among twenty snowy mountains
RAT 421; Voi III 155

BLACKSMITHS

The Blacksmiths (anon,
Anglo-Saxon)
Swarthy smoke-blackened smiths,
smudged with soot
In O I 16
Swart swarthy smiths besmattered
with smoke
Rat 82; Touch II 41

The Blacksmith's Song or
Twankydillo (anon)
Here's a health to the blacksmith,
the best of all fellows
Fab PV 208; Puf SB 143

Felix Randal (Gerard Manley
Hopkins)
Felix Randal the farrier, O he is
dead then? my duty all ended
Choice 114; Fab Mod 65; Plea 186;
PW 265; Voi III 171

The Forge (Seamus Heaney)
All I know is a door into the dark
Seven 110; Tel 76; Touch IV 98

The Village Blacksmith (Henry
Wadsworth Longfellow)
Under a spreading chestnut tree
CTV 77; EGV 177; Fab PR 131

BLENHEIM

The Battle of Blenheim (Robert
Southey)
It was a summer evening
By 143; Fab PR 74

BLINDNESS

The Astigmatic or *With Half an*
Eye (Philip Hobsbaum)

At seven the sun that lit my world
blew out
*Gold IV 31; Hap 92; Liv 10; Poems II
102*

The Blind Boy (James Kirkup)
Alone, in the unseeing crowd, he
walks with eyes
RR 194

The Blind Men and the Elephant
(John Godfrey Saxe)
It was six men of Indostan
*CBC 119; Come 202; CTV 46; DP I
21; Gold I 54; Once 22*

The Fog (W. H. Davies)
I saw the fog grow thick
*DP I 17; GV V 16; J Vo III 98; Out
70; P Life IV 28; Poems II 38; Rhy
104*

BOARS

from *Venus and Adonis* (William
Shakespeare)
'Thou hadst been gone', quoth she,
'sweet boy, ere this'
Venus and Adonis, line 613; FM 13

BOATS

See also Canal Boats, Canoes,
Coracles. Life Boats, Tugs
Made a Boat (Michael Rosen)
Made a boat
Ros W 31; Ros Y

from *Paper Boats* (Rabindranath
Tagore)
Day by day I float my paper boats
*Bite I 47; Flock 236; Out Sc 67;
R Eig 36*

Rowboats (Max Fatchen)
I like rowboats, little rowboats
Fat W 52

Sampan (Tao Lang Pee)
Waves lap lap/Fish fins clap clap
Al II 28

Where go the Boats? (Robert
Louis Stevenson)
Dark brown is the river
*CTV 71; Fab CV 99; Like 49; Ox
CV 294; P Life I 60; Ste CG 14;
WAS 71*

BODY SNATCHERS

The Doctor Outwitted (anon)
I'll tell you a trick that was played
t'other evening
Brit 24

Mary's Ghost (Thomas Hood)
'Twas in the middle of the night
Ev 176; My V 85

The Resurrectionists (anon, 1832)
Come listen awhile and a story I'll
tell
Bal 106

BONFIRES

See also Guy Fawkes Night

Autumn Fires (Robert Louis
Stevenson)
In the other gardens
P Life 257; Ste CG 72; Tap 32

Bonfire (Jean Kenward)
There's a great wild beast in my
garden
Third 72

For Bonfires (Edwin Morgan)
The leaves are gathered, the trees
are dying
Drag 79–83; Seven 248

Our Bonfire (Brian Lee)
Our bonfire still smoulders as we
start back for home
Lee L 14

from *The Burning of the Leaves*
(Laurence Binyon)
Now is the time for the burning of
the leaves
EGV 301

BOOKS

See also: Fab UV 229–233
Useful for Book-Plates (anon)
Who folds a leafe down
Fab UV 229

BOREDOM

Bored (John Kitching)
I'm ten and I'm bored
Third 22

Boredom (Eleanor Farjeon)
Oh dear! What shall I do?
Far M 68

Boredom (Gareth Owen)
Boredom/Is/Me/Gloomy as
Monday
Owe S 37

The Camel's Hump (Rudyard
Kipling)
The camel's hump is an ugly lump
Young 70

Nothing to do? (Shelley
Silverstein)
Nothing to do?
ADT 75; BBGG 15; CBC 16

Rain (Brian Lee)
The lights are all on, though it's
just past midday
Lee L 12; Poems 68; Sort 37

Right Now (Michael Rosen)
Right now/I'd like best of all not to
be here
Ros M 11

Some Days (Kit Wright)
I didn't find it interesting
Wri R 40

Sometimes (Lesley Miranda
Agard, child)
Sometimes
Stuf 14

Tired Tim (Walter de la Mare)
Poor tired Tim! It's sad for him
de la M Col 247

What shall I do? (Brian Lee)
The wind pulls the smoke from the
chimney-pots
Lee L 37; Sort 78

BORES

Hot Dog (Kit Wright)
My Dad can't stand my sister's
latest boyfriend
Wri H 11

BOUNCING BALLS

The Blue Ball (John Walsh)
With many a bump
World 12

Child's Bouncing Song (Tony
Conner)
Molly Vickers

*Imp 37; Prel I 31; Touch II 55; Voi I
23*

Song for a Ball-Game (Wilfred
Thorley)
Bounce ball! Bounce ball!
Come 64; Rhyme II 25; R Six 63

BOXING

Comeback (Vernon Scannell)
The wind is in a whipping mood
tonight
Nar 175

First Fight (Vernon Scannell)
Tonight, then, is the night
*Bite II 1; My V 72; Sca A 7; Theme V
15*

Last Fight (Vernon Scannell)
This is one you know that you can't
win
Sca A 32

The Loser (Charles Bukowski)
And the next I remembered I'm on
a table
Imp 75

Peerless Jim Driscoll (Vernon
Scannell)
I saw Jim Driscoll fight in
nineteen-ten
DP II 49

Who killed Davey Moore? (Bob
Dylan)
Who killed Davey Moore?
Imp 58

BOYS

A Boy's Head (Miroslav Holub)
In it there is a space-ship
*Flock 71; J Vo IV 79; Like 156; Liv
104; Touch III 138; Voi III 167*

The Explorers (Brian Lee)
At three o'clock yesterday, not long
before tea
Lee L 15

Legend (Judith Wright)
The blacksmith's boy went out
with a rifle
*BE 60; Flock 192; Poems 93; Rain 91;
Rat 233; Str 35; Sun 178; Tho 98*

from *The Naughty Boy* (John
Keats)
There was a naughty boy

Come 198; CTV 73; Deli 131; Fab CV
284; Fab NV 97; Like 79; Merry 204;
Mov 121; My V 107; ND 97; Once
107; Ox CV 148; P Life III 37; P Scot
41; Puf V 122; Trad 92

Nooligan (Roger McGough)
I'm a nooligan
McRo 25

from *Return Journey* (Dylan
Thomas)
O yes, yes I remember him well
DP II 7

Saturdays I put on my Boots
(Michael Rosen)
Saturdays I put on my boots and
go wading down the River Pinn
Poems II 22

The Tunnel (Brian Lee)
This is the way that I have to go
Lee L 10

BREAKFAST

The King's Breakfast
(A. A. Milne)
The King asked/The Queen and
*Fab NV 266; Mil VY 55; My R 56;
Ox CV 341; Pac 14*

The Meal (Karla Kuskin)
Timothy Tompkins had turnips
and tea
Pac 28

BROADCASTING

Here is the News (Michael
Rosen)
Here is the News
Ros W 76

BROTHERS

I share my bedroom (Michael
Rosen)
I share my bedroom with my
brother
Full 60; Ros M 67

The Quarrel (Eleanor Farjeon)
I quarrelled with my brother
Far M 40

BUFFALOES

Buffalo (Yoruba, trans Ulli
Beier)
The buffalo is the death
Rat 199; Rhy 80

Buffalo Dusk (Carl Sandburg)
The buffaloes are gone
BE 30

The Buffalo Skinners (anon)
Come all you jolly cowboys and
listen to my song
Fab PV 220; Peng B 336; Rat 88
'Twas in the town of Jacksboro in
the year of seventy-three
Gold IV 25

The Flower-fed Buffaloes (Vachell
Lindsay)
The flower-fed buffaloes of the
spring
*BE 30; In O I 23; Rat 158; Theme VII
62; This W 123; World 88*

BUGLES

from *The Princess* (Alfred, Lord
Tennyson)
The splendour falls on castle walls
*By 166; Choice 83; CTV 77; DP III
65; EGV 206; Fab CV 36; Ox PC
142; Plea 239; Prel IV 40; PW 217;
R Nine 68; This W 86; Touch II 46;
Voi I 120*

BULLDOZERS

*The Chant of the Awakening
Bulldozers* (Patricia Hubbell)
We are the bulldozers, bulldozers,
bulldozers
J Vo I 44; Theme VII 49

BULLFIGHTING

Bullfight (Miroslav Holub, trans
I. and J. Milner)
Someone runs about
Rat 90

Bullfight in the Sun (Dannie
Abse)
The public matador in his arrogant
yellow suit
Theme I 65

The Matador (Elizabeth Jennings)
He will come out with grace and music
Tel 13

Novillada (James Kirkup)
Madrid is on the Manzanares
Theme V 20

BULLFINCHES

The Bullfinch (Betty Hughes)
I saw upon a winter's day
F Feet 75; WAS 148

The Bullfinches (Thomas Hardy)
Brother Bulleys, let us sing
Bir 35

Bullfinches (Ted Hughes)
A mournful note, a crying note
Hug M 21

BULLFROGS

See Frogs

BULLS

The Bull (Ralph Hodgson)
See an old unhappy bull
Bat A 38

A Bull in a China Shop (anon)
You've heard of a frog in an opera hat
Voi I 44

The Bull Moses (Ted Hughes)
A hoist up and I could lean over
Bill 130; Hug SP 45; Touch V 179

The Magnificent Bull (Dinka Tribe, Africa)
My bull is white like the silver fish in the river
Dis 68; Stuf 50

BUREAUCRACY

In the Playground (Michael Rosen)
In the playground
Four 27

This Letter's to say (Raymond Wilson)
Dear Sir or Madam
Four 62

BUSES

The Bold Bad Bus (Wilma Horsburgh)
Pimpernel Petroleum is a bold, bad bus
Hor B 7

Bus Home (John Walsh)
The school bus now
World 17

A Bus Ride (U. I. Ukwu)
Two ample women, somewhat past their primes
Att 44

Bus to School (John Walsh)
Rounding a corner
Prel II 2; Rhyme IV 69; TD 74; Word 149; World 10

Conductress (J. K. Annand)
When I growe up and leave the schule
Scot 16

Jamaican Bus Ride (A. S. J. Tessimond)
The live fowl squatting on the grapefruit and bananas
Rhy 88

No One can Call Me (Phoebe Hesketh)
Here is my heaven – on the top of a bus
Hes S 28

On the Motor Bus (A. D. Godley)
What is this that roareth thus?
Fab Non 241; Ox LV 170

Standing at a Bus Stop (Caroline Freeman Sayer)
Standing at a bus stop
Here 48

Walking Song (William E. Hickson)
We waited for an omnibus
Ox CV 230

BUSHRANGERS

Cf. Highwaymen, USA: Pioneers of the West
[Bold] Jack Donahue (anon)
Attend ye valiant highwaymen and outlaws of disdain
Peng B 308

Come all you gallant bushrangers
that gallop on the plain
Gold I 52
In Dublin town I was brought up
Brit 134

A Bushranger (Kenneth Slessor)
Jackey Jackey gallops on a horse
like a swallow
SAS 152

The Bushrangers (Edward
Harrington)
Four horsemen rode out from the
heart of the range
SAS 80

The Death of Ben Hall (Will
Ogilvie)
Ben Hall was out on the Lachlan
side
Nar 97; Theme III 12

The Death of Ned Kelly (John
Manifold)
Ned Kelly fought the rich men in
country and in town
J Vo IV 32

The Ned Kelly Song (anon)
Ned Kelly was born in a
ramshackle hut
Imp 46

The Wild Colonial Boy (anon)
'Tis of a wild Colonial boy, Jack
Doolan was his name
*BHL 11; Bk Bal 100; Ev 132; Fab
Bal 229; Gold II 7; In O I 33; Nar 91;
Peng B 304; Theme III 11*

BUSINESS

*An Old-Fashioned American
Business Man* (Richard
Eberhart)
I asked no quarter and I gave none
RR 13

BUSTLE MAKERS

I was a Bustle-Maker once, Girls
(Patrick Barrington)
When I was a lad of twenty
Plea 274

BUSYNESS

Busy (trans from Mbundu)
I've got some dust in my eye
Afr I 15

A Busy Day (Michael Rosen)
Pop in/pop out
Drum 94; McRo 36

BUTTERFLIES

Adventure (Louis Untermeyer)
The moon said
Stuf 36

Blue-Butterfly Day (Robert
Frost)
It is blue-butterfly day here in
spring
Like 36

Butterfly (D. H. Lawrence)
Butterfly, the wind blows seaward
Tap 85

Butterfly (S. Thomas Ansell)
Down the air
F Feet 71

Flying Crooked (Robert Graves)
The butterfly, a cabbage white
*Choice 236; Fab Mod 233; Flock 208;
Rat 160; Tam 61; Young 24*

Sulphur Butterfly (Teresa
Hooley)
Out of its dark cocoon
Bk S 24

Was Worm (May Swenson)
Was worm/swaddled in white
Full 124; Voi I 10

CAGES

The Red Cockatoo (Po Chü-I,
trans, Arthur Waley)
Sent as a present from Annam
*ADT 32; Bric 44; Gold III 20; Hap
16; Iron II 45; Pluc 29; Touch III 39;
Voi III 149; Zoo 70*

CAIN AND ABEL

See also Adam

Cainsmorning (Dom Moraes)
Having eliminated his dear brother
By 308

CAMBRIDGE

*Inside of King's College Chapel,
Cambridge* (William
Wordsworth)

Tax not the royal saint with vain
expense
Bat R 46

King's College Chapel (Charles
Causley)
When to the music of Byrd or
Tallis
*Cau C 37; In O I 8; Isle 86; PT IV 12;
Time 19*

*Sunday Morning, King's
Cambridge* (John Betjeman)
File into yellow candelight fair
choristers of King's
Time 7

CAMELS

Camel (J. K. Annand)
The camel has a humpy back
Ring 94

Camel (William Jay Smith)
The camel is a long-legged
humpbacked beast
Puf Y 109

Camel (Mary Britton Miller)
O camel in the zoo
Full 32

Exile (Virna Sheard)
Ben-Arabie was the Camel
P Life III 76

The Plaint of the Camel (Charles
Edward Carryl)
Canary-birds feed on sugar and
seed
*CBC 147; Come 158; Fab NV 80; FV
16; If 41; Ox CV 305; P Life III 84;
Rhyme III 29*

CAMPING

Camping Pie (Julie Holder)
The wind roared up
Third 60

CANADA

The Alberta Homesteader (anon)
My name is Dan Gold, an old
bach'lor I am
Gold II 11

The Shooting of Dan McGrew
(Robert Service)
A bunch of the boys were
whooping it up in the Malamute
saloon
Bill 94; EGV 313; Nar 100; Rat 381

The Squad of One (Robert Stead)
Sergeant Blue of the Mounted
police was a so-so kind of guy
Nar 92

CANAL BOATS

The Barge Horse (Sean Jennett)
The brasses jangle and the hawsers
tighten
Bill 129

Legging the Tunnel (Gregory
Harrison)
I don't know whether I believe
Sec 20

CANNIBALISM

The Yarn of the 'Nancy Bell'
(W. S. Gilbert)
'Twas on the shores that round our
coast
*Bat L 38; Bill 31; CBC 115; DP II
34; EGV 258; Nar 116; Ox LV 148;
Peng B 322; Touch I 70*

CANOES

Canoe Story (Geoffrey
Summerfield)
We went in a long canoe, two of us
Theme V 30

CAREERS

The Fist Lord's Song
(W. S. Gilbert)
When I was a lad I served a term
Bat C 42

CARS

See Motor Cars, Motoring

CATERPILLARS

Caterpillar (Christina Rossetti)
Brown and furry
*Blow 11; Come 141; Croc 40; CTV 66;
Fan 32; F Feet 130; Like 30; Merry
92; My R 38; Ox CV 279; Puf Y 93*

The Tickling Rhyme (Ian
Serraillier)
'Who's that tickling my back?' said
the wall
*Bits p; Croc 41; Fab NV 57; Fan 18;
Hap II 79; Like 12; Once 124; P Life
III 87; Puf Q 174; R Six 9; Zoo 22*

CATS (L AND D)

See also Death of Cats, Kittens
Apartment Cats (Thom Gunn)
The Girls wake, stretch, and pad
up to the door
Gold II 6; R Ten 67; Seven 79

Auntie Agnes's Cat (Colin West)
My Auntie Agnes has a cat
Wes N 50

Can it be? (Stevie Smith)
Can it be, can it be
Hap 59

The Cat (Richard Church)
Hark! she is calling to her cat
Tap 28

The Cat (W. H. Davies)
Within that porch, across the way
*Cat 38; Fan 12; Gold I 17; GV III 24;
Merry 257; Ox PC 109; PT II 29; Tap
28*

Cat! (Eleanor Farjeon)
Cat!/Scat!
*Drum 60; Far M 33; Hap 65; Once
45; Ox PC 104; P Life III 82; PT II
26; Puf Q 38; R Eig 20*

Cat (Mick Gowar)
He hasn't got a name/the cat who
owns me
Gow S 12

The Cat (W. Adolphe Roberts)
Pleasures that I most enviously
sense
NS 52

Cat (Vernon Scannell)
My cat has got no name
Sca A 27

A Cat (Edward Thomas)
She had a name among the
children
*Gold I 16; Hap 57; Iron II 45; ND 83;
Ox PC 109; RR 183; Theme I 16*

Cat (J. R. R. Tolkien)
The fat cat on the mat
Tol T 48; Zoo 38

The Cat and the Moon
(W. B. Yeats)
The cat went here and there
*Cat 31; Fab CV 69; Flock 57; Iron II
54; J Vo II 28; Shad 104; This W 23;
Touch I 80*

Cat and the Weather (May
Swenson)
Cat takes a look at the weather
J Vo II 50

Cat-Goddesses (Robert Graves)
A perverse habit of cat-goddesses
Voi III 84

Cat in the Dark (John Agard)
Look at that
Stuf 44

Catnap (Max Fatchen)
My cat sleeps
Fat S 10

The Cat of Cats (William
Brighty Rands)
I am the cat of cats, I am
Duck 53; Ox CV 236

Cats (Phoebe Hesketh)
Cats are contradictions; tooth and
claw
Theme I 18; Touch III 127

*Cats no less Liquid than their
Shadows* (A. S. J. Tessimond)
Cats no less liquid than their
shadows
Cat 40; ND 81: Touch III 129

Cats of Kilkenny (anon)
There were two cats of Kilkenny
Croc 49; Ev 61

Cats Sleep Anywhere (Eleanor
Farjeon)
Cats sleep/Anywhere
*Al II 43; Cat 24; Croc 47; Fir 58; Like
26; P Life II 23; Puf Y 104; Rhyme I
33: Zoo 30*

Cosy Cat-Nap (James Kirkup)
Pussy-kitten, pussy-cat
BE 10

Diamond cut Diamond (Ewart Milne)
Two cats/One up a tree
Cat 36; Fab CV 76

Double Dutch (Walter de la Mare)
That crafty cat, a buff-black Siamese
Hap 50

Esther's Tomcat (Ted Hughes)
Daylong this tomcat lies stretched flat
Cat 20; Drag 33; Hug SP 41; Ox Con 235; Seven 147; Time 76; Touch IV 152

Farm Cat (Paul Hyland)
Silly to say that butter would not melt
Over 102

Fat Cat (Mary Rayner)
Siamese have cobalt eyes, their tails are thin and kinky
Sort 60

Five Eyes (Walter de la Mare)
In Hans' old mill his three black cats
Cat 23; de la M Col 100; DP I 2; Duck 40; Fab NV 28; Gold I 16; Like 90; Merry 108

Fourteen Ways of Touching the Peter (George MacBeth)
You can push/your thumb
Flock 59

French Persian Cats having a Ball (Edwin Morgan)
chat/shah shah/chat
J Vo III 15; Mod 207; World 119

'Good-night Mouser' (John Walsh)
'Good-night, Mouser'
Drum 48

The Happy Cat (Randall Jarrell)
The cat's asleep; I whisper *kitten*
Bat A 24

from *Lady Feeding the Cats* (Douglas Stewart)
Shuffling along in her broken shoes from the slums
Flock 61; (part) *PT V 20*

London Tom-Cat (Michael Hamburger)
Look at the gentle savage, monstrous gentleman
Lon 58

The Lost Cat (E. V. Rieu)
She took a last and simple meal, when there were none to see her steal
Puf Q 102

Milk for the Cat (Harold Munro)
When the tea is brought at five o'clock
BB 50; By 238; Cat 26; Come 138; Gold I 17; My V 130; Ox PC 109; Poems II 27; Theme I 8; This W 21; Touch I 81

Mort aux Chats (Peter Porter)
There will be no more cats
Ox Con 221

Mouser (James Kirkup)
The cat, black-masked, trots with level back
BE 11

The Mysterious Cat (Vachell Lindsay)
I saw a proud mysterious cat
Fab NV 174

On a Cat, Ageing (Sir Alexander Gray)
He blinks upon the hearth rug
Cat 92; F Feet 97; Gold II 5

On a Night of Snow (Elizabeth J. Coatsworth)
Cat, if you go outdoors you must walk in the snow
F Feet 187; P Life IV 17; PT II 27; Say 50; Shad 105; Young 30

On Mrs Reynolds's Cat (John Keats)
Cat! who hast pass'd thy grand climacteric
BB 38; Fab CV 75; F Feet 114; FM 133; Iron I 7

Pangur Bán (Gaelic, trans Robin Flower)
I and Pangur Bán my cat
Fab CV 70; Rat 333

from *Rejoice in the Lamb* (Christopher Smart)
For I will consider my cat Jeoffry
Cat 65; DT 48; Fab CV 72; FM 70; In O II 34; Ox PC 107; PW 145; Rat 301; Touch III 129; Voi I 88

The Tom Cat (Don Marquis)
At midnight in the alley
Drum 62; J Vo IV 46; P Life IV 16; PT III 26; Touch II 69

The Tortoiseshell Cat (Patrick Chalmers)
The tortoiseshell cat
Cat 82; P Life II 24; R Nine 8

CATS (N)

Cat meets Hedgehog (Christopher de Cruz)
Cat sees round prickly ball
Drum 56

from *The Everlasting Mercy* (John Masefield)
I told a tale to Jim's delight
Round 6

The Galloping Cat (Stevie Smith)
Oh I am a cat that likes to
Mus 18

Glasgow October 1972 (Edwin Morgan)
At the Old Ship Bank pub in Saltmarket
Poems II 26

The Matron-Cat's Song (Ruth Pitter)
So once again the trouble's o'er
By 281

Mother Tabbykins (Elizabeth Anna Hart)
Sitting at a window
Ox CV 268

Mrs McGinty (Michael Johnson)
Mrs McGinty
Prel I 33

The Rescue (Hal Summers)
The boy climbed up into the tree
Dawn 58; DP I 42; Gold I 18; Poems 88; Prel I 16; Tap 29

The Retired Cat (William Cowper)
A poet's cat, sedate and grave
Cat 53; FM 77

Sad Memories (C. S. Calverley)
They tell me I am beautiful; they praise my silken hair
FM 191

The Singing Cat (Stevie Smith)
It was a little captive cat
Cat 43; Dawn 21; Hap 69; PT IV 24; Say 38

Yellow Cat (Gregory Harrison)
'There he is', yells Father
Fir 60

CATS (ELIOT)

See also Eli OP throughout
The Ad-dressing of Cats
(T. S. Eliot)
You've read of several kinds of cat
FM 260

Growltiger's Last Stand
(T. S. Eliot)
Growltiger was a Bravo Cat, who lived upon a barge
DP I 3; Ev 74; Fab CV 182; Hap 19; Plea 271; Str 87; Touch I 114

Macavity: the Mystery Cat
(T. S. Eliot)
Macavity's a mystery cat: he's called the Hidden Paw
Bat C 24; By 264; Choice 225; CBC 64; GV V 22; Like 45; My V 132; ND 82; Once 110; Ox CV 346; Ox LV 216; Rain 49; Rat 255; Touch I 116

The Old Gumbie Cat (T. S. Eliot)
I have a Gumbie Cat in mind
Fab NV 168; FV 19

The Rum Tum Tugger
(T. S. Eliot)
The Rum Tum Tugger is a Curious Cat
Fab Non 282; F Feet 117; Hap II 34

Skimbleshanks the Railway Cat
(T. S. Eliot)
There's a whisper down the line at 11.49
DP II 21; Fab CV 285; Ox LV 218; P Rail 67; Rail 32; Touch II 53; Young 14

The Song of the Jellicles
(T. S. Eliot)
Jellicle Cats come out tonight
Cat 14; EGV 339; Fab CV 75; Fab Non 280; Fab NV 175; Ox CV 347; Ox PC 105; Plea 50

CATTLE

See also Bulls

Bags of Meat (Thomas Hardy)
'Here's a fine bag of meat'
FM 201; Iron IV 17; Rat 60; Touch V 181; Voi II 62

Birth of Rainbow (Ted Hughes)
This morning blue vast clarity of
March sky
Hug M 19; Hug SP 185

Cow (George Barker)
I am the Cow
Bar A 'C'

Cow (Alan Brownjohn)
You wouldn't think so solid an
animal could be so learned
Full 34; R Nine 27

The Cow (Robert Louis
Stevenson)
The friendly cow all red and white
*CTV 62; F Feet 30; FM 222; My V
124; Ox CV 296; Ox PC 116; P Life I
46; Puf V 46; Ste CG 24*

Cow in Calf (Seamus Heaney)
It seems she has swallowed a barrel
Bat A 62; Touch III 29

Cow in Meadow (Clive Sansom)
All day
San E 16

Cows (James Reeves)
Half the time they munched the
grass and all the time they lay
*Duck 50; Ox PC 118; Puf Q 64; Ree C
79; Zoo 32*

Devon Cattle (Brian Jones)
They lug their churning bellies
Jon S 17

Fetching Cows (Norman
MacCaig)
The black one, last as usual, swings
her head
*Flock 227; Liv 52; Ox Con 21; Poems
II 30; Round 75*

Hay in Winter (Gregory
Harrison)
The bullocks trample at the gate
Full 98

A Jersey Heifer (Peter
Hopegood)
A jolly little dame is Molly
SAS 47

Madam (Zulfikar Ghose)
One day grandfather came home
with a calf
Deli 44

Man and Cows (Andrew Young)
I stood aside to let the cows
Dawn 63

A March Calf (Ted Hughes)
Right from the start he is dressed in
his best
*Deli 46; Hug S 13; Hug SP 143; Mus
107; WAS 32*

Milking before Dawn (Ruth
Dallas)
In the drifting rain the cows in the
yard are black
Theme VII 32

Speaking of Cows (Kaye
Starbird)
Speaking of cows
Hi 30

CELANDINES

from *To the Small Celandine*
(William Wordsworth)
Pansies, lilies, kingcups, daisies
Bk S 22

CENSORSHIP

The Wicked Words (Vernon
Scannell)
The wicked words corrupt. The young
are gorged
Gold IV 41

CENTIPEDES

The Centipede (anon)
A centipede was quite content
Tale 47

CHAMELEONS

Chameleon (Alan Brownjohn)
I can think sharply
Fan 102; Four 73

CHANGELINGS

The Changeling (Shirley
Toulson)
Mary's mother is tall and fair
Puf M 94

The Stolen Child (W. B. Yeats)
Where dips the rocky highland
Puf M 90

The Three Beggars (Walter de la
Mare)
'Twas autumn daybreak gold and
wild
Puf M 92

CHARLES I

As I was going by Charing Cross
(anon)
As I was going by Charing Cross
*Fab CV 139; Fab NV 261; Fab PV
188; Merry 45; Ox Dic 114; Ox NR
81; Ox PC 146; Puf NR 53; Trad 98*

CHARLES II

Epitaph on Charles II (John
Wilmot, Earl of Rochester)
Here lies a Great and Mighty King
By 95; ND 151; Ox LV 19

The Royal Patient Traveller
(Henry Jones)
God hath preserved our Royal
King
Bal 26

*When the King enjoys His Own
again* (Martin Parker)
What Booker can prognosticate
Fab CV 140

CHARLIE, BONNIE PRINCE

Hieland Laddie (anon)
Where have ye been all the day?
Puf SB 164

Johnnie Cope (Adam Skirving)
Hey, Johnnie Cope, are ye wauking
yet?
Ring 111

O'er the Water to Charlie (Robert
Burns)
We'll o'er the water and o'er the
sea
Fab CV 141

The Skye Boat Song (Robert
Louis Stevenson)
Sing me a song of a lad that is gone
By 199; Puf V 181

Will ye no come back again? (anon)
Royal Charlie's noo awa'
By 99

CHARMS AND SPELLS

See also Dis, Hist, Puf M
throughout; *Deli 110; Fab CV
221–30; Fab UV 64–5, 106–7; J Vo
I 47–9; J Vo II 64–5; Ox NR
74–5; Rat 105, 401; Tale 48–50;
Voi I 66–8*

Charm for the Coming Day
(Robert Herrick)
In the morning when ye rise
Hist 37; PT II 5

A Charm for the Ear-ache (James
Kirkup)
Now let music, light as an
enchanter's hands
Time 103

from *Comus* (John Milton)
Sabrina fair,/Listen where thou art
sitting
Fab CV 217; Puf M 199

Cushy Cow (anon)
Cushy cow, bonny, let down thy
milk
Ox Dic 137; PT II 4

Good Apple Tree (trad)
Here's to thee, good apple tree
Croc 80; Ox PC 139; Puf NR 29

Good Wish (Gaelic, trans
Alexander Carmichael)
Power of raven black be thine
Dis 48; Fab CV 229

from *Macbeth* (William
Shakespeare)
Round about the cauldron go
Macbeth IV i 4; PT II 8; Wit 12

The Mulla-Mulgars Journey Song
(Walter de la Mare)
That one/Alone
de la M Col 294

The Nativity Chant (Sir Walter
Scott)
Canny moment, lucky fit
Fab CV 221

New Year's Water (anon)
Here we bring new water from the
well so clear
Fab PV 297

from *The Night-Piece to Julia*
(Robert Herrick)
Her eyes the glow-worm lend thee
Drum 17

A Song of Enchantment (Walter de
la Mare)
A song of enchantment I sang me
there
Drum 148

A Spell for Sleeping (Alastair Reid)
Sweet william, silverweed, sally-my-handsome
Shad 21

Spells (James Reeves)
I dance and dance without any feet
My V 43; Puf M 51; Puf Q 66; Ree C 4

This is the Key (anon)
This is the Key of the Kingdom
Bat L 97; Deli 134; Fab CV 227; Merry 287; Ox NR 125; Ox PC 158; P Life III 63; Rhyme II 59; R Nine 46; Star 49; Tap 2; This W 43; Trad 169

Three (Peter Fallon)
Where three fields meet
Strict 38

Thrice toss these Oaken Ashes (Thomas Campion)
Thrice toss these oaken ashes in the air
Fab CV 226; Hist 46; Iron III 64; Plea 234

Warts (Jeni Couzyn)
You can sell them for a penny to
Deli 111; Puf M 26

Witches' Charm (Ben Jonson)
The owl is abroad, the bat and the toad
Deli 126; Fab CV 224; F Feet 158; FM 17; Hist 16; Iron I 48; Merry 361; Ox PC 88; Poems II 122; PT II 7; Rat 469; Say 26; Shad 94; TD 83; This W 36 (part) *Plea 44*

CHAUCER, GEOFFREY

Sir Geoffrey Chaucer (Robert Greene)
His stature was not very tall
Fab CV 116

CHEESE

Say Cheese (Kit Wright)
At Christmas the Stilton
Wri R 72

CHERRY TREES

The Cherry Trees (Walter de la Mare)
Under pure skies of April blue I stood
P Life I 55

Loveliest of Trees (A. E. Housman)
Loveliest of trees, the cherry now
DP IV 28; EGV 279; Flock 13; My V 142; ND 9; Out 29; Ox PC 136; Puf V 23; Rat 253; WAS 45; (part) *Bk S 20*

CHESTNUTS

Sweet Chestnuts (John Walsh)
How still the woods were! Not a redbreast whistled
Duck 33

CHICKENS

The Chickens (anon)
Said the first little chicken
Puf Y 120; R Six 27

CHILDREN

See also Ros M, Ros W, Ros Y throughout
See also Boys, Families, Growing Up, Japanese, Tales Cautionary (Belloc), (Hoffmann)

from *The Babees Book, 1475* (anon)
Children, attend!
Duck 42

Bunches of Grapes (Walter de la Mare)
'Bunches of grapes', says Timothy
de la M Col 26; Fab NV 123; Ox CV 326

The Child is Father to the Man but with More Authority (Ogden Nash)
Once there were some children and they were uninterested in chores
Hap 71

Child on Top of a Greenhouse (Theodore Roethke)
The wind billowing out the seat of my britches
Bric 22; Burn 12; Duck 40; Gold II 38; Hap 22; J Vo III 90; Out Sc 21; Poems II 33; Say 26; Theme III 3; Theme V 64; Touch I 157; Voi I 132

Children's Song (R. S. Thomas)
We live in our *own* world
Choice 305; PC 39

Don't Cry, Darling, It's Blood All Right (Ogden Nash)
Whenever poets want to give you the idea
Nas C 70

Good and Bad Children (Robert Louis Stevenson)
Children, you are very little
BBGG 98; Fab CV 94; FV 49; Ox CV 296; Ox PC 31; Puf V 145; Ste CG 27; (part) *Trad 76*

The Good Little Girl
(A. A. Milne)
It's funny how often they say to me
'Jane?'
BBGG 37; Mil NS 66

The Hero (Robert Graves)
Slowly with bleeding nose and aching wrists
Bric 20

My Parents kept me from Children who were Rough (Stephen Spender)
My parents kept me from children who were rough
Bite II 11; Bric 21; Conf 46; Dawn 79; Deli 12; DP 4; Flock 62; Liv 14; ND 119; PC 67; PT V 7; Rhyme IV 71; Theme III 28; Touch 155

The Place's Fault (Philip Hobsbaum)
Once, after a rotten day at school
Conf 45; DP I 41; Liv 22; RR 191; Theme III 27; Touch IV 94

The Sweet-shop round the Corner (Robert Graves)
The child dreaming along a crowded street
Hap II 85

from *Upon the Disobedient Child* (John Bunyan)
Children become, while little, our delights
PC 76

from *Wit without Money*
(F. Beaumont and J. Fletcher)
What benefit can children be?
PC 65

CHILDREN, AWKWARD

Children's Party (Ogden Nash)
May I join you in the doghouse, Rover?
Touch I 143

Children when they're very sweet
(John Ciardi)
Children when they're very sweet
BBGG 40

Ermyntrude (Roy Fuller)
A little girl named Ermyntrude
Ful S 23

Extremely Naughty Children
(Elizabeth Godley)
By far/the naughtiest
Puf Y 146

The National Union of Children and *The National Association of Parents* (Roy Fuller)
NUC has just passed a weighty resolution
Ful S 10; Like 123

An Only Son (Harry Graham)
Augustus was a sober child
Prel I 7

Social Studies (Mary Neville)
Woody says, 'Let's *make* our soap
Al III 6; J Vo II 31

Tableau at Twilight (Ogden Nash)
I sit in the dusk. I am all alone
Nas C 40

To a Small Boy Standing on my Shoes (Ogden Nash)
Let's straighten this out, my little man
Nas C 56

Tom's Bomb (David Hornsby)
There was a boy whose name was Tom
Sort 88

CHILDREN, ILL-TREATED

Arithmetic (Gavin Ewart)
I'm 11. And I don't really know
Hap II 59

Fourpence a Day (anon)
The ore's awaiting in the tubs; the snow's upon the fell
DP I 37

The Orphan (Chinese, trans Arthur Waley)
To be an orphan
Hap II 31; Iron III 64; Pluc 100

from *Peter Grimes* (George Crabbe)

Peter had heard there were in
London then
DP I 38

Puffing Billy (Mary Sullivan)
My father, kind man, opening his
hands in autumn mornings
Gold III 24

Timothy Winters (Charles
Causley)
Timothy Winters comes to school
*Bill 22; Cau C 77; Conf 49; Gang 38;
Mod 67; My V 100; ND 113; Rat 433;
Theme IV 43; Touch III 142; Voi II 90*

The Workhouse Boy (anon)
The cloth was laid in the
Workhouse hall
Bill 49; Fab PV 265; Peng B 315

CHIMNEY SWEEPS

The Chimney Sweeper (William
Blake)
A little black thing among the snow
DP I 36; EGV 114

The Chimney Sweeper (William
Blake)
When my mother died I was very
young
*Ox CV 86; Prel II 44; Puf V 211;
Rhyme III 48; This W 142*

'Sooeep! (Walter de la Mare)
Black as a chimney is his face
de la M Col 268

Wm. Brazier (Robert Graves)
At the end of Tarrier's Lane, which
was the street
Ox LV 230

CHOICE

The Choosing (Liz Lochhead)
We were first equal Mary and I
Strict 22

The Road not Taken (Robert
Frost)
Two roads diverged in a yellow
wood
*EGV 311; Fab CV 292; Gold III 4;
GV V 17; Poems 85; PW 285*

CHRIST

See also Christmas, Crucifixion,
Easter, Epiphany, Judas

Iscariot, Religious Themes:
New Testament

All in the Morning (anon)
It was on Christmas Day
Sun 127

As Dew in Aprille (anon)
I sing of a maiden
Fab CV 354; Flock 288; Wind 71

As Joseph was a-walking (anon)
As Joseph was a-walking
*Merry 163; Puf V 263; Rhyme IV 122;
Wind 72*

As Mary was a-walking (Spanish,
trans Edith C. Batho)
As Mary was a-walking
Sun 118

Ballad of the Bread Man (Charles
Causley)
Mary stood in the kitchen
*Cau C 165; DP I 72; Gang 53; Mod
198; Rat 64; Sun 132; Voi III 63*

Ballad of the Goodly Fere (Ezra
Pound)
Ha' we lost the goodliest fere o'all
P Tale 171

The Birds (Hilaire Belloc)
When Jesus Christ was four years
old
Rhyme III 68; Sun 120

The Bitter Withy (anon)
As it fell out on a Holy Day [bright
holiday]
*Fab Bal 152; Fab PV 303; Gold I 7;
Iron II 2; Nar 8; Peng B 27; Sun 121;
Wind 74*

Carol (John Short)
There was a boy bedded in bracken
In O I 39

The Carpenter's Son
(A. E. Housman)
Here the hangman stops his cart
Bill 117

The Cherry Tree Carol (anon)
When Joseph was an old man
*Brit 71; DP I 70; Fab Bal 151; Fab
PV 299; Iron IV 99; Peng B 21; Touch
I 15; Voi I 134*

Footnote to John ii, 4
(R. A. K. Mason)
Don't throw your arms around me
in that way
Voi III 60

The Holy Well (anon)
As it fell out one May morning
Bat S 32; Fab CV 360; Fab PV 305; Peng B 34; Sun 122

In the Wilderness (Robert Graves)
Christ of his gentleness
RR 166

Jesus Christ (Woody Guthrie)
Jesus Christ was a man that travelled through the land
Oral 380

Jesus and His Mother (Thom Gunn)
My only son, more God's than mine
Voi III 60

My Dancing Day (anon)
Tomorrow shall be my dancing day
Merry 296

On the Morning of Christ's Nativity (John Milton)
But peaceful was the night
Fab CV 355

The Riddles of Christmas (James Kirkup)
How can a boy
Round 86

Woefully Arrayed (John Skelton)
Woefully arrayed
Touch IV 66

Yet if His Majesty (anon)
Yet if His Majesty, our Sovereign Lord
DP IV 154; Fab CV 364; Gold III 13; Plea 328; RR 156

CHRISTMAS: RELIGIOUS

African Christmas (John Press)
Here are no signs of festival
Dawn 109

The Animals' Carol (Charles Causley)
Christus natus est! the cock
Cau C 278; Sun 102; WAS 164

The Burning Babe (Robert Southwell)
As I in hoary winter's night
Fab CV 358; Flock 288; Rat 98; Sun 101

Carol of the Field Mice (Kenneth Grahame)
Villagers all, this frosty tide
Star 24

Chester Carol (anon)
He who made the earth so fair
TD 107

The Children's Song of the Nativity (Frances Chesterton)
How far is it to Bethlehem?
Rhyme I 46

Christ Climbed Down (Lawrence Ferlinghetti)
Christ climbed down
Touch IV 72

Christmas (John Betjeman)
The bells of waiting Advent ring
Like 127; Time 11

A Christmas Carol (G. K. Chesterton)
The Christ-child lay on Mary's lap
Come 226

Christmas Day (Andrew Young)
Last night in the open shippen
Dawn 108; DT 25; R Nine 32

Christmas Eve at Sea (John Masefield)
A wind is rustling 'south and soft'
Sun 94

A Christmas Hymn (Richard Wilbur)
A stable-lamp is lighted
Mod 100

Christmas Landscape (Laurie Lee)
Tonight the wind gnaws
Out 92

Christmas Star (Boris Pasternak, trans Lydia Pasternak)
It was winter
Flock 282

Eddi's Service (Rudyard Kipling)
Eddi, priest of St Wilfrid
Plea 218; Star 26

The Eve of Christmas (James Kirkup)
It was the evening before the night
Dawn 107; DP I 69; Star 28

How Grand and how Bright
(anon)
How grand and how bright that
wonderful night
Fab PV 302

In Freezing Winter Night or *New
Prince New Pomp* (Robert
Southwell)
Behold, a silly tender babe
*Flock 281; Rhyme IV 120; Star 36;
This W 94*

from *Joly Joly Wat* (anon)
The shepherd upon a hill he sat
By 14

My Father played the Melodeon
(Patrick Kavanagh)
My father played the melodeon
Sun 110

The Oxen (Thomas Hardy)
Christmas Eve, and twelve of the
clock
*Come 224; DP I 68; F Feet 173; Rat
331; RR 165; Touch III 73; WAS 159*

St Joseph and God's Mother
(Spanish, trans Edith C.
Batho)
St Joseph and God's Mother
Sun 92

The Shepherds' Carol (anon)
We stood on the hills, Lady
Sun 98

The Shepherds' Play (anon)
Hankin: Oh, I've been walking on
wolds full wild
Voi I 137

The Shepherd's Tale (R. Pouchon,
trans J. Kirkup)
Woman, you'll never credit what
Round 13; Str 67; Time 102

Take Heart, Sweet Mary (Old
French, trans Eleanor Farjeon)
Joseph: Take heart, the journey's
ended
Str 63

from *The Witnesses* (Clive
Sansom)
The Innkeeper's Wife: It was a
night in winter
Flock 287

CHRISTMAS: SECULAR

*The Boy who Laughed at Santa
Claus* (Ogden Nash)
Rhyme IV 74
In Baltimore there lived a boy
Rhyme IV 74

from *Christmas* (Leigh Hunt)
Christmas comes! He comes, he
comes
Star 14

Christmas at Sea (Robert Louis
Stevenson)
The sheets were frozen hard, and
they cut the naked hand
Gold II 18, Nar 107; Prel I 46; RR 33

The Christmas Exchange (Arthur
Guiterman)
When Bill gives me a book, I know
CTV 31

Christmas Family Reunion (Peter
de Vries)
Since last the tutelary hearth
Ox LV 277

Christmas Mummers' Play (anon)
Here come I, Old Father
Christmas
Voi II 167

Christmas Shopping (Louis
MacNeice)
Spending beyond their income on
gifts for Christmas
Touch IV 76

Christmas Thank Yous (Mick
Gowar)
Dear Auntie/Oh, what a nice
jumper
Gow S 76

*The Computer's First Christmas
Card* (Edwin Morgan)
jollymerry/hollyberry
*Drag 86; J Vo III 101; Mod 208; Star
16; Touch II 34*

Keepen up o' Chris'mas (William
Barnes)
And zoo you didden come athirt
[across]
Voi I 133

Make we Merry (anon)
Make we merry, both more and
less
Star 58

My Christmas List (Gyles Brandreth)
A police car/A helicopter
Sec 94

from *The Shepherd's Calendar: December* (John Clare)
The shepherd now no more afraid
Voi II 165

Snapdragon (anon)
Here he comes with flaming bowl
Star 63

Trio (Edwin Morgan)
Coming up Buchanan Street, quickly, on a sharp winter evening
Look 38; Mod 183; Seven 240

The Twelve Days of Christmas (trad)
The first day of Christmas
Bat L 68; Merry 238; Ox Dic 119; Ox NR 198; P Life III 56; Puf NR 184; Rhyme III 76; TD 110; Trad 142

A visit from St Nicholas (Clement Moore)
'Twas the night before Christmas, when all through the house
CTV 32; Ox CV 154; P Life 173

Welcome Yule (George Wither)
Now thrice welcome Christmas
Star 18

The Wicked Singers (Kit Wright)
And have you been out carol singing?
Wri R 10

CHRISTMAS TREES

The Christmas Tree (C. Day Lewis)
Put out the lights now!
R Nine 92; Star 72

The Cultivation of Christmas Trees (T. S. Eliot)
There are several attitudes towards Christmas
Gold III 16

Little Tree (E. E. Cummings)
little tree
Flock 286; R Eig 84; Young 51

To a Young Wretch (Robert Frost)
As gay for you to take your father's axe
Sun 105

CHURCH-GOING

A Boy in Church (Robert Graves)
'Gabble-gabble . . . brethren . . . gabble-gabble!'
ND 100

Churchgoing (Philip Larkin)
Once I am sure there is nothing going on
Many 99; Touch V 80

Diary of a Church Mouse (John Betjeman)
Here among long-discarded cassocks
ND 75; Time 9; Touch I 85

In Church (Thomas Hardy)
'And now to God the Father', he ends
Touch IV 104

In Church (William Barnes)
The Church do seem a touching sight
Sun 218

In Westminster Abbey (John Betjeman)
Let me take this other glove off
Ox LV 249; Touch IV 105

CHURCHILL, WINSTON

from *Letters to Malaya* (Martyn Skinner)
How close to miracle seemed that retreat [Dunkirk]
TR 47

CIRCUSES

See also Elephants, Lions

The Big Tent under the Roof (Ogden Nash)
Noises new to sea and land
Nas C 109

The Circus Band (Charles E. Ives)
All summer long, we boys
J Vo IV 75

Clowns (Louis MacNeice)
Clowns, Clowns and
Dawn 82

Clowns (Margaret Mahy)
Zing! goes the cymbal. Bang! goes
the drum
Like 172

Hazardous Occupations (Carl
Sandburg)
Jugglers keep six bottles in the air
Voi III 162

Horses (Louis MacNeice)
The long whip lingers
Dawn 61; Hor 25; Mov 12

*In Memory of the Circus Ship
'Euskera'* (Walker Gibson)
The most stupendous show they
ever gave
Sea 160

The Leopards (Bernard Spencer)
One of them was licking the bars of
its circus cage
(*Tel 22; Theme I 69*

Nino, the Wonder Dog (Roy
Fuller)
A dog emerges from the flies
Dawn 60; Dog 84; Theme I 68

Unemployable (Gareth Owen)
'I usth thu workth in the thircusth'
Owe S 60; Strict 157

CITIES AND TOWNS

See also Belfast, Cambridge,
Dublin, Dunwich, Hiroshima,
London, Venice, York
See also Parks, Skyscrapers,
Slums, Suburbs, Tower Blocks,
Town and Country

Beleaguered Cities (F. L. Lucas)
Build your houses, build your
houses, build your towns
Conf 108; Ev 57; Theme VII 63

The Capital (W. H. Auden)
Quarter of pleasures where the rich
are always waiting
Lon 15

Hotel Room, 12th Floor (Norman
MacCaig)
This morning I watched from here
Many 141

I like the Town (D. J. Enright)
Kids are supposed to like the
country
Full 84

I went out (Michael Rosen)
I went out and looked about
Ros W 11

On Roofs of Terry Street (Douglas
Dunn)
Television aerials, Chinese
characters
Drag 44

Pioneer (Mick Gowar)
Who needs jungles for excitement
Gow S 7

Preludes I (T. S. Eliot)
The winter evening settles down
*Bric 58; Choice 217; Dawn 105; DP
III 29; Lon 14; PW 306; TD 138;
Touch I 94*

Preludes II (T. S. Eliot)
The morning comes to
consciousness
Choice 217; DP III 29; Lon 14

A Removal from Terry Street
(Douglas Dunn)
On a squeaking cart they push the
usual stuff
*Drag 39; Fab Mod 420; Liv 89; Ox
Con 279*

Sing a Song of People (Lois
Lenski)
Sing a song of people
Puf Y 31; R Six 87

Slough (John Betjeman)
Come friendly bombs and fall on
Slough
Touch III 90

Up at a Villa – Down in the City
(Robert Browning)
Had I but plenty of money
Puf V 124; Theme VII 18

We are going to see the Rabbit
(Alan Brownjohn)
We are going to see the rabbit
*DP I 12; Ev 271; Hap 36; Mod 106;
ND 85; Tel 40; Theme VII 60; Touch
II 74; WAS 98*

CLARE, JOHN

At the Grave of John Clare
(Charles Causley)
Walking in the scythed
churchyard, around the locked
church
*Cau C 34; Flock 171; Many 134; Seven
40*

Entering the City (Tony Connor)
The city lies ahead. The vale
Tel 37

Helpston (Charles Causley)
Hills sank like green fleets on the
land's long rim
Seven 45

CLAVERHOUSE

Bonnie Dundee (Sir Walter Scott)
To the Lords of Convention 'twas
Claver'se who spoke
Scot 72

CLEOPATRA

from *Antony and Cleopatra*
(William Shakespeare)
The barge she sat in, like a
burnished throne
Antony & Cleopatra II ii 191; Mov 42

CLERGYMEN

The Country Clergy
(R. S. Thomas)
I see them working in old rectories
Theme VI 18

A Priest (L. A. G. Strong)
A little liked, more feared, his dark
Touch III 7

from *The Deserted Village: The
Village Preacher* (Oliver
Goldsmith)
Near yonder copse, where once the
garden smiled
Theme VI 17
A man he was to all the country
dear
RR 164

CLERIHEWS

Clerihews (E. C. Bentley)
The Art of Biography
Ox LV 208

*On Clive, Mahomet, George III,
William Rufus, Charles Peace,
General Sherman*
Ox LV 208–9

*On George III, Sir Christopher
Wren*
GV V 24

*On George Hirst, Lord Clive, Prof.
Dewar*
Plea 313

CLOUDS

The Black Cloud (W. H. Davies)
Little flocks of peaceful clouds
Rat 81

The Cloud-Mobile (May
Swenson)
Above my face is a map
J Vo II 10

Clouds (Aileen Fisher)
Wonder where they come from?
Out 31

White Sheep (W. H. Davies)
White sheep, white sheep
Al I 8; Here 42; Hi 13

COCKATOOS

The Red Cockatoo (Po Chu-I,
trans Arthur Waley)
Sent as a present from Annam
*ADT 32; Bric 44; Gold III 20; Hap
16; Iron II 45; Pluc 29; Touch III 39;
Voi III 149; Zoo 70*

COCKFIGHTING

Wedgebury Cocking (trad)
At Wedgebury there was a cocking
Fab Bal 191; Touch III 66; Voi III 151

COCKS

from *Canterbury Tales* (Geoffrey
Chaucer)
A yeerd she hadde, enclosed al
aboute
Bir 77
(trans Nevill Coghill)
Chanticleer and Pertelote: She had
a yard
ND 74
(trans Frank Ernest Hill)
Once, long ago, set close beside a
wood
DP II 15

Cock-Crow (Edward Thomas)
Out of the wood of thoughts that
grows by night
*Choice 174; F Feet 159; Iron III 46;
ND 73; PW 292; Rat 110; Theme II
44; Touch III 39; Voi I 110; WAS 112*

Doubt (anon)
I sometimes think I'd rather crow
CBC 39

from *An Evening Walk* (William
Wordsworth)
Sweetly ferocious, round his native
walks
Zoo 74

He leaves the Nest (Sanskrit, trans
John Brough)
He leaves the nest
Rhy 44

COCOA

Lament for Cocoa (John Updike)
The scum has come
Hap 79

COLLECTING

Hector the Collector (Shel
Silverstein)
Hector the collector
Gang 32

Johnny's Pockets(Alison Winn)
Johnny collects
Puf Y 37; R Six 39

COLOURS

Golden Glories (Christina
Rossetti)
The buttercup is like a golden cup
Full 112

Grandpa dropped his Glasses
(Leroy F. Jackson)
Grandpa dropped his glasses once
OSF 13

Grey (James Reeves)
Grey is the sky, and grey the
woodman's cot
Ree C 17; Tap 16; Word 123

The Paint Box (E. V. Rieu)
Cobalt and umber and ultramarine
Like 158; Puf Q 106; R Six 80

Symphony in Yellow (Oscar
Wilde)
An omnibus across the bridge
Fan 96

Uncle Edward's Affliction
(Vernon Scannell)
Uncle Edward was colour-blind
Prel IV 10; Strict 68

from *What is Blue?* (Mary
O'Neill)
Blue is a lake
Bits b

What is Grey? (Mary O'Neill)
Grey is the colour of an elephant
Fan 94

What is Pink? (Christina
Rossetti)
What is pink? A rose is pink
*Croc 45; Fan 74; Once 59; Ox CV 280;
Puf Y 68; Rhyme II 48*

What is Red? (Mary O'Neill)
Red is a sunset
Fir 80

What is White? (Mary O'Neill)
White is a dove
Word 6

COLUMBUS

from *Christopher Columbus* (Louis
MacNeice)
Your Catholic Majesties . . . it is
hard for me
DP II 65

Discovery (Sir John Squire)
There was an Indian, who had
known no change
*Bite III 44; Deli 116; Mov 38;
ND 136; NS 14; P Life IV 50;
Sea 60; Tam 42*

The Emigrants: Columbus
(Edward Braithwaite)
Columbus from his after–
Tam 31

For Christopher Columbus (A. J.
Seymour)
Music came thundering through
the North-East trades
Bite III 17; Cari I 74
(part) And so they came upon San
Salvador
Tam 11

COMPUTERS

The Computer's First Christmas Card (Edwin Morgan)
jollymerry/hollyberry
Drag 86; J Vo III 101; Mod 208; Star 16; Touch II 34

The Computer's Spring Greeting (Gary Lewis, aged 9)
Spring gling
J Vo II 25

Dial Love (Gerda Mayer)
Father Christmas brought me a private computer
May K 23

COOK, CAPTAIN JAMES

from *The Great South Land* (Rex Ingamells)
Cook shortened sail
Aus 26

COOKING

Girl Making Pies (Roy Fuller)
When my mother's making pies
Ful S 12

CORACLES

The Coracle (Sir Walter Raleigh, after Lucan)
The moistened osier of the hoary willow
Mov 32

CORAL

Coral (Christina Rossetti)
O sailor, come ashore
FM 187; Full 116; PT I 30; Tap 68

from *Coral Grove* (James Gates Percival)
Deep in the wave is a coral grove
Fan 124

CORBIES

See Ravens

CORMORANTS

The Common Cormorant (anon)
The common cormorant or shag
CBC 143; Fab CV 88; Fab Non 292; Fab NV 82; FV 20; If 27; In O I 29; My V 158; Ox PC 66; Plea 47; R Eig 66; Touch I 118: Trad 109

The Cormorant (John Heath-Stubbs)
A lone black crag stands offshore
Hea P 17; Sea 46

Cormorants (John Blight)
The sea has it this way: if you see
Flock 94

CORTEZ

Cortez (William Kean Seymour)
Cortez one night trod
My V 50

COUNTING-OUT RHYMES

See also Fab NV 19; Fab PV 20–1; J Vo I 80–1; Trad 14
If one is one (Michael Rosen)
If one is one/if two is two
Ros M 22

COUNTING RHYMES

See Puf Y 169–81

COUNTING RHYMES (DOWN)

Ten Little Indian Boys (M. M. Hutchinson)
Ten little Indian boys making a canoe
Come 55; Fab NV 110

Ten Little Indian Boys (Septimus Winner)
Ten little Indian boys standin' in a line
Ox Dic 328; Puf NR 68

Twelve huntsmen with horns and hounds (trad)
Twelve huntsmen with horns and hounds
Fab NV 141; In O II 41; Iron II 78; Merry 240; R Eig 54; Say 34

COUNTING RHYMES (UP)

Black Monkeys (Ruth Ainsworth)
One black monkey swinging on a tree
Five 8

Cottage (Eleanor Farjeon)
When I live in a cottage
Croc 58; Puf Q 45

A Gaping Wide-Mouthed Waddling Frog (trad)
A gaping, wide-mouthed, waddling frog
J Vo I 73; Ox Dic 181; P Life III 60

Green grow the Rushes-O (trad)
I'll sing you one-O!
Fab PV 28; P Life IV 80

A New Dial (anon)
In those twelve days let us be glad
Sun 79

One More River (trad)
The animals came in two by two
DT 52; Ev 254; Fab PV 75; P Life IV 78; Puf V 158; Rain 28; Rhyme III 65

One Old Ox (trad)
One old ox opening oysters
Word 115
One old Oxford ox opening oysters
Fab Non 76; If 54; Puf NR 164

One, Two, Buckle my Shoe (trad)
One, two, buckle my shoe
Come 14; Fab NV 34; Merry 62; Ox Dic 333; Ox NR 112; Puf NR 165; Trad 20

Over in the Meadow (trad)
Over in the meadow in the sand in the sun
Fab NV 24; Rhyme II 39

Ten Little Dicky-Birds (A. W. I. Baldwin)
One little dicky-bird
Five 12

This Old Man (trad)
This old man, he played one
Fab NV 125; Merry 74; P Life II 62; Rhyme II 27

The Twelve Days of Christmas (trad)
The first day of Christmas
Bat L 68; Merry 238; Ox Dic 119; Ox NR 198; P Life III 56; Puf NR 184; Rhyme III 76; TD 110; Trad 142

The Yule Days (anon)
The king sent his lady on the first Yule day
Fab PV 47

COUNTRIES

See Australia, England: History (chronological), Ireland, Jamaica, New Zealand, Scotland, South Africa, Ulster

COUNTRY LIFE

See also Farming
Country Lunch (Max Fatchen)
The basket is a big one, the billy can immense
Fat W 68

The Pasture (Robert Frost)
I'm going out to clear the pasture spring
Al III 17; Bits p; By 230; Choice 277; Deli 44; F Feet 26; Gold I 20; Hap II 71; PT VI 12; R Eig 115; Rhyme II 20

COURAGE

If (Rudyard Kipling)
If you can keep your head when all about you
CTV 109; EGV 290; Fab PR 228; Like 165; Ox CV 324

Still Here (Langston Hughes)
I've been scarred and battered
Burn 151

COURTSHIP (L & D)

See also Love, Lovers, Love Songs, Marriage
Being-in-love (Roger McGough)
you are so very beautiful
Strict 107

Courting Song and Reply (New Guinea Ceremony)
Oh, my handsome boy!
RR 151

The Foggy Dew (anon)
When I was a bachelor I lived all alone
GV III 4; Iron IV 65; Peng B 276

*I will give you the Keys of Heaven
[Canterbury]* (anon)
I will give you the keys of heaven
*DT 80; Rhyme II 22; Rhyme III
60*

Johnnie Groat Says (Charles
Causley)
Johnnie Groat says my eyes are
blue
Cau F 30

John to Joan (anon)
Quoth John to Joan, 'Wilt thou
have me'
Merry 286

The Key of my Heart (anon)
Madam, I will give you a new lace
cap
Puf NR 82

Leezie Lindsay (anon)
Will you gang wi' me, Leezie
Lindsay
Fab CV 350

Love Letter (Louise Bennett)
Me darlin' love, me little dove
Afr II 43

Mary Ann (Joseph Tabrar)
He's bought a bed and a table too
Iron I 14; World 130

Old Man's Courtship (anon)
Old man come courtin' me one day
Gold IV 26

O No, John (anon)
On yonder hill there stands a
creature
Rhyme III 4

Paper of Pins (anon)
I'll give to you a paper of pins
Gold I 28

Soldier, Soldier (trad)
O soldier, soldier, won't you marry
me?
*Blow 30; DP I 77; Duck 94; Merry
142; Ox PC 35; P Life II 60; Puf NR
176; Puf SB 78; Puf Y 142; Rain 31;
Rhyme III 20; RR 143*

A Thunderstorm in Town
(Thomas Hardy)
She wore a new 'terra-cotta' dress
Fab LP 97; Iron IV 119

To his Coy Mistress (Andrew
Marvell)
Had we but world enough and time
*EGV 84; Fab LP 53; Plea 97; Poems
II 96; PW 118; Touch V 48*

from *The Yeomen of the Guard*
(W. S. Gilbert)
A man who would woo a fair maid
Fab UV 61

COURTSHIP (N)

The Braw Wooer (Robert Burns)
Last May a braw wooer cam' down
the lang glen
Scot 49

The Courtship of Billy Grimes
(anon)
Tomorrow, Pa, I'm sweet sixteen,
and Billy Grimes the drover
Gold IV 27

Flowers in the valley (anon)
O there was a woman and she was
a widow
Ev 105; Gold I 26; Ox PC 40

Green Broom (anon)
There was an old man lived out in
the wood
Gold I 27; Merry 187; Ox PC 38

The Laird o' Cockpen (Lady
Nairne)
The Laird o' Cockpen, he's proud
and he's great
Scot 61

The Magpie said 'Come in' (anon)
I lingered near a cottage door
Brit 174

COWBOYS

See also Buffaloes

Bow Down your Head and Cry
(anon)
I went down to the river, poor boy
Oral 365

Cowboys (Jon Stallworthy)
Panther-footed saunter in the street
ND 139; Voi II 120

Cowboy Song (Charles Causley)
I come from Salem County
*Cau C 60; Like 92; Poems 60; Strict
152; Time 27; Voi II 132*

The Cowboy's Lament (anon)
As I walked out in the streets of
Laredo
*Bite I 6; Bk Bal 110; Deli 98; Fab PV
321; Imp 56; Iron III 12; Peng B 338;
Rat 409; Rhyme IV 63; Say 81; Touch
I 45; Wind 83*
As I rode out by Tom Sherman's
bar-room
Fab Bal 242

Lament for the Cowboy Life
(Julian Mitchell)
Where the trails met, our herds
met too
Theme VI 36

*Whoopee Ti Y Yo, Git Along Little
Dogies* (anon)
As I was a-walking one morning
for pleasure
Imp 26

COWS

See Cattle

CRABS

Crabs (Katherine Tyrrell)
Crabs, hiders in rock pools
Tho 22

The Dead Crab (Andrew Young)
A rosy shield upon its back
*Bat A 81; Bite II 29; FM 249; Rat
122; RR 53; Ten 164*

The Giant Crab (John Walsh)
Along the steep wall at the old
pier's side
Out Sc 50; Theme VI 32; World 94

Hermit Crab (Helen Frye)
His year is a long search for the
perfect armour
Ev 79

CRANES (BIRDS)

The Cranes (Anne Ridler)
We thought they were gulls at first,
while they were distant
DP IV 14

CRANES (MACHINES)

The Crane (John Redwood
Anderson)
It stuns/The rapt attention
DP IV 90

The Crane (Charles Tomlinson)
That insect, without antennae
Touch IV 97

Cranes (J. R. S. Davies)
Across a sky suddenly
mid-February blue
Drag 41

CREATION

The Creation (James Weldon
Johnson)
And God stepped out on space
Rhyme IV 1; Sun 46

The Fulani Story of the Creation
(trad Fulani)
At the beginning there was a huge
drop of milk
Dis 109; Many 87; Rhy 71

In the beginning (from Boluba)
In the beginning
Afr I 66

from *Paradise Lost: Creation of the
Animals* (John Milton)
And God said, Let the waters
generate
FM 1

CRIES OF LONDON

See Street Cries

CRICKET

At Lord's (Francis Thompson)
It is little I repair to the matches of
the Southron folk
By 206

Batsman-with-Music Sobers
(James Barry)
That man with a ball and bat
Blue 42

Cricket at Brighton (Alan Ross)
At night the Front like coloured
barley-sugar; but now
Time 133

Cricketer (R. C. Scriven)
Light/as the flight
Drum 138

Cricket for Christmas (Brian
Jones)
These players like white legends of
themselves
Jon S 29

How McDougal topped the score
(Thomas E. Spencer)
A peaceful spot is Piper's Flat. The folk that live around
Nar 52; Tam 49

from *Rites* (Edward Braithwaite, West Indies)
Look wha' happen las' week at de O-
Many 116

Village Cricket (Gerald Bullett)
Flowing together by devious channels
Theme V 7

Vitai Lampada (Sir Henry Newbolt)
There's a breathless hush in the close tonight
EGV 283: (part) *Like 38*

CRICKETS

The Cricket (John Fuller)
The cricket, like a knuckled rubber band
Over 99

To a Cricket (William Cox Bennett)
Voice of summer, keen and shrill
Come 145

CRITICISM

Hear the Voice of the Critic (Adrian Mitchell)
There are too many colours
Seven 222

CROCODILES

from *The Cheerful Crocodile* (Thomas Bolt)
Upon the sacred river Nile
GV V 18

A Crocodile (Thomas Love Beddoes)
Hard by the lilied Nile I saw
Bat A 65; FM 142; Rat 114

Crocodile (Mary Innes)
Loglike the crocodile lies on the banks
Inn B 'C'

The Crocodile (Hilaire Belloc)
Whatever our faults we can always engage
Bat L 125

How doth the little crocodile (Lewis Carroll)
How doth the little crocodile
Croc 36; CTV 71; Fab Non 113; F Feet 115; Lolli III 13; Merry 276; My R 48; Ox LV 125; Ox PC 116

If You should meet a Crocodile (anon)
If you should meet a crocodile
Croc 36; F Feet 106; Full 24; If 98; Lolli III 12; Once 101; Rhyme II 34; R Six 37

On the Crocodile (Thomas Heyrick)
I am the Terrour of the Sea
FM 42

CROWS

The Answer is 'N' (E. B. White)
What answer maketh the crow?
BB 23

The Carrion Crow (anon)
A carrion crow sat on an oak
Merry 144; My V 148; Ox Dic 111; Ox NR 186; Ox PC 21

Crow (Alasdair MacLean)
Crow, crow, crow. Was here on the first day
Hap II 84

The Crow (Barnabas J. Ramon-Fortuné)
Crows on the wing!
Cari I 90

The Crow (Russell Hoban)
Flying loose and easy, where does he go?
Hob P 2; Zoo 75

Doubt (anon)
I sometimes think I'd rather crow
CBC 39

Horrible Song (Ted Hughes)
The Crow is a wicked creature
Hug M 29; Poems 70

Night Crow (Theodore Roethke)
When I saw that clumsy crow
Poems 73

CRUCIFIXION, THE

Friday Morning (Sydney Carter)
It was on a Friday morning that
they took me from the cell
Liv 68; Poems II 40

The Killing (Edwin Muir)
That was the day they killed the
Son of God
Touch V 89

The Merchants' Carol (Frank
Kendon)
As we rode down the steep hill-side
Sun 137

O, My Heart is Woe! (anon)
'O, my heart is woe!' 'Mary' she
said so
Sun 145

The Seven Virgins (anon)
All under the leaves, the leaves of
life
Peng B 25; Sun 143

The Song of the Hours (German,
trans James Kirkup)
In the first hour of the day
Sun 136

The Wood Fire (Thomas Hardy)
'This is a brightsome blaze you've
lit, good friend, tonight'
Sun 141; WAS 53

CUCKOOS

The Cuckoo (John
Heath-Stubbs)
The cuckoo and the warty toad
Hea P 12

The Cuckoo (anon)
The cuckoo comes in April
Bat L 106

The Cuckoo (trad)
Cuckoo, cuckoo
*Fab NV 76; P Life II 51; Puf V 16;
Rhyme I 21; Word 113*

The Cuckoo (anon)
The cuckoo is a pretty bird
*Fab PV 60; Iron II 55; Ox Dic 139;
Plea 47; Rat 119; R Eig 34*

The Cuckoo (Patrick
R. Chalmers)
The cuckoo when the lambkins
bleat
PT VI 7

Cuckoo Song (Rudyard Kipling)
Tell it to the locked-up trees
Puf M 168

Hearing the Cuckoo (John
Heath-Stubbs)
Cuckoo, bubbling your green
words across half Berkshire
Dawn 95

Summer is icumen in (anon)
Summer is icumen in
*By 13; Duck 29; EGV 1; Fab PV 40;
Flock 34*

To the Cuckoo (William
Wordsworth)
O blithe New-comer! I have heard
Bir 56

When daisies pied (William
Shakespeare)
When daisies pied and violets blue
*Love's Labour's Lost V ii 902; BB 17;
Plea 107; P Life II 45; This W 72;
(part) Trad 47*

The Woods and Banks
(W. H. Davies)
The woods and banks of England
now
WAS 43

CULLODEN

*The Soldier's Praise of Duke
William* (anon, 1746)
Good news is arrived
Bal 52

CUMULATIVE VERSES

Bread-Fruit (trad Ibo)
What happened to Nweke
Njeghiliona?
RAP 83

Chain-Song (anon Fulani)
If a jackal bothers you, show it a
hyena
Afr I 10

Chain-Song (anon)
Ukwa killed Nwaka Dimkpolo
Afr I 5

A Farmyard Song (anon)
I had a cat and the cat pleased me
J Vo I 52; Ox NR 182

The House that Jack Built (trad)
This is the house that Jack built
Come 16; GV II 2; If 57; Merry 32; Ox Dic 229; Ox NR 47; P Life 1 22; Puf NR 23; Trad 56

John Ball (trad)
John Ball shot them all
Fab NV 189; P Life III 54

The Old Woman who bought a Pig (anon)
An old woman went to market and bought a pig
Bat L 54; Brit 42; Ox NR 207

There was an old Woman (anon)
There was an old women who swallowed a fly
Blow 42; CBC 144; CTV 94; GV II 20; J Vo I 24; Rhy 32; R Six 60; Word 116

The Train to Glasgow (Wilma Horsbrugh)
Here is the train to Glasgow
CBC 40; Fab NV 251; Hor B 32; Once 11; Young 90

CURSES

See also Puf M 57–68
A Curse on the Cat (John Skelton)
O cat of churlish kind
RR 170

Curses (Michael Patrick Hearn)
Ragwort, tansy, parsley, pea
Wit 10

A Glass of Beer (James Stephens)
The lanky hank of a she in the inn over there
Bill 23; Rat 179

Goody Blake and Harry Gill (William Wordsworth)
Oh what's the matter? what's the matter?
Iron I 33; Poems II 18

Soliloquy of the Spanish Cloister (Robert Browning)
GR-R-R – there go, my heart's abhorrence!
Ox LV 105

Traveller's Curse after Misdirection (Robert Graves)
May they stumble, stage by stage
Hist 50; Poems 59; Voi II 87

The wicked who would do me harm (Gaelic, trans A. Carmichael)
The wicked who would do me harm
Rat 462

CUTTY SARK, THE

Dreams of a Summer Night: The Cutty Sark (George Barker)
I think of her where she lies there on her stone couch by the Thames
Flock 51

DAFFODILS

The Lent Lily (A. E. Housman)
'Tis spring, come out to ramble
WAS 51

To Daffodils (Robert Herrick)
Fair daffodils, we weep to see
EGV 66; Ev 50; Fab CV 51; Puf V 22

DAISIES

Daisies (Andrew Young)
The stars are everywhere tonight
Say 47

Daysies (Geoffrey Chaucer)
Now have I thereto this condicioun
Poems II 34

DANCING (L & D)

Amongst my friends (Colin West)
Amongst my friends
Wes N 41

Chorus from 'Atalanta' (Algernon Swinburne)
When the hounds of spring are on winter's traces
Plea 136

The Dancing Cabman (J. B. Morton)
Alone on the lawn
Fab NV 213; Ox LV 228

Fancy's Knell (A. E. Housman)
When lads were home from labour
Fab CV 43; Plea 132

The Fiddler of Dooney
(W. B. Yeats)
When I play on my fiddle in
Dooney
*BE 52; Deli 104; Plea 130; P Life III
42; RR 167; Theme VI 18*

from *Hansel and Gretel*
(Engelbert Humperdinck, trans
Constance Bache)
Gretel: Brother, come and dance
with me
PT IV 26

Lachlan Gorach's Rhyme (anon)
First the heel
Plea 134

Negro Lass (William Arthur)
Hear the crash of the jungle trees
Cari I 12

Nutcracker Suite: Chinese Dance
(Ogden Nash)
You wouldn't think a Chinese fan
PT IV 20

Nutcracker Suite: Russian Dance
(Ogden Nash)
The Russian moujik is mad for
music
Nas C 107; PT IV 4

*Nutcracker Suite: Sugar Plum
Dance* (Ogden Nash)
The sugar plums began to dance
PT IV 4

*Nutcracker Suite: Waltz of the
Flowers* (Ogden Nash)
Strike up the waltz, the flowers all
PT IV 4

Rumba (Jose Tallet)
Zumba, mama, la rumba y tambo!
Afr II 12

Rural Dance (anon)
Come lasses and lads
Fab PV 40

Tarantella (Hilaire Belloc)
Do you remember an Inn
*Bite II 37; EGV 302; Fab CV 45;
Gold II 30; Like 111; PT IV 17; Rat
416; Touch II 52*

Tribal Dance (Martin Brennan)
They sat in the shade of a
cotton-silk tree
Rhy 55

DANCING (N)

Lord of the Dance (Sydney
Carter)
I danced in the morning
Liv 67

The Lost Shoe (Walter de la
Mare)
Poor little Lucy
de la M Col 79; Fab NV 95; FV 99

My Dancing Day (anon)
Tomorrow shall be my dancing
day
Merry 296

Off the Ground (Walter de la
Mare)
Three jolly farmers
*de la M Col 23; Down 47; Fab NV 60;
P Life III 32*

DANDELIONS

Time Child (Gareth Owen)
Dandelion, dandelion
Strict 60

A Yellow Circle (May Swenson)
A green/string
J Vo IV 18

DANGER

Good Taste (Christopher Logue)
Travelling, a man met a tiger, so
*BE 18; Dawn 69; GV V 29; Poems II
109; Prel IV 25; R Eig 95; Say 30;
Tap 13*

Traveller's Choice (Jon
Stallworthy)
Counsel yourself that traveller
J Vo IV 88

DANIEL

from *Daniel: a Sermon*
(W. H. Auden)
The plotting princes approach the
king
Sun 73

The Daniel Jazz (Vachell
Lindsay)
Darius the Mede was a king and a
wonder
*BE 24; Bite I 3; My V 59; ND 126;
PW 293; Touch II 15; Voi I 39*

DARTS

Darts (Louis MacNeice)
Begin and end with a double. He places his feet
Hap II 64

DAVID AND GOLIATH

David and Goliath (Nathaniel Crouch)
When Israel against Philistia
Ox CV 41

The David Jazz (Edwin Meade Robinson)
David was a Young Blood, David was a striplin'
Bite I 17; Str 29

Goliath and David (Robert Graves)
Once an earlier David took
Bat S 48

Goliath and the Pebble (Michael Baldwin)
David looking on Goliath saw
Sun 70

King David (Walter de la Mare)
King David was a sorrowful man
Sun 70

from *A Metrical Version of the Bible* (A Negro 1858)
David was a shepherd lad, sheep tended night and day
Fab UV 199

DAWN

Dawn is a Fisherman (Raymond Barrow)
Dawn is a fisherman, his harpoon of light
NS 84; Tam 54

Hark! Hark! the Lark (William Shakespeare)
Hark! Hark! the lark at heaven's gate sings
Cymbeline II iii 21; Fab CV 47; Merry 272; My V 16; Ox PC 94; TD 54

DAYDREAMS

Jenny the Pirate (Bertolt Brecht, trans H. R. Hays)
Good sirs, today you see me rinsing out the glasses
Theme VI 44

DEATH

See also Dying, Mortality, Time

American Gothic (Samuel Allen [Paul Vesey])
Sometimes I feel like I will *never* stop
Burn 178

Calchas speaks over the body of Ajax (James Shirley)
The glories of our blood and state
By 70; EGV 71; Ev 277; Fab PR 39; ND 241; Plea 287; PW 104; RR 103

Dance Song (Gond Aboriginal, India)
The bed says to the carpenter, 'Do not make me'
Dis 81

Death (Welsh, Aneirin, trans Talfan Davies)
One night as I lay on my bed
Rat 122

Death in Leamington (Sir John Betjeman)
She died in the upstairs bedroom
Rat 123; Theme IV 65; Touch IV 43

Death of an Old Woman (Alasdair MacLean)
She lived too much alone to be aware of it
Tel 53

Five Minutes (Norman Nicholson)
'I'm having five minutes', he said
DP IV 123

Holy Sonnet X (John Donne)
Death, be not proud, though some have called thee
DP IV 144; Ev 278; PW 88; RR 104; Say 127; Touch V 15

How Death Came (Hottentot, trans Jack Cope)
The moon, they say, called Mantis
Att 59

Jill's Death (George Buchanan)
After Jill died they remembered how she liked this chair
Over 53

Let me Die a Youngman's Death (Roger McGough)
Let me die a youngman's death
Mer 91; Mer R 96; Mer RR 105

Lights Out (Edward Thomas)
I have come to the borders of sleep
Flock 177; Rain 123; RR 112; Ten 138

Mid-Term Break (Seamus Heaney)
I sat all morning in the college sick bay
DP III 4; Touch V 9

My Busconductor (Roger McGough)
My busconductor tells me
DP III 117; In O I 36; Liv 76; Many 34; Mer 75; Mer R 84; Mer RR 90; Voi III 50

Prospice (Robert Browning)
Fear death? – to feel the fog in my throat
Theme II 70

A Recollection (Frances Cornford)
My father's friend came once to tea
DP III 2

The Squirrel (Iain Crichton Smith)
The squirrel lay on the cold stone
Theme I 51

There was a Lady (anon)
There was a lady all skin and bone
Brit 172; My V 84; Ox Dic 260

Upon a Dead Man's Head (John Skelton)
Your ugly token
Touch IV 71

Verses on the Death of Dr Swift (Jonathan Swift)
. . . The time is not remote when I
RR 105

DEATH OF CATS

A Case of Murder (Vernon Scannell)
They should not have left him there alone
DP II 23; Strict 78; Theme I 15

Cat's Funeral (E. V. Rieu)
Bury her deep, down deep
Croc 48; P Life III 83; Puf Q 147

Death of a Cat (Brian Jones)
Always fastidious, it removed its dying
Liv 54

from *The Death of a Cat* (Louis MacNeice)
For he was our puck, our miniature lar, he fluttered
Cat 18

The Early Purges (Seamus Heaney)
I was six when I first saw kittens drown
Seven 107; Theme I 57

Ode on the Death of a Favourite Cat (Thomas Gray)
'Twas on a lofty vase's side
Cat 57; EGV 104; FM 68; Ox LV 46; Plea 60

DECEMBER

December (Robert Southey)
A wrinkled crabbéd man they picture thee
Like 122

DEER

The Deerstalker (L. E. Jones)
The shadow of the mountains lay
Theme V 20

The Fallow Deer at the Lonely House (Thomas Hardy)
One without looks in tonight
Bat A 85; F Feet 148; Ox PC 124; Rat 151; Rhyme III 43; Tap 44; TD 144

The First Day (Phoebe Hesketh)
The spotted fawn
Hes S 17

Hunting Song (Papago Indians)
Here I come forth
Dis 61

Roe-Deer (Ted Hughes)
In the dawn-dirty light, in the biggest snow of the year
Hug M 13; Hug SP 184

The Shot Deer (anon Hindi, India)
Tear on tear/Weeps the dew
Dis 60

DEMOLITIONS

Bradford, June 1972 (Edwin Morgan)
Dusty, bruised and grazed, and cut about a bit, but
Seven 258

Demolition of a Crescent (Marion Lines)
Families gone/Boards in the windows
Lin T 36

Demolitions (Robert Jones)
Change down to second, indicator right
Gold IV 11

from *For Bonfires II* (Edwin Morgan)
An island in the city, happy demolition men
Drag 80; Seven 249

House Coming Down (Eleanor Farjeon)
They're pulling down the house
Puf Y 16

DENTISTS

Dentist at Work (Keith Harrison)
Mister, if I could illustrate this moment
Theme VI 14

Going to the Dentist (Gareth Owen)
After tea/Trev and me
Owe S 9

Oh, I wish I'd looked after me Teeth (Pam Ayres)
Oh, I wish I'd looked after me teeth
Like 68

This is going to hurt just a little bit (Ogden Nash)
One thing I like less than most things is sitting in a dentist's chair
Ev 106; Theme VI 54

DESERT

Green, Green is El Aghir (Norman Cameron)
Sprawled on the crates and sacks in the rear of the truck
TR 105

DESERT ISLANDS

The Castaways or Vote for Caliban (Adrian Mitchell)
The Pacific Ocean –
Gang 86; Seven 208

Emperors of the Island (Dannie Abse)
There is the story of a deserted island
Dawn 87; Ev 262; Four 32; Hist 65; In O I 7; Poems 64; Shad 70

The Man on the Desert Island (Gerda Mayer)
The man on the desert island
May K 17

DEVIL, THE

See also Satan
The devil in Texas (anon)
He scattered tarantulas over the roads
Bill 105; Rat 127

DIGGING

Digging (Seamus Heaney)
Between my finger and my thumb
PT V 29; Seven 106; Tel 81; Touch IV 33

Digging (Edward Thomas)
Today I think
Choice 174; Iron I 53; Prel IV 44; Tap 35; Touch II 179; Voi I 112; WAS 138

Muckers (Carl Sandburg)
Twenty men stand watching the muckers
Theme VI 40

DINGOES

High Explosive (A. B. Paterson)
'Twas the dingo pup to his dam that said
Pat A 17

DINOSAURS

See also Dino throughout
The Dinosaur (Bert Leston Taylor)
Behold the mighty dinosaur
Ev 83

Iguanadon (Mary Innes)
When all the world was young and new
Inn B 'I'

So Big! (Max Fatchen)
The dinosaur, an ancient beast
AM 64; Fat S 14

The Tale of the Trinosaur (Charles Causley)
In Dunborough town
Cau T

To the Skeleton of a Dinosaur in the Museum (Lilian Moore)
Hey there, Brontosaurus!
Dino 19

DIRGES AND LAMENTS

Anthem for Doomed Youth (Wilfred Owen)
What passing-bells for these that die as cattle
Burn 106; Choice 158; Fab Mod 192, Flock 250; Like 169; ND 183; PW 319; Voi III 125

Arthur: Constance's Lament (William Shakespeare)
Grief fills the room up of my absent child
King John III iv 93; PC 61

Bells for John Whiteside's Daughter (John Crowe Ransom)
There was such speed in her little body
Rat 72

The Bonnie Earl of Moray (anon)
Ye Highlands and ye Lowlands
BHL 50; Fab Bal 144; Fab CV 270; Ox PC 152; Plea 253; Puf V 97; Scot 36

Bonnie George Campbell (anon)
Hie upon Hielands and laigh upon Tay
BHL 49; Fab Bal 145; Fab PV 250; Gold II 7; Peng B 188; Plea 259; Scot 5; Trad 34

Burial Songs (Arthur Waley)
How swiftly it dries
PW 315

Cock Robin (trad)
Who killed Cock Robin?
Fab NV 114; Merry 9; Non 192; Ox Dic 131; Ox NR 166; P Life I 28; Puf NR 76; Puf SB 94; Puf V 38; Trad 159

David's Lament over Saul and Jonathan (Bible, A. V.)

The beauty of Israel is slain upon thy high places
Samuel II, I 19; Dis 96

A Dirge (John Webster)
Call for the robin redbreast and the wren
Deli 101; DP II 97; Fab CV 265; Ox PC 153; PW 93; Rat 99; This W 30

A Dirge (Kofi Awoonor, Ghana)
Tell them, tell it to them
Afr II 57

Elegy for Tom Roding (John Pudney)
After the death spelt out in headlines, after the gains
Mod 32

Elegy Written in a Country Churchyard (Thomas Gray)
The curfew tolls the knell of parting day
EGV 150; Fab PR 52; PW 140; (part) Bat R 13

The Exequy (Henry King)
Accept, thou shrine of my dead saint!
Fab LP 360
(part) Sleep on, my love, in thy cold bed
Plea 304

The Falcon (anon)
Lully, lullay! lully, lullay!/The falcon hath borne my make away
Duck 84; Flock 257; Trad 154

Fear no more the Heat o' the Sun (William Shakespeare)
Fear no more the heat o' the sun
Cymbeline IV ii 259; By 41; DP IV 137; EGV 56; Fab CV 265; Fab LP 346; Like 154; ND 242; Plea 285; Puf V 244; PW 61; Rain 113; Rat 151; WAS 180

Fighting South of the Ramparts [Castle] (Chinese, trans Arthur Waley)
They fought south of the ramparts [castle]
Flock 249; Gold III 9; PW 314; Voi II 69

The Flowers of the Forest (Jean Elliot)
I've heard them lilting at the yowe-milking
Fab CV 269; Plea 266; Scot 109

For the Fallen (September 1914)
(Laurence Binyon)
With proud thanksgiving, a mother
for her children
EGV 300; ND 182

Full Fathom Five (William
Shakespeare)
Full fathom five thy father lies
*The Tempest I ii 394; Blow 37; Deli
114; DP II 67; DT 39; EGV 57; Fab
CV 268; Flock 42; Merry 270; My V
29; Ox PC 52; Plea 160; PW 60;
Rhyme IV 56; This W 83; Touch I 131;
Trad 147*

In Time of Pestilence (Thomas
Nashe)
Adieu, farewell earth's bliss
*By 27; Fab CV 274; Fab PR 36; Plea
326; PW 75; Rat 21; RR 98*

Lament of Hsi-Chün (Hsi-Chün,
trans Arthur Waley)
My people have married me
Iron I 28; Pluc 95

Lament of the Border Widow
(anon)
My love he built me a bonny bower
Merry 328; Peng B 85

The Lyke-Wake Dirge (anon)
This ae night, this ae night
*Deli 100; DP I 90; EGV 4; Fab CV
264; Fab PV 322; Flock 258; Iron II
74; Puf V 204; PW 1; Tale 105; Voi II
156*

Missing (John Pudney)
Less said the better
TR 78

McPherson's Rant (anon)
Fareweel, ye dungeons dark an'
strong
Brit 116; In O II 17

The Night is Freezing Fast
(A. E. Housman)
The night is freezing fast
Plea 195

A Nocturnal upon St Lucy's Day
(John Donne)
'Tis the year's midnight, and it is
the day's
Fab LP 67

On my First Son (Ben Jonson)
Farewell, thou child of my right
hand, and joy
PC 24

Rattler Morgan (Charles
Causley)
Now his eyes are bright farthings
Cau C 30

Requeim (Robert Louis
Stevenson)
Under the wide and starry sky
EGV 271; My V 177

The Soldier's Death (Anne,
Countess of Winchelsea)
Trail all your pikes, dispirit every
drum
DP IV 59; RR 46

Stop all the Clocks
(W. H. Auden)
Stop all the clocks, cut off the
telephone
Rat 406; RR 202

Tom Bowling (Charles Dibdin)
Here, a sheer hulk, lies poor Tom
Bowling
Sea 143

The Wilderness (Sidney Keyes,
killed in action 1943)
The red rock wilderness
TR 111

DISLIKES

I don't like Beetles (Rose
Fyleman)
I don't like beetles though I'm sure
they're very good
Ox CV 338

They'll None of 'Em be Missed
(W. S. Gilbert)
As some day it must happen that a
victim must be found
Bat C 20

Wishes at a Garden Party
(Professor Walter Raleigh)
I wish I loved the human race
By 206; GV IV 9; Ox LV 183

DISOBEDIENCE

Disobedience (A. A. Milne)
James James/Morrison Morrison
Mil VY 30

When I'm Ready (Max Fatchen)
Doing things immediately
Fat S 26

DIVES AND LAZARUS

Dives and Lazarus (anon)
As it fell out upon a day
Fab Bal 153; Flock 165; Sun 163

DIVING

The Diver (Ian Serraillier)
I put on my aqua-lung and plunge
Ev 237; Hap II 23; PT V 14; Theme V 37

The Diver (W. W. E. Ross)
I would like to dive
P Life IV 60; Tel 18

DODOS

The Dodo (Hilaire Belloc)
The dodo used to walk around
Lolli I 15

DOGS (L & D)

See also Foxhounds, Greyhounds, Hounds, Pets, Sheepdogs, Spaniels

Bad Dog (Brian Lee)
All day long, Bones hasn't been seen
Lee L 11

Canine (Thomas Blackburn)
You were lifted two yards from that mountain
Bla D 19

The Country Dog (Max Fatchen)
The country dog with his eager grin
Fat S 8

Dog (George Barker)
Dog I am Dog
Bar A 'D'

Dog! (Scott Fitzgerald and Edmund Wilson)
In sunny Africa they have the elephant
Bat A 68

The Dog on the Beach (John Walsh)
As we sit on the beach
Gold I 1

Down behind the Dustbin (Michael Rosen)
Down behind the dustbin
McRo 41

An Introduction to Dogs (Ogden Nash)
The dog is man's best friend
Round 30; Young 9

Lone Dog (Irene McLeod)
I'm a lean dog, a keen dog, a wild dog and lone
Blow 40; Duck 52; Hap 93; Like 35; Rhy 87; Puf V 42

Mick (James Reeves)
Mick my mongrel-o
Out Sc 57; Ree C 62

My Dog Dash (John Ruskin aged 11)
I have a dog of Blenheim birth
FM 159

My Dog Robbo (Gareth Owen)
Mongrel dog Robbo up got
Owe S 12

Night Song (Frances Cornford)
On moony nights the dogs bark shrill
Gold I 1

Night Walk (Max Fatchen)
What are you doing away up there?
Fat S 12

A Popular Personage at Home (Thomas Hardy)
I live here. 'Wessex' is my name
Bat A 16; Dog 66; FM 202; Gold II 4

The Rainwalkers (Denise Levertov)
An old man whose black face
Theme I 6

Roger the Dog (Ted Hughes)
Asleep he wheezes at his ease
Fir 56

Snoozing by the Boozer (Kit Wright)
All day outside the boozer snores
Wri R 64

Today was not (Michael Rosen)
Today was not/very warm
Ros W 80

Tom's Little Dog (Walter de la Mare)
Tom told his dog called Tim to beg
de la M Col 100; P Life I 42

Who rolled in the Mud (Michael Rosen)
Who rolled in the mud
Ros M 62; Ros Y

The Wild Dog (Stevie Smith)
The city dog goes to the drinking trough
Dog 13

The Wire-Haired Fox Terrier
(Leslie Norris)
I am a blithe/Fox Terrier
Drum 58

DOGS (N)

An Addition to the Family (Edwin Morgan)
A musical poet, collector of basset-horns
In O I 43; Mod 181; Ring 114

The Darlaston Dog Fight (trad)
Down Sewerage Street where the smell ain't so sweet
Voi II 66

A Dog in the Quarry (Miroslav Holub, trans George Theiner)
The day was so bright
J Vo IV 16

Elegy on the Death of a Mad Dog
(Oliver Goldsmith)
Good people all, of every sort
Dog 46; Fab CV 82; Plea 48

Fidele's Grassy Tomb (Sir Henry Newbolt)
The Squire sat propped in a pillowed chair
Nar 56

Fidelity (William Wordsworth)
A barking sound the Shepherd hears
FM 97; Gold III 33

Of the Aweful Battle of the Pekes and the Pollicles(T. S. Eliot)
The Pekes and the Pollicles, everyone knows
Bat A 32

PC Plod versus the Dale Street Dogstrangler (Roger McGough)
For several months
McRo 14

The Rescue (Ian Serraillier)
The wind is loud
Fir 52; Tale 28

DOMESTIC SERVANTS

Madam and her Madam
(Langston Hughes, USA)

I worked for a woman
Afr I 57; Ima 67

The Washerwoman's Prayer
(Oswald Mtshali, South Africa)
Look at her hands
Ima 68

DONKEYS

Ass in Retirement (C. Day Lewis)
Ass/orbits/a firm stake
Bat A 63

Aubade: Dick the Donkey-Boy
(Osbert Sitwell)
Tall, with tow-hair, the texture of hide
Dawn 76; Mov 24; Prel II 45

The Donkey (G. K. Chesterton)
When fishes flew and forests walked
Bat A 19; By 221; Deli 81; EGV 309; Fab PR 232; Like 137; ND 76; Rain 53; Rat 133; Rhyme IV 118; Sun 132; TD 92; WAS 52

Francis Jammes: A Prayer to go to Paradise with the Donkeys
(Richard Wilbur)
When I must come to you, O my God, I pray
Rat 166

Frustrated Virtuoso (Norman MacCaig)
In the corner of Crombie's field
Seven 176

DOWSERS

The Diviner (Seamus Heaney)
Cut from the green hedge a forked hazel stick
Seven 107; Touch III 58

DRAGON-FLIES

The dragonfly (Libby Houston)
There was once a terrible monster
Gang 89

The Dragon-fly (Alfred, Lord Tennyson)
Today I saw the dragon-fly
P Life III 71; Zoo 21

A Dragon-fly (Eleanor Farjeon)
When the heat of the summer
Far M 15; P Life III 71

DRAGONS

Custard the Dragon and the Wicked Knight (Ogden Nash)
Guess what happened in the little white house
Nas C 96

The Dragon of Death (Jack Prelutsky)
In a faraway, faraway forest
Night 18

The Dragon of Wantley (English folk song)
Old stories tell how Hercules
Voi II 29
(part) This dragon had two furious wings
Drum 69; Duck 103

Fafnir and the Knights (Stevie Smith)
In the quiet waters
ND 189; World 84

from *The Hoard*
(J. R. R. Tolkien)
There was an old dragon under grey stone
AM 48; Drum 72

Jocelyn, my Dragon (Colin West)
My dragon's name is Jocelyn
Wes N 86

The Lambton Worm (folk song)
Whisht lads, haud your gobs
Duck 109

St Martha and the Dragon (Charles Causley)
In far Provence, where runs the brawny river
Cau C 208; Cau N 65

Sir Eglamore (Samuel Rowlands)
Sir Eglamore that valiant [worthy] knight
Fab CV 170; Fab Non 25; Merry 324; Ox PC 25

A Small Dragon (Brian Patten)
I've found a small dragon in the woodshed
AM 20; Drag 28; Drum 70; Duck 85; Gang 112; Liv 43; Mer R 125; Mer RR 130; ND 190; Puf M 174; Ten 3; Tho 150; World 59

The Tale of Custard the Dragon (Ogden Nash)

Belinda lived in a little white house
Fab NV 170; Hap II 36; Nas C 42; Once 130; Rhyme III 25; Touch I 112; (part) Croc 95

DRAKE, SIR FRANCIS

A Ballad of Sir Francis Drake (John Masefield)
Before Sir Francis put to sea
Sea 188

Drake's Drum (Sir Henry Newbolt)
Drake he's in his hammock an' a thousand mile away
By 208; EGV 282; Fab CV 246; Fab PR 208; Sea 139

Epitaph on Drake (Thomas Beedome)
Drake, who the world hast conquered like a scroll
By 31

Of the Great and Famous . . . Drake (Robert Hayman)
The Dragon that our Seas did raise his crest
Fab CV 145

Upon Sir Francis Drake's Return (anon)
Sir Francis, Sir Francis, Sir Francis is come
Fab CV 144

DREAMS

See also Nightmares
Fever Dream (Edward Lowbury)
Tossed with fever on my bed
Sort 69

I often meet a Monster (Max Fatchen)
I often meet a monster
Fat W 11

Portrait of a Boy (Stephen Vincent Benet)
After the whipping he crawled into bed
Touch II 143

What did I dream? (Robert Graves)
What did I dream? I do not know
Theme II 37; Voi I 112; World 58

DRESSMAKERS

The Dressmaker (Jean Kenward)
Mrs Binns
My V 83; PT V 18

DRINKING

A Catch (Henry Aldrich)
If it be true that I do think
PW 128

Drinking (Abraham Cowley)
The thirsty earth soaks up the rain
Plea 138

Jolly Good Ale and Old (William
Stevenson)
I cannot eat but little meat
PW 46

DROUGHT

Drought (George Campbell,
Caribbean)
No love in my heart
Cari I 33

Drought (Flexmore Hudson)
Midsummer noon, and the
timbered walls
Prel III 8

Drought (Denys Lefebvre)
Heat, all-pervading, crinkles up
the soil
Bite II 36

The Dry Season (Kwesi Brew)
The year is withering; the wind
RAP 35

We sat down there (Kofi Say,
Africa)
We sat down there
RAP 36

DROVERS, AUSTRALIAN

Ballad of the Drover (Henry
Lawson)
Across the stony ridges
SAS 83

The Billy-Goat Overland
(A. B. Paterson)
Come all ye lads of the droving
days, ye gentlemen unafraid
Pat A 59

The Drovers (Roland Robinson)
Over the plains of the whitening
grass
SAS 3

The New-Chum's First Trip
(anon)
Now if you will listen I'll tell you a
story
Bk Bal 90; Fab Bal 232

Windy Gap (David Campbell)
As I was going through Windy
Gap
SAS 116

DROWNING

The Banished Duke of Grafton or
Six Dukes went a-fishing (anon)
As two men were a-walking down
by the seaside
Deli 21; Fab PV 320; Peng B 154
Six dukes went a-fishing
*Bk Bal 180; Deli 20; Fab Bal 130;
Gold IV 58; Voi III 86*
Three youths went a-fishing
Iron IV 58; Sea 55

Life Saver (Elizabeth Riddell)
He was brought up out of the sea
Imp 53

*On a Friend's Escape from
Drowning* (George Barker)
Came up that cold sea at Cromer
like a running grave
DP III 17; Mod 61; Say 127

The Sands of Dee (Charles
Kingsley)
O Mary go and call the cattle home
*Deli 16; EGV 228; Fab PR 171; Ox
PC 153; Plea 162*

from *The Waste Land, Part IV*
(T. S. Eliot)
Phlebas the Phoenician, a fortnight
dead
Dawn 38

Willie Leonard or *The Lake of Cold
Finn* (anon)
It was early Monday morning
Willie Leonard arose
Bat S 107

DRUMS

The Drum (John Scott)
I hate that drum's discordant
sound
Theme III 61; Voi II 73

from *Jazz for Five: Colin Barnes,
Drums* (John Smith)
Listen, listen/there's walking in the
world
Mod 186; PT IV 14

DRUNKENNESS

Blaming Sons A.D. 406 (T'ao
Ch'ien, trans Arthur Waley)
White hairs cover my temples
Pluc 78; Voi II 96

Good Friday (Edwin Morgan)
Three o'clock. The bus lurches
Look 76; Ring 10

Officers' Mess (Gavin Ewart)
It's going to be a thick night
tonight, (and the night before was
a thick one)
TR 129

The Pig got up (anon)
'Twas an evening in November
Blow 55; CBC 81; GV V 21; Imp 34

from *A Satirical Poem*
(Chimedun Figmed, Mongol)
There is drink fermented
Oral 53

Saunders Mac Siccar (Hamish
Hendry)
Ae müneless nicht in a blear
October
Ring 20

DUBLIN

No Place so Grand (anon)
Oh! Dublin sure there is no
doubtin'
Oral 184

DUCKS

See also Mallard

The Duck (Ogden Nash)
Behold the duck
CBC 133; Nas C 74; Rat 137; Zoo 76

Ducks (Frederick William
Harvey)
From troubles of the world
Once 40; Rain 66; Touch I 88; (part)
DT 57

Ducks (Phoebe Hesketh)
A small procession waddles single
file
Tap 60

Ducks' Ditty (Kenneth
Grahame)
All along the backwater
*Come 130; Fab NV 78; Like 114; Ox
CV 328; Plea 49; Young 29*

Feeding Ducks (Norman
MacCaig)
One duck stood on my toes
Drag 12

Flo, the White Duck (Gwen
Dunn)
All white and smooth is Flo
F Feet 67

*O, what have you got for dinner,
Mrs Bond?* (anon)
O, what have you got for dinner,
Mrs Bond?
*Merry 16; Ox Dic 91; Ox NR 171; Puf
SB 42*

Quack! (Walter de la Mare)
The duck is whiter than whey is
*de la M Col 266; Merry 218; Rhyme I
24; R Six 57*

Winter Ducks (Russell Hoban)
Small in the shrink of winter, dark
of the frost and chill
Hob P 29

DUELS

The Duel (Thomas Hardy)
I am here to time, you see
TCN 66

Incident in Hyde Park 1803
(Edmund Blunden)
The impulses of April, the
rain-gems, the rose-cloud
P Tale 105; TCN 62

DUNWICH

At Dunwich (Anthony Thwaite)
Fifteen churches lie here
Mod 176; Round 24; World 82

DUSTMEN

The Dustbin Men (Gregory
Harrison)
The older ones have gone to school
Fir 38

The Dustman (Clive Sansom)
Every Thursday Morning
TD 72

DWARFS

The Dwarf (Walter de la Mare)
Now, Jinnie, my dear, to the dwarf be off
DP I 83

Far Over the Misty Mountains
(J. R. R. Tolkien)
Far over the misty mountains cold
Like 135

DYING

See also Death, Mortality, Time
Aunt Abigail (Ada Jackson)
Aunt Abigail was practical
DP IV 139

The Death-Bed (Siegfried Sassoon)
He drowsed and was aware of silence heaped
Plea 302

The Death of a Peasant
(R. S. Thomas)
You remember Davies? He died, you know
DP IV 142; Ima 131

Do not go gentle into that good night
(Dylan Thomas)
Do not go gentle into that good night
Bite III 63; Touch V 12

The Dying Airman (anon)
A handsome young airman lay dying
Bat C 64

The Dying Stockman (anon)
A strapping young stockman lay dying
Bk Bal 117; Imp 57

Eighty-One Years Old (Elizabeth Jennings)
She wanted to die and all of us
Theme IV 67

EAGLES

The Eagle (Alfred, Lord Tennyson)
He clasps the crag with crooked hands
Bir 40; Bite III 33; By 164; Come 131; CTV 65; Deli 80; DP II 9; DT 58; Fab CV 89; FM 154; Gold I 57; GV IV 21; Iron I 12; Lolli I 2; ND 64; Ox PC 66; Plea 53; P Life IV 18; Rhyme

IV 105; Tam 79; Theme I 25; This W 120; Touch I 78; Word 51; Zoo 66

The Eagle (Andrew Young)
He hangs between his wings outspread
P Life IV 18; Touch I 78

The Eagles (John Heath-Stubbs)
Where the Roman legions tramped
Hea P 7

EARTHQUAKES

Earthquake (James Kirkup)
An old man's flamingo-coloured kite
Time 90; Touch III 92

EARTHWORMS

The Earthworm
(H. E. Martinson, trans Robert Bly)
Who really respects the earthworm
Rat 139

EARWIGS

The Horny-Goloch [Earwig] (trad Scottish)
The horny-goloch is an awesome beast
AM 38; Fab CV 92; Hist 86; J Vo II 57; Scot 5

EASTER

Easter (Gerard Manley Hopkins)
Break the box and shed the nard
Sun 152

Easter Eggs (trad Russian)
Easter eggs! Easter eggs! Give to him that begs
Sun 154

Easter Hymn (Henry Vaughan)
Death and darkness, get you packing
Plea 340

Easter Song (George Herbert)
I got me flowers to straw thy way
Come 232; Fab CV 362; Sun 152; TD 94

Easter Sunday (Edmund Spenser)
Most glorious Lord of Life! that, on this day
Sun 151

Good Friday (Edwin Morgan)
Three o'clock. The bus lurches
Look 76; Ring 10

The world itself keeps Easter Day
(J. M. Neale)
The world itself keeps Easter Day
TD 95

ECHO

Echo (Sara Asheron)
Hello! (Hello!)
GP 9

A Gentle Echo on Woman
(Jonathan Swift)
Echo, I ween, will in the wood
reply
RR 144

EDEN

Eden (Bible)
And the Lord God planted a
garden in Eden
Genesis II 8; DT 68

*They wondered why the fruit had
been forbidden* (W. H. Auden)
They wondered why the fruit had
been forbidden
Sun 49

EDUCATION

See also School
Night School in the Black Country
(D. J. Enright)
Silent the playground, dark and
empty
Enr R 27

Oh bring back higher standards
(Peter Dixon)
Oh bring back higher standards
Strict 18

With Every Regret (Morris
Bishop)
For many years the undersigned
CBC 97

EELS

from *Elvers* (F. W. Harvey)
Up the Severn river from Lent to
Eastertide
DT 47

EGOISTS

How I See It (Kit Wright)
Some say the world's
Four 7; Wri H 72

Me (Kit Wright)
My Mum is on a diet
ADT 16; Sec 8; Wri R 8

Perfect Arthur (N. M. Bodecker)
'Nowhere in the world'/said
Arthur
Bod L 70

EGRETS

Egrets (Judith Wright)
Once as I travelled through a quiet
evening
BE 17; SAS 145

Egrets (Tu Mu, trans
A. C. Graham)
Snowy coats and snowy crests
BE 17

EL ALAMEIN

El Alamein (John Jarmain,
killed in action 1944)
There are flowers, now, they say, at
Alamein
TR 100

ELEPHANTS

The Blind Men and the Elephant
(John Godfrey Saxe)
It was six men of Indostan
*CBC 119; Come 202; CTV 46; DP I
21; Gold I 54; Once 22*

The Elephant (Herbert Asquith)
Here comes the elephant
Come 140

Elephant (George Barker)
Elephants are elephants
Bar A 'E'

Elephant (Alan Brownjohn)
It is quite unfair to be
*Bat L 128; Full 36; Hap II 15; Once
33*

Elephant (Mary Innes)
Of course the elephant must be
Inn B 'E'

Elephant (Yoruba, trans Ulli Beier)
Elephant, a spirit in the bush
Rat 201

Elephant (Yoruba, trans)
Elephant, death-bringer
Afr I 23

Elephants (Louis MacNeice)
Tonnage of instinctive
Touch IV 159

Elephant Song or *Hunting Song*
(anon, Gabon Pygmy)
On the weeping forest, under the
evening wind
Rhy 84
On the weeping forest, under the
wing of the evening
Afr II 23; Dis 57

*Elephants are different to different
people* (Carl Sandburg)
Wilcer and Pilcer and Snack stood
before the zoo elephant
Four 68; J Vo III 17; World 71

Elephants in the Circus
(D. H. Lawrence)
Elephants in the circus
Bric 44; Voi I 93

Oliphant (J. R. R. Tolkien)
Grey as a mouse
AM 14; Drum 65; Rhy 45; Tol T 47;
(part) *J Vo II 49*

Salute to the Elephant (Yoruba,
Odeniyi Apolebieji, trans
A. Babalowa)
O elephant, possessor of a savings
basket full of money
AP 10; Oral 161

Two Performing Elephants
(D. H. Lawrence)
He stands with his forefeet on the
drum
Drag 27; Rat 442; Touch II 72;
Voi I 92

ELIZABETH I

A Ditty (Edmund Spenser)
See where she sits upon the grassy
green
Fab CV 137
The Looking-Glass (Rudyard
Kipling)
Queen Bess was Harry's daughter.
Stand forward partners all
Shad 24

ELMS

The Elm Tree (Eleanor Farjeon)
One November morning clean and
cold
Puf Q 43

EMIGRANTS

from *The Emigrant* (Alexander
McLachlan 1818–96)
Old England is eaten by knaves
Root 60

Sailing to Australia, 1949 (Peter
Skrzynecki, Germany)
Tired, embittered
Root 64

ENGINE DRIVERS AND
FIREMEN

Casey Jones (anon)
Come all you rounders, listen here
*Bat C 46; Bite I 14; Bk Bal 93; DP II
75; Duck 91; Gold I 33; Iron IV 6; Ox
PC 76; P Rail 58; Rail 66; Touch II
106; Wind 85*

The Engine Driver (Clive
Sansom)
The train goes running along the
line
R Six 20

ENGINEERS

Engineers (Jimmy Garthwaite)
Pistons, valves and wheels and
gears
Mov 86

ENGLAND

The Englishman (W. S. Gilbert)
He is an Englishman!
Ox LV 146

Gaunt's Dying Speech (William
Shakespeare)
Methinks I am a prophet
new-inspir'd
Richard II II i 31; ND 6
This royal throne of kings, this
sceptred isle
*Richard II II i 40; EGV 38; Fab PR
32*

In England (Robert Frost)
Alone in rain I sat today
Hi 4

The Roman Centurion's Song
(Rudyard Kipling)
Legate, I had the news last night –
my cohort ordered home
Scene 66

This England (William
Shakespeare)
This England never did, nor never
shall
King John V vii 112; Come 212

ENGLAND: HISTORY

See also Bal throughout, Roman
Britain

English History (Guy Boas)
Remember, boys, when studying
the story of your land
Ev 215

Puck's Song (Rudyard Kipling)
See you the ferny ride that steals
Fab CV 129; Ox CV 320; Plea 250
(part) See you the dimpled track
that runs
DP I 81; P Life IV 72

The Secret people
(G. K. Chesterton)
Smile at us, pay us, pass us, but do
not quite forget
Fab PR 237; Scene 68

ENGLAND: HISTORY –
DARK AGES

Abbey Tomb (Patricia Beer)
I told them not to ring the bells
Ev 206

ENGLAND: HISTORY –
KING JOHN

Runnymede (Magna Carta)
(Rudyard Kipling)
At Runnymede, at Runnymede
Ev 212

The Danes (George Walter
Thornbury)
Their sails, as black as a starless
night
Ev 209

ENGLAND: HISTORY –
PLANTAGENETS

See also Agincourt

*King Edward IV and the Tanner of
Tamworth* (anon)
In summer time, when leaves grew
green
Peng B 244

Young Edgcumbe (Charles
Causley)
Young Edgcumbe spoke by the
river
Cau N 23

ENGLAND: HISTORY –
TUDORS

See also Armada, Drake,
Elizabeth I
Bad Bishop Jegon (1550–1618)
(anon)
Our short fat lord bishop
Fab PV 186

The Death of Queen Jane (anon)
Queen Jane was in labour
Iron IV 113
Queen Jane was in labour full six
weeks and more
Iron IV 115

ENGLAND: HISTORY –
STUARTS

See also Benbow, Charles I,
Charles II, London: Fire 1666,
Sole Bay
The Song of Samuel Sweet
(Charles Causley)
As I leaned at my window
Cau N 51

The Song of the Western Men
(Robert Stephen Hawker)
A good sword and a trusty hand
Merry 225

The Vicar of Bray (anon)
In good King Charles' golden days
EGV 96; Fab PV 198; Ox LV 36

ENGLAND: HISTORY –
THE GEORGES

See also Charlie, Bonnie Prince,
Nelson
The Press-Gang (anon)
Here's the tender coming
Rhyme IV 52

Rule, Britannia (James Thomson)
When Britain first, at Heaven's command
Fab PR 50

A Smuggler's Song (Rudyard Kipling)
If you wake at midnight and hear a horse's feet
DP I 60; Duck 96; Ox CV 322; Ox PC 52; Plea 168; P Life III 92; Rhyme IV 54

Sonnet: England in 1819 (Percy B. Shelley)
An old, mad, blind, despised and dying king
Iron IV 3

ENGLAND: HISTORY – VICTORIA

See also Body-Snatchers, Grinders

The Distressed Sempstress (E. Hodges, 1849)
You gentles of England, I pray give attention
Bal 130

The Song of the Shirt (Thomas Hood)
With fingers weary and worn
EGV 164; Fab PR 100; Theme V 41

The Watercress Girl (anon)
One day I took a ramble down by a running stream
Brit 189

The Watercress Seller (Thomas Miller)
Now all aloud the wind and rain
Ox CV 211

ENGLISH LANGUAGE, THE

See ONe W throughout
As (anon)
As wet as a fish – as dry as a bone
Rhyme III 3

As I went down the cat-walk (Charles Causley)
As I went down the cat-walk
Cau F 55

Blue Umbrellas (D. J. Enright)
The thing that makes a blue umbrella with its tail
Say 120; Voi III 156

but (Paul Coltman)
The other day while I was writing
Hap II 80

The Cheetah, my dearest, is known not to cheat (George Barker)
The cheetah, my dearest, is known not to cheat
Bar R 59; Hap II 33

English (Eleanor Farjeon)
As gardens grow with flowers
Rhyme III 1

Feelings about Words (Mary O'Neill)
Some words clink
ONe W 32

Foolish Questions (Folk rhymes adapted by W. Cole)
Where can a man buy a cap for his knee?
OSF 40

Hints on Pronunciation for Foreigners (anon)
I take it you already know
Fab UV 141

A New Song of New Similes (John Gay)
My passion is as mustard strong
Ox LV 33

Old Mrs Thing-um-e-bob (Charles Causley)
Old Mrs Thing-um-e-bob
Cau F 36; Sort 104; Tap 74

The Parts of Speech (anon)
Three little words you often see
Fab UV 142

The Song of the Dumb Waiter (James Reeves)
Who went to sleep in the flower-bed?
Hap 89; Ree C 8

Speak! (Rhodri Jones)
How many synonyms for the verb to speak
Prel IV 40

Tottie [Rhyming slang] (G. R. Sims 1847–1922)
As she walked along the street
Lon 62

Typo (Russell Hoban)
'Nitgub' said the typewriter
Hob P 12

What's the plural? (anon)
No one for spelling at a loss is
Fab UV 145

Why English is so hard (anon)
We'll begin with a box, and the
plural is boxes [cf. ox, oxen]
CTV 70; Fab UV 143

Words (Edward Thomas)
Out of us all
DP IV 1; Iron II 41

EPIPHANY

Epiphany (Charles Williams)
It was a king of negro-land
TD 88

The Gifts (John Heath-Stubbs)
Three kings stood before the
manger
Ox Con 106

Journey of the Magi (T. S. Eliot)
A cold coming we had of it
*Choice 219; EGV 338; Fab CV 359;
Fab Mod 135; Gold IV 6; Iron III 9;
ND 225; P Tale 169; PW 308; Star
81; TCN 132; Ten 64*

Three Kings came riding (Henry
W. Longfellow)
Three kings came riding from far
away
Star 76

EPITAPHS

*See also BE 58–9; Ful S 31–2; Plea
316–320; Poems II 8–9; RR 97–8;
Sea 228; Touch III 77–8; Voi II
161–4*

Charley Lamb (Henry S. Leigh)
Charley Lamb while yet a child
CBC 95

A Dream of Death (W. B. Yeats)
I dreamed that one had died in a
strange place
Fab LP 331

An Epitaph (Walter de la Mare)
Here lies a most beautiful lady
GV V 44; Rat 142

Epitaph on an Army of Mercenaries
(A. E. Housman)
These, in the day when Heaven
was falling

EGV 281; ND 183; Rat 142

*Another Epitaph on an Army of
Mercenaries* (Hugh
Macdiarmid)
It is a God-damned lie to say that
these
Rat 35

Epitaph on an Auctioneer (anon)
Beneath this stone facetious white
Voi I 94

Epitaph on a Tyrant
(W. H. Auden)
Perfection, of a kind, was what he
was after
*Choice 239; GV V 38; Rat 142; Voi III
58*

Epitaph on Salathiel Pavy (Ben
Jonson)
Weep with me, all you that read
Plea 318

Here lies a poor woman (anon)
Here lies a poor woman who
always was tired
*CBC 55; GP 15; GV V 27; My V 91;
Poems II 45; Rhy 68; Theme VI 11*

In Memoriam: Easter 1915
(Edward Thomas)
The flowers left thick at nightfall in
the wood
Choice 172; RR 52

An Inscription by the Sea (after the
Greek of Glaucos)
No dust have I to cover me
Poems II 45

A Jacobite Epitaph (Thomas
B. Macaulay)
To my true king I offered free from
stain
Fab PR 125

Knowlt Hoheimer (Edgar Lee
Masters)
I was the first-fruits of the battle of
Missionary Ridge
Gold III 7

On a Dead Statesman (Rudyard
Kipling)
I could not dig; I dared not rob
Iron IV 19; RR 168; Touch V 112

Requiem (Robert Louis
Stevenson)
Under the wide and starry sky
Fab PR 205; Poems II 45

Shipwreck (George Mackay Brown)
Paul grounded at Braga, a gull on his shoulder
Liv 70

Voices from Things growing in a Churchyard (Thomas Hardy)
These flowers are I, poor Fanny Hurd
Touch IV 81

EQUALITY

From *The Gondoliers* (W. S. Gilbert)
There lived a king, as I've been told
Plea 280

ESKIMOS

See also Oral 229–254
Bear Hunting (Aua, Eskimo)
I spied a bear
Oral 239

Eskimo Chant (trans Knud Rasmussen)
There is joy in
BE 14

Eskimo Hunting Song (trans Sir Maurice Bowra)
I wanted to use my weapon
J Vo II 54

The Father's Song (Eskimo, trans Peter Freuchen)
Great snowslide
Dis 47; Prel III 45; Voi I 129

Glorious it is (trans Dr Edmund Carpenter)
Glorious it is to see
Rhyme III 44

The Mother's Song (anon, Eskimo)
It is so still in the house
Dis 48; Oral 236; Voi III 12

Song to a Miser (Eskimo, trans T. Lowenstein)
I put some words together
Rhy 37

Upstream (Ikinilik, trans Tom Lowenstein)
I often go back
Poems II 100

EVE

See Adam and Eve

EVENING

Elegy in a Country Churchyard (Thomas Gray)
The curfew tolls the knell of parting day
EGV 150; Fab PR 52; PW 140; (part) *Bat R 13*

The Evening Comes (Matthew Arnold)
The evening comes, the fields are still
PT VI 31

Evening Quatrains (Charles Cotton)
The Day's grown old, the fainting Sun
Voi I 119

Summer Evening (Walter de la Mare)
The sandy cat by the Farmer's chair
Bits b; de la M Col 239; F Feet 147; WAS 96

EVEREST

from *Everest Climbed: the Icefall* (Ian Serraillier)
It was April when they came to the Icefall
Ev 248; Puf Q 183; Theme V 52

A Prayer for Everest (Wilfrid Noyce)
That I may endure
Ev 247

EXILE

The 137th Psalm Paraphrased (John Heath-Stubbs)
By foreign waters
Sun 32

One Exile to Another (David Evans, South Africa)
That old sage
Root 34

EXPLOITS

The Green Eye of the Little Yellow God (Milton Hayes and Cuthbert Clarke)

There's a one-eyed yellow idol to
the north of Katmandu
Bat C 16; EGV 293

EXPLORERS

See also Columbus, Cook,
Cortez, Drake, Magellan,
Stanley, Ulysses

from *The Ballad of Kon-Tiki* (Ian
Seraillier)
All day the plane had searched for
them, the wild
Mov 46; Puf Q 177
They were not lonely. They found
the sea
PT I 14

FABLES

The Ant and the Cricket (anon)
A silly young cricket accustomed to
sing
Rain 44

Belinda and Jill (Diana Harland)
There once were two cows named
Belinda and Jill
Sort 58

A Bush Lawyer (A. B. Paterson)
When Ironbark the turtle came to
Anthony's lagoon
Pat A 30

Cat into Lady (La Fontaine,
trans Edward Marsh)
A Man possessed a Cat on which
he doted
Cat 76

Crow and Fox (Krylov, Russia,
trans Bernard Pares)
How often have they told us, please
Rhyme IV 109

Diary of a Church Mouse (John
Betjeman)
Here among long-discarded
cassocks
ND 75; Time 9

*The Fable of the Trained White
Horses* (Jiri Filip)
The trained white horses
Ev 261; Theme III 59

Fishes' Heaven or *Heaven* (Rupert
Brooke)
Fish, fly-replete, in depth of June
By 259; Ev 142; ND 59; Plea 51

The Fox and the Grapes (La
Fontaine, trans Marianne
Moore)
A fox of Gascon, though some say
of Norman descent
FM 260

The Frog and the Ox (Ian
Seraillier)
Two frogs
Third 100

The Hare and the Tortoise (Ian
Seraillier)
'You can't race me,' said Johnny
the hare
Puf Q 165

The Hoopoe (John
Heath-Stubbs)
A rare one with us –
Hea P 8

The Jigsaw Puzzle (Russell
Hoban)
My beautiful picture of pirates and
treasure
Sort 81

Little Fable (Roy Fuller)
The mouse like halting clockwork,
in the light
Dawn 60

The Mountain and the Squirrel
(Ralph Waldo Emerson)
The mountain and the squirrel had
a quarrel
BB 13; Come 202; CTV 17; Ev 80

*The Nightingale and the
Glow-worm* (William Cowper)
A nightingale that all day long
CTV 16

Saint (Robert Graves)
This Blatant Beast was finally
overcome
Voi III 130

warty bliggens the toad (Don
Marquis)
i met a toad
In O II 44

The Wolf and the Stork (La
Fontaine, trans Marianne
Moore)
Wolves can outeat anyone
FM 259

FACTORIES

Factory Windows (Nicholas Vachell Lindsay)
Factory windows are always broken
RR 68

FAIRIES

See also *Plea 230–251*
See also Dwarfs, Goblins, Ogres, Robin Goodfellow

The Ballad of Minepit Shaw (Rudyard Kipling)
About the time that taverns shut
Plea 244

Bonny Kilmeny (James Hogg)
Bonny Kilmeny gaed up the glen
Scot 95

The Fairies (William Allingham)
Up the airy mountain
Fab CV 209; Merry 97; Ox CV 215; Ox PC 92; Plea 233; Puf V 190

The Fairies of the Caldon Low (Mary Howitt)
And where have you been, my Mary
Merry 100

The Fairy Queen (anon)
Come follow, follow me
My V 32; Merry 104; Plea 230; Puf M 215

Fairy Song (Stevie Smith)
I went into the wood one day
Drum 151

Farewell Rewards and Fairies (Bishop Richard Corbet)
Farewell rewards and fairies
Fab Bal 175; Fab CV 205; Merry 265; Plea 231

The Host of the Air (W. B. Yeats)
O'Driscoll drove with a song
DP III 128; Isle 28; TCN 104

I'd love to be a Fairy's Child (Robert Graves)
Children born of fairy stock
Come 66; Croc 92

from *The Satyr* (Ben Jonson)
This is Mab, the mistress-fairy
DP III 101; Puf M 211

The Stolen Child (W. B. Yeats)
Where dips the rocky highland
Isle 57

Tam Lin (anon)
O I forbid you, maidens a'
Fab Bal 129

Thomas Rhymer (anon)
True Thomas lay on Huntlie [yon grassie] bank
Fab Bal 127; Fab CV 213; Flock 181; Isle 38; Peng B 65; Puf V 94; Rat 425; Scot 41; Wind 31

FAIRIES' SONGS

Come unto these Yellow Sands (William Shakespeare)
Come unto these yellow sands
Fab CV 216; Merry 259; Ox PC 90; Plea 131; Puf M 213; This W 74

Fairy Song (George Darley)
We the sun's bright daughters be
Hi 8

Fairy's Song (John Keats)
Shed no tear – O shed no tear
Puf M 212

Full Fathom Five (William Shakespeare)
Full fathom five thy father lies
Tempest I ii 394; Blow 37; Deli 114; DP II 67; DT 39; EGV 57; Fab CV 268; Flock 42; Merry 270; My V 29; Ox PC 52; Plea 160; PW 60; Rhyme IV 56; This W 83; Touch I 131; Trad 147

Now the Hungry Lion roars (William Shakespeare)
How the hungry lion roars
Midsummer Night's Dream V i 360; Duck 78; Flock 125; Hist 11; Isle 55; My V 34; Poems II 122; Puf M 219; R Nine 78; TD 100; This W 40; Touch I 161

Over Hill, Over Dale (William Shakespeare)
Over hill, over dale
Midsummer Night's Dream II i 2; Come 78; Ox PC 90; Plea 235; P Life III 70; This W 75

Where the Bee Sucks (William Shakespeare)
Where the bee sucks, there suck I
Tempest V i 88; BB 43; DT 75; EGV 58; Isle 15; Merry 348; My V 26; ND 8; Ox PC 91; P Life III 70; PW 59;

Rhyme III 53; TD 120; This W 76; Touch IV 19

You Spotted Snakes (William Shakespeare)
You spotted snakes with double tongue
Midsummer Night's Dream II ii 9; BB 27; By 40; DP I 80; F Feet 157; Isle 53; Merry 367; My V 27; Ox PC 160; P Life II 78; PT II 6; Rhyme II 52; This W 37; Touch I 172

FAIRS

Back to the Fair (John Arlott)
Tonight a cloud-rimmed flowering of the air
Gold II 29

Bartleme Fair (George Alexander Stevens)
While gentlefolks strut in their silver and satins
Voi II 21

Fairground (Marion Lines)
Organ-shout music, kaleidoscope streamers
Lin T 5

Fairground (W. H. Auden)
Thumping old tunes give a voice to its whereabouts
Liv 60

Good Friday Fair (Michael Rosen)
Good Friday fair
Ros W 93

Home from the Carnival (Russell Hoban)
Gone all the lights and all the noise
Hob P 26

from *Music* (Kenneth Slessor)
In and out the country folk, the carriages and carnival
SAS 138

from *The Prelude: St. Bartholomew's Fair* (William Wordsworth)
What say you, then
Theme VII 15

Roundabout (James Reeves)
At midsummer fair on a galloping pony
Puf Q 70; Ree C 11; Say 39

Scarborough Fair (trad)

Where are you going? To Scarborough Fair?
Wind 79

The Showman's Song (adapted from J. H. Byron)
If you step into my show, sir
CBC 9

Strawberry Fair (trad)
As I was going to Strawberry Fair
DT 59; Merry 334; P Life IV 76

FAIRY TALES

After Ever Happily (Ian Seraillier)
And they both lived happily ever after
Poems 65

Any Prince to any Princess (Adrian Henri)
August is coming
Gang 145; NV 68

Ballad of the Frog Princess (Charles Causley)
A young prince rode the partridge wood
Nar 18

The Builders [Three Pigs] (Sara Henderson Hay)
I told them a thousand times if I told them once
Bite I 43

Cinderella (Roald Dahl)
I guess you think you know this story
Dah R

Goldilocks and the Three Bears (Roald Dahl)
This famous wicked little tale
Dah R

The Goose (Alfred, Lord Tennyson)
I knew an old wife lean and poor
Nar 25

Jack and the Beanstalk (Roald Dahl)
Jack's Mother said, 'We're stony broke!'
Dah R

Little Red Riding-Hood and the Wolf (Roald Dahl)
As soon as Wolf began to feel
Dah R

from *The Sleeping Beauty* (Edith Sitwell)
The wicked fay descended, mopping, mowing
PT II 18

The Sleeping Beauty (Alfred, Lord Tennyson)
Year after year unto her feet
Isle 60

Snow White and the Seven Dwarfs (Roald Dahl)
When little Snow White's mother died
Dah R

Tails on Fairy Tales (Roy Fuller)
What would the bears have done
Ful S 62

Tell me a Story (Dennis Doyle)
Tell me a story
Stuf 80

The Three Little Pigs (Roald Dahl)
The animal I really dig
Dah R

FAMILIES

See also Hug F, Ros M, Ros W, Ros Y throughout; *Touch V 116–130*
See also Brothers, Fathers, Fathers and Daughters, Fathers and Sons, Grandparents, Mothers and Sons, Nonsense: Hughes, Twins, Uncles

Among Ourselves (Alasdair Maclean)
Among ourselves we rarely speak
Tel 27

The Drawer (George MacBeth)
Their belongings were buried side by side
Touch IV 43

Emma Hackett's Newsbook (Allan Ahlberg)
Last night my mum
Ahl P 18

I've heard so much (Ted Hughes)
I've heard so much about other folks' folks
Bits y; Hug F 11; R Six 36

Protest of a Sixth-Former (Robert Hayes aged 17)
Oh Father can cease to exist
Theme IV 38

She's leaving home (John Lennon and Paul McCartney)
Wednesday morning at five o'clock, as the day begins
GV IV 36

FANTASY

The Butterfly's Ball (William Roscoe)
Come take up your hats and away let us haste
If 74; Non 201; Once 35; Ox CV 131

A Child's Thought (Robert Louis Stevenson)
At seven, when I go to bed
Come 69

Errantry (J. R. R. Tolkien)
There was a merry passenger
Isle 16

If All the Seas (trad)
If all the seas were one sea
Bat L 91; Blow 22; Come 8; CTV 70; Fab NV 132; GV III 7; Merry 38; Once 120; Ox Dic 379; Ox NR 137; P Life I 15; Puf NR 150; Puf Y 196; Trad 102

If All the World (trad)
If all the world were paper
EGV 70; Iron I 16; Fab Non 32; Fab NV 119; Fab PV 91; Non 190; Ox NR 135; Ox PC 20; P Life II 76; Puf NR 150; Trad 70

I'll buy a Peacock Bird (Modwena Sedgwick)
When I have a beard that is curly and weird
Sort 47

In the Fashion (A. A. Milne)
A lion has a tail and a very fine tail
Mil VY 95; Puf Y 121

I saw a Peacock with a Fiery Tail (anon)
I saw a peacock with a fiery tail
Deli 114; Fab CV 276; Fab PV 90; Merry 282; My V 22; Non 254; Ox Dic 342; Ox PC 26; Plea 237; Puf NR 106; Rat 205

Jim Jay (Walter de la Mare)
Do diddle di do/Poor Jim Jay

de la M Col 267; My V 169; Puf V 207

John Mouldy (Walter de la Mare)
I spied John Mouldy in his cellar
de la M Col 169; Iron IV 93; Plea 239; Puf Y 49

Kubla Khan (S. T. Coleridge)
In Xanadu did Kubla Khan
Bat R 70; By 125; Deli 118; EGV 134; Fab CV 201; Iron II 29; ND 201; Puf V 195; PW 177; Scene 111; This W 173; Touch II 141

The Legend (Judith Wright)
The blacksmith's boy went out with a rifle
BE 60; Flock 192; Poems 93; Rain 91; Rat 233; Str 35; Sun 178; Tho 98

Lucy in the Sky with Diamonds (John Lennon and Paul McCartney)
Picture yourself in a boat on a river
In O II 4

My Hat (Stevie Smith)
Mother said if I wore this hat
Gang 28; My V 62

Romance (W. J. Turner)
When I was but thirteen or so
EGV 341; Like 130; Puf V 209; R Ten 89; TD 18; This W 135

Snail of the Moon (Ted Hughes)
Saddest of all things on the moon is the snail without a shell
ND 192

Song of the Mad Prince (Walter de la Mare)
Who said 'Peacock Pie?'
de la M Col 305; DP III 119; Fab CV 282; Iron IV 68; My V 32; Ox CV 327; Puf V 203; RR 115; TD 163

Still the Dark Forest (W. H. Auden)
Still the dark forest, quiet the deep
BE 7

Tartary (Walter de la Mare)
If I were Lord of Tartary
de la M Col 234; Like 73; ND 111; Ox CV 325; P Life IV 92

The Ups and Downs of the Elevator Car (Caroline D. Emerson)
The elevator car in the elevator shaft
Mov 104; Young 83

Warning to Children (Robert Graves)
Children, if you dare to think
BE 32; Choice 257; Deli 136; Fab CV 98; Flock 195; Ox PC 32

Who's Scared Now? (Max Fatchen)
I'm warning you./Don't scare me
Fat S 28

You'd better believe him (Brian Patten)
Discovered an old rocking-horse in Woolworth's
Drag 9; Gang 12; Hap II 43; Liv 59; Poems II 108; World 62

FARMING

See also Fab UV 36–55
See also Barley, Farmworkers, Hay, Haystacks, Mowing, Ploughing, Wheat

Burning the Stubble (Jon Stallworthy)
Another harvest gathered in
ND 25

Churning Day (Seamus Heaney)
A thick crust, coarse-grained as limestone rough-cast
Scene 51

Harvest Hymn (John Betjeman)
We squirt the fields and scatter
Touch II 119

The Hill Farmer speaks (R. S. Thomas)
I am the farmer, stripped of love
Choice 309; Mod 53; RR 196

Hymn of the Scientific Farmer (Clive Sansom)
We squirt the fields and scatter
RR 22

The Wife's Tale (Seamus Heaney)
When I had spread it all on linen cloth
Look 37; Touch V 141

FARMWORKERS

See also Tractors
Cultivators (Susan Taylor)
We
Strict 134

68

Drumdelgie (anon)
There's a farmer up in Cairnie
Fab PV 210

Farmer's Boy (John Clare)
He waits all day beside his little
flock
DP II 26; Rhy 93

The Farmer's Boy (anon)
The sun went down beyond yon
hill, across yon dreary moor
DT 83

Farm Woman (Maurice Lindsay)
She left the warmth of her body
tucked round her man
Theme VI 57

The Foddering Boy (John Clare)
The foddering boy along the
crumping snows
Prel II 47

The Herdboy (Lu Yu, trans
Arthur Waley)
In the southern village the boy who
minds the ox
Flock 76; (part) *PT VI 27*

The Herdboy's Misery
(R. Oler-Opyaha)
Happy are the blacksmith's
children
Rhy 94

The Herd boy's Song (Chen
Shan-Shih, trans R. C
Trevelyan)
Splashing Water
Stuf 82

Milkin' ('P')
It was a sunburnt farmer who was
leaning on a plough
SAS 101

Pastures of Plenty (Woody
Guthrie)
It's a mighty hard road that my
poor hands have hoed
Oral 379

The Rest of the Day's Your Own
(anon)
One day when I was out of work a
job I went to seek
Deli 28

Soil (R. S. Thomas)
A field with tall hedges and a
young
Choice 305; Drag 65; Touch IV 89

FATHERS

My Dad's Thumb (Michael
Rosen)
My dad's thumb
*Deli 92; Poems 46; Ros M 30; World
45*

My Father (Ted Hughes)
Some fathers work at the office,
others work at the store
*Hug F 41; Poems 48; PT III 9; Voi I
58*

Our Father (Ray Mathew)
She said my father had whiskers
and looked like God
Flock 63; Theme IV 46; Voi II 92

When Father papered the Parlour
(Weston and Barnes)
Our parlour wanted papering, and
pa said it was waste
Prel I 18

FATHERS AND
DAUGHTERS

Father and Child (W. B. Yeats)
She hears me strike the board and
say
Gold IV 9; Voi III 70

A Prayer for my Daughter
(W. B. Yeats)
Once more the storm is howling,
and half-hid
Ten 154

from *Remembering Golden Bells*
(Po-Chü-i, trans Arthur
Waley)
When I was almost forty
Iron IV 136; Pluc 76
Ruined and ill – a man of two-score
Iron IV 137; Pluc 90

*Student Daughter Home for the
Weekend* (David Holbrook)
Arriving home – boots and a black
ankle-coat
Mus 90

You Being Born (Brian Jones)
I saw you born
Jon S 7

FATHERS AND
SONS (L & D)

Blaming Sons: A. D. 406 (T'ao
Ch'ien, trans Arthur Waley)

White hairs cover my temples
Pluc 78; Voi II 96

*Boy Driving his Father to
Confession* (Seamus Heaney)
Four times now I have seen you as
another
Burn 23

Digging (Seamus Heaney)
Between my finger and my thumb
*PT V 29; Seven 106; Tel 81; Touch IV
33*

End of a Holiday (Ian Hamilton
Findlay)
My father climbs the stairs
Al III 7

Father Says (Michael Rosen)
Father says/Never
*ADT 116; CC 9; Fir 12; Poems 46;
Ros M 72*

Follower (Seamus Heaney)
My father worked with a horse
plough
*DP II 4; Liv 26; RR 201; R Ten 58;
Seven 108; Theme IV 63; Touch IV 42;
Voi III 14*

For my Son (Alan Brownjohn)
Not ever to talk when merely
requested
Touch V 125

The Identification (Roger
McGough)
So you think it's Stephen?
NV 102

If you don't put your shoes on
(Michael Rosen)
If you don't put your shoes on
before I count fifteen
*Drum 124; Duck 38; Ros M 24; Ros
Y; Sec 14*

I say: What are you doing?
(Michael Rosen)
I say:/What are you doing? And
our little boy Joe says/Mm?
Ros Y

*The Man who finds his Son has
become a Thief* (Raymond
Souster)
Coming into the store at first angry
Gold III 26; Theme III 5

The Modern Man (Basil
McFarlane)
I came/And laughed at my father
Cari I 11; NS 90

Morning Glory (Michael Raper)
My father would begin each day
Bric 29; Touch II 166; Word 86

My Dad, Your Dad (Kit Wright)
My dad's fatter than your dad
Poems 47; Sec 10; Wri R 31

My Papa's Waltz (Theodore
Roethke)
The whiskey on your breath
*Bric 28; Flock 64; Theme IV 46; Word
87*

*A Parental Ode to my Son, Aged
Three* (Thomas Hood)
Thou happy, happy elf!
Prel I 2

This morning my father
(Michael Rosen)
This morning my father looks out
the window
Ros M 31

Walking Away (C. Day Lewis)
It is eighteen years ago, almost to
the day –
Conf 114

FATHERS AND SONS (N)

Sohrab and Rustum (Matthew
Arnold)
And the first grey of morning fill'd
the east
P Tale 105

FAUNS

The Faun (Ezra Pound)
Ha! sir, I have seen you sniffing
and snoozling about among my
flowers
Fab CV 68; Flock 112

FEAR

The Barn (Seamus Heaney)
Threshed corn lay piled like grit of
ivory
Full 78; Theme VII 32

Bayonet Charge (Ted Hughes)
Suddenly he awoke and was
running – raw
*Conf 28; Hug SP 30; Theme III 62;
Touch V 64*

Cold Feet (Brian Lee)
They have all gone across

Fir 116; Lee L 22; Poems 67; Sort 82

Coming Home (Mick Gowar)
It's not really scary
Gow S 71

The Fear (Andrew Young)
How often I turn round
Tap 21

Fear (Gillian Anderson, aged
15)
Walking through the park
Theme II 27

Fear by Moonlight (Phoebe
Hesketh)
The bullion-moon tonight is
profligate
Theme II 33

Gunpowder Plot (Vernon
Scannell)
For days these curious cardboard
buds have lain
*Flock 267; Mod 64; Theme II 58;
Touch III 61; Voi II 17*

The Quarry or *O What is that
Sound?* (W. H. Auden)
O what is that sound which so
thrills the ear
*Bite I 16; Choice 237; Dawn 42; DP I
61; Flock 254; Ima 101; Mod 15; P
Tale 186; Say 77; Theme I 32; Touch
II 50; Wind 93*

The Queer Moment (Brian Lee)
It was a queer moment when all on
my own
Lee L 39

The Silent Spinney (Seamus
Redmond)
What's that rustling behind me?
ADT 105

The Song of the Little Hunter
(Rudyard Kipling)
Ere Mor the Peacock flutters, ere
the Monkey People cry
P Life IV 13

Warning to Parents (Elizabeth
Jennings)
Save them from terror; do not let
them see
Conf 62

Windy Boy in a Wind-Swept Tree
(Geoffrey Summerfield)
The branch swayed, swerved
*Liv 6; Out Sc 22; PT V 15; Theme V
51; Word 142*

FEBRUARY

At Middle-field Gate in February
(Thomas Hardy)
The bars are thick with drops that
show
Conf 92

FEMINISM

*Her brains have been eaten away by
the termites of education* (Joseph
Buruga, East Africa)
Sometimes I think
Many 109

The New Bloomer Costume: c. 1851
(anon)
Listen females all, no matter what
your trade is
Bal 131

Ragtime Suffragette: 1906 (Harry
Williams and Nat D. Ayer)
What's that noise upon the avenue
Bal 163

FENS, THE

The Powte's Complaint [on
draining the fens] (anon 1611)
Come brethren of the Water, and
let us all assemble
Bal 13; Fab PV 173

FERRETS

The Ferret (Lord Alfred
Douglas)
There is one animal of merit
Bat L 117

FERRYMEN

The Ferryman (Christina
Rossetti)
Ferry me across the water
*Fab NV 240; Merry 107; Ox CV 277;
P Life I 58*

The Jolly Young Waterman
(Charles Dibdin)
And did you not hear of a jolly
young waterman
Plea 273

FIDDLERS

The Fiddler of Dooney
(W. B. Yeats)

When I play on my fiddle in
Dooney
*BE 52; Deli 104; Plea 130; P Life III
42; RR 167; Theme VI 18*

The Fiddlers (Walter de la
Mare)
Nine feat Fiddlers had good Queen
Bess
P Life II 18

Pat's Fiddle (James Reeves)
When Pat plays his fiddle
PT IV 15

The Penny Fiddle (Robert
Graves)
Yesterday I bought a penny fiddle
Merry 133; Rhyme II 21

FIDDLES

See Violins

FIGHTING

Against Quarrelling and Fighting
(Isaac Watts)
Let dogs delight to bark and bite
Ox CV 49; (part) ADT 65

The Combat (Edwin Muir)
It was not meant for human eyes
Ev 156; TCN 136; Ten 113

*The fox-coloured pheasant enjoyed
his peace* (Peter Levi)
The fox-coloured pheasant enjoyed
his peace
Dawn 36

FINANCIERS

Thrushes (Humbert Wolfe)
The City Financier
*Bric 15; Drag 39; P Life III 72; PT
III 28; Touch II 169*

FIRE (L & D)

See also London: Fire 1666
from *Banza* (Paul
Keens-Douglas, Caribbean)
How yu mean
Stuf 20

A City Fire (John Gay)
But hark! distress with screaming
voice draws nigh'r
Iron II 4; RR 64; Say 84

Fire Down Below (trad)
Fire in the galley, fire down below

Merry 179; P Life III 65; Puf SB 123;
Rain 19; Rhyme II 6

FIRE (N)

The Progress of the Fire (Michael
Baldwin)
John struck a match or two then
tossed them away
Ev 196

Matilda (Hilaire Belloc)
Matilda told such dreadful lies
*BE 48; Bel CV 26; CBC 102; DP I
24; EGV 304; FAB CV 96; Ox CV
314; Ox PC 30; P Life IV 90; Puf V
152; Rhyme IV 79*

FIREFLIES

Fireflies in the Garden (Robert
Frost)
Here come real stars to fill the
upper skies
F Feet 149; Zoo 18

The Firefly (Edward Lowbury)
This beast is real, but fabulous
Low G 30

FIREWORKS

See also Guy Fawkes' Night

After the Fireworks (Vernon
Scannell)
Back into the light and warmth
DP IV 110; Touch IV 54

Fireworks (James Reeves)
They rise like sudden fiery flowers
*Croc 105; Once 17; P Life II 56; Poems
75; Puf Q 59; Ree C 95; Tap 32; TD
104; WAS 134*

FISHERMEN

Fisherman (George Mackay
Brown)
The west flushed, drove down its
shutter
Sea 97

The Fisher's Life (anon)
What joys attend the fisher's life
Fab PV 216

A Fisher-Wife (Christina
Rossetti)
The soonest mended, nothing said
Theme VI 58

I sit up here at Midnight (Robert
Louis Stevenson)

I sit up here at midnight
Sea 101

Nile Fishermen (Rex Warner)
Naked men, fishing in Nile without
a licence
Ima 97

The Three Fishers (Charles
Kingsley)
Three fishers went sailing away to
the west
Blow 41; Fab PR 168

Uncle Roderick (Norman
MacCaig)
His drifter swung in the night
Mod 180; PT V 11; Sea 97

We'll go to Sea no more (anon)
Oh blythely shines the bonnie sun
Fab PV 215

FISHES AND SEA CREATURES

See also Fat S 36–41
See also Crabs, Eels, Flounders,
Flying-Fish, Goldfish,
Lobsters, Mackerel, Pike,
Sardines, Seals, Sea Monsters,
Sharks, Skates, Squids,
Swordfish, Trout, Turtles,
Whales

Alas! Alack! (Walter de la
Mare)
Ann, Ann!/Come! quick as you can
Croc 21; de la M Col 268; Fab NV 64;
Merry 88; Ox CV 327; Trad 111

from *The Ballad of Kon-Tiki* (Ian
Serraillier)
Then did ocean
P Life IV 58

Fish (Ivor Cutler)
Fish/are not/very bright
Gang 124

Fish (John Donne)
Is any kind subject to rape like fish
RR 173

The Fish (Rupert Brooke)
In a cool curving world he lies
Bat A 70; FM 256

Fishes' Heaven or *Heaven* (Rupert
Brooke)
Fish (fly-replete, in depth of June
By 259; Ev 142; ND 59; Plea 51

Four Fish (Ted Walker)

Still as a stone
Sec 78

If I were a fish (Alison Winn)
Splash! Splosh!
Al I 28

from *I stood tiptoe* (John Keats)
. . . Swarms of minnows show their
little heads
F Feet 69

from *The Rime of the Ancient
Mariner* (S. T. Coleridge)
Beyond the shadow of the ship
P Life IV 56

Some Sea Creatures (Ogden
Nash)
Who wants my jellyfish?
PT I 13

FISHING

from *The Angler's Song* (Isaac
Walton)
As inward love breeds outward talk
Ev 236

Ballade to a Fish of the Brooke
(John Wolcot)
Why flyest thou away with fear?
RR 174; Voi II 41

Blackfriars (Eleanor Farjeon)
Seven Black Friars sitting back to
back
Ox CV 330

The Boy Fishing (Edith J.
Scovell)
I am cold and alone
Bite I 61; Bits g; Drag 11; F Feet 146;
Gold I 5; My V 150; Out Sc 35; Prel II
22; Theme V 31; This W 14; WAS 93;
World 25

Dibby Dubby Dhu (George
Barker)
Dibby Dubby Dhu rose one
night/to sail his boat in the sky
Bar R 21

The Fish (Elizabeth Bishop)
I caught a tremendous fish
Gang 126; Rat 153; Touch III 114; Voi
II 45

Fishing (Marion Lines)
A line below a bridge
Lin T 40

Fishing (Thomas Blackburn)
A stream called the Devil's Water
Bla D 8

Fishing Song (anon, Maori)
Pull in the net!
Oral 313

The Giant Crab (John Walsh)
Along the steep wall at the old
pier's side
Out Sc 50; Theme V 32; World 94

Going Fishing (Lexie Griffiths)
When it's dull, or if the sun is
gleaming
R Eig 32

from *The Nightfishing*
(W. S. Graham)
We are at the hauling then hoping
for it
Flock 48

One Evening in the Bay of Lipari
(Michael Rosen)
One evening in the Bay of Lipari
Ros W 40

The One that Got Away (Leslie
Pickett)
Don't talk to me about the one
Bric 1

The Pond (Anthony Thwaite)
With nets and kitchen sieves they
raid the pond
Gold I 6; Liv 54

from *Rural Sports I* (John Gay)
When a brisk gale against the
current blows
FM 51

The Salmon Fisher to the Salmon
(Seamus Heaney)
The ridged lip set upstream, you
flail
Seven 110

Trout Fisher (George Mackay
Brown)
Semphill, his hat stuck full of hooks
Ox Con 123

FISHMONGERS

Cockles and Mussels (trad)
In Dublin's fair city, where the
girls are so pretty
P Life III 68; Puf SB 67

FLEAS

from *On Poetry* (Jonathan Swift)
So, naturalists observe, a flea
Bat A 58

FLIES

from *The Fly* (Anthony
Thwaite)
The fly's sick whining buzz
Word 144

The Fly (Walter de la Mare)
How large unto the tiny fly
*By 228; de la M Col 89; Deli 58; DP I
6; DT 76; F Feet 186; Once 38; Plea
42; Poems 28; Touch I 30; Trad 83*

A Fly (Ruth Dallas, New
Zealand)
If I could
Stuf 36

The Fly (William Blake)
Little fly/Thy summer's play
*Bat A 59; FM 88; Ox PC 130; Puf V
47; Touch III 120*

FLOOD, THE

See Noah

FLOODS

The Flood (John Clare)
On Lolham Brigs in wild and
lonely mood
Rat 156

*The High Tide on the Coast of
Lincolnshire* (Jean Ingelow)
The old mayor climbed the belfry
tower
Rhyme IV 30

The Hump-backed Bridge (Wilma
Horsbrugh)
Here is a hump-backed bridge
Hor B 12

Twentieth Century Flood (Alison
Bielski)
When the rain started to fall it was
Wednesday
Prel III 17

FLOUNDERS

St Columba and the Flounder
(anon, Gaelic)
Columba passing on his way
Dis 77

FLOWERS

See also Celandine, Daffodils,
Daisies, Dandelions, Gentians,
Nettles, Snowdrops, Sweet

Peas, Thistles, Water Lilies,
Window Boxes

Bridal Song (? John Fletcher)
Roses, their sharp spines being
gone
BB 16

Flower in the Crannied Wall
(Alfred Lord Tennyson)
Flower in the crannied wall
Sun 23

from *Thyrsis* (Matthew Arnold)
Soon will the high midsummer
pomps come on
Bk S 34

FLUTES

The Flutes (Ogden Nash)
How happy are the fruity flutes
PT IV 30

Little Ben Bute (W. B. Rands)
O little Ben Bute
Rhyme I 11

FLYING

Boy Flying (Leslie Norris)
Flying/He saw the earth flat as a
plate
Drum 38; Over 91

Cloud Clipper (R. C. Scriven)
Beneath our wing
Mov 98

Honeymoon Flight (Seamus
Heaney)
Below, the patchwork earth, dark
hems of hedge
Mov 101

Song of the Gremlins (anon)
When you're seven miles up in the
heavens
Puf M 224

Up in the Air (James S. Tippett)
Zooming across the sky
Hi 25

FLYING-FISH

The Flattered Flying-Fish
(E. V. Rieu)
Said the Shark to the Flying-Fish
over the phone
Puf Q 122; R Ten 67; Tam 84

FOG

*Early Shift on the Evening Standard
Newsdesk* (Adrian Mitchell)
Fog Chaos Grips South
Out 69

The Fog (W. H. Davies)
I saw the fog grow thick
*DP I 17; GV V 16; J Vo III 98;
Out 70; P Life IV 28; Poems II 38;
Rhy 104*

Fog (Crosbie Garstin)
Over the oily swell it heaved, it
rolled
RR 38

The Fog (F. R. McCreary)
Slowly, the fog
Drag 34

Fog (Carl Sandburg)
The Fog comes
*Al II 6; CTV 150; DP I 18; Drag 34;
Flock 266; GV I 24; Hap II 39; Out
68; Poems II 39; R Eig 56; TD 46;
Touch II 130; Voi I 124; Word 36;
(part) Bits g*

November Night, Edinburgh
(Norman MacCaig)
The night tinkles like ice in glasses
Poems II 39

Railway Note (Edmund
Blunden)
The station roofs curve off and line
is lost
Rail 45

FOOD

*See also Pac throughout
See also* Baking, Breakfast,
Cheese, Cooking, Fruit, Greed,
Honey, Soup

Any Part of Piggy (Noel Coward)
Any part of piggy
Bat L 123

The Clean Platter (Ogden Nash)
Some singers sing of women's eyes
Nas C 65

Dinner Party Blues (Mick
Gowar)
I eat/Children's food
Gow S 61

Figgie Hobbin (Charles Causley)

The Fox (Phoebe Hesketh)
It was twenty years ago I saw the fox
Theme VII 30; Touch IV 160

The Fox (C. D. Lewis)
'Look, it's a fox!' their two hearts spoke
Drag 27

The Fox (Adrian Mitchell)
A fox among the shadows of the town
Theme I 26

A Fox came into my Garden (Charles Causley)
A fox came into my garden
Cau F 17; Sort 53

A Fox jumped up (trad)
A fox jumped up on a moonlight [winter's] night
Bk Bal 174; Blow 18; Down 15; Merry 109 and 111; My V 57; Ox Dic 173; Ox NR 190; Ox PC 114; P Life III 88; Puf V 50; Rain 26

The Fox Rhyme (Ian Serraillier)
Aunt was on the garden seat
Al I 27; Lolli III 14; My V 160; Puf Q 168

Fox-Trot (John Fuller)
As the earth's turning darkness ends
Ful C 7

A Moon Man-Hunt (Ted Hughes)
A man-hunt on the moon is full of horrible sights and sounds
Theme I 64

Reynard (Gwen Dunn)
Round Miss Bell's pond the grasses and weeds
Duck 49

from *Reynard the Fox* (John Masefield)
At Ghost Heath Wood on Ghost Heath Down
Round 72
For a minute he ran and heard no sounds
TCN 99; Theme I 63
The fox was strong, he was full of running
Rhyme IV 111; Theme I 63
On Ghost Heath turf was a steady drumming
Rain 62

The pure clean air came sweet to his lungs
DP IV 21; Touch I 46

The Thought-Fox (Ted Hughes)
I imagine this midnight moment's forest
Drag 91; Hug SP 13; Touch IV 31; Voi I 108

The Three Foxes (A. A. Milne)
Once upon a time there were three little foxes
Mil VY 38; Ox CV 341

The Tod (anon)
'Eh' quo' the tod, 'it's a braw licht nicht'
Scot 14

The Vixen (John Clare)
Among the taller wood with ivy hung
Bat A 12; Ev 62; Rat 451

FOXHOUNDS

from *Reynard the Fox* (John Masefield)
But now the resting hounds gave cheer
Dog 68
The hounds drew round him on the green
Dog 21

FRIENDS

Auld Lang Syne (? Robert Burns)
Should auld acquaintance be forgot
EGV 117; Scot 154

A boy's friend (Roy Fuller)
I have a secret friend
Ful S 21; PT V 9

Friends (Elizabeth Jennings)
I fear it's very wrong of me
Full 64; Liv 34

If I had a Hammer (Pete Seeger and Lee Hayes)
If I had a hammer
GV III 8

Us Two (A. A. Milne)
Wherever I am there's always Pooh
Mil NS 33; Ox CV 345

FROGS

Bullfrog (Ted Hughes)
With their lithe long strong legs
Bat A 20; Dawn 65; DP II 8; Gold II 46

Death of a Naturalist (Seamus Heaney)
All year the flax-dam festered in the heart
DP IV 36; Theme VII 25; Touch V 185; Voi II 51

The Frog (John Bunyan)
The frog by nature is both damp and cold
Bat A 20

A Frog he would a-wooing go and *The Frog and the Mouse* (trad)
A frog he would a-wooing go
Fab NV 114; If 84; Merry 25; Ox Dic 177; Ox NR 172; P Life I 37; Puf SB 104; Rhyme I 25; Trad 58
There was a frog lived in a well
Merry 183 and 200; P Life II 74

Frogs (Norman MacCaig)
Frogs sit more solid
Touch IV 158; Voi III 11

Frogs (Louis Simpson)
The storm broke, and it rained
Rhy 105

Frogs in Chorus (A. B. Paterson)
The chorus frogs in the big lagoon
Pat A 15

The Frog's Lament (Aileen Fisher)
I can't bite/like a dog
Fir 70

The Puddock (J. M. Caie)
A Puddock sat by the lochan's brim
Like 95; Scot 22

Speckle-black Toad and Freckle-green Frog (George Darley)
Speckle-black toad and freckle-green frog
FM 134

FROST AND ICE

The Eye marvels (Ecclesiasticus xliii 18–20)
The eye marvels at the beauty of its whiteness
Fan 68

Ice (Walter de la Mare)
The North Wind sighed
Drum 26; P Life IV 30

Frost on the Shortest Day (Patricia Beer)
A heavy frost last night
Strict 131

Hard Frost (Andrew Young)
Frost called to water 'Halt!'
BE 15; Drag 11; Like 129; Out 88; Prel III 39; Ring 17; Ten 168; Touch II 129; Voi I 124; Word 23

The Warm and the Cold (Ted Hughes)
Freezing dusk is closing
Hug S 74; WAS 152

From *Winter* (Alfred Lord Tennyson)
Bite, frost, bite!
Drum 112

FRUIT

See also Apples, Bilberries, Lychees
from *Goblin Market* (Christina Rossetti)
Morning and evening
Come 210; EGV 243; Rhyme III 56

In the Street of Food Stalls (Jon Stallworthy)
Wicks balance flame, a dark dew falls
Prel IV 21

This is Just to Say (William Carlos Williams)
I have eaten/the plums
Al I 31; BE 18; Bits p; Flock 232; Hap II 54; Prel IV 24; Tap 13; Word 13

FUNERALS

The Choirmaster's Burial (Thomas Hardy)
He often would ask us
TCN 56; Ten 99; Theme II 10; Voi II 154; WAS 120

Father Dunman's Funeral (Thomas Hardy)
'Bury me on a Sunday'
Voi III 106

Home Burial (Robert Frost)
He saw her from the bottom of the stairs
Voi III 98

In the Cemetery (Thomas Hardy)
You see those mothers squabbling
there?
Iron III 85

Roman Holiday (Frank
Collymore)
O, it was a lovely funeral!
NS 88; Tam 68

GAMEKEEPERS

The Gallows (Edward Thomas)
There was a weasel lived in the sun
*DP III 25; Drag 14; FM 244; Gold
IV 52; Iron IV 53; PT VI 25; Touch I
87; Voi I 74*

GAMES

See also Bouncing Balls, Cricket,
Darts, Football, Golf, Hide and
Seek, Marbles, Monopoly,
Polo, Rugby League, Snakes
and Ladders, Table Tennis

Confessions of a Born Spectator
(Ogden Nash)
One infant grows up and becomes
a jockey
Ev 249; Theme V 69

Those were the Games!
(R. N. Curry)
Now that our fertile acres yield
Theme V 60

GARAGES

Filling Station (Elizabeth Bishop)
Oh, but it is dirty!
Fab Mod 294

GARDENERS

Dad's Garden (Mick Gowar)
My Dad's very keen on gardening
Gow S 8

Garden Lore (Juliana Horatia
Ewing)
Every child who has gardening
tools
Ox CV 260

He Was (Richard Wilbur)
a brown old man with a green
thumb
Voi III 48

My Aunt (Ted Hughes)
You've heard how a green thumb
Gold I 41; Hug F 29; Shad 87; Str 7

Tom Rich (Phoebe Hesketh)
Tom Rich, the gardener
Hes S 12

GARDENING

See Fab UV 36–55
See Digging, Sowing,
Transplanting

GARDENS

The Garden (Andrew Marvell)
How vainly men themselves amaze
PW 115; Scene 138

A Garden Song (Austin Dobson)
Here in this sequestered close
BB 47

GASWORKS

The Gasworks (Terry aged 12)
The smell like rotten eggs
Tho 48

GEESE

Goose (Ted Hughes)
The White Bear, with smoking
mouth, embraces
Hug SP 151; Hug U 41

Something told the Wild Geese
(Rachel Field)
Something told the wild geese
*CTV 27; My V 114; Once 51; Out 60;
Rhyme IV 13; R Nine 91; TD 130;
WAS 109*

GENERALS

See Hannibal, Napoleon

GENTIANS

Bavarian Gentians
(D. H. Lawrence)
Not every man has gentians in his
house
Choice 198; Fab CV 54; Fab Mop 180

GERBILS

My Gerbil (John Kitching)
Once I had a gerbil
Sec 76

GHOSTS (L & D)

See also GP, Night throughout;
Hist 31–42, Puf M 99–128

Explanation of a News Item
(Dannie Abse)
He leading, they floated up
Tel 68

The Garden Seat (Thomas
Hardy)
Its former green is blue and thin
Rat 175; Shad 31

The Ghost (Walter de la Mare)
'Who knocks?' 'I who was beautiful
Ten 47

Ghosts (Elizabeth Jennings)
Those houses haunt in which we
leave
Look 68

Ghosts (Kit Wright)
That's right. Sit down and talk to
me
Wri R 54

The Ghosts' High Noon
(W. S. Gilbert)
When the night wind howls
Puf M 127; R Ten 74

The Ghost's Song (anon)
Woe is me! Woe is me! *or* Wae's
me! Wae's me!
*Fab CV 228; Fab PV 284; Hist 81;
Merry 346; Ox PC 156; Puf V 186;
Rat 455; R Eig 105; Shad 53; Trad 90*

The Haunted House (Thomas
Hood)
Unhinged the iron gates half-open
hung
Theme II 3

The House of Ghosts (Humbert
Wolfe)
First to describe the house. Who
has not seen it
Theme II 3

Lord Cozens Hardy (John
Betjeman)
Oh Lord Cozens Hardy
Puf M 112

The Man who wasn't There (Brian
Lee)
Yesterday upon the stair
Lee L 29; Poems 33

No Room for Ghosts (Laurence
Lerner)
This house has no room for ghosts
Theme II 5

Something tapped (Thomas
Hardy)
Something tapped on the pane of
my room
Theme II 17

Unwelcome (Mary Coleridge)
We were young, we were merry, we
were very, very wise
Shad 61

Who? (Charles Causley)
Who is that child I see wandering,
wandering?
Cau F 96

The Wicked Hawthorn Tree
(W. B. Yeats)
O, but I saw a solemn sight
Shad 51

GHOSTS (N)

The Choirmaster's Burial
(Thomas Hardy)
He often would ask us
*TCN 56; Ten 99; Theme II 10; Voi II
154; WAS 120*

Colonel Fazackerly (Charles
Causley)
Colonel Fazackerly
Butterworth-Toast
*Cau F 50; Hap II 57; Like 116; Once
118; OSF 24; Puf M 103; Round 8;
Sort 22; Str 11; Tap 27*

Daniel Webster's Horses
(Elizabeth Coatsworth)
If when the wind blows
Hist 40; Shad 56

Dicky (Robert Graves)
O what a heavy sigh!
Puf M 107; Shad 29; Theme II 8

Emperors of the Island (Dannie
Abse)
There is the story of a deserted
island
*Dawn 87; Ev 262; Four 32; Hist 65;
In O I 7; Poems 64; Shad 70*

The Fakenham Ghost (Robert Bloomfield)
The lawns were dry in Euston park
Rain 39

The Ghosts' Walk (John Kendall)
They came with lorries, they came with vans
Hist 68; Shad 84

The Glimpse (Thomas Hardy)
She sped through the door
Puf M 118

The Haunted Lift (James Kirkup)
On the ground floor
Third 38

The Holland Handkerchief (trad from Packie Byrne)
A wealthy squire lived in our town
Brit 51

Lo, the ghost of our least favourite uncle (Ray Bradbury)
Lo, the ghost of our least favourite uncle
Gang 66

Lowery Cot (L. A. G. Strong)
This is the house where Jesse White
Dawn 56

Miller's End (Charles Causley)
When we moved to Miller's End
Cau C 237; Cau F 81; Tel 67

Old Mother Laidinwool (Rudyard Kipling)
Old Mother Laidinwool had nigh twelve months been dead
Puf M 99; (part) *Iron II 78*

The Old Wife and the Ghost (James Reeves)
There was an old wife and she lived all alone
GP 19; Hap II 51; P Life II 37; Puf Q 76; Ree C 63; R Eig 70; Shad 80

The Paphian Ball (Thomas Hardy)
We went our Christmas rounds once more
TCN 121

Prince Kano (Edward Lowbury)
In a dark wood Prince Kano lost his way
Four 86; Low G 17; Hist 39

A Shropshire Lad (Sir John Betjeman)
The gas was on in the Institute
Gang 70

Singing Ghost (Stephen Kroll)
At the circus I was watching
GP 16

Sweet William's Ghost (anon)
There came a ghost to Margaret's door
Bk Bal 31; Hist 34; Puf M 123; Tale 87

The Two Old Women of Mumbling Hill (James Reeves)
The two old trees on Mumbling Hill
Poems 26

Two's Company (Raymond Wilson)
They said the house haunted, but
Rhyme IV 83

Unfortunate Miss Bailey (George Colman the Younger)
A Captain once in Halifax that dwelt in country quarters
Bk Bal 34; Fab Bal 194; Fab PV 293; Peng B 286

The Visitor (Ian Serraillier)
A crumbling churchyard, the sea and the moon
Sec 30

Whose Boo is whose? (X. J. Kennedy)
Two ghosts I know once traded heads
GP 24

Widdecombe Fair (trad)
Tom Pearse, Tom Pearse, lend me your grey mare
Down 7; Duck 106; Merry 350; P Life IV 75; Puf SB 109

The Wife of Usher's Well (trad)
There lived a wife at Usher's Well
Bk Bal 29; Brit 44; Fab Bal 58; Isle 88; Peng B 75; P Life IV 48; P Tale 21; PW 2; Rat 464; Scot 94; Shad 36; Theme II 18; Touch IV 23; Wind 7

GIANTS

See Gi throughout
See also Ogres

The Giant Follderowe (Leslie Norris)
Who uses a mountain as his bed
Drum 76

Giant's Delight (Steven Kroll)
Vats of soup
Pac 23

Giant Thunder (James Reeves)
Giant Thunder, striding home
Al III 19; Drum 77; My V 120; Pac 105; Ree C 105; TD 39

Grim (Walter de la Mare)
Beside the blaze as of forty fires
de la M Col 271; Gi 9; Trad 165

In the Orchard (James Stephens)
There was a giant by the orchard wall
Gi 11; J Vo IV 44; Puf M 159

Momstara (Japanese, trans Rose Fyleman)
Where did Momstara go
Gi 26

My Brother dreams of Giants (Bernard Logan)
My brother dreams the world is the size of a football
Gang 129

Song of the Giant-Killer (Leslie Norris)
Poor giant, I see you still don't know
Drum 80

from *Verses on 'Gulliver's Travels'* (Alexander Pope)
From his nose
Drum 75; R Nine 19; Say 18
See! and believe your eyes!
Deli 61

GIPSIES

See Gypsies

GIRAFFES

Conversation with a Giraffe (Douglas Livingstone)
Hail, lofty/necking quizzically
Liv 57; Mod 189

The Giraffe (Geoffrey Dearmer)
Hide of a leopard and hide of a deer
Rain 60

Giraffe (Mary Innes)
Giraffes when they feed eat the leaves of the trees
Inn B 'G'

The Giraffe (George Wyndham)
A doubtful friend is the giraffe
CBC 111; Dou T 40

The Giraffes (Roy Fuller)
I think before they saw me the giraffes
Bat A 18

GIRLS

See also Tales, Cautionary (Belloc)
Adventures of Isabel (Ogden Nash)
Isobel met an enormous bear
Croc 22; Fab NV 105; My R 33; Nas C 88; Once 143; P Life II 10; Young 72

Blue Girls (John Crowe Ransom)
Twirling your blue skirts, travelling the sward
PW 313; Rat 82; Theme IV 8

Lullaby for a Naughty Girl (E. V. Rieu)
O peace, my Penelope, slaps are the fate
Fab NV 271; P Life III 91; Puf V 148

Pooh! (Walter de la Mare)
Dainty Miss Apathy
Bat L 140; de la M Col 40

GLIDING

In a Sailplane (James Kirkup)
Still as a bird
J Vo II 13; Mov 92; Tel 11; Touch II 157

GLOW-WORMS

Glow worms (Andrew Young)
As though the dark had called
DT 70

GNATS

The Gnats (Odette Tchernine)
The gnats are dancing in the sun
Fan 24; My V 147

GOATS

The Beard (Proscovia Rwakyaka)
In the pulpit he swayed and turned
Att 36

The Goat (John Redwood Anderson)
It dwelt upon the very edge of things
DP IV 16

The Goat (anon)
There was a man, now please take note
Once 139
There was a man/named Ikey Small
Imp 27

The Goat-Paths (James Stephens)
The crooked paths
Bite I 34; Gold I 59; PT VI 16

Old Hogan's Goat (anon)
Old Hogan's goat was feeling fine
Third 97

GOBLINS

from *Goblin Market* (Christina Rossetti)
Evening by evening
Puf M 217

Little Orphant Annie (James Whitcomb Riley)
Little Orphant Annie's come to our house to stay
BBGG 113; Ox CV 300

Overheard on a Saltmarsh (Harold Munro)
Nymph, nymph, what are your beads?
Bite I 55; Drum 146; J Vo I 16; Like 104; Puf M 207; This W 33

GODS, ANCIENT AFRICAN

Eshu (anon, Yoruba)
Eshu, who muddles men's minds!
Afr II 27

Ogun (Obutunde Ijimere, Nigeria)
Ogun is not like pounded yam
RAP 26

Ogun (anon, Yoruba)
Ogun kills on the right and ruins on the right
Afr II 29

Oshun [Water goddess curing diseases] (anon, Yoruba)
Bronze and parrot feathers
Afr II 28

GOLDFINCHES

A Goldfinch (Walter de la Mare)
This feather-soft creature
de la M Col 118

Goldfinches (John Keats)
Sometimes goldfinches one by one will drop
Bat A 11

GOLDFISH

Goldfish (Alan Jackson)
the scene of the crime
Four 71; Strict 47

GOLF

Seaside Golf (John Betjeman)
How straight it flew, how long it flew
Theme V 9

GOLIATH

See David and Goliath

GORILLAS

Au Jardin des Plantes (John Wain)
The gorilla lay on his back
Deli 50; Ev 81; Flock 220; Full 12; Tel 23; Theme I 70

GOSSIPING

Cooking Woman (trad, Ibo)
When woman cooks, cooks, and the food is never done
RAP 78

Keep it Dark! (anon, Zezuru)
Keep it dark!
Afr II 65

Scandal (John Clare)
She hastens out and scarcely pins
her clothes
Iron IV 118

Tattle (Godfrey Turner)
A scandal or two
Ox LV 140

They Walked and Talked (Uche
Okeke)
They talked and walked
Bite I 8; RAP 76; Rhy 62

GRACES

A Grace (Robert Herrick)
Here a little child I stand
*CTV 161; My V 176; Ox CV 31; Plea
15; This W 98*

Grace for Children (Robert
Herrick)
What God gives, and what we take
Ox CV 31; Plea 15; Sun 32

GRANDPARENTS

Bucket (Roger McGough)
Every evening after tea
CC 15; Look 46; McRo 54

Church Steeples and Grandad
(Marian Lines)
Grandad to the barber goes
Lin T 34

Dreaming in the Shangai Restaurant
(D. J. Enright)
I would like to be that elderly
Chinese gentleman
Mod 119

Gran (John Kitching)
'My goodness! what a big boy you
are!
Sec 18

Grandad (Brian Jones)
My grandad sailed in clipper ships
Jon S 11

Grandad (Kit Wright)
Grandad's dead
Wri R 28

Grandpa (Paul Chidyansiku)
They say they are healthier than
me
GV IV 34; RAP 11; Rhy 66

A Moment of Respect (Edwin
Brock)
Two things I remember about my
grandfather
Prel I 49; Touch III 72

Mountain Road (Mary Oliver)
My grandfather kept no
PT VI 18

My Gramp (Derek Stuart)
My gramp has got a medal
Sec 19

My Grandmother (Elizabeth
Jennings)
She kept an antique shop – or it
kept her
*DP III 11; Liv 32; Look 49; Mod 89;
PT V 26; RR 202; Touch V 129*

A Striking Old Man (Alasdair
Aston)
When grandfather first came to us
Hap II 42

GRASSHOPPERS

The Grasshopper (Richard
Lovelace)
O thou that swing'st upon the
waving hair
Bat A 76

GREED

A-Apple Pie (Walter de la Mare)
Little Polly Pillikins
R Six 53

The Avaricious Boy (Colin West)
Oh, see the sun above us shine
Wes N 52

from *The Faerie Queene* (Edmund
Spenser)
And by his side rode loathsome
Gluttony
Touch III 22

The Glutton (Spike Milligan)
O Molly, Molly, Molly
Pac 67

Greedyguts (Kit Wright)
I sat in the café and sipped at a
Coke
Wri H 32

Greedy Jane (anon)
Pudding *and* pie
Ox CV 328

Greedy Richard (Jane Taylor)
'I think I want some pies this morning'
Fab NV 100, Puf V 136

Griselda (Eleanor Farjeon)
Griselda is greedy, I'm sorry to say
Far M 62; Young 53

Ice-Cream Poem (Gerda Mayer)
The chiefest of young Ethel's vices
May K 26; Poems 19

Jimmy Jupp, who died of Overeating (H. A. C. Evans)
O shed no tears for Jimmy Jupp
OSF 37

Little Thomas (F. Gwynne Evans)
Thomas was a little glutton
BBGG 45

The Notorious Glutton (Ann Taylor)
A duck who had got such a habit of stuffing
Ox CV 118

The other day when I met Dick (John Ciardi)
The other day when I met Dick
Pac 54

Robbin the Bobbin (trad)
Robbin the Bobbin the big fat [big-bellied] Ben
Fab NV 59; GV III 31; Ox Dic 372; Ox NR 84; Pac 88; P Life I 27; Puf NR 133

Sneaky Bill (William Cole)
I'm Sneaky Bill. I'm terribly mean and vicious
FV 47; Pac 87

Three Little Puffins (Eleanor Farjeon)
Three little puffins
Hi 17; Pac 92

UCKG! (Michael Rosen)
Once I went to the fridge
Pac 40

A Whitebait Feast (Thomas Love Peacock 1785–1866)
All day we sat, until the sun went down
Lon 48

GREYHOUNDS

A Ballad of Master McGrath (anon)
Eighteen sixty-nine being the date of the year
Fab Bal 215

The Properties of a Good Greyhound (Dame Juliana Berners)
A greyhound should be headed like a snake
Rat 352; (part) Al II 36; Voi II 49

To a Black Greyhound (Julian Grenfell)
Shining black in the shining light
Dog 25; Rain 59

GRIFFINS

The Griffin (or Gryphon) (Edward Lowbury)
The griffin was a strange device
Low G 35

GRINDERS

The Grinders
The Sheffield Grinder's a terrible blade
Fab PV 222

GROWING UP

All the World's a Stage (William Shakespeare)
All the world's a stage
As You Like It II vii 139; EGV 42; Ev 276; Fab PR 31; Rat 27; RR 99; Touch I 146

Autobiography (Louis MacNeice)
In my childhood trees were green
Flock 193

Can't Wait (John Kitching)
Not having much fun/At one
Fir 7

Every Few Weeks (Michael Rosen)
Every few weeks someone looks at me and says
Ros M 27; Ros Y

Growing (Max Fatchen)
When I grow up I'll be so kind
Fat S 18

If Things Grew Down (Robert D. Hoeft)
If things grew down
OSF 69

I'm a Man (Michael Rosen)
I'm a man./A grown-up man?
Ros M 37

I'm the Youngest (Michael Rosen)
I'm the youngest in our house
Fir 28; Ros W 35; Ros Y

Nursery Rhyme of Innocence and Experience (Charles Causley)
I had a silver penny
Cau C 16; Dawn 31; Hap 32; Liv 11; Sea 251; Str 32; Time 29

Schooldays End (Ewan MacColl)
Schooldays over – come on, then, John
Gold II 42

When I was One (A. A. Milne)
When I was One
Like 82; Mil NS 102

GUY FAWKES' NIGHT

See also Fireworks
Anagram for Guy Fawkes' Night (Frances Cornford)
Give me crowding children. A front lawn damp
Gold II 1

Gunpowder Plot (Vernon Scannell)
For days these curious cardboard buds have lain
Flock 267; Mod 64; Theme II 58; Touch III 61; Voi II 17

The Gunpowder Plot (anon)
Remember, remember/The fifth of November
Fab UV 159

A Guy (Stanley Cook)
Burglar alarming to find a man in the hall
Gold II 1

Guy Fawkes' Day (Charles Causley)
I am the caught, the cooked, the candled man
Voi II 19

November Story (Vernon Scannell)
The evening had caught cold
Poems 74; Sca A 16

November the Fifth (Leonard Clark)
And you, big rocket
Puf Y 72

November 3rd (Mick Gowar)
A rocket with its stick
Gow S 67

Please to Remember (Walter de la Mare)
Here am I
Croc 106; de la M Col 50; Gold II 3; P Life II 55

GYPSIES

Gipsies (John Clare)
The snow falls deep; the forest lies alone
Ev 111; Gold II 14; ND 136; Theme III 37
The gipsies seek wide sheltering woods again
DT 81; Rain 97; Rhyme IV 17; R Nine 14; Tho 88

The Gipsy Laddie (anon)
It was late in the night when the squire [my lord] came home
Come 196; Fab CV 173; Gold II 13; Ox PC 70

Gypsies (Rachel Field)
Last night the gypsies came
PT V 19

The Gypsy Countess (anon)
There cam' seven Egyptians on a day
Plea 255

The Idlers (Edmund Blunden)
The gipsies lit their fires by the chalkpit gate anew
Come 164; Gold II 12; Hap 34; ND 137; Say 47; Theme VI 23

Meg Merrilies (John Keats)
Old Meg she was a gipsy
Fab CV 117; Like 162; Merry 293; My V 88; Ox CV 147; Ox PC 149; Plea 117; Prel I 53; Puf V 235; RR 124; This W 137

The Romanies in Town (Anne Beresford)
Let us leave this place, brother
Liv 91

'Travellers' (Clive Sansom)
Gypsies are camped in Morton's
lot this morning
San E 8

The Wraggle-Taggle Gypsies
(trad)
Three gypsies stood at the castle
gate
Blow 46; Brit 118; Merry 246; P Life
IV 22; This W 157; Wind 81;
(variants) DP II 79; Duck 104
The gypsies they cam' to my lord
Cassilis' yett
Fab Bal 72; Peng B 53

HALLOWEEN

Halloween (Marie A. Lawson)
'Granny I saw a witch go by
Out Sc 78

Hallowe'en (John Ciardi)
Ruth says apples have learned to
bob
PT II 14; Shad 98

HANGING

from The Ballad of Reading Gaol
(Oscar Wilde)
He did not wear his scarlet coat
EGV 273

Ballad of the Long Drop (John
Pudney)
We dropped a chap that raped a
child
Bill 109; DP IV 119

Billy in the Darbies (Herman
Melville)
Good of the Chaplain to enter Lone
Bay
DP II 67

Clever Tom Clinch going to be
Hanged 1727 (Jonathan Swift)
As clever Tom Clinch, while the
rabble was bawling
Bill 121; DP IV 118; Fab Bal 182;
Theme III 19

Danny Deever (Rudyard
Kipling)
'What are the bugles blowin' for?'
said Files-on-Parade
Bill 120; EGV 284; Fab Bal 195; Fab
PR 223; Peng B 328; TCN 58

Eight O'Clock (A. E. Housman)
He stood, and heard the steeple
Bill 112; Gold IV 61; Touch II 170

The Epitaph in form of a Ballade
(F. Villon, trans A. C.
Swinburne)
Men, brother men, that after us yet
live
Bill 113

The Faking Boy (anon)
The Faking boy to the trap is gone
Bill 111; Rat 150

The Hangman at Home (Carl
Sandburg)
What does the hangman think
about
Theme III 21

The Hangman's Tree (anon)
Hangman, hangman, hold your
hand
Tale 30
O the prickly briar
Bk Bal 159
O good Lord Judge, and sweet
Lord Judge
Iron IV 109

Killers (Carl Sandburg)
I am put high over all others in the
city today
Gold III 9

A London Fête (Coventry
Patmore 1823–96)
All night fell hammers, shock on
shock
Lon 82; Theme III 19

This Malefactor (John Pudney)
This malefactor dies how many
times a day
Bill 110; Theme III 21

Murder (Edward Lucie-Smith)
For weeks we've had them, all the
photographs
DP IV 118

The Night before Larry was
Stretched (anon)
The night before Larry was
stretched
Fab Bal 208; Fab PV 161; Ox LV 54;
Peng B 299

Rizpah (Alfred, Lord
Tennyson)
Wailing, wailing, wailing, the wind
over land and sea
Poems II 116

A Shropshire Lad
(A. E. Housman)
On moonlit heath and lonesome
bank
Bill 117; Poems II 115

To Hang a Man (Ralph
Hodgson)
To hang a man
Theme III 22

HANNIBAL

Hannibal (Eleanor Farjeon)
Hannibal crossed the Alps!
P Life II 43

HARDY, THOMAS

Afterwards (Thomas Hardy)
When the Present has latched its
postern behind my tremulous stay
*Choice 144; ND 237; Plea 211; PW
261; Rat 23; Ten 98; Touch IV 40*

Birthday Poem for Thomas Hardy
(C. Day Lewis)
Is it birthday weather for you, dear
soul?
EGV 348

HARES

The Christmas Hare (anon)
It was one chilly Christmas Eve
Brit 33

Epitaph on a Hare (William
Cowper)
Here lies whom hound did ne'er
pursue

*Bat A 22; FM 76; OX PC 121; Plea
55; Puf V 55; RR 108; Voi I 84*

Hares at Play (John Clare)
The birds are gone to bed, the cows
are still
Ev 65; Rat 184

How Death Came (Hottentot,
trans Jack Cope)
The moon, they say, called Mantis
Att 59

March Hares (Andrew Young)
I made myself as a tree
Prel IV 8; Ten 163; Theme I 39

Two Songs of a Fool
(W. B. Yeats)
A speckled cat and a tame hare
F Feet 127; Rat 443; Voi I 83

from *Venus and Adonis* (William
Shakespeare)
By this, poor Wat [hare] far off
upon a hill
Venus and Adonis 697; Deli 87
But if thou needs wilt hunt, be
ruled by me
Venus and Adonis 673; FM 14; RR 171

The White Hare (Lilian Bowes
Lyon)
At the field's edge
Bat A 47; Plea 56

Your Own Way (John
Montague)
I heard this sound one night
Over 37

HATE

Fire and Ice (Robert Frost)
Some say the world will end in fire
GV IV 13

You! (Igbo, trans)
You!/Your head is like a hollow
drum
Afr I 9

HAWKS

The Hawk (Richard Church)
The hawk! He stands on air
Theme I 24

The Hawk (George Mackay
Brown)
On Sunday the hawk fell on
Bigging
Rat 184; Touch III 133

Hawk (George Rostrevor
Hamilton)
Things motionless were felt to
move
Tel 12; Touch III 133

Hawk Roosting (Ted Hughes)
I sit in the top of the wood, my eyes
closed
*Bir 84; Deli 88; Ev 101; Hug SP 43;
Mod 81; Tel 12; Theme I 24; Time 72;
Touch IV 155*

Hurt Hawks (Robinson Jeffers)
The broken pillar of the wing jags
from the clotted shoulder
Rat 204; Voi III 143

The Sparrow Hawk (Russell
Hoban)
Wings like pistols flashing at his
sides
Hob P 3; Zoo 71

HAY

The Hayloft (Robert Louis
Stevenson)
Through all the pleasant
meadow-side
P Life II 47; Ste CG 41

The Haystack (Andrew Young)
Too dense to have a door
Bits b; Dawn 99; Poems 24

HEDGEHOGS

Cat meets Hedgehog (Christopher
de Cruz)
Cat sees round prickly ball
Drum 56

Hedgehog (Chu Chen Po, trans
K. Rexroth)
He ambles along like a walking
pincushion
BE 37

The Hedgehog (John Clare)
The hedgehog hides beneath the
rotten hedge
Voi I 105

Hedgehog (Clive Sansom)
His back's all prickles, but his
pointed face
San E 10

Hedgehog (Anthony Thwaite)
Twitching the leaves just where the
drainpipe clogs
*Bat A 50; Dawn 64; Deli 49; DP I 7;
Drag 52; Gold II 36; Hap 17; Theme
VII 59; Touch II 68*

Hog (Roy Fuller)
'Erratic and eccentric in every way'
Ful P 62

HELICOPTERS

Helicopter (Gregory Harrison)
Heli, Heli, Heli/Copter
Mov 102

from *Precision* (Peter Collenette)
A small red-painted helicopter
Mov 103

HENS

See also Chickens, Cocks
The Clucking Hen
(A. Hawkshawe)
'Pray will you take a walk with me'
Fab NV 28; Puf V 35

The Hens (Elizabeth Madox
Roberts)
The night was coming very fast
Say 46

Hen's Nest (John Clare)
Among the orchard weeds, from
every search
Ev 91

Song of the Battery Hen (Edwin
Brock)
We can't grumble about
accomodation
*DP IV 15; Liv 83; Mod 112; Poems II
74; RR 18; Theme I 58*

HEROD

Innocents' Day (Norman
Nicholson)
And Herod said 'Sup-
Time 127

Innocents' Song (Charles
Causley)
Who's that knocking on the
window?
*Cau C 95; Dawn 110; DP I 75;
Mod 102; Shad 19; Star 83; Sun
112; Time 20*

The Miraculous Harvest (anon)
Rise up, rise up, you merry men all
Sun 113

HERONS

Boy into Heron (Celia Randall)
High on a stilt-raised bed above
the reeds
Gold I 56; My V 152; Theme V 44

The Heron (Gregory Harrison)
I said to the heron, 'Why do you
stand
Sec 81

The Heron (Phoebe Hesketh)
On lonely river-mud a heron alone
Touch II 74

The Heron (Ted Hughes)
The Sun's an iceberg
Hug U 28

Heron (John Normanton)
Flaps away north
Sun 27

The Heron (Theodore Roethke)
The heron stands in water where
the swamp
Gold II 45; Touch II 73

The Heron (Vernon Watkins)
The cloud-backed heron will not
move
Sea 45

Night Herons (Judith Wright)
It was after a day's rain
Sort 41

HIAWATHA

from *Hiawatha* (Henry
W. Longfellow)
By the shores of Gitche Gumee
CTV 75; EGV 185
First he danced a solemn measure
PT IV 13
Gitche Manito the mighty
Like 65
Swift of foot was Hiawatha
Touch II 120
Then the little Hiawatha
Once 46; Puf V 57
When he heard the owls at
midnight
FM 145

HIDE & SEEK

Hide and Seek (Robert Graves)
The trees are tall, but the moon
small
Fir 115

Hide and Seek (Vernon Scannell)
Yoo-Hoo! Call out. Call loud. I'm
ready! Come and find me!
*DP III 13; Drum 134; Duck 81; Ev
202; Gang 60; Hap 29; J Vo IV 70;
Liv 7; ND 99; Out Sc 34; Prel II 32;
R Nine 77; Theme V 59; Word 154;
World 20*

HIGHWAYMEN

Brennan on the Moore (anon)
It's of a fearless highwayman a
story I will tell
*Bk Bal 138; Fab Bal 204; Fab PV
254; Mov 14; Nar 89*

The Crafty Farmer (anon)
Farmer Jupp on a country road
Tale 96

The Female Highwayman (anon)
Priscilla on one summer's day
Brit 191

The Highwayman (Alfred Noyes)
The wind was a torrent of darkness
among the gusty trees
DP I 54; EGV 319; Like 145; ND 140

The Highwayman Outwitted
(anon)
It's of a rich farmer in Cheshire
Brit 141

HIPPOPOTAMI

I had a Hippopotamus (Patrick
Barrington)
I had a hippopotamus, I kept him
in a shed
*Blow 50; Ev 72; Fab NV 181; Hap II
81; Rhyme IV 90*

The Hippopotamus (Hilaire
Belloc)
I shoot the hippopotamus
*Bat A 14; Bat L 129; Bal CV 102;
CBC 51; Merry 191*

The Hippopotamus (Ogden Nash)
Behold the hippopotamus!
Nas C 33; Once 27

The Hippopotamus (Jack
Prelutsky)
The huge hippopotamus hasn't a
hair
Sec 69; Zoo 46

Our Hippopotamus (Colin West)
We thought a lively pet to keep
Wes N 68

HIROSHIMA

Ghosts, Fire, Water (James
Kirkup)
These are the ghosts of the
unwilling dead
Time 88

Hiroshima (Angela M. Clifton)
The bomb burst like a flower
Conf 11

The Monuments of Hiroshima
(D. J. Enright)
The roughly estimated ones, who
do not sort well
Gold IV 53

No More Hiroshimas (James
Kirkup)
At the station exit, my bundle in
hand
*Conf 12; Theme III 70; Touch V 66;
Time 89*

Relative Sadness (Colin
Rowbotham)
Einstein's eyes
Burn 119; Touch V 68

HOBOES

The Big Rock Candy Mountains
(trad)
One evenin' as the sun went down
*Duck 100; Fab PV 228; Imp 91; Iron I
38; J Vo II 36; ND 112; PW 22;
Touch I 158*

Hallelujah, Bum Again (anon)
O why don't I work like other men
do?
Fab PV 231

An Invitation to Lubberland (anon)
There's all sorts of fowl and fish
Fab Non 40

Two Hoboes (anon)
Railroad look so pretty
Oral 367

HOHENLINDEN

Hohenlinden (Thomas
Campbell)
On Linden, when the sun was low
Fab CV 256; Fab PR 81

HOLLY TREES

The Holly (Walter de la Mare)
The sturdiest of forest trees
Bk S 69

HOMELESSNESS

Not Sixteen (Ian Serraillier)
I wasn't sixteen when I left school
Tale 69

Song (John Clare)
I've wandered many a weary mile
Bat C 27

HOMESICKNESS

Home Thoughts from Abroad
(Robert Browning)
O to be in England
*BB 31; By 173; EGV 222; Fab PR
162; ND 7; P Life IV 71; Puf V 177;
Rain 82; Root 48; Scene 64*

Home Thoughts from Home (Rick
Ferreira)
The sunlight is pierced with
screams
Root 49

I am Two Islands (Rick Ferreira)
I am two islands
Root 90

My Heart's in the Highlands
(Robert Burns)
My heart's in the Highlands, my
heart is not here
*Ox PC 141; Plea 106; Rhyme III 43;
Root 47*

The Old Vicarage, Grantchester
(Rupert Brooke)
Just now the lilac is in bloom
EGV 329

Postcard from Kashmir (Agha
Shahid Ali)
Kashmir shrinks into my mailbox
Root 26

To S. R. Crockett (Robert Louis
Stevenson)
Blows the wind today, and the sun
and the rain are flying
Puf V 201

The Tropics in New York (Claude
McKay)
Bananas ripe and green, and
ginger-root
Cari I 82

HONESTY

Telling lies to the young is wrong
(Y. Yevtushenko)
Telling lies to the young is wrong
Conf 3

HONEY

See also Bees

Sing a song of honey (Barbara Euphan Todd)
Honey from the white rose, honey from the red
Puf V 143; Rhyme II 31

HOOPOES

The Hoopoe (John Heath-Stubbs)
A rare one with us
Sun 72

HOPPING

Hoppity (A. A. Milne)
Christopher Robin goes/Hoppity, hoppity
Mil VY 60

HORATIUS

from *Horatius* (Lord Macaulay)
Lars Porsena of Clusium
EGV 168; Fab CV 150; Fab PR 106; ND 164

HORRORS

Alternative Endings to an Unwritten Ballad (Paul Dehn)
I stole through the dungeons while everyone slept
Gang 47

HORSES (L & D)

See also Hor throughout, *Plea 166–187*
See also Hunting, Polo, Ponies, Racehorses

The Barge Horse (Sean Jennett)
The brasses jangle and the hawsers tighten
Bill 129

The Clipper that stands in the stall at the top (G. J. Whyte-Melville)
Go strip him, lad! Now, sir, I think you'll declare
Hor 68

The Dauphin's Horse (William Shakespeare)
I will not change my horse with any that treads
Henry V III vii 11; Bat A 31

The Horses (Ted Hughes)
I climbed through woods in the hour-before-dawn dark
Drag 15; Hor 36; Hug SP 19; Time 71; Touch V 203

Horses (Edwin Muir)
Those lumbering horses in the steady plough
Fab CV 78; Hor 78; Plea 166; Ten 115

Horses Aboard (Thomas Hardy)
Horses in horsecloth stand in a row
Voi I 92

The Horses of the Sea (Christina Rossetti)
The horses of the sea
Bat A 30; Rain 48; Rhyme II 42

Horses on the Camargue (Roy Campbell)
In the grey wastes of dread
Dawn 88; Hor 63; ND 78; Plea 167; Touch V 204

Old Horse (Phoebe Hesketh)
He's worked out
Hes S 19

Poor Old Horse (anon)
My clothing was once of the linsey woolsey fine
Gold I 40; Hor 35; Iron I 21; Merry 216

from *Song of Myself* (Walt Whitman)
A gigantic beauty of a stallion
Bat A 30; FM 162; Hor 45; Theme I 7

Title of a Swift Horse (anon, Mongol)
This truly wonderful steed
Oral 51

from *Venus and Adonis* (William Shakespeare)
But lo, from forth a copse that neighbours by
Venus and Adonis 259; FM 11; Hor 12; Plea 180

War God's Horse Song (Navajo, trans Louis Watchman)
I am the Turquoise Woman's son
Dis 121; Rat 455

War-Horse (Book of Job A.V.)
Hast thou given the horse strength?
Job 39 19; Bat A 31; DP II 97; FM 5; Hor 11; Iron II 15; PW 83; Rhyme III 54

The Wild, the Free (Lord Byron)
With flowing tail and flying mane
Like 145

HORSES (N)

Birth of the Foal (Ferenc Juhász, trans David Wevill)
As May was opening the rosebuds
Rat 79; Stuf 47

The Horses (Edwin Muir)
Barely a twelvemonth after
Conf 21; Ima 114; Rat 191; Ring 115; RR 185; Ten 120; Touch V 74

The Horse's Revenge (La Fontaine, trans Edward Marsh)
Not from the first were Horses born for Men
Hor 48

How they brought the Good News from Ghent to Aix (Robert Browning)
I sprang to the stirrup, and Joris, and he
By 169; Down 35; EGV 219; Fab PR 163; (part) Hor 65

from *How we beat the Favourite* (Adam Lindsay Gordon)
Dark brown with tan muzzle, just stripped for the tussle
Hor 56

The Man from Snowy River (A. B. 'Banjo' Paterson)
There was movement at the station for the word had passed around
Nar 44; SAS 13; Tam 19

HOSPITALS

See also Illness, Nurses

from *Air-Raid Casualties: Ashridge Hospital* (Patricia Ledward)
On Sundays friends arrive with kindly words
TR 128

Sick Visits (R. S. Thomas)
They keep me sober
Theme IV 67

Surgical Ward: Men (Robert Graves)
Something occurred after the operation
Fab Mod 238

Ten Types of Hospital Visitor (Charles Causley)
The first enters wearing the neon armour
Cau C 245; Mus 53; Ox Con 81

Vigil (W. E. Henley)
Lived on one's back
Theme II 36

Visiting Hour (Norman MacCaig)
The hospital smell
GV V 34; Liv 82; Look 50; Seven 173

Ward F4 (Phoebe Hesketh)
There is no weather in my room
Hes S 13

HOUNDS

Hounds (William Shakespeare)
I was with Hercules and Cadmus once
Midsummer Night's Dream IV i 109; Dog 77
My hounds are bred out of the Spartan kind
Midsummer Night's Dream IV i 116; Plea 54

HOUSES

See also Demolitions, Tower Blocks
A Cornish Cottage (Crosbie Garstin)
Beside the clock two spaniels stand
RR 43

Portrait of a House (E. V. Rieu)
The house that we live in was built in a place
Hap II 90

HOUSES, LONELY

The Deserted House (Mary Coleridge)

There's no smoke in the chimney
Blow 8; Deli 67; Ev 167; Merry 175; Puf Y 18; R Eig 63; This W 110; Tho 55

The Empty House (Russell Hoban)
Where the lone wind on the hilltop
Hist 62; Hob P 10

The Haunted House (Jack Prelutsky)
On a hilltop bleak and bare
Night 6

House Fear (Robert Frost)
Always – I tell you this they learned –
Hap II 61; Puf M 146

House for Sale (Vernon Scannell)
The wind is loud, wraps noise about the house
Drag 37

I know some lonely Houses (Emily Dickinson)
I know some lonely houses off the road
Iron II 22; J Vo III 73; PW 246; Theme III 5; Touch II 163

The Old Stone House (Walter de la Mare)
Nothing on the gray roof, nothing on the brown
Shad 35

The Shepherd's Hut (Andrew Young)
The smear of blue peat smoke
Dawn 48; GP 14; ND 213; Shad 34

Silences (Thomas Hardy)
There is the silence of a copse or croft
Prel IV 36

HOUSEWIVES

From the Train (Kenneth Hopkins)
From this slow train I see the terraced backs
Theme VI 32

The Housewife's Lament (trad)
One day I was walking, I heard a complaining
Theme VI 10; Voi I 45

Ire (R. S. Thomas)
Are you out, woman of the lean pelt
RR 95

On a Poor Woman (anon)
Here lies a poor woman who always was tired
CBC 55; GP 15; GV V 27; My V 91; Poems II 45; Rhy 68; Theme VI 11

Sall Scratch (Charles Causley)
Sall Scratch
Cau F 22

'Urry! (C. J. Dennis)
Now, ma-til-der! Ain't yer dressed yet? I declare, the girl ain't up!
Aus 43

The Wider Life (Celia Fremlin)
I once was a dull, narrow housewife
PT V 18

HUMMING-BIRDS

Humming-Bird
(D. H. Lawrence)
I can imagine in some otherworld
Gold IV 1; ND 66; Rat 197; Touch V 167

On an Indian Tomineois (Thomas Heynick)
I'm made in sport by Nature, when
FM 41

HUMP, THE

The Hump (Rudyard Kipling)
The Camel's hump is an ugly lump
Fab NV 104; Ox CV 319

HUNGER

Hunger (trad Yoruba)
Hunger makes a person climb up to the ceiling
Att 79
Hunger makes a person lie down
Oral 166; Rhy 52

Lazy Morning (Jacques Prevert, trans Lawrence Ferlinghetti)
It's terrible
Prel IV 25

Starvation in de Market-Place
(Glyne Walrond, Caribbean)
All kind of breadfruit, pumpkin,
potato and melon
Stuf 54

HUNTING

See also 'Hunter Poems of the
Yoruba' *Rat 197–203*
See also Foxes, Foxhounds,
Hares, Hounds, Shooting,
Stags

Big Game Hunter (Alexander
Resnikoff)
My father goes to Africa
OSF 71

from *Don Juan* (Lord Byron)
A fox-hunt to a foreigner is strange
Hor 44

Drink, Puppy, Drink
(G. J. Whyte-Melville)
Here's to the fox in his earth below
the rocks
Dog 64

The Fox-Hunt (Stanley Cook)
They hunt the fox today
Four 78

Hi! (Walter de la Mare)
Hi! handsome hunting man
Bat L 124; de la M Col 104

The Hunt (Walter de la Mare)
Tallyho! Tallyho!
de la M Col 22

Hunting Songs (trad North
American Indian)
One I have wounded, yonder he
moves *and* Lo, surely I shall die
Deli 86

The Lord of the Valley
(G. J. Whyte-Melville)
Hunters are fretting, and hacks in a
lather
Hor 84

The Mare and her Master
(R. E. Egerton-Warburton)
Though my sight is grown dim,
though my arm is grown weak
Hor 42

The Old Squire (Wilfrid Scawen
Blunt)
I like the hunting of the hare
Fab PR 199

The Runnable Stag (John
Davidson)
When the pods went pop on the
broom, green broom
EGV 272; Fab PR 195; FM 230

from *St Valentine's Day* (Wilfrid
Scawen Blunt)
Today, all day, I rode upon the
down
Hor 75

Three Jovial Welshmen (trad)
There were three jovial Welshmen
[huntsmen]
*Fab NV 140; Fab PV 86; Gold I 11;
Merry 337; Ox Dic 421; Ox NR 116;
Ox PC 24; P Life III 48; Puf V 162;*
(part) *Lolli II 12; My V 17*
Three jolly huntsmen
Puf Y 156

HYENAS

The Hyaena (Lord Alfred
Douglas)
A curious beast is the hyaena
Dou T 10

Hyena (Edwin Morgan)
I am waiting for you
Ima 122; Strict 41

Hyena (Yoruba, trans Ulli
Beier)
The scruffy one
Rat 202

ICE

See Frost and Ice

IGUANAS

*Australian Transcripts: Mid-Noon
in January* (William Sharp)
Upon a fibry fern-tree bough
FM 225

ILLNESS

The Battle (Edward Lowbury)
Not Alamein or Waterloo
Low G 31

Bones (Walter de la Mare)
Said Mr Smith, 'I really cannot
CC 48

A Child Ill (John Betjeman)
Oh, little body, do not die
PC 37; Ten 39

Evans (R. S. Thomas)
Evans? Yes, many a time
Choice 308; Poems II 98

Fever Dream (Edward Lowbury)
Tossed with fever on my bed
Low G 28

Head Injury (Roger McGough)
I do not smile because I am happy
Mer R 95; NV 104

Poor Henry (Walter de la Mare)
Thick in its glass/The physic
stands
de la M Col 270

The Watch (Frances Cornford)
I wakened on my hot hard bed
RR 117

IMAGINATION

*The Aging Poet Sees a Sinister
Being* (Roy Fuller)
A motor waiting by the library
Ful P 26

In the Bathroom (Roy Fuller)
What is that bloodstained thing
Ful P 18; Sec 37

IMAGINATION,
CHILDREN'S

The Balloon (Karla Kuskin)
I went to the park
Here 70

The Bedpost (Robert Graves)
Sleepy Betsy from her pillow
Isle 67

Busy (A. A. Milne)
I think I am a Muffin man. I
haven't got a bell
Mil NS 7

The Centaur (May Swenson)
The summer that I was ten –
Nar 34

The Commentator (Gareth Owen)
Good afternoon and welcome
ADT 79; Third 32

The End of the World (Basil
Dowling)
I was but nine years old
Theme IV 5

A Good Play (Robert Louis
Stevenson)
We built a ship upon the stairs
ADT 77; Ste CG 14; Young 82

Halfway Down (A. A. Milne)
Halfway down the stairs
Mil VY 81

The Hamspringer (George
Barker)
The Hamspringer jumps about in
the bed
Bar R 14

I'll Stand the Lot of You (Martin
Hall)
I'll stand the lot of you
ADT 84

The Land of Counterpane (Robert
Louis Stevenson)
When I was sick and lay a-bed
*CTV 128; Ox CV 295; PC 42; Rain
95; Ste CG 16; WAS 62*

The Land of Story-Books (Robert
Louis Stevenson)
At evening when the lamp is lit
CTV 125; Duck 108; Ste CG 58

Lines and Squares (A. A. Milne)
Whenever I walk in a London
street
Mil VY 12; Non 224

The Marrog (R. C. Scriven)
My desk's at the back of the class
*AM 11; Drum 104; Duck 72; Fir 108;
Hist 85; Like 85*

Once a Stone was a Car (Edmond
Leo Wright)
Once a stone was a car. It only
need be
Over 21

The Secret Brother (Elizabeth
Jennings)
Jack lived in the greenhouse
Prel I 14

A Sick Child (Randall Jarrell)
The postman comes when I am
still in bed
Theme IV 4

Skilly Oogan (Russell Hoban)
Skilly Oogan's no one you can see
Hob P 4

The Toaster (William Jay Smith)
A silver-scaled dragon with jaws
flaming red
*ADT 13; Drum 83; Fab NV 173; J Vo
III 7; Sec 66; Zoo 57*

You were the Mother last time
(Mary Anne Hoberman)
You were the mother last time
CC 9

IMMIGRANTS

*Four Epigrams on the
Naturalisation Bill* (John Byrom,
1692–1763)
Come all ye foreign strolling gentry
Ox LV 42

On Seeing my First Snowfall
(P. S. Guptara, India)
'Terrible weather,' he said, 'and
you
Root 24

Questionnaired (Tessa Stiven,
India)
'Tell me again – the name of your
wife
Root 30

INDEPENDENCE

I'm the Youngest (Michael
Rosen)
I'm the youngest in our house
Ros W 35; Ros Y

INDIA

The Night of the Scorpion (Nissim
Ezekiel, India)
I remember the night my mother
*Att 18; Bite I 21; Ev 112; Ima 34;
Many 65*

INDIANS, RED

See also Buffaloes, Hiawatha
*The Bad Boy of the North-West
Coast* (Dannie Abse)
Before the grown-ups awake –
haaya
Over 67

Circles (Carl Sandburg)
The white man drew a small circle
in the sand
Flock 134

INDUSTRIAL SOCIETY

Going Anywhere? (Richard Kell)
The limousine that Mr L. S. Dee
Conf 100; Gold IV 12

An Importer (Robert Frost)
Mrs Someone's been to Asia
Iron IV 31; PW 287

The Marunouchi Building
(Nakahara Chuya)
Ah! lunch and/There goes the siren
Al III 13

INGRATITUDE

Blow, blow, thou winter wind
(William Shakespeare)
Blow, blow, thou winter wind
*As You Like It II vii 174; DP IV 35;
EGV 43; Fab LP 317; Merry 255; P
Life IV 33 Puf V 30; PW 58*

INSECTS AND RELATED
CREATURES

See also Bees, Beetles,
Butterflies, Caterpillars,
Centipedes, Crickets,
Dragon-Flies, Earwigs,
Fireflies, Fleas, Flies,
Glow-worms, Gnats,
Grasshoppers, Ladybirds,
Locusts, Mosquitoes,
Scorpions, Spiders, Wasps

Advice to Children (Roy Fuller)
Caterpillars living on lettuce
Ful S 56

An August Midnight (Thomas
Hardy)
A shaded lamp and a waving blind
Iron III 11; Ten 101; Theme I 53

Flea, Bee, Moth, Termite, etc
(Frank Collymore)
I think that I shall never see
Cari I 80–81; Tam 44–46

The Insect World (John Clare)
The insect world amid the suns
and dew
DT 71

June Bug (Edward Lucie-Smith)
Bug like a coffee bean
Cari I 65

Termite, Firefly (Ogden Nash)
Some primal termite knocked on wood
Touch II 117

INVENTIONS

Fruitless Fable (Muriel Spark)
Mr Chiddicott, being a bachelor
Hap II 74

The Microscope (Maxime Kumin)
Anton Leuwenhoek was Dutch
BE 36; PT V 28

IRELAND

See also Ulster

The Croppy Boy 1798 (anon)
It was early, early all in the spring
DP II 82

Easter 1916 (W. B. Yeats)
I have met them at close of day
Fab Mod 74; Fab PR 214; Ten 148

No Irish need apply (anon)
I'm a decent boy just landed
Oral 187

The Shan Van Vocht (anon 1797)
O the French are on the sea
Fab PV 194

The Wearing of the Green (Dion Boucicault)
O Paddy dear, and did you hear the news that's going round?
Fab PR 175; Fab PV 193; Oral 185

JACKDAWS

The Jackdaw (William Cowper)
There is a bird who, by his coat
Bir 62

The Jackdaw of Rheims (Richard Harris Barham)
The Jackdaw sat on the Cardinal's chair!
ND 67; Touch I 50

JACOBITES

See Charlie, Bonnie Prince

JAGUARS

The Jaguar (Ted Hughes)
The apes yawn, and adore their fleas in the sun
Gold III 28; Hug SP 15; Many 64; Seven 141; Theme I 71; Time 70; Touch II 65

Second Glance at a Jaguar (Ted Hughes)
Skinfull of bowl, he bowls them
Seven 151; Touch V 178

JAMAICA

Ballad of Sixty-Five (Alma Norman)
The roads are rocky and the hills are steep
Stuf 87

Jamaican Market (Agnes Maxwell-Hall)
Honey, pepper, leaf-green limes
Bite I 49

Jamaica Wanderers (Alma Norman)
You'll find us in Nigeria, you'll see us in Colon
NS 57

Lament of the Banana Man (Evan Jones)
Gal, I'm tellin' you, I'm tired fo' true
Cari I 86; Mod 165; NS 29; PT III 20

A Letter to Jo in Jamaica (Joan Davidson)
The wind blows sweetly
Blue 28

Revolt of Chief Tacky (Alma Norman)
Tacky the chieftain decided to fight
Bite I 2; NS 26

Song of the Banana Man (Evan Jones)
Touris', white man wipin' his face
Afr II 52; Bite I 9; Cari I 4; Many 17; Mod 162; NS 46; Tam 34

JAMES, JESSE

Cf. Bushrangers, Highwaymen

Jesse James (anon)
It was on a Wednesday night, the moon was shining bright
Gold II 8

Jesse James was a lad that killed
many a man
BHL 9
Jesse James was one of his names
Bk Bal 119
Yes, I went down to the depot
Iron II 88

JANUARY

from *Odes of the Months*
(Aneirin, trans W. Probert)
Month of January – smoky is the
vale
Flock 4

JAPAN

Japanese Children (James
Kirkup)
The round, calm faces rosy with
the cold
Flock 68; R Eig 125

JAYS

Jay (George Barker)
Jays are birds
Bar A 'J'

JAZZ

J is for Jazz-Man (Eleanor
Farjeon)
Crash and/CLANG!
J Vo I 14; Pt IV 10

Jazz Fantasia (Carl Sandburg)
Drum on your drums, batter on
your banjos
*Bite II 9; Tho 97; Touch II 44;
Voi III 79*

from *Jazz for Five: Colin Barnes,
Drums* (John Smith)
Listen, listen/There's walking in
the world
Mod 186; PT IV 14

from *Jazz for Five: Shake Keane,
Trumpet* (John Smith)
Have you ever heard the sun in the
sky
Mod 188; PT IV 21

JEALOUSY

The First Tooth (Charles and
Mary Lamb)
Through the house what busy joy
Ox CV 143

Jealousy (Ian Serraillier)
Who lived in the empty house
Tale 84

My Last Duchess (Robert
Browning)
That's my last Duchess painted on
the wall
Plea 281; PW 227

The Two Sisters of Binnorie
(anon)
There were two sisters sat in a
bower
*Bk Bal 14; Fab Bal 32; Plea 257;
Wind 14*
There were twa sisters sat in a
bower
Scot 89; Touch I 11

JERUSALEM

Jerusalem (William Blake)
And did those feet in ancient time
*By 111; Come 215; DP IV 155; EGV
116; Fab CV 126; Fab PR 62; Hymn
78; ND 5; P Life IV 74; Puf V 247;
PW 156; Rat 221; Scene 176*

Jerusalem or *Hierusalem* (anon)
Jerusalem, my happy home
Fab CV 370; Fab PR 19; Voi II 149

Jerusalem the Golden (Bernard of
Cluny, trans J. M. Neale)
Jerusalem the golden
Hymn 14

JERVIS BAY, THE

The Jervis Bay (Michael
Thwaites)
The *Jervis Bay* was a liner in the
proper days of peace
Hap 74; RR 35

JEWELS

Flint (Christina Rossetti)
An emerald is as green as grass
Merry 268; Ox CV 277; Rain 111

Precious Stones (Walter de la
Mare)

Ruby, amethyst, emerald,
diamond
de la M Col 95; P Life III 89

JONAH

Jonah (Aldous Huxley)
A cream of phosphorescent light
Sea 163

Jonah (Thomas Blackburn)
He stands in rags upon the heaving
prow
Dawn 38; Sun 76

Jonah and the Whale (Gareth
Owen)
Well to start with/It was dark
Nar 20; Owe S 41

The Whale and Jonah (Viola
Meynell)
He sported round the watery world
By 254

JOSEPH

Joseph Fell A-Dreaming (Eleanor
Farjeon)
Joseph fell a-dreaming
Puf Q 20

JOSEPH, SAINT

Carpenter (George Mackay
Brown)
Workman, what will you make on
the bench today?
Ox Con 127

Joseph (Gilbert Thomas)
Who has not carolled Mary
Hap II 60

Joseph and Jesus (Spanish, trans
Robert Graves)
Said Joseph unto Mary
Star 84

JUDAS ISCARIOT

Jack o'Lent (Charles Causley)
Where are you running to, Jack o'
Lent?
Cau C 265; WAS 28

Judas (anon, 13th century)
It was upon a Maundy Thursday
that our Lord arose
Flock 160

Judas Iscariot (R. W. Buchanan)
'Twas the soul of Judas Iscariot
Sun 168

JUGGLERS

Juggler (Richard Wilbur)
A ball will bounce, but less and
less. It's not
Voi III 161

JULY

from *The Shepherd's Calendar*
(John Clare)
. . . noon burns with its blistering
breath
Touch III 102

JUNE

June Thunder (Louis MacNeice)
The Junes were free and full,
driving through tiny
Mod 20

KANGAROOS

Kangaroo (Mary Innes)
The kangaroo proceeds by hops
Inn B 'K'

Kangarooo (D. H. Lawrence)
In the northern hemisphere
Flock 214; Touch IV 162; Voi I 81
(part) Delicate mother kangaroo
World 68

The Kangaroo (singing game,
Australian)
Old Jumpety-Bumpety-Hop
and-Go-One
*Al II 34; Fab NV 74; F Feet 80; FV
10; Rain 54; Rhyme I 30*

KARATE

Bradford, June 1972 (Edwin
Morgan)
Dusty, bruised, and grazed, and
cut about a bit, but
Seven 258

KEATS, JOHN

Keats at Teignmouth 1818
(Charles Causley)
By the wild sea-wall I wandered
By 301; Cau C 13

KESTRELS

K is for Kestrel (Eleanor Farjeon)
Still hangs the kestrel there
Far M 13

The Kestrel (John Heath-Stubbs)
The small falcon, with sharp pointed wings
Hea P 7

KEW GARDENS

The Barrel Organ (Alfred Noyes)
Go down to Kew in lilac-time, in lilac-time, in lilac-time
Come 82

KIDD, CAPTAIN

Captain Kidd (R. and S. V. Benét)
This person in the gaudy clothes
Fab NV 40; P Life III 11

Captain Robert Kidd (anon)
You captains brave and bold, hear our cries
Peng B 266

KIDNAPPING

John Polrudden (Charles Causley)
John Polrudden/All of a sudden
Cau C 186; Cau N 9; Drag 57; Ev 124

KILLING

Five Ways to Kill a Man (Edwin Brock)
There are many cumbersome ways to kill a man
Look 83; Tam 27; Touch V 16

KINGFISHERS

Kingfisher (Phoebe Hesketh)
Brown as nettle-beer, the stream
Hes S 21

The Kingfisher (John Heath-Stubbs)
When Noah left the Ark, the animals
Sun 55

Kingfishers (Percy Bysshe Shelley)
I cannot tell my joy when o'er a lake
Bat A 52

from *Upon Appleton House* (Andrew Marvell)
So when the shadows laid asleep
Bir 29

KINGS AND QUEENS

See also Fab NV 258–272; Fab UV 160–68 and Ox NR 113 for mnemonics for order and dates of English rulers
See also Charles I, Charles II, Elizabeth I, Mary Queen of Scots, Queens

The King's Breakfast (A. A. Milne)
The King asked/the Queen and
Fab NV 266; Mil VY 55; My R 56; Ox CV 341; Pac 14

Old King Cole (anon)
Old King Cole
Fab NV 265

KITES

The Kite (Harry Behn)
How bright on the blue
Hi 12

Kite (Miles Gibson)
When steel winds wiped
Drag 66

from *Reflection on Wrecked Kites* (Frank Collymore)
On the sagging telephone wires
Bite I 30

KITTENS

Choosing their Names (Thomas Hood)
Our old cat has kittens three
ADT 24; Blow 26; Cat 44; Puf Y 105; Rain 38; Rhyme II 41

from *The Kitten and the Falling Leaves* (William Wordsworth)
See the kitten on the wall
Cat 33; Ox PC 106; Puf V 48

The Kitten in Falling Snow (James Kirkup)
The year-old kitten
Out 78; Sec 100

Miss Tibbles (Ian Serraillier)
Miss Tibbles is my kitten; white
Puf Q 155

The Three Little Kittens
Three little kittens/They lost their mittens
Bat L 58; Ox Dic 256; Ox NR 65

Two Little Kittens (Jane Taylor)
Two little kittens one stormy night
Blow 12; Come 54; Fab NV 166; F Feet 111; Ox CV 285; Rhyme I 31; R Six 30

KNIGHTS AND LADIES (L & D)

See also Arthur, King
Advice to a Knight (T. H. Jones)
Wear modest armour; and walk quietly
Flock 245; Poems II 16

All in Green (e. e. cummings)
All in green went my love riding
Flock 203; This W 149

from *The Canterbury Tales* (Geoffrey Chaucer)
A Knyght ther was, and that a worthy man
Duck 64; EGV 2; Flock 19
(trans N. Coghill)
There was a knight, a most distinguished man
Flock 18

Eldorado (Edgar Allen Poe)
Gaily bedight/A gallant knight
CTV 53; Fab CV 187; Like 117; P Life IV 96; Puf V 86; Stuf 81

from *The Faerie Queene* (Edmund Spenser)

A gentle knight was pricking o'er the plain *and* The knight of the Redcrosse when him he spied
Hor 38

Fafnir and the Knights (Stevie Smith)
In the quiet waters
ND 189; World 84

The Knight in Prison (William Morris)
Wearily, drearily
J Vo III 83; PW 255; World 83

KNIGHTS AND LADIES (N)

The Enchanted Knight (Edwin Muir)
Lulled by La Belle Dame Sans Merci he lies
Isle 43; Shad 43

The Knight's Leap (Charles Kingsley)
So the foemen have fired the gate, men of mine
DP II 43

La Belle Dame Sans Merci (John Keats)
'O what can ail thee, knight-at-arms
By 141; DP IV 127; EGV 157; Fab CV 202; Hist 54; Isle 41; My V 36; ND 195; Plea 243; Puf M 62; Puf V 107; PW 212; Rat 71; This W 164

The Lady of Shalott (Alfred, Lord Tennyson)
On either side the river lie
DP IV 130; EGV 198; Isle 69; ND 204; Puf V 197; Rhyme III 6
(part) A bow-shot from her bower-eaves
P Life IV 36
(part) On either side the river lie
Like 155
(part) That she weaves by night and day
Puf M 54

Shameful Death (William Morris)
There were four of us about that bed
Bat S 84

Sir Eglamour (Samuel Rowlands)
Sir Eglamour that worthy knight

Fab CV 170; Fab Non 25; Merry 324;
Ox PC 25

Young Waters (anon)
About Yule when the wind blew
cule
Bat S 64

KNITTING

The Useful Art of Knitting
(Katherine Craig)
When Mum sits down to knit at
night
Sort 75

KRAKEN

The Kraken (Alfred, Lord
Tennyson)
Below the thunders of the upper
deep
AM 51; ND 191; P Life IV 59; This
W 119

LADYBIRDS

Clock-a-Clay [Ladybird] (John
Clare)
In the cowslip pips I lie
DP I 6; Drum 51; Merry 258; Ox PC
119; Rain 47; R Nine 45; Say 44; This
W 118

Ladybird (Clive Sansom)
Tiniest of turtles
Drum 50

LAMBS

See also Sheep

A Child's Voice (Andrew Young)
On winter nights shepherd and I
Out Sc 81

First Sight (Philip Larkin)
Lambs that learn to walk in snow
By 303

Herding Lambs (Ruth Pitter)
In the spring, in the morning
Dawn 96

The Lamb (William Blake)
Little lamb, who made thee?
By 113; EGV 112; Fab CV 353; Ox
CV 85; R Eig 78; Say 70; Trad 141;
WAS 49

The Lambs of Grasmere, 1860
(Christina Rossetti)

The upland flocks grew starved
and thinned
Ev 29; F Feet 33; FM 186

Woolly White Lambs (Wilma
Horsburgh)
Woolly white Lambs with black
legs and faces
Hor B 17

LAMENTS

See Dirges

LANDSCAPES

See P Scot throughout
The Cuillin Hills (Andrew
Young)
Each step a cataract of stones
P Scot 72

Landscape as Werewolf (William
Dunlop)
Near here, the last grey wolf
DP IV 51

from *Marmion: St Mary's Lake*
(Sir Walter Scott)
Thou know'st it well – nor fen nor
sedge
P Scot 33

Rocky Acres (Robert Graves)
This is a wild land, country of my
choice
Choice 258; DP IV 49; Theme VII 39

Under the Mountain (Louis
MacNeice)
Seen from above
Touch I 28

Wuthering Heights (Sylvia Plath)
The horizons ring me like faggots
Touch III 94

LARKS

A Green Cornfield (Christina
Rossetti)
The earth was green, the sky was
blue
F Feet 55; Rain 48; R Eig 26

The Lark Ascending (George
Meredith)
He rises and begins to round
Ev 94; Prel IV 31

The Sea and the Skylark (Gerard Manley Hopkins)
On ear and ear two noises too old to end
FM 212; PW 264; Voi I 116

The Skylark (John Heath-Stubbs)
'There's a sparrer up there', said the Cockney boy
Hea P 31

Skylarks (Ted Hughes)
The lark begins to go up
Hug SP 102

To a Skylark (Percy Bysshe Shelley)
Hail to thee, blithe spirit!
Bir 46; (part) *F Feet 54*

LAUGHTER

Mrs Reece Laughs (Martin Armstrong)
Laughter, with us, is no great undertaking
Prel IV 43

LAZARUS

See also Dives and Lazarus

Lazarus (Elizabeth Jennings)
It was the amazing white, it was the way he simply
Theme II 22

The Little Family (anon)
There was a little family
Bat S 99

LAZINESS

Go to the Ant (The Bible A.V.)
Go to the ant, thou sluggard
Proverbs VI 6; RR 172

Lazy (Mary O'Neill)
Lazy is a word
ONe 44

Lazy Lou (Mary Mapes Dodge)
Lazy Lou, Lazy Lou
BBGG 39

The Lazy Man (trad Yoruba)
When the cock crows
Rhy 39

Lazy Man's Song (Po Chu-I, trans Arthur Waley)
I could have a job but am too lazy to choose it
Full 42; Hap 72; Imp 84; Iron IV 90;

Pluc 26; Rhy 38; Theme VI 22

Pooh! (Walter de la Mare)
Dainty Miss Apathy
Bat L 140; de la M Col 40

The Old Sailor (A. A. Milne)
There was once an old sailor my grandfather knew
Fab NV 36; Mil NS 36

Reply of the Sluggard (Christine Morley, aged 14)
Working, that's not for me
Theme VI 21

The Sluggard (Isaac Watts)
'Tis the voice of the sluggard; I heard him complain
EGV 89; Ox CV 51; Puf V 147; Theme VI 20

LEAR, EDWARD

Edward Lear (Edward Lear)
How pleasant to know Mr Lear!
Bat C 36; Fab CV 124; OX LV 103; P Life III 30

LEGS

The Legs (Robert Graves)
There was this road
BE 42; J Vo III 61; Rat 235

LEISURE

Leisure (W. H. Davies)
What is this life if, full of care
Come 102; CTV 40; Deli 68; DP II 25; EGV 306; GV III 14; My V 145; ND 222; TD 10

LEOPARDS

Leopard (Yoruba, trans Ulli Beier)
Gentle hunter
Rat 203

Leopard (Sotho)
See the golden Leopard with the spots!
Afr I 25

LEPANTO

from *Lepanto* (G. K. Chesterton)
White founts falling in the courts of the sun
EGV 310; Fab PR 233; Rat 236; TCN 22

LEPROSY

The leper (Ka-'ehu, Hawaii)
What will become of Hawaii?
Oral 287

LIFEBOATS

The Lifeboat 'Mona' (Peggy
Seeger)
Remember December, fifty-nine
Mov 44

LIGHTHOUSES

Skerryvore: the Parallel (Robert
Louis Stevenson)
Here all is sunny, and when the
truant gull
Sea 88

LIMERICKS

*See AM 65, 77; Bat A 15; Bat C
23; Bat L 154–5; BBGG 29; Bill
58; CBC 18, 22, 29, 46, 65, 81, 91,
101, 105, 110, 135, 141; CC 16;
Croc 16, 20; CTV 92, 93, 96, 127;
Deli 77; Dog 81; Duck 70; Fab
Non throughout; Fab NV
218–24; Fab UV 120; Fat S 15, 24,
25, 32, 46–7, 62; Fat W 50; Four
41, 42; FV 9, 68–70, 95; Gold IV
57–8; GV I 5, 21; GV II 14; GV
III 10, 30; GV V 25; Here 128;
Hor 16, 17; If 39, 56; In O II
24–6; Iron III 11; J Vo III 44;
Lolli I 8; Lolli II 6, 8; Lolli III 2,
10; Low G 14; Merry 131, 150,
208–9, 264, 306; Mov 22, 25, 42,
45, 54, 73, 95, 106, 107, 119; My V
164, 165; Nas C 64; Non 121–45,
247–8, 257; Once 73, 124, 133,
134; Ox CV 151–3, 183–4; Ox Dic
91, 241, 267, 359, 407; Ox LV
104–5, 222–3; Ox PC 11, 14, 17;
Pac 20, 31, 63, 68, 69, 79, 86, 92,
95–7; Plea 314–5; P Life III 31,
47; P Life IV 89; Poems II 6–7;
Puf V 36, 168; Puf Y 192; Rail
30; Rhyme III 31, 32; R Six 15,
29; R Ten 68; Sec 51, 56, 68, Tale
38; Third 108; Touch II 118;
Young 31, 32, 36, 39; Zoo 34*

LINCOLN, ABRAHAM

Nancy Hanks (Rosemary Benet)
If Nancy Hanks
P Life IV 43

LIONS

Circus (Margaret
Stanley-Wrench)
Saucer of sand, the circus ring
Ev 82; Rhyme IV 115

Circus Lion (C. Day Lewis)
Lumbering haunches, pussyfoot
tread, a pride of
Mod 110; Plea 52

The King (Douglas Livingstone)
Old Tawny's mane is moth-
Zoo 47

The Lion (Lord Alfred Douglas)
The lion is an awful bore
Bat A 86; Dou T 26

The Lion and Albert (Marriott
Edgar)
There's a famous seaside place
called Blackpool
CBC 89; Deli 37

LIZARDS

Gecko (Noel Lloyd)
There was a lizard kept me
company
Deli 52

Lizard (D. H. Lawrence)
A lizard ran out on a rock and
looked up, listening
Gold III 29; Rat 248; Touch IV 169

The Lizard (Theodore Roethke)
He too has eaten well
Bat A 34; Deli 53

LLAMAS

The Lama (Ogden Nash)
The one-l lama
Fab CV 90; Imp 24; R Eig 17

The Llama (Hilaire Belloc)
The llama is a woolly sort of fleecy,
hairy goat
Fab CV 90

LOBSTERS

The Lobster Pot (John Arden)
Who can tell how the lobster got
PT I 21

A Lobster Quadrille (Lewis
Carroll)
'Will you walk a little faster?' said a
whiting to a snail
*CBC 130; Come 199; DP II 37; Fab
Non 119; Merry 353; Ox CV 240; Plea
134; P Life II 26*

LOCUSTS

The Locust (Malagasy, trans
A. Marre and W. R. Trask)
What is a locust?
J Vo III 13; Rat 249

LOGGERS

The Jam on Gerry's Rock (anon)
Come all ye true born shanty boys,
whoever that ye be
Fab Bal 240; Iron III 17

LONDON

See also Lon throughout
See also Kew Gardens; London:
Fire 1666; Street Cries
Composed upon Westminster Bridge
(William Wordsworth)
Earth hath not anything to show
more fair
*By 124; Choice 28; DP IV 88; EGV
131; Fab CV 128; Fab PR 71; Iron IV
10; ND 11; Prel IV 8; Puf V 249;
Rain 114; Touch I 94*

Days and Seasons in London 1715
(John Gay)
Experienced men, inured to city
ways
DP III 30; Iron III 24

A Description of a City Shower
(Dean Swift)
Careful observers may foretell the
hour
PW 129

In London (Philip Hobsbaum)
In London again, my nostrils seal
with soot
Theme VII 5

London (William Blake)
I wander thro' each chartered
street
Choice 47; Lon 38; PW 157; Scene 155

London at my Feet (John
Betjeman)
Great was my joy with London at
my feet
Theme VII 4

London Bridge (anon)
London Bridge is broken down
*Fab PV 24; Ox Dic 270; Ox NR 76;
Puf NR 49; Puf Y 188; Rain 24; Trad
60*

London City (Russell Hoban)
I have London, London, London
Drum 97

London Eclogue (F. J. Osborn)
The buses trundle
PT III 8

London is a little bit of all right
(Noel Coward)
I was born and bred in London
Lon 21

The Ocean in London (Harold
Monro)
In London while I slowly wake
Theme II 43

The Streets of Laredo (Louis
MacNeice)
O early one morning I walked out
like Agag
Bill 172; Mod 36; Peng B 356

LONDON: FIRE OF, 1666

from *The Fire of London* (John
Dryden)
At length the crackling noise and
dreadful blaze
RR 61
Night came, but without darkness
or repose
Flock 244

The New London (John Dryden)
Methinks already, from this
Chymick flame
Fab CV 126

London Mourning in Ashes 1666
(anon)
Of fire, fire, fire I sing
Bal 30; Nar 135
The crackling flames do fume and
roar
Say 80

LONELINESS

Alone (Ivor Cutler)
If
Strrict 89

Alone (Stella Gibbons)
Twilight over the sea and no ship
in sight
Tap 18

The Boarder (Louis Simpson)
The time is after dinner. Cigarettes
Theme III 40

Business Girls (John Betjeman)
From the geyser ventilators
Lon 54; PT III 7

Come out with Me (A. A. Milne)
There's sun on the river and sun on
the hill
Mill NS 57

Desert Places (Robert Frost)
Snow falling, and night falling,
fast, oh fast
PW 288; Rat 125; Voi III 140

Eleanor Rigby (John Lennon and
Paul McCartney)
Ah, look at all the lonely people
Oral 385
Eleanor Rigby picks up the rice in
the church
Imp 51

Footpath (Stella Ngatho, Kenya)
Path-let . . . leaving home, leading
out
Att 29

The Hill Wife (Robert Frost)
It was too lonely for her there
Imp 48

I'm alone in the evening (Michael
Rosen)
I'm alone in the evening
Ros M 95

In this City (Alan Brownjohn)
In this city, perhaps a street
*Al III 14; Drum 94; Hap II 73; PT V
27; Theme III 41*

Lament of Hsi-Chun (Arthur
Waley)
My people have married me
Imp 49

The lamplighter (Robert Louis
Stevenson)
My tea is nearly ready and the sun
has left the sky
Ox CV 297; Ste CG 31

Let me tell you a little story
(W. H. Auden)
Let me tell you a little story
Theme III 43

Loneliness (Margaret Taylor)
Nightmare town
Tel 51

The Lonely Farmer
(R. S. Thomas)
Poor hill farmer astray in the grass
Word 93

Miss Hamilton in London (Fleur
Adcock)
It would not be true to say she was
doing nothing
Lon 43

Mr Bleaney (Philip Larkin)
'This was Mr Bleaney's room. He
stayed
*Burn 33; DP IV 141; Look 70; ND
145; Ox Con 155; Theme III 41; Touch
V 24*

Not Waving but Drowning (Stevie
Smith)
Nobody heard him, the dead man
*Burn 40; Ev 147; GV IV 40; Like 105;
Many 54; ND 234; Tel 67; Theme III
46; Touch V 28*

The Old Field (D. J. Enright)
The old field is sad
Enr R 12

P. C. Plod at the Pillar Box
(Roger McGough)
It's snowing out
NV 106

The Rat (W. H. Davies)
That woman there is almost dead
Theme I 23

*The River-Merchant's Wife: a
Letter* (?Ezra Pound,? Arthur
Waley)
While my hair was still cut straight
across my forehead
Pluc 72; Rat 357

Simple Lyric (Brian Patten)
When I think of her sparkling face
NV 125

Song of the Unloved (Sotho, trans Jack Cope)
I could have wept and howled
Att 51

The Two of Us (Hsing Kao)
Who are the companions sitting alone at the bright window
Tel 48

Vinegar (Roger McGough)
Sometimes i feel like a priest
Mer 90

LOONS

The Loon (Ted Hughes)
The Loon, the Loon
Hug U 12

LORRIES

Long-distance Lorry (Philip Callow)
Red truck slumbering in an alley
Mov 76; PT III 8

LORRY DRIVERS

Song of the Wagondriver (B. S. Johnson)
My first love was the ten-ton truck
Many 50; Theme VI 5; Touch V 133; World 110

LOSING THINGS

Anyone seen my . . .? (Max Fatchen)
The people who keep losing things
Fat S 20

Missing Objects (Roy Fuller)
Expect it's a fairy pinched my comb
Ful P 9

LOT'S WIFE

Lot's Wife (Karen Gershon)
My home, my lovely home, she wept
Sun 59

LOVE

See also Courtship, Lovers, Marriage

The Clod and the Pebble (William Blake)
Love seeketh not itself to please
Choice 44; Rat 108; RR 146; Touch V 194; Voi III 97

Cokkils (Sydney Goodsir Smith)
Doun throu the sea
Ring 62

The Confirmation (Edwin Muir)
Yes, yours, my love, is the right human face
Ring 58; Ten 115

Fain would I change that note (anon)
Fain would I change that note
Fab LP 184

First Love (John Clare)
I ne'er was struck before that hour
DP IV 100; Fab LP 92; Poems II 92

Love (Philip Larkin)
The difficult part of love
Touch V 195

Love (George Herbert)
Love bade me welcome; Yet my soul drew back
By 68; Iron IV 101; ND 231; Plea 336; Sun 78; Touch IV 69

Love will find out the Way (anon)
Over the Mountains
Fab CV 332; Fab LP 24; Voi III 74

The Mesh (Kwesi Brew, Ghana)
We have come to the cross-roads
Ima 30

Never seek to tell thy love (William Blake)
Never seek to tell thy love
Plea 77

No Loathsomeness in Love (Robert Herrick)
What I fancy, I approve
Bat L 100; Fab LP 197

Not to Sleep (Robert Graves)
Not to sleep all the night long, for pure joy
Burn 52

Part of Plenty (Bernard Spencer)
When she carries food to the table and stoops down
DP IV 105; Look 36

A Ring presented to Julia (Robert Herrick)
Julia, I bring
Bat L 98

She tells her love while half-asleep (Robert Graves)
She tells her love while half-asleep
Fab LP 119

Shepherdess (Norman Cameron)
All day my sheep have mingled with yours. They strayed
Fab LP 189; Ima 29

Sonnett 116 (William Shakespeare)
Let me not to the marriage of true minds
By 37; EGV 33; Ev 256; Fab LP 229; Iron IV 29; PW 63; Theme IV 20; Touch V 37

Walsingham (Sir Walter Raleigh)
As you came from the holy land
Bat C 44; Fab CV 336; Fab LP 64; Iron I 4; Plea 86; PW 48; Rat 43

LOVERS

See also Courtship, Love, Marriage

At Castle Boterel (Thomas Hardy)
As I drive to the junction of lane and highway
Ten 107

from *The Caucasian Chalk Circle* (Bertolt Brecht, trans Eric Bentley)
Simon Shashava, I shall wait for you
DP IV 101

A Frosty Night (Robert Graves)
Alice, dear, what ails you?
Theme IV 25

The Girl's Confession (Eric Millward)
He loves me for imagined excellences
Gold IV 8; Mus 115

Gone are the Days (Norman MacCaig)
Impossible to call a lamb a lambkin
Ox Con 27

The Good-Morrow (John Donne)
I wonder, by my troth, what thou and I
Plea 87

Hesitant (Brian Patten)
He sees beyond her face another face
Look 18

Incident (Norman MacCaig)
I look across the table and think
Seven 183

Lullaby (W. H. Auden)
Lay your sleeping head, my love
EGV 355; Ten 21

Meeting at Night (Robert Browning)
The grey sea and the long black land
EGV 223; Fab LP 200; Gold IV 16; Iron II 57; Plea 158; Poems II 88

Meeting Point (Louis MacNeice)
Time was away and somewhere else
By 291; TR 143

Plucking the Rushes (Chinese, trans Arthur Waley)
Green rushes with red shoots
Burn 48; Iron IV 87; Pluc 64; PW 317; RR 194; Touch V 38; Voi III 73

Scaffolding (Seamus Heaney)
Masons, when they start upon a building
Liv 34; Theme IV 30

Strawberries (Edwin Morgan)
There were never strawberries
Voi III 70

The Sun Rising (John Donne)
Busy old fool, unruly sun
Plea 82

Tam i' the Kirk (Violet Jacob)
O Jean, my Jean, when the bell ca's the congregation
Fab LP 87

When you go (Edwin Morgan)
When you go
Look 32

White an' Blue (William Barnes)
My love is of comely height, an' straight
Fab LP 86

Who? (Adrian Henri)
Who can I/spend my life
Mer R 37; Mer RR 36

LOVERS: FAITHLESS

Ballad (anon)
A faithless shepherd courted me
Voi III 80

Donal Og (Irish, trans Lady
Augusta Gregory)
It is late last night the dog was
speaking of you
Rat 132
O Donal Og if you go across the
sea
Fab LP 302; In O I 47

The Foreboding (Robert Graves)
Looking by chance in at the open
window
Fab LP 277

Frankie and Johnnie [Albert]
(anon)
Frankie and Johnnie were lovers
*Bill 54; Bk Bal 78; EGV 256; GV V
30; Iron IV 85; Peng B 342; Rat 167;
Voi III 88*

I loved a Lass (George Wither)
I loved a lass, a fair one
Plea 28

Love from Arthur Rainbow
(Adrian Henri)
In a villa called 'Much Bickering'
Mer R 43; Mer RR 42

On the Oldpark Road (anon)
On the Oldpark Road where I did
dwell
Bat S 60

On Top of Old Smoky (anon)
On top of Old Smoky, all covered
with snow
GV V 6; Iron IV 44

Ou Phrontis (Charles Causley)
The bells assault the maiden air
Cau C 58; Voi III 90

Polly Perkins (anon)
I'm a broken-hearted milkman, in
grief I'm arrayed
Bat C 72

Poor but Honest (anon)
She was poor, but she was honest
*Bill 35; Fab PV 260; GV IV 11; Ox
LV 163; Peng B 330*

The Scrutiny (Richard Lovelace)
Why should you swear I am
forsworn)
Fab LP 273

Sea Love (Charlotte Mew)
Tide be runnin' the great world
over
Gold III 3

William Taylor (anon)
William Taylor was a brisk young
sailor
RR 136

LOVERS: REUNITED

The Bailiff's Daughter of Islington
(anon)
There was a youth, a well-beloved
youth
Bk Bal 71; Brit 190; Fab Bal 67

Hynd Horn (anon)
Hynd Horn's bound, love, and
Hynd Horn's free
Bk Bal 59
In Scotland there was a baby born
Merry 278

Lochinvar (Sir Walter Scott)
O Young Lochinvar is come out of
the west
*By 119; EGV 132; ND 133; P Life IV
68; Puf V 92*

The Simple Ploughboy (anon)
O the Ploughboy was a-ploughing
Fab CV 349

*The Valiant Seaman's Happy
Return* (anon)
When Sol did cast no light
Fab PV 119; Peng B 257

LOVERS: UNHAPPY (L & D)

Beyond the Last Lamp (Thomas
Hardy)
While rain, with eve in partnership
Ten 103

The Broken-Hearted Gardener
(anon)
I'm a broken-hearted gardener
and don't know what to do
Fab PV 115

Down by the Salley Gardens
(W. B. Yeats)
Down by the salley gardens my
love and I did meet
EGV 295; Iron I 10

For No One (John Lennon and
Paul McCartney)
The day breaks, your mind aches
Oral 384

Li Fu-Jên (Wu-Ti, trans Arthur Waley)
The sound of her silk skirt has stopped
Pluc 110
(trans Ezra Pound)
The rustling of the silk is discontinued
Touch III 39

Lost Love (Robert Graves)
His eyes are quickened so with grief
By 279; Deli 61; Fab CV 346; Theme II 48

Love without Hope (Robert Graves)
Love without hope, as when the young bird-catcher
Choice 256; Iron II 37; Touch III 74

Mariana (Alfred, Lord Tennyson)
With blackest moss the flower-pots
Choice 84; Plea 192

My Version (Kit Wright)
I hear that since you left me
Strict 124

Neutral Tones (Thomas Hardy)
We stood by a pond that winter day
Touch V 52

No One so much as You (Edward Thomas)
No one so much as you
Fab LP 268

O the Valley in the Summer (W. H. Auden)
O the valley in the summer where I and my John
Theme IV 22

Rosimaya (Atukwei Okai)
You stone/my Saturdays
AP 206

Sometimes it Happens (Brian Patten)
Sometimes it happens that you are friends and then
Strict 122

The Stone (Wilfrid Gibson)
And will you cut a stone for him?
TCN 78

LOVERS: UNHAPPY (N)

The Ballad of Charlotte Dymond (Charles Causley)
It was a Sunday evening
Cau C 120; Time 31; Voi II 112

Barbara Allen (anon)
Down in London where I was raised
Fab Bal 235
In Scarlet town, where I was born
Bk Bal 65; Brit 82; EGV 8; Wind 24
It was in and about the Martinmas time
Peng B 193

The Brown Girl (anon)
I am as brown as brown can be
Tale 103

Clark Sanders (anon)
Clark Sanders and May Margret
Peng B 87

The Cruel Brother (anon)
There was three ladies playd at the ba'
Peng B 94

The Despairing Lover (William Walsh)
Distracted with care
Fab CV 345; Ox LV 24

The Douglas Tragedy (anon)
'Rise up, rise up, Lord Douglas,' she says
DP IV 123; Fab Bal 29; Nar 61; Peng B 155; Scot 84

Fair Annie (anon)
It's narrow, narrow make your bed
Fab Bal 44

The Haystack in the Floods (William Morris)
Had she come all the way for this
P Tale 141

Lord Thomas and Fair Annet (anon)
Lord Thomas and Fair Annet
Brit 79; Fab Bal 122; Peng B 114; Tale 11

Lord Thomas and Fair Eleanor (anon)
Lord Thomas he was a bold forester
Bk Bal 19; Nar 69; Rhyme IV 22

Lord Ullin's Daughter (Thomas Campbell)
A chieftain to the Highlands bound
Fab PR 79; Nar 58; P Life IV 65; Wind 68

The Ratcatcher's Daughter (anon)
In Westminster not long ago
Fab PV 134

The Unquiet Grave (anon)
The wind is blowing today, my love
Fab Bal 146; Fab PV 131; Gold IV 64; Iron IV 132; Isle 91; Peng B 93; Plea 293; Rat 446; Tale 82; Touch I 37; Voi III 76

LOVE SONGS

The Baite (John Donne)
Come live with me, and be my love
Iron IV 9; Rat 338

Come Live with Me (David Campbell)
Come live with me and we'll be drovers
Poems II 95

The Gourmet's Love-Song (P. G. Wodehouse)
How strange is Love; I am not one
Ox LV 213

If You'll give Me a kiss (Leo Aylen)
If you'll give me a kiss and be my girl
Theme V 63

Love is . . . (Adrian Henri)
Love is feeling cold in the back of vans
Mer 19; Mer R 21; Mer RR 21; Strict 108

The Lover's Shirt (anon)
As I was washing under a span
Burn 53

My true love hath my Heart (Sir Philip Sidney)
My true love hath my heart and I have his
EGV 21; Fab LP 227; Plea 77

The Nymph's Reply to the Shepherd (Sir Walter Ralegh)
If all the world and love were young
EGV 29; Rat 337; RR 138

Of a' the airts (Robert Burns)
Of a' the airts the wind can blaw
Ring 59

O mistress mine (William Shakespeare)
O mistress mine, where are you roaming?
Twelfth Night II iii 38; By 39; Fab LP 52; Iron IV 43; PW 60

O my luve is like a red red rose (Robert Burns)
O my luve is like a red red rose
By 114; DP IV 104; EGV 118; Fab CV 335; Fab LP 100; GV IV 2; Poems II 91; PW 160; RR 146

The Passionate Shepherd to his Love (Christopher Marlowe)
Come live with me and be my love
BB 58; By 23; EGV 28; Poems II 94; Rat 336; RR 137; This W 55; Touch V 47

Revelation (H. A. Vaughan)
Turn sideways now and let them see
Cari I 63; Tam 41

See the Conkering Heroine Comes (Adrian Henri)
Thinking about you
Mer RR 51

Song (John Clare)
I'll come to thee at eventide
Voi III 84

Song (Jacques Prevert, trans Lawrence Ferlinghetti)
What day is it
Look 66

Song (Edmund Waller)
Go, lovely rose
Fab LP 52; Plea 39

When I see the beauty (Acoli, trans Okot p'Bitek)
When I see the beauty on my beloved's face
Att 51

Will you come? (Edward Thomas)
Will you come?
By 235; Say 55

LOVE SONGS: HAPPY

A Birthday (Christina Rossetti)
My heart is like a singing bird

BB 33; EGV 244; Ev 188; Ox PC 41; This W 62

Galactic Lovepoem (Adrian Henri)
Warm your feet at the sunset
Mer R 42; Mer RR 41

It was a lover and his lass (William Shakespeare)
It was a lover and his lass
As You Like it V iii 15; EGV 44; Fab LP 21; Merry 194; Rat 218

Jarri's love song (Kath Walker, Australia)
Outside his new-made gunya Jarri
Many 41

Pot Pourri from a Surrey Garden (John Betjeman)
Miles of pram in the wind and Pam in the gorse track
Ox LV 253

Sally in our Alley (Henry Carey)
Of all the girls that are so smart
Plea 35

A Subaltern's Love-Song (John Betjeman)
Miss J. Hunter Dunn, Miss J. Hunter Dunn
EGV 349; Ox LV 251

LOVE SONGS: UNHAPPY

Adrian Henri's Talking After-Christmas Blues (Adrian Henri)
Well I woke up this mornin' it was Christmas Day
Burn 73; Liv 41; Mer 31; Mer R 17; Mod 201

Car Crash Blues (Adrian Henri)
You make me feel like
Mer RR 59

Come away, come away, Death (William Shakespeare)
Come away, come away, Death
Twelfth Night II iv 50; Fab LP 341; Plea 305

In my Dreams I searched for you (anon, Gond)
The wind and the rain are beating down
Oral 25

The Lament of Barbara Douglas (anon)
O waly, waly up the bank
Fab Bal 143; Plea 254

The Lazy Wave (anon, Somerset)
The lazy wave slides over the sand
Dis 32

A New Courtly Sonnet of the Lady Greensleeves (anon)
Alas, my love, you do me wrong
DP I 79; EGV 12; Fab CV 338; Fab LP 143; Puf SB 28

One-and-Twenty (A. E. Housman)
When I was one-and-twenty
GV III 3; Plea 31

O Open the door to Me, O! (Robert Burns)
O open the door, some pity to show
Fab CV 347

O Western Wind (anon)
O western wind, when wilt thou blow
Fab CV 351; Fab LP 243; Fab PV 118

The Seeds of Love (anon)
I sowed the seeds of love
Dis 31; Fab CV 334; Fab PV 137; PW 165

A Song in April (Adrian Henri)
The buds of April bursting
NV 63

Tonight at Noon (Adrian Henri)
Tonight at Noon
Mer 11; Mer R 13; Mer RR 13; Mod 184

The Voice (Thomas Hardy)
Woman much missed, how you call to me, call to me
Plea 100

Waly, Waly (anon)
The water is wide, I cannot cross [get o'er]
Dis 29; Fab PV 144; Iron IV 129; Tale 8
Down in the meadows the other day
PW 164
O waly, waly up the bank
Ring 64

Winter Night (Chien Wên-Ti, trans Arthur Waley)
My bed is so empty that I keep on waking up
Pluc 52

Ye Flowery Banks (Robert Burns)
Ye flowery banks o' bonnie Doon
Bat R 33

LULLABIES

All the Pretty Little Horses (anon)
Hushaby, don't you cry
Bat A 29

Baby, Baby, Naughty Baby (anon)
Baby, baby, naughty baby
Ox LV 48; Ox NR 20; Trad 6

Can ye sew Cushions? (anon)
O can ye sew cushions?
Fab CV 93

Cradle Hymn (Martin Luther)
Away in a manger, no crib for a bed
Come 220; CTV 30

Golden Slumbers (Thomas Dekker)
Golden slumbers kiss your eyes
Merry 271; My V 177; Ox CV 17; Ox PC 161; This W 89; Trad 2

Hush, Little Baby (anon)
Hush little baby, don't say a word
Al II 17; Ox NR 18; Rhyme I 23; Trad 1; Young 52

Lullaby (Frank Collymore)
Darkness broods on earth and air
Cari I 101

Lullaby (Gerda Mayer)
Go to sleep, the moon in amber
May K 8

Lullaby for a Naughty Girl (E. V. Rieu)
O peace, my Penelope, slaps are the fate
Fab NV 271; P Life III 91; Puf V 148

Nurse's Song (anon, German)
Sleep, baby, sleep!
My V 186

Rocking (anon, Czechoslovakia)
Little Jesus, sweetly sleep, do not stir
DT 28

A Rocking Hymn (George Wither)
Sweet baby, sleep: what ails my dear?
DT 32; Ox CV 28; Trad 9

Sweet and Low (Alfred, Lord Tennyson)
Sweet and low, sweet and low
Come 221; CTV 111; DT 29; GV I 27; My V 185; Ox CV 212; Ox PC 160; P Life II 77; This W 87; Trad 4

Sweet Dreams, form a Shade (William Blake)
Sweet dreams, form a shade
Hymn 75

Sweet was the Song (anon)
Sweet was the song the Virgin sang
Star 37

Wynken, Blynken and Nod (Eugene Field)
Wynken, Blynken and Nod one night
Fab NV 244; Merry 80; Ox CV 303

You Spotted Snakes (William Shakespeare)
You spotted snakes with double tongue
Midsummer Night's Dream II ii 9; BB 27; By 40; DP I 80; F Feet 157; Isle 53; Merry 367; My V 27; Ox PC 160; P Life II 78; PT II 6; Rhyme II 52; This W 37; Touch I 172

LYCHEES

The Lychee (Wang I, trans Arthur Waley)
Fruit white and lustrous as a pearl
Fab CV 110

MACHINES

See also Bulldozers, Cranes, Lorries, Motor Cars, Motor Cycles, Steam Shovels, Tar Boilers, Tractors, Trains, USA Railroads, Washing (Clothes)

The Army Horse and the Army Jeep (John Ciardi)
'Where do you go when you go to sleep?'
Mov 90

Concrete Mixers (Patricia Hubbell)

The drivers are washing the
concrete mixers
Full 88

The Excavation (Max Endicoff)
Clusters of electric bulbs
DP IV 95; RR 72; Tho 14; Touch I 92

The Guillotine (Wilfrid Gibson)
Obedient to the will of men
Gold III 23

An Importer (Robert Frost)
Mrs Someone's been to Asia
Iron IV 31; PW 287

Portrait of a Machine (Louis
Untermeyer)
What nudity as beautiful as this
DP IV 94; RR 73; Touch IV 92

from *The Secret of the Machines*
(Rudyard Kipling)
We were taken from the ore-bed
and the mine
RR 74; Tho 11

Sewing Machine (Gwen Dunn)
I'm faster, I'm faster than fingers
Drum 83

The Toaster (William Jay Smith)
A silver-scaled dragon with jaws
flaming red
*ADT 13; Drum 83; Fab NV 173; J Vo
III 7; Sec 66; Zoo 57*

MACKEREL

Mackerel Song (Ted Hughes)
While others sing the mackerel's
armour
Hug S 29

MADNESS

Counting the Mad (Donald
Justice)
This one was put in a jacket
Liv 81; Theme III 31

In a Hospital Sitting-Room
(Elizabeth Jennings)
Utrillo on the wall. A nun is
climbing
Liv 81

Mental Cases (Wilfred Owen)
Who are these? Why sit they here
in twilight?
Choice 157; Theme II 57

Sad Aunt Madge (Roger
McGough)

As the cold winter evenings drew
near
Mer 74;P Mer R 83; Mer RR 80

Snipers (Roger McGough)
When I was knee-high to a
table-top
Mer R 74; Mer RR 78

Veteran with a Head Wound
(Adrian Mitchell)
Nothing to show for it at first
Seven 210

MAGELLAN

from *The Voyage of Magellan*
(Laurie Lee)
So we avoided that island
Sea 255

MAGI, THE

See Epiphany

MAGIC

See Puf M throughout
See also Charms and Spells,
Changelings, Sorcerers,
Witches

The Frog and the Golden Ball
(Robert Graves)
She let her golden ball fall down
the well
Hap II 29

Kiph (Walter de la Mare)
My Uncle Ben, who's been
R. Ten 71

On a Night of Snow (Elizabeth
J. Coatsworth)
Cat, if you go outdoors you must
walk in the snow
*F Feet 187; P Life IV 17; PT II 27;
Say 50; Shad 105; Young 30*

The Song of Wandering Aengus
(W. B. Yeats)
I went out to the hazel wood
*Fab CV 211; Iron II 31; Isle 44; R
Nine 89; Say 114*

MAGICIANS

The Magician's Attic (Harold
Massingham)
The woodwork's musty as the
russet smell of old burnt toast
BE 47

The Two Magicians (anon)
The lady stands in her bower door
Fab PV 278; Peng B 77
O she looked out of the window
Hist 26; Merry 341
She becam' a girdle, An' he becam'
a cake
Brit 59

MAGPIES

Magpies (anon)
I saw eight magpies in a tree
Lolli I 4

MALLARD

The Mallard (Phoebe Hesketh)
Brown-checked, neat as new spring
tweed
Touch III 134

Mallard (Rex Warner)
Squawking they rise from reeds
into the sun
Drag 24; RR 183; Touch III 135

MAN

The Mystery Creatures (Wes
Magee)
They dwell on a planet not far from
the sun
Third 7

The Newcomer (Brian Patten)
There's something new in the river
Four 50

MANNERS

See also Ox NR 115
See also Table Manners

A Children's Don't (Harry
Graham)
Don't tell Papa his nose is red
BBGG 90

Etiquette (W. S. Gilbert)
The *Ballyshannon* foundered off the
coast of Cariboo
P Tale 147

How to Get On in Society (John
Betjeman)
Phone for the fish-knives, Norman
Ox LV 254

Manners for a Child of 1918
(Elizabeth Bishop)
My grandfather said to me
Ox Con 35; Rat 268

A Matter of Taste (Gerda
Mayer)
It is good taste to have
May K 18

Politeness (A. A. Milne)
If people ask me
Mil VY 41

Too Polite (Ian Serraillier)
Broad met Stout
Al II 46

MARBLES

Marbles (R. N. Currey)
Now that our fertile acres yield
Prel II 24

MARCH

All Sorts (Leonard Clark)
In March, all sorts of weather
Out 25

Early March (Norman
Nicholson)
We did not expect this; we were not
ready for this
Prel III 3

March Morning unlike Others
(Ted Hughes)
Blue haze. Bees hanging in air at
the hive-mouth
Hug S 16; Out 26

Written in March (William
Wordsworth)
The cock is crowing
*Bat C 17; CTV 22; Merry 362; P Life
II 46; Rain 81; Rhyme II 49; Say 29;
TD 117; This W 103; (part) Lolli I
11*

MARCHING

*March for Drum, Trumpet and 21
Giants* (C. S. Lewis)
With stumping stride in pomp and
pride
Voi I 65

*March for Strings, Kettledrums and
63 Dwarfs* (C. S. Lewis)
With plucking pizzicato and the
prattle of the kettledrum
Voi I 65

The Song of Soldiers (Walter de la Mare)
As I sat musing by the frozen dyke
de la M Col 60

MARKETS

The Caledonian Market (William Plomer)
A workbasket made of an old armadillo
Lon 75

The Hausa Trader (J. H. Sackey)
Beneath the trees along the highway
Afr II 17

Jamaican Market (Agnes Maxwell-Hall)
Honey, Pepper, leaf-green limes
Bite I 49

The Market (Ann Berry)
The stall are set in the market-place
Rhy 57

Market Square (Marion Lines)
Take your basket to the market square
Lin T 8

Marketwomen (Daisy Myrie, Caribbean)
Down from the hills, they come
Cari I 10

MARRIAGE

See also *Fab UV 74–80*
An Arundel Tomb (Philip Larkin)
Side by side, their faces blurred
Look 54; Mod 74; Theme IV 33

Bound to be a Row (anon)
I am an unlucky married man, I've such an awful wife
Brit 207

The Cooper of Fife (anon)
There was a wee cooper that lived in Fife
Brit 213; DP III 99

The Daughter of the Farrier (anon)
The daughter of the farrier
FV 43

An Elder's reproof to his Wife ('Abdillaahi Muuse)
A stream flowing steadily over a stone does not wet its core
Att 36

from *Epithalamion* (Edmund Spenser)
Wake now, my love, awake, for it is time
Fab LP 59

Get up and Shut [Bar] the Door (anon)
It fell about the Martinmas time
Bk Bal 167; Duck 98; Fab Bal 77; Ox PC 19
It happened one December night
Brit 211; Nar 23; Str 24; Tale 95

In the Room of the Bride-Elect (Thomas Hardy)
'Would it had been the man of our wish!'
Burn 84

Ire (R. S. Thomas)
Are you out, woman of the lean pelt
RR 95

Jack and Joan (Thomas Campion)
Jack and Joan they think no ill
Fab CV 348

from *The lion and the jewel* (Wole Soyinka, Nigeria)
When we are wed, you shall not walk or sit
Att 10

Olive and Davy (James Simmons)
When conversation failed
Over 55

One Flesh (Elizabeth Jennings)
Lying apart now, each in a separate bed
DP IV 111; Look 60; Mod 90; Strict 72; Touch V 51

Self's the Man (Philip Larkin)
Oh, no one can deny
Theme IV 31

She Vowed Him This (William Box)
Constant I will be
Burn 90

Single Girl (anon)
Single girl, single girl
Theme IV 31
When I was single, went dressed
all so fine
Iron III 76; Say 86

A Slice of Wedding-Cake (Robert
Graves)
Why have such scores of lovely,
gifted girls
Burn 87; Many 42

A Small Keen Wind (Thomas
Blackburn)
My wife for six months now in
sinister
Theme IV 27

Songs for a Coloured Singer
(Elizabeth Bishop)
A washing hangs upon the line *and*
The time has come to call a halt
Rat 402

Les Sylphides (Louis MacNeice)
Life in a day; he took his girl to the
ballet
Burn 81; Theme IV 29; Touch V 45

The Tired Man (Anna
Wickham)
I am a quiet gentleman
My V 19

from *To His Wife on the Fourteenth
Anniversary* (Samuel Bishop)
'Thee, Mary, with this ring I wed
WAS 122

To My Dear and Loving Husband
(Anne Bradstreet)
If ever two were one, then surely
we
Voi III 87

Wedding Wind (Philip Larkin)
The wind blew all my wedding day
Burn 86; Say 100; Theme IV 26

When I'm sixty-four (John
Lennon and Paul McCartney)
When I get older, losing my hair
GV V 8

The Whitsun Weddings (Philip
Larkin)
That Whitsun, I was late getting
away
*Fab Mod 354; Look 26; Scene 162;
Touch V 31*

MARTENS

The Marten Cat (John Clare)
The marten cat long-shagged, of
courage good
FM 132; Iron IV 49; Voi II 49

MARTHA OF BETHANY

Martha of Bethany (Clive
Sansom)
It's all very well
Tam 23; Theme VI 31

MARTYRDOM

From *William Tyndale to John
Frith* (Edgar Bowers)
The letters I, your lone friend,
write in sorrow
Voi III 44

The Martyrdom of Bishop Farrar
(Ted Hughes)
Bloody Mary's venomous flames
can curl
Hug SP 33

MARY MAGDALENE

Magdalen at Michael's Gate
(Henry Kingsley)
Magdalen at Michael's Gate
By 188; Sun 185

Mary, Mary Magdalene (Charles
Causley)
Mary, Mary Magdalene
*Cau C 239; Cau F 87; Look 13; Seven
53; Wind 76*

MARY, QUEEN OF SCOTS

Alas! Poor Queen (Marion
Angus)
She was skilled in music and the
dance
Ring 29

MATHEMATICS

See also Fab UV 186–191
New Maths (Tom Lehrer)
You can't take three from two, two
is less than three
Fab UV 189

MAY

Corinna's Going A-Maying
(Robert Herrick)
Get up, get up for shame! The
blooming morn
Plea 119; PW 98

Home Pictures in May (John
Clare)
The sunshine bathes in clouds of
many hues
WAS 75

The May Magnificat (Gerard
Manley Hopkins)
May is Mary's month and I
Iron III 33; Sun 154; WAS 72

On May Morning (John Milton)
Now the bright morning star, day's
harbinger
TD 97

MEN VERSUS WOMEN

*The Old Man who lived in the
Woods* (anon)
There was an old man who lived in
the woods
Once 78

MERMAIDS AND MERMEN

The Eddystone Light (anon)
My father was the keeper of the
Eddystone Light
Peng B 355; Puf M 195; Voi II 25

The Forsaken Merman (Matthew
Arnold)
Come, dear children, let us away
*Fab CV 325; Fab PR 176; My V 68;
ND 197; Ox PC 59; Plea 151; PW
239; Rhyme IV 44*
(part) Children dear, was it
yesterday?
DT 41; Sea 177

Little Fan (James Reeves)
I don't like the look of little Fan,
mother
*Out Sc 52; PT I 23; Puf Q 87; Ree C
6; Rhyme IV 50; Shad 82*

A Mermaiden (Thomas Hennell)
Chilled with salt dew, tossed on
dark waters deep
Theme II 15

The Merrymaid (Charles
Causley)
Robert Stephen Hawker
Cau F 68

Sam (Walter de la Mare)
When Sam goes back in memory
de la M Col 76

MERRY-GO-ROUNDS

Merry-go-round (Clive Sansom)
Red horse! . . . . green! . . . The
Cambridge horse
Mov 21

The Roundabout (Clive Sansom)
Round and round the roundabout
Rhyme I 36

MICE

Anne and the Field Mouse
(Ian Serraillier)
We found a mouse in the chalk
quarry today
*Hap 15; Out Sc 59; Prel I 20; R Eig
106; Say 51*

*The Country Mouse and the City
Mouse* (R. S. Sharpe)
In a snug little cot lived a fat little
mouse
Ox CV 139

Diary of a Church Mouse (John
Betjeman)
Here among long-discarded
cassocks
ND 75; Time 9; Touch I 85

The Fieldmouse (Cecil Frances
Alexander)
Where the acorn tumbles down
Ox CV 204

Harvest Mouse (Clive Sansom)
A sleek brown acrobat, he climbs
San E 17

Leaving School (Roy Fuller)
Our Blackheath Comprehensive
School (for mice)
Bat L 120; Ful P 57

Madame Mouse Trots (Edith
Sitwell)
Madame Mouse trots
Dawn 23; Fab CV 78

119

The Meadow Mouse (Theodore Roethke)
In a shoe box stuffed in an old nylon stocking
Gang 22; Hap II 64; J Vo IV 15; Rat 282

Moose (Mary Innes)
There's a certain confusion when I say a moose
Inn B 'M'

The Mouse (Elizabeth Coatsworth)
I hear a mouse
Puf V 45

The Mouse in the Wainscot (Ian Serraillier)
Hush, Suzanne!
My R 86; Rhyme III 28; R Six 18

The Mouse that Gnawed the Oak Tree Down (Vachell Lindsay)
The mouse that gnawed the oak-tree down
J Vo II 6

The Mouse's Invitation Cards (Brian Patten)
'Come at seven', 'Come at nine'
Poems 82

Mouse's Nest (John Clare)
I found a ball of grass among the hay
DT 78; Rat 299; World 124

The Needless Alarm (John Ruskin, aged 6)
Among the rushes lived a mouse
FM 158

To a Mouse (Robert Burns)
Wee, sleekit, cowerin', tim'rous beastie
Bat A 56; BB 18; EGV 118; FM 95; Scot 30

MILLERS

from *The Canterbury Tales* (Geoffrey Chaucer)
The Miller was a stout carl for the nones
Flock 31; Iron III 58; Touch I 149
(trans) *Touch I 149*
(trans Nevill Coghill)
The Miller was a chap of sixteen stone
Flock 30; ND 133

The Jolly Miller (trad)
There dwelt a miller hale and bold
Fab PV 214
There was a jolly miller once
Bat L 138; EGV 110; Merry 194; Ox NR 83; P Life II 61; Puf SB 30; Trad 48

The Miller's Song (anon)
There was an old miller and he lived all alone
Gold IV 37

The Unfortunate Miller (A. E. Coppard)
On windy days the mill
Touch II 167

MINERS

See also Accidents: Mines, Gold Rush

Caliban in the Coal-Mines (Louis Untermeyer)
God, we don't like to complain
PT V 24

The Collier (Vernon Watkins)
When I was born on Amman hill
Dawn 80; DP III 6; Flock 197; Mod 9; Tel 74

The Collier's Rant (anon 1793)
As me and my marrow was ganging to wark
Bal 78

The Durham Lock-Out 1892 (anon)
In our Durham County I am sorry for to say
DP IV 82; Theme VI 47

The First Snow (Wilfrid Gibson)
From the pit's mouth men pour, a stream of black
Gold II 16

Fourpence a Day (anon)
The ore's awaitin' in the tubs; the snow's upon th' fell
DP I 37

The Image o' God (Joe Corrie)
Crawlin' aboot like a snail in the mud
Scot 75
Crawling about like a snail in the mud
GV IV 23

Miners (Wilfrid Owen)

There was a whispering in my hearth
DP IV 79; Iron IV 127

Mother Wept (Joseph Skipsey)
Mother wept and father sigh'd
Prel II 50

Schooldays End (Ewan MacColl)
Schooldays over – come on then, John
Gold II 42

MISFITS

Adjust your Dress before Leaving (Anthony Edkins)
The man who is sidling towards me
Gold III 19

The Hunchback in the Park (Dylan Thomas)
The hunchback in the park
DP II 95; Theme III 30

My Friend Maloney (Charles Causley)
My friend Maloney, eighteen
Cau C 113; DP IV 114; Time 28

Not Waving but Drowning (Stevie Smith)
Nobody heard him, the dead man
Burn 40; Ev 147; GV IV 40; Like 105; Many 54; ND 234; Tel 67; Theme III 46; Touch V 28

Picking Teams (Allan Ahlberg)
When we pick teams in the playground
Ahl P 35

The place's fault (Philip Hobsbaum)
Once, after a rotten day at school
Conf 45; DP I 41; Liv 22; RR 191; Theme III 27; Touch IV 94

Richard Cory (Edward Arlington Robinson)
Whenever Richard Cory went downtown
EGV 299; GV IV 41; Ima 130; Theme VI 40

The White Blackbird (Andrew Young)
Gulls that in meadows stand
Theme III 33

You and I (Roger McGough)
I explain quietly. You
NV 96

MISSEL THRUSHES

The Missel Thrush (John Heath-Stubbs)
February brings its storms and rain
Hea P 25

Missel Thrush (Walter de la Mare)
When from the brittle ice the fields
Iron II 80

MIST

Kingdom of Mist (Edward Storey)
I ride through a kingdom of mist
Puf M 186

Mist (Andrew Young)
Rain, do not fall
Flock 119

Mist (Douglas Gibson)
Subtle as an illusionist
TD 33

MOLE-CATCHERS

The Mole-Catcher (John Clare)
When melted snow leaves bare the black-green rings
Iron III 78

Mole-Catcher (Edmund Blunden)
With coat like any mole's, as soft and black
Gold III 17; RR 127; Touch II 156

MOLES

A Dead Mole (Andrew Young)
Strong-shouldered mole
Drag 72; FM 250; Say 20; Touch I 82

Mole (Alan Brownjohn)
To have to be a mole?
Drum 47

MONEY

The Hardship of Accounting (Robert Frost)
Never ask of money spent
Fab CV 374

£.S.D (Robert Graves)
When *libra, solidus, denarius*
Mus 15

Money (Richard Armour)
Workers earn it
Imp 85

New Rich (Arthur Hugh
Clough)
I cannot but ask, in the park and
the streets
Bat C 52

Wages (D. H. Lawrence)
The wages of work is cash
Conf 98; Gold III 98

MONKEYS

See Apes and Monkeys

MONOPOLY

It's a Bit Rich (Max Fatchen)
Playing Monopoly's
Fat W 55

MONSTERS

Be a Monster (Roy Fuller)
I am a frightful monster
AM 10; Ful P 24; Poems 52; Sec 35

The Bunyip (Douglas Stewart)
The water down the rocky wall
AM 60

The Marrog (R. C. Scriven)
My desk's at the back of the class
*AM 11; Drum 104; Duck 72; Fir 108;
Hist 85; Like 85*

The Mewlips (J. R. R. Tolkein)
The shadows where the Mewlips
dwell
AM 32; Shad 72

Nessie (Ted Hughes)
No, it is not an elephant or any
such grasshopper
AM 52; Hug M 8

MONTHS

See also January, February,
March, April, May, June, July,
August, September, October,
November, December

A Child's Calendar (George
Mackay Brown)
No visitors in January
Sun 126

The Death of Cold (anon,
Punjab)
Cold in August is conceived
Dis 86

Here we go round the Roundhouse
(Charles Causley)
Here we go round the roundhouse
Bat S 37

Labours of the Months (anon)
January: By this fire I warm my
hands
Fab PV 205

The Months (Christina Rossetti)
January cold desolate
Ev 15; Like 37; Puf Y 55

The Months of the Year (Sara
Coleridge)
January brings the snow
*Croc 68; CTV 33; Fab NV 227; Ox
CV 169; P Life I 54; Puf V 15; Rain
78; TD 113; Trad 26*

MOON

*See also Hug, M 12, 16, 22, 26–8,
32*

Above the Dock (T. E. Hulme)
Above the quiet dock in midnight
*ADT 124; Deli 123; Fab Mod 87; PW
297; Sea 94; Touch I 19*

Autumn (T. E. Hulme)
A touch of cold in the autumn
night
*ADT 103; Bric 54; Deli 123; Fab
Mod 87; My V 10; PW 297; TD 132;
Touch I 27*

The Cat and the Moon
(W. B. Yeats)
The cat went here and there
*Cat 31; Fab CV 69; Flock 57; Iron II
54; J Vo II 28; Shad 104; This W 23;
Touch I 80*

The Dog (Anton Buttigieg, trans
F. Ebejer, Malta)
On the roof of a farmhouse
Stuf 45

Flying (J. M. Westrup)
I saw the moon
Come 122; Fir 87; Hi 42; Once 57

Four Moons (Dennis Doyle)
The cowboy's moon is thin and
clear
Stuf 69

Full Moon (Walter de la Mare)
One night as Dick lay fast asleep
de la M Col 258

Full Moon Rhyme (Judith
Wright)
There's a hare in the moon tonight
Deli 124; R Nine 16; SAS 32; Shad 52

The Hare in the Moon (Ryokan)
Long long ago, they say
Deli 125

The Harvest Moon (Ted Hughes)
The flame-red moon, the harvest
moon
*Four 105; Hug S 38; Hug SP 148;
Strict 133*

Is the Moon tired? (Christina
Rossetti)
Is the Moon tired? She looks so
pale
Come 115; Merry 193

The Man in the Moon
(J. W. Riley)
(part) And the man in the moon
has a boil on his ear
CBC 114

from *The Merchant of Venice*
(William Shakespeare)
The moon shines bright. In such a
night as this
Merchant of Venice V i 1; Plea 220

The Moon (Percy Bysshe
Shelley)
And like a dying lady lean and pale
Fab CV 49

The Moon (Robert Louis
Stevenson)
The moon has a face like the clock
in the hall
*Croc 85; My R 18; P Life I 68; Puf V
225; Ste CG 33*

The Moon and a Cloud
(W. H. Davies)
Sometimes I watch the moon at
night
Rat 291

The Moon and the Sun
(Anglo-Saxon, trans K.
Crossley-Holland)
I saw a strange creature)
Puf M 183; Tap 31
(trans Alexander Bone)
I saw a creature sally forth with
booty
PW 27

Moon in the Bucket (Gabriel
Imomotiure Okara, Nigeria)
Look! Look out there
AP 50; Ima 112

*The Moon's the North Wind's
Cooky* (Vachell Lindsay)
The Moon's the North Wind's
cooky
Croc 86; In O II 27

Moon-Wind (Ted Hughes)
There is no wind on the moon at all
Hug M 26; Poems 56

Night Song (Frances Cornford)
On moony nights the dogs bark
shrill
F Feet 153; TD 62

Silver (Walter de la Mare)
Slowly, silently, now the moon
*Come 116; CTV 151; de la M Col 256;
Like 144; Merry 323; P Life III 90;
Rhyme IV 10*

Washed in Silver (James
Stephens)
Gleaming in silver are the hills
P Life III 90

who knows if the moon's
(e. e. cummings)
who knows if the moon's
BE 26; Full 134

The Wind and the Moon (George
Macdonald)
Said the Wind to the Moon
Bits b

The Wise Men of Gotham
(Thomas Love Peacock)
In a bowl to sea went wise men
three
Fab Non 84

MOOSES

Moose (Mary Innes)
There's a certain confusion when I
say a moose
Inn B 'M'

Mooses (Ted Hughes)
The goofy Moose, the walking
house frame
Hug U 36

MORTALITY

See also Plea 284–308
See also Time

Alexander the Great (anon)
Four men stood by the grave of a
man
PW 28

As I walked out (W. H. Auden)
As I walked out one evening
Rat 39

Elegy for Himself or *Lines before
Execution* (Chidiock Tichborne)
My prime of youth is but a frost of
cares
Rat 140; Voi II 149

Gone (Walter de la Mare)
Where's the Queen of Sheba?
de la M Col 304; Fab NV 263; TD 161

Last Lauch (Douglas Young)
The Minister said it wald dee
Ring 141

Let us Drink and be Merry
(Thomas Jordan)
Let us drink and be merry, dance
joke and rejoice
Plea 140

Like to the Grass (anon)
Like to the grass that's newly
sprung
TD 153

Lucy (William Wordsworth)
A slumber did my spirit seal
*Bat C 74; EGV 124; Fab CV 273; Iron
IV 4; Plea 299*

Man's Mortality (anon)
Like as the damask rose you see
Fab CV 381

My Bus Conductor (Roger
McGough)
My bus conductor tells me
Many 34; Mer 84

Proud Maisie (Sir Walter Scott)
Proud Maisie is in the wood
*Fab CV 267; Ox PC 154; Puf V 192;
RR 110*

Rising Five (Norman Nicholson)

'I'm rising five', he said
Look 42; Touch IV 113

To Daffodils (Robert Herrick)
Fair daffodils, we weep to see
EGV 66; Ev 50; Fab CV 51; Puf V 22

Virtue (George Herbert)
Sweet day, so cool, so calm, so
bright
*EGV 68; Iron I 42; Plea 323; PW 101;
Touch IV 68*

MOSES

The Burning Bush (Norman
Nicholson)
When Moses, musing in the desert,
found
Sun 65

MOSQUITOES

The Mosquito (Ted Hughes)
To get into life
Hug U 44

Mosquito (D. H. Lawrence)
When did you start your tricks
*Choice 191; Plea 63; Rat 294; Touch II
23; Voi II 42*

Mosquito (John Updike)
On the fine wire of her whine she
walked
Flock 206

MOTHERS AND
DAUGHTERS

A Frosty Night (Robert Graves)
'Alice, dear, what ails you?
Liv 28

MOTHERS AND SONS

Footnote to John ii 4
(R. A. K. Mason)
Don't throw your arms around me
in that way
Voi III 60

Little Johnny's Final Letter (Brian
Patten)
Mother/I won't be home this
evening, so
GV IV 38; Liv 27

Mother and Son (R. S. Thomas)
At nine o'clock in the morning
Burn 21; Theme IV 40

Mothering Sunday
(G. H. Leonard)
It is the day of all the year
Sun 130; WAS 34

Mum'll be coming Home today
(Michael Rosen)
Mum'll be coming home today
Ros W 36

To My Mother (George Barker)
Most near, most dear, most loved
and most far
*By 296; Fab Mod 312; Flock 63; Liv
27; Prel I 26*

The Widow's Plot (William
Plomer)
Troubled was a house in Ealing
Bill 39

MOTOR CARS

See also Accidents: Road,
Garages
Autobahnmotorwayautoroute
(Adrian Mitchell)
Around the gleaming map of
Europe
Rat 52

Carbreakers (Marian Lines)
There's a graveyard in our street
Lin T 15; Poems 39

My Uncle's Car (Brian Jones)
Once upon a time when cars
Jon S 12

she being Brand (e. e. cummings)
she being Brand/– new
Mov 78

Southbound on the Freeway (May
Swenson)
A tourist came in from Orbitville
J Vo IV 54

*The Testament . . . concerning
Automobilism* (John Davidson
1857–1908)
That railways are inadequate
appears
Rail 37

To Lizzie, My Old Car (anon)
I love you though your radiator's
busted
CBC 59

MOTOR CYCLES

Fifteen (William Stafford)
South of the Bridge on Seventeenth
Bite III 26; Imp 73; Voi II 89

Hitting the Moon (Phoebe
Hesketh)
I'm Rodney on my redhot
motorbike
Hes S 10

Leather-jackets Bikes and Birds
(Robert Davies)
The streets are noisy
Mov 72

A motorbike (Ted Hughes)
We had a motorbike all through
the war
Gang 16; Hug SP 213

Oh, Brother! (Max Fatchen)
My brother's a motorbike freak
Fat W 36

On the Move (Thom Gunn)
The blue jay scuffling in the bushes
follows
Seven 76

MOTORWAYS

Merritt Parkway (Denise
Levertov)
As if it were
Gold IV 11; Scene 166; Voi III 28

Motorway (Marian Lines)
Motorway – motorway – motorway
Lin T 26

MOUNTAINEERING

See also Everest

Alpine (R. S. Thomas)
About mountains it is useless to
argue
RR 42

Breathless (Wilfrid Noyce)
(written at 21,200 feet)
Heart aches/Lungs pant
RR 41; Touch II 3; Word 130

from *Burning* (Gary Snyder)
After scanning its face again and
again
Flock 141

Climbing Suilven (Norman MacCaig)
I nod and nod to my own shadow and thrust
Theme V 51

De Gustibus (St John E. C. Hankin)
I am an unadventurous man
Ev 250; Theme V 70

The Devil's Kitchen (Thomas Blackburn)
There's a crag, The Devil's Kitchen
Bla D 20

An Expedition (Thomas Blackburn)
We had a drink in the inn called La Stanga
Bla D 24

Having Climbed to the Topmost Peak (Po Chü-I, trans Arthur Waley)
Up and up, the Incense-Burner Peak!
Pluc 37

MOUNTAIN LIONS

Mountain Lion (D. H. Lawrence)
Climbing through January snow, into the Lobo Canyon
Drag 10; Iron III 15; Rat 297; RR 180; Theme I 43; Touch II 26

MOVEMENT

Jump or Jiggle (Evelyn Beyer)
Frogs jump/Caterpillars hump
Al II 31; FV 11; Word 112

MOWING

Mowing (Robert Frost)
There was never a sound beside the wood but one
Ten 78

MUD

Mud (Polly Chase Boyden)
Mud is very nice to feel
Here 16

Mud (John Smith)
I like mud
My R 55

The Mud (Andrew Young)

This glistening mud that loves a gate
Gold I 25

MURDER

The Ballad of Charlotte Dymond (Charles Causley)
It was a Sunday evening
Cau C 120; Time 31; Voi II 112

By the Exeter River (Donald Hall)
What is it you're mumbling, old father, my Dad?
Mod 141

The Cruel Mother (anon)
I looked over the castle wall
Tale 112
There was a lady lived in York
Brit 54

The Dorking Thigh (William Plomer)
About to marry and invest
Bill 71

Edward, Edward! (anon)
Why does your brand so drip with blood
Bk Bal 142; EGV 6; Fab PR 21; Peng B 203; P Tale 25; Wind 11
Why dois your brand sae drap wi' bluid
Bk Bal 189; Fab Bal 119; PW 4; Scot 91
How comes this blood on your shirt sleeve?
Iron II 20

The Flower of Serving Men (Lawrence Price)
My father he built me a shady bower
Brit 187

Fragment of an Agon (T. S. Eliot)
Oh Mr Sweeney, please don't talk
Iron IV 40

Homecoming (Jacques Prevert, trans Lawrence Ferlinghetti)
A Breton returns to his birthplace
Bat S 88

The Inquest (W. H. Davies)
I took my oath I would enquire
Rat 213

Johnny Sands (anon)
A man whose name was Johnny Sands
Bk Bal 151; Str 9; Touch I 41

The Lady Isabella's Tragedy
(anon)
There was a lord of worthy fame
Fab PV 251

Life of the Mannings (anon 1849)
See the scaffold it is mounted
Fab Bal 188

Little Johnny's Confession (Brian
Patten)
This morning/being rather young
and foolish
*Gang 123; Imp 85; Mer 96; Mer R
110; Mer RR 110*

Little Musgrave (anon)
As it fell one holy day
Peng B 106
The people went to church one day
Tale 51

Lizzie Borden (anon)
Lizzie Borden with an axe
GV III 29; Tale 21

Lord Randal (anon)
O where have you been Lord
Randal my son?
*Bk Bal 164; Blow 52; EGV 9; Fab
Bal 34; PW 14; RR 26; Say 73; Tale
18; Voi II 133; Wind 23*

May Colvin (anon)
False Sir John a-wooing came
Bk Bal 156; Wind 17; Tale 60

Mrs Dyer the Baby Farmer (anon)
The old baby farmer has been
executed
Brit 130

Notting Hill Polka (W.
Bridges-Adam)
We've – had –/A Body in the
house
Bill 43; Lon 63

from *Peter Grimes* (George
Crabbe)
Old Peter Grimes made fishing his
employ
P Tale 44

The Rich Old Lady or
Marrowbones (anon)
A rich old lady in our town
Iron IV 52; Tale 99
Now there was an old woman in
Ireland
Brit 210

The Sacrilege (Thomas Hardy)
I have a Love I love too well
TCN 68

Shooting of his Dear or *Molly
Bawn* (anon)
Come all you young people that
handle the gun
*Bat S 86; Bk Bal 36; Brit 55; Fab Bal
206; Peng B 294; PW 19*

A Small Tragedy (Sally Roberts)
They came up in the evening
Theme III 10

The Swan swims so Bonny (anon)
A Farmer there lived in the North
Country
Brit 91

The Two [Twa] Sisters of Binnorie
(anon)
There were two sisters sat in a
bower
*Bk Bal 14; Fab Bal 32; Plea 257;
Wind 14*
There were twa sisters sat in a
bower
Scot 89; Touch I 11

Victor was a Little Baby
(W. H. Auden)
Victor was a little baby
Bill 58; Peng B 358

Young Hunting
(anon)
The lady stood at her castle door
Tale 42

MUSHROOMS

Mushrooms (Sylvia Plath)
Overnight, very/whitely, discreetly
*Drag 68; Gold III 42; MyV 150; Rat
299; Theme II 66; Touch III 50; Voi II
52; World 122*

MUSIC

See also PT IV throughout
See also Banjos, Bugles, Drums,
Fiddlers, Flutes, Jazz, Singing,
Spirituals, Violins

The hurdy-gurdy (Jacques
Prevert)
I play the piano/said one
Gang 114

Interruption at the Opera House
(Brian Patten)
At the very beginning of an
important symphony
Liv 73; Mer R 150; Nar 41; NV 126

Jukebox (Mervyn Morris)
Jammed with Culture, they
Bite III 39

Music (William Shakespeare)
How sweet the moonlight sleeps
upon this bank
Merchant of Venice V i 54; PW 69

Music (Amy Lowell)
The neighbour sits in his window
and plays the flute
Imp 39

*On hearing Dvorak's 'New World'
Symphony* (John Figueroa)
The chestnut trunks are dark
Cari I 52

Orpheus with his Lute (William
Shakespeare)
Orpheus with his lute
Henry VIII III i 3; Fab CV 36

Piano and Drums (Gabriel
Okara, Nigeria)
When at the break of day at a
riverside
Bite III 39; Many 129

The Release (Wilfrid Wilson
Gibson)
All day he shoves the pasteboard in
Bite III 5; GV V 37; Theme VI 37

Song for St Cecilia's Day (John
Dryden)
From harmony, from heavenly
harmony
PW 123

There is Sweet Music here (Alfred,
Lord Tennyson)
There is sweet music here that
softer falls
PT IV 13

A Wish (John Norris)
Whatever blessing you my Life
deny
Say 130

MYSTERY (L & D)

At the Keyhole (Walter de la
Mare)
'Grill me some bones', said the
Cobbler
de la M Col 158; Shad 23

Green Candles (Humbert Wolfe)

'There's someone at the door', said
gold candlestick
Shad 76

Hawthorn White (Charles
Causley)
Hawthorn white, hawthorn red
Burn 35; Cau C 79; Ev 38; Hap 64

The Way through the Woods
(Rudyard Kipling)
They shut the road through the
woods
*DP IV 38; EGV 289; Fab CV 377;
Gold I 25; Hist 67; Isle 81; Like 96;
ND 18; Ox CV 323; Plea 240; P Life
IV 26; Rain 80; Rhyme IV 16; Theme
II 6; This W 163; Touch I 156*

MYSTERY (N)

*Childe Roland to the Dark Tower
came* (Robert Browning)
My first thought was, he lied in
every word
P Tale 131

Flannan Isle (Wilfrid Wilson
Gibson)
Though three men dwell on
Flannan Isle
*Nar 104; Ox PC 78; P Tale 152; RR
29; Str 47; TCN 116; Touch I 168*

He's Behind Yer or *Pantomime
Poem* (Roger McGough)
HE'S BEHIND YER!
*Gang 98; Mer R 63; NV 77; Strict 33;
Third 48*

The Huntsman (Edward
Lowbury)
Kagwa hunted the lion
Many 86; Nar 36

John Grimaldi or *The Sailor's
Return* (John Masefield)
Not all forgotten yet in London
town
Bat S 123

The Listeners (Walter de la
Mare)
'Is there anybody there?' said the
Traveller
*Bite I 19; By 228; de la M Col 154;
DP IV 43; Drag 52; EGV 306; GV V
42; Isle 83; Like 177; ND 209; Plea
247; P Life IV 42; Prel IV 35; Shad
38; TCN 120; Ten 46; This W 147;
Touch I 166*

Lollocks (Robert Graves)
By sloth on sorrow fathered
Choice 262; Flock 196; Rat 249; Theme II 14; Touch II 154

The Mistletoe Bough
(T. H. Bayly)
The mistletoe hung in the castle hall
Blow 56

The Strange Visitor (trad)
A wife was sitting at her reel ae nicht
Fab CV 195; Fab PV 290; Hist 31; J Vo III 63; Ox PC 86; P Life IV 45; Puf M 101; Str 83

The Trap (Jon Stallworthy)
The first night that the monster lurched
Ev 168; ND 210; Theme II 64; Voi III 142

Welsh Incident (Robert Graves)
But that was nothing to what things came out
EGV 345; ND 212; P Tale 185; RR 178; Str 27; Theme II 51; Voi II 11

What has happened to Lulu?
(Charles Causley)
What has happened to Lulu, Mother?
ADT 17; Cau C 227; Cau F 16; Duck 77; Full 50; Hap II 83; Strict 34

NABARA, THE

The Nabara (C. Day Lewis)
Freedom is more than a word, more than the base coinage
P Tale 174

NAMES

The American Traveller (Robert H. Newell)
To Lake Aghmoogenagamook
Bat S 23

Boys' and Girls' Names (Eleanor Farjeon)
What splendid names for boys there are!
P Life II 9

Cat (Vernon Scannell)
My cat has got no name
Fir 59

Choosing a Name (Charles and Mary Lamb)
I have got a new-born sister
Ox CV 141

Choosing their Names (Thomas Hood)
Our old cat has kittens three
ADT 24; Blow 26; Cat 44; Puf Y 105; Rain 38; Rhyme II 41

Infant Joy (William Blake)
I have no name
By 112; PC 15; This W 52; Trad 125

Jargon (James Reeves)
Jerusalem, Joppa, Jericho
Hap 51; Ree C 156; Rhyme III 1; Word 107

Kariuki (Joseph Gatuiria)
T he hour of midnight met with a gathering of mothers
Att 47; Rhy 62

Names (Roy Fuller)
Before I was christened my grandfather said
Ful S 43

Names (Roy Fuller)
A skein of suns, the uncut stones of night
Voi III 141

The Naming of Cats (T. S. Eliot)
The Naming of Cats is a difficult matter
Eli OP 11

Picnic (Hugh Lofting)
Ella, fella/Maple tree
BE 12; FV 112

Stately Verse (anon, USA)
If Mary goes far out to sea
FV 39

What? (Ivor Cutler)
Where
Strict 88

What's Your Name? (Michael Rosen)
When they said
McRo 13

NAPOLEON

Baby, Baby, Naughty Baby (anon)
Baby, baby, naughty baby
Ox LV 48; Ox NR 20; Trad 6

129

Boney was a Warrior (anon)
Boney was a warrior
PW 21

An Incident of the French Camp
(Robert Browning)
You know, we French stormed
Ratisbon
DP III 74

Napoleon (Miroslav Holub)
Children, when was
Gang 99

Napoleon (Walter de la Mare)
What is this world, O soldiers?
Fab CV 147; Rat 307

A Saint Helena Lullaby (Rudyard
Kipling)
How far is Saint Helena from a
little child at play?
Fab CV 147

We Be the King's Men (Thomas
Hardy)
We be the King's Men, hale and
hearty
Merry 346

NATIVITY, THE

See Christmas: Religious

NEIGHBOURS

Here is a note (Michael Rosen)
Here is a note from Head Office
Ros W 70

Mending Wall (Robert Frost)
Something there is that doesn't
love a wall
*Choice 278; EGV 312; Ima 53; In O II
38; Iron III 52; Ten 76; Touch V 139*

Neighbour, tenth floor
(A. L. Hendriks, West Indies)
Beyond a span of wall
Many 26

Parable (William Soutar)
Two neighbours who were rather
dense
Conf 14; Ima 56

The People Upstairs (Ogden
Nash)
The people upstairs all practice
ballet
Nas C 105; Prel IV 30; Rhyme IV 82

The Unexploded Bomb (C. Day
Lewis)
Two householders (semi-detached)
once found
Ev 134; Conf 15

NELSON, LORD

See also Trafalgar
The Death of Nelson (anon)
Come all gallant seamen that unite
a meeting
P Tale 27

from *Nationality in Drinks*
(Robert Browning)
Here's to Nelson's memory
Sea 140

Nelson at Palermo (Alan Ross)
Monte Pellegrino, mauve, bald and
granite skull
Time 138

Nelson's Death (anon)
Old England's long-expected
heavy news from our fleet
Bal 88

The Sentinel's Story 1805 (Charles
Causley)
Three days below Trafalgar
Cau C 178

1805 (Robert Graves)
At Viscount Nelson's lavish funeral
*Fab CV 146; PW 320; RR 51; Theme
VI 73*

NETTLES

Tall Nettles (Edward Thomas)
Tall nettles cover up, as they have
done
*Choice 169; Gold III 41; In O II 1;
Iron I 43; Out 44; Say 52; Tap 53; Ten
128; Touch I 102; Voi I 113; Word 71*

NEWSBOYS

Fleet Street (Shane Leslie)
I never see the newsboys run
Lon 34; PT III 22

NEWTS

My Newts (Clarissa Hinsley)
One night in thunder
Drum 71

NEW YEAR

A New Year Carol (anon)
Here we bring new water
Flock 3; Merry 300; R Nine 96; TD 87; This W 96

New Year Song (Ted Hughes)
Now there comes
Hug S 71; Sun 108

Ring Out, Wild Bells (Alfred, Lord Tennyson)
Ring out, wild bells, to the wild sky
EGV 208; Fab PR 160; GV IV 44; Rain 73; (part) *Bk S 76*

NEW ZEALAND

A Beginning (Peter Blond)
Who am I? What am I doing here
Root 46

Farewell to New Zealand (Wynford Vaughan Thomas)
Super-suburbia of the Southern Seas
Ox LV 274

NIGHT

See also Bedtime, Stars

Check (James Stephens)
The night was creeping on the ground
Drum 8; Once 66; P Life III 95; Puf M 189; R Nine 22

The Country Bedroom (Frances Cornford)
My room's a square and candle-lighted boat
By 254; Ox PC 137

In Teesdale (Andrew Young)
No, not tonight
Gold III 45

Night (William Blake)
The sun descending in the west
Ox CV 88; Say 54; TD 81

Night Sounds (Thomas Middleton)
Midnight's bell goes ting, ting, ting, ting, ting
R Eig 124; TD 67

Out in the Dark (Edward Thomas)
Out in the dark over the snow
BB 60; DT 35; F Feet 154; Iron IV 111; Plea 227; Rat 329; Ten 143

Shadow March (Robert Louis Stevenson)
All round the house is the jet-black night
P Life III 94

Switch on the Night (Ray Bradbury)
Once there was a little boy
Drum 10

NIGHTINGALES

The Nightingale and the Glow-worm (William Cowper)
A nightingale that all day long
CTV 16

Ode to a Nightingale (John Keats)
My heart aches, and a drowsy numbness pains
Bat R 97; Bir 68; By 136; Choice 67; EGV 159; Puf V 222; Scene 96; (part) *F Feet 208*

NIGHTMARES

Dreadful Dream (Kit Wright)
I'm glad to say/I've never met
Wri H 27

My Garden (Paul Evans)
The plants in my garden
Imp 68

Nightmare (W. S. Gilbert)
When you're lying awake with a dismal headache
Bat C 40; Ev 164; Fab Non 174; Gold IV 29; Ox LV 151; Theme II 39; Touch II 138

The Nightmare (Elizabeth Jennings)
The dream was that old falling one
Theme II 38

The Nightmare (Wang-Yen-Shou, trans, A. Waley)
Once, as in the darkness I lay asleep by night
Pluc 87; Touch II 145; Voi II 13

NOAH

The Animals in the Ark (anon)
Noah: Have done, you men and women all!
Fab PV 74

The Ark (Elizabeth Jennings)
Nobody knows just how they went
Sea 121

The Ballad of Mrs Noah (Robert Duncan)
Mrs Noah in the Ark
Mod 103

Didn't it Rain (trad American)
Now, didn't it rain, chillun
Duck 93

The History of the Flood (John Heath-Stubbs)
Bang Bang Bang
Down 55; Flock 38; Imp 28; Str 38; Sun 51; Touch I 54

The Late Passenger (C. S. Lewis)
The sky was low, the sounding rain was falling dense and dark
Str 81

Measles in the Ark (Susan Coolidge)
The night it was horribly dark
Ox CV 282

Noah (Roy Daniels)
They gathered around and told him not to do it
Theme III 57

Noah (Siegfried Sassoon)
When old Noah stared across the floods
Blow 54; Prel III 19; Tho 106

Noah and the Rabbit (Hugh Chesterman)
'No land', said Noah
By 232

One More River (trad)
The animals came in two by two
P Life IV 78; Puf V 158
In come de animals two by two
Ev 254; Fab PV 75
Old Noah once he built the ark
DT 52; Rain 28; Rhyme III 65

'Twas when the Rain fell steady (Rudyard Kipling)
'Twas when the rain fell steady an' the Ark was pitched an' ready
Sea 121

When the Animals left the Ark (anon, 14th century)
There was scurrying and scrimmage when the wild ones all escaped
R Eig 113

NOISES

A Big Noise (W. B. Rands)
Twenty whales
P Life II 17

Half Asleep (Gareth Owen)
Half asleep
Third 24

In the Kitchen (John Cotton)
In the kitchen
ADT 14

Night Music (Brian Lee)
The mail train south fades out into the dark
ADT 117

Noise (anon)
Billy is blowing his trumpet
Duck 41

Noises in the Night (Thomas Middleton)
Midnight's bell goes ting, ting, ting, ting, ting
R Eig 124; TD 67

The Ocean in London (Harold Monro)
In London while I slowly wake
Theme II 43

Sounds (Alastair Reid)
PLOO is breaking your shoelace
J Vo III 39

The Sounds in the Evening (Eleanor Farjeon)
The sounds in the evening
Far M 74; Fir 18

NONSENSE

See also *Bod L, Fab Non, McG S, Mil SV, Nas C, Non, Wes N* throughout

Adventures of Isabel (Ogden Nash)
Isabel met an enormous bear
Croc 22; Fab NV 105; My R 33; Nas C 88; Once 143; P Life II 10; Young 72

anyone lived (e. e. cummings)
anyone lived in a pretty how town
EGV 343; Rat 35; (part) *Trad 113*

The Bionic Boy (Charles Connell)
It really fills me full of joy
CC 6

The Comic Adventures of Old Mother Hubbard (Sarah Catherine Martin)
Old Mother Hubbard
Non 198; Ox CV 125; Ox Dic 317; Ox NR 28; Puf NR 146

Eletelephony (Laura Richards)
Once there was an elephant
Al II 35; CBC 36; CC 40; CTV 63; Fab NV 56; Once 142; Ox CV 289; P Life III 87; Young 22; (part) *GV V 20*

The Headless Gardener (Ian Serraillier)
A gardener, Tobias Baird
Puf Q 162; Sort 93; Tale 87

If I were an Elephant (N. M. Bodecker)
If I were an elephant
Bod L 12

The Man in the Moon came down too soon (J. R. R. Tolkien)
The Man in the Moon had silver shoon
Tol T 32

The Man in the Moon stayed up too late (J. R. R. Tolkien)
There is an inn, a merry old inn
Hap 60; Tol T 31

Martin said to his Man (anon 1609)
Martin said to his Man
Fab Non 27

Mr Kartoffel (James Reeves)
Mr Kartoffel's a whimsical man
Hap II 68; My V 93; Ree C 31; Tap 75

Night Starvation or *The Biter Bit* (Carey Blyton)
At night, my uncle Rufus
Sec 23

Oh, such silliness! (William Cole)
Oh, such silliness!
OSF 11

The Old Sussex Road (Ian Serraillier)
'Do I see a hat in the road?' I said
Fir 42

Poor old Lady [Woman] (anon)
Poor old lady she swallowed a fly
Blow 42; CBC 144; CTV 94; GV II 20; J Vo I 24; Rhy 32; R Six 60; Word 116

A Reply from the Akond of Swat
(E. T. Scheffauer)
Mr Lear, I'm the Akond of Swat
CBC 74

Sky in the Pie! (Roger McGough)
Waiter, there's a sky in my pie
McG S 11

Song of the Pop-Bottles (Morris Bishop)
Pop-bottles, pop-bottles
CC 24

Tam o' the Linn or *Tommy O'Linn* or *Brian O'Linn* (anon)
Tam o' the Linn cam' up the gait
Scot 1
Tommy O'Linn was a Scotsman [Dutchman] born
Merry 233; Ox NR 202
Brian O'Linn was a gentleman born
Fab Non 43; Rat 86; (part) *Puf NR 102*
Brian O'Linn has no breeches to wear
Fab Bal 199

Three Jovial Welshmen (trad)
There were three jovial Welshmen
Fab NV 140; Fab PV 86; Gold I 11; Merry 337; Ox Dic 421; Ox NR 116; Ox PC 24; P Life III 48; (part) *Lolli II 12; My V 17*
Three jolly huntsmen
Puf Y 156

Topsyturvey World (William Brighty Rands)
If the butterfly courted the bee
Ox CV 232

A Tragic Story (W. M. Thackeray)
There liv'd a sage in days of yore
Come 192; CTV 97; Fab NV 197; J Vo II 38; P Life III 44

NONSENSE: LEWIS CARROLL

Beautiful Soup (Lewis Carroll)
Beautiful soup, so rich and green
ADT 54; Bat L 92; Croc 26; Fab Non 118; Merry 340; My V 160; Ox PC 12; Pac 31; P Life II 28

Brother and Sister (Lewis Carroll)
'Sister, sister, go to bed
Fab Non 94; P Life IV 87; Prel I 8

How doth the Little Crocodile
(Lewis Carroll)
How doth the little crocodile
*Croc 36; CTV 71; Fab Non 113; F
Feet 115; Lolli III 13; Merry 276; My
R 48; Ox LV 125; Ox PC 116*

Humpty Dumpty's Song (Lewis
Carroll)
In winter when the fields are white
*Fab NV 130; Ox PC 14; Puf V 75;
Trad 118* (part) *Tap 9*

Jabberwocky (Lewis Carroll)
'Twas brillig, and the slithy toves
*AM 44; Bat A 78; BE 13; CTV 124;
Deli 36; Duck 71; EGV 247; Fab Non
134; Like 51; Merry 283; ND 191;
Non 1; Ox CV 241; Ox LV 127; P Life
IV 10; PW 252; Rat 219; Rhyme IV
87; Tap 76; Touch II 9; Voi I 19*
(part) *Al III 39*
Jabberwocky explained: Non 118

A Lobster Quadrille (Lewis
Carroll)
'Will you walk a little faster?' said a
whiting to a snail
*CBC 130; Come 199; DP II 37; Fab
Non 119; Merry 353; Ox CV 240; Plea
134; P Life II 26*

The Mad Gardener's Song (Lewis
Carroll)
He thought he saw an Elephant
[Banker's Clerk]
*Bat L 72; By 190; Fab Non 207; Fab
NV 144; If 48; Non 58; Once 140; Ox
CV 249; P Life IV 85; Puf V 169;
Rain 42; Rat 256;* (parts) *DP II 32*

The Pig-Tale (Lewis Carroll)
There was a pig that sat alone
Ev 121

'Tis the Voice of the Lobster (Lewis
Carroll)
'Tis the voice of the Lobster, I
heard him declare
*Bat C 32; Fab Non 117; Fab NV 146;
If 65; Non 47; Ox CV 241; Ox LV
126; Trad 114*

The Walrus and the Carpenter
(Lewis Carroll)
The sun was shining on the sea
*CBC 56; Down 39; EGV 248; Fab
Non 138; Fab NV 245; Non 48; Ox CV
242; Ox LV 128; Ox PC 125; Touch I
119*

The White Knight's Song (Lewis
Carroll)
I'll tell thee everything I can
*Fab CV 277; Fab Non 132; Fab NV
142; Ox CV 247; Ox LV 131*

You are Old, Father William
(Lewis Carroll)
'You are old, Father William,' the
young man said
*CBC 149; Fab Non 113; GV IV 32;
Iron I 62; Merry 366; ND 150; Ox CV
239; Ox LV 125; P Life IV 84; Rhyme
IV 77*

NONSENSE: TED HUGHES

See also Hug F throughout
Folks (Ted Hughes)
I've heard so much about other
folks' folks
Hug F 11; R Six 36; (part) *Bits y*

Moon-Hops (Ted Hughes)
Hops are a menace on the moon, a
nuisance crop
J Vo III 65

My Aunt (Ted Hughes)
You've heard how a green thumb
Gold I 41; Hug F 29; Shad 87; Str 7

My Brother Bert (Ted Hughes)
Pets are the Hobby of my Brother
Bert
*BBGG 27; Duck 58; Hug F 25;
Out Sc 60; Rhyme III 23; R Six 78;
Theme I 3*

My Father (Ted Hughes)
Some fathers work at the office,
others work at the store
*Hug F 41; Poems 48; PT III 9; Voi I
58*

My Grandma (Ted Hughes)
My grandmother's a peaceful
person and she loves to knit
Hap II 54; Hug F 21; PT V 25

My Grandpa (Ted Hughes)
The truth of the matter, the truth
of the matter
Hug F 17; My R 20

My Mother (Ted Hughes)
All Mothers can serve up a bit of
buttered toast
Hug F 37

My Sister Jane (Ted Hughes)
And I say nothing – no, not a word

ADT 18; BE 19; CC 12; DP I 32;
Flock 95; Hap 16; Hug F 13; Once 70;
Prel I 11; Rhyme IV 98; (part)
Croc 11

My Uncle Dan (Ted Hughes)
My Uncle Dan's an inventor, you
may think that very fine
FV 51; Hug F 33

NONSENSE: EDWARD LEAR

See also Lear, Edward
The Akond of Swat (Edward
Lear)
Who, or why, or which, or what, is
the Akond of Swat?
*CBC 72; Fab CV 121; Fab Non 205;
GV II 10; My V 80; P Life III 27 (see
Nonsense: A Reply)*

An Animal Alphabet (Edward
Lear)
The Absolutely Abstemious Ass
Rat 32

Calico Pie (Edward Lear)
Calico Pie/The little birds fly
*Bat L 79; Croc 52; Fab CV 85; Fab
NV 88; If 44; Non 85; Ox PC 12;
R Eig 109; Trad 39*

*The Courtship of the
Yonghy-Bonghy-Bo* (Edward
Lear)
On the coast of Coromandel
Fab Non 153; Non 88; P Life III 22

The Dong with a Luminous Nose
(Edward Lear)
When awful darkness and silence
reign
*AM 34; Bat L 46; DP II 38; Fab Non
148; P Life II 29; Touch I 122*

The Duck and the Kangaroo
(Edward Lear)
Said the Duck to the Kangaroo
*Bat A 72; FV 84; Ox CV 186; Puf Y
122; Ten 46*

*Incidents in the Life of my Uncle
Arly* (Edward Lear)
O my aged Uncle Arly!
*CBC 38; Fab Non 203; P Life II 33;
Prel I 39*

The Jumblies (Edward Lear)
They went to sea in a sieve, they
did
*Bat L 63; CTV 126; Deli 33; EGV
225; Fab Non 170; Fab NV 248; FV
100; Merry 195; My V 104; Non 78;*

Ox CV 187; Ox PC 54; P Life III 16;
Puf V 77; Rain 34

The New Vestments (Edward
Lear)
There lived an old man in the
kingdom of Tess
CC 20

The Owl and the Pussy-Cat
(Edward Lear)
The Owl and the Pussy-Cat went
to sea
*Bat L 116; By 174; CBC 83; Come
191; Croc 19; CTV 123; DT 30; EGV
224; Ev 60; Fab CV 87; Fab Non 116;
Fab NV 250; GV III 38; If 20; Like
11; Merry 214; My V 163; Non 75; Ox
CV 185; Ox PC 117; P Life I 52; Puf
V 167; Puf Y 150; Rhyme II 43; Tap
73; Touch I 126; Trad 42*

The Pelican Chorus (Edward
Lear)
King and Queen of the pelicans we
Bir 53; Ev 86; Fab Non 159

The Pobble who has no Toes
(Edward Lear)
The Pobble who has no toes
*AM 56; Fab CV 91; Fab Non 199;
Fab NV 153; Non 93; Ox CV 198; Ox
PC 16; P Life III 20; Puf V 80*

The Quangle Wangle's Hat
(Edward Lear)
On top of the Crumpetty tree
*AM 69; Fab NV 59; Merry 219; Non
98; Once 126; P Life I 49; Rhyme IV
85*

The Table and the Chair (Edward
Lear)
Said the Table to the Chair
Fab NV 235

NOSTALGIA

Flame-Heart (Claude McKay)
So much have I forgotten in ten
years
Bite I 70; Tam 89

Nostalgia: for Railway-lovers only
(Gilbert Thomas)
You loved them too; those locos
motley gay
P Rail 13

Oft, in the Stilly Night (Thomas
Moore)
Oft, in the stilly night
Bat R 54

Soap Suds (Louis MacNeice)
This brand of soap has the same
smell as once in the big
Fab Mod 282

NOVEMBER

from *Marmion: November* (Sir
Walter Scott)
November's sky is chill and drear
P Scot 38

from *November* (John Clare)
The landscape sleeps in mist from
morn till noon
Flock 266

November (John Clare)
The shepherds almost wonder
where they dwell
Prel III 34; RR 88

November (Thomas Hood)
No sun – no moon!
*CBC 24; CTV 28; Ev 26; Ox PC 99;
Poems 43; Prel III 35; RR 89*

November (Ted Hughes)
The month of the drowned dog.
After long rain the land
Hug SP 51; Touch IV 86

November (Edward Thomas)
November days are thirty
WAS 140

November Night, Edinburgh
(Norman MacCaig)
The night tinkles like ice in glasses
Prel III 34

NUCLEAR POWER

Windscale (Norman Nicholson)
The toadstool towers infect the
shore
Tel 38; Theme VII 54

NUCLEAR WAR

See also Hiroshima
Death in the Suburbs (Adrian
Henri)
The end of the world will surely
come
NV 13

Defence (Jon Silkin)
She arrived late, with this motto
Voi III 130

Fifteen Million Plastic Bags
(Adrian Mirchell)
I was walking in a government
warehouse
Conf 18; Peng B 364

The H-Bomb's Thunder (John
Brunner 1959)
Don't you hear the H-Bomb's
thunder
Bal 179

Icarus Allsorts (Roger
McGough)
A little bit of heaven fell
Mer 71, Mer RR 100; Poems II 86

*Mother the wardrobe is full of
infantry men* (Roger McGough)
Mother the wardrobe is full of
infantry men
Burn 117; Mer 88; Mer RR 104

Noah's Arc (Roger McGough)
In my fallout shelter I have enough
food
NV 100

Noon Hour (Joan Finnigan)
Noon-hour/and the children
come in
Burn 115

The Responsibility (Peter
Appleton)
I am the man who gives the word
Conf 22; Ev 275; RR 58; Touch IV 134

This excellent machine (John
Lehmann)
This excellent machine is neatly
planned
Conf 17

Your Attention Please (Peter
Porter)
The Polar DEW has just warned
that
*Conf 19; DP IV 68; Liv 100; Look 82;
Touch V 70*

NUMBERS

Arithmetic (Carl Sandburg)
Arithmetic is where numbers fly
like pigeons in and out of your head
*Drum 101; Flock 238; Four 12; Gold I
3; Hap II 16; J Vo III 50; Prel II 10;
World 16*

How many apples grow on the tree?
(George Barker)

How many apples grow on the tree?
Bar R 13

Stable's Tables (Roy Fuller)
There was a girl called Sheila Stables
Ful S 33; Sort 92

The Will (Ian Serraillier)
There was an old man that had three sons
Tale 78

NUNS

The Young Nuns (Alex Comfort)
All night I've heard the sea on Bunduff strand
Theme V 56

NURSES

Night Sister (Elizabeth Jennings)
How is it possible not to grow hard
Theme VI 55

OAKS

The Oak and the Ash (anon)
A north countrymaid up to London had strayed
Fab CV 131

OCCUPATIONS

See also Fab NV 36–46, Puf Y 39–41, Theme VI throughout
See also Acrobats, Bananamen (*see* Jamaica), Barbers, Blacksmiths, Buses, Bushrangers, Business, Bustle-makers, Chimneysweeps, Circuses, Clergymen, Cowboys, Dentists, Dowsers, Dressmakers, Dustmen, Engine Drivers and Firemen, Engineers, Ferrymen, Financiers, Fishermen, Fishmongers, Grinders, Highwaymen, Jugglers, Loggers, Lorrydrivers, Millers, Miners, Molecatchers, Newsboys, Nuns, Nurses, Pedlars, Pilgrims, Pipers, Poachers, Poets, Politicians, Porters, Postmen, Roadmakers, Roadmenders, Sailors, Shearers, Shepherds, Shopkeepers, Smugglers, Soldiers, Steeplejacks, Tailors, Tattooists, Tramps, Watchmen, Whaling, Woodmen

Cherrystones (A. A. Milne)
Tinker, Tailor, Soldier, Sailor
Mil NS 19

Hay for the Horses (Gary Snyder)
He had driven half the night
RR 200; Theme V 48; Voi III 15

Hazardous Occupations (Carl Sandburg)
Jugglers keep six bottles in the air
Voi III 162

When I grow up (William Wise)
When I grow up
Puf Y 130

OCEANS

The Eye (Robinson Jeffers)
The Atlantic is a stormy moat; and the Mediterranean
Theme VII 65

OCTOBER

October (Christina Rossetti)
I've brought you nuts and hops
Come 87; Say 34; WAS 122

October (Clive Sansom)
The year slows down. The swallows go
San E 22

October (Edward Thomas)
The green elm with the one great bough of gold
Scene 31; Ten 131

October Dawn (Ted Hughes)
October is marigold, and yet
Hug SP 29; Touch III 108

OGRES

The Ogre (Jack Prelutsky)
In a foul and filthy cavern
Night 24

Song of the Ogres (W. H. Auden)
Little fellow, you're amusing
Hap II 78; Hist 79; Puf M 160;
(part) *Drum 80*

OLD AGE

See also Grandparents

The Auld Man o'Muckhart
(William Soutar)
The auld man o'Muckhart
Ring 95

Beautiful Old Age
(D. H. Lawrence)
It ought to be lovely to be old
Theme IV 69; Voi III 56

A Country Death (B. S. Johnson)
And when her husband died, of
course she went
Many 55

Crowsfeet Splaying round his Eyes
(L. Paul Lloyd-Evans)
Crowsfeet splaying round his eyes
Burn 162

Dick Straightup (Ted Hughes)
Past eighty, but never in eighty
years
Theme IV 71

Geriatric Ward (Phoebe
Hesketh)
Feeding time in the Geriatric Ward
Theme IV 68; Touch V 110

I Look into my Glass (Thomas
Hardy)
I look into my glass
Theme IV 58

In Oak Terrace (Tony Connor)
Old and alone, she sits at nights
Prel I 49; Touch V 196

In the Snack-Bar (Edwin
Morgan)
A cup capsizes along the formica
Ring 1; Seven 243; Touch V 19

The Little Chapel (Suniti
Namjoshi, Pakistan)
When I am old and rich and
gracious
Many 33

Lore (R. S. Thomas)
Job Davies, eighty-five
Choice 311

Note for the Future (Jim Burns)
When I get old
Strict 70

The Old Fools (Philip Larkin)
What do they think has happened,
the old fools
Mus 76

An Old Man's Winter Night
(Robert Frost)
All out-of-doors looked darkly in at
him
Choice 280

Old Men (Tony Connor)
When there was a war they went to
war
Look 47; Strict 69

*The Old Men admiring themselves
in the Water* (W. B. Yeats)
I heard the old, old men say
*BE 62; Fab CV 379; Gold III 36; GV
III 18; Imp 89; RR 198; TD 152;
Third 114; Touch I 145*

The Old Ones (Frances Bellerby)
In the May evening
Dawn 98

An Old Woman of the Roads
(Padraic Colum)
Oh, to have a little house!
*Come 178; Like 131; Puf V 135; Puf Y
14; Theme IV 57; Word 88*

The Old Wood-seller (Chinese,
trans John Scott)
Just an old man from the
mountains
Rhy 100

Poem for Kids (John Wain)
An old, old man lived down our
street
Over 78

The Song of the Old Mother
(W. B. Yeats)
I rise in the dawn and I kneel and
blow
Bric 30; Iron I 17; Theme IV 58

A Striking Old Man (Alasdair
Aston)
When grandfather first came to us
Hap II 42

A Summer Storm (William
Plomer)
This is the voluntary patients' wing
Theme IV 60

Warning (Jenny Joseph)
When I am an old woman I shall
wear purple
*Full 48; In O I 28; Liv 59; Mod 144;
PT V 20; Round 57; World 133*

When I'm Sixty-Four (John
Lennon and Paul McCartney)
When I get older, losing my hair
GV V 8

When You are Old (W. B. Yeats)
When you are old and grey and full
of sleep
*By 216; EGV 296; Fab LP 321; Flock
289; GV V 11; Touch V 51*

2001 – The Tennyson/Hardy Poem
(Gavin Ewart)
When I am old and long turned
gray
Mus 51

OLD AND YOUNG

The Boys (Anthony Thwaite)
Six of them climbed aboard
DP IV 112

Childhood (Frances Cornford)
I used to think that grown-up
people chose
*DP II 1; Gold III 36; Theme IV 6;
Touch I 150*

It is Impossible (Ross Falconer)
It is impossible
Burn 9

When I was Your Age (Michael
Frayn)
When I was your age, child
Sort 14

Witch (Marian Lines)
There was this old lady on the bus
. . . (Old cat! Sourpuss!)
Lin T 14

The Young Ones (Elizabeth
Jennings)
They slip on the bus, hair piled up
high
Gold III 51; Theme IV 9

OPTIMISTS

The Difference (anon)
'Twixt optimist and pessimist
CTV 47

Say not the Struggle naught availeth
(Arthur Hugh Clough)
Say not the struggle naught
availeth
Ev 260; Fab PR 172

ORIENTAL POEMS, BRIEF

See Flock (throughout); *Imp
9–10, 21, 23, 65, 67, 68; J Vo I 10,
67, 72; J Vo II 17, 26, 46; J Vo III
14, 22, 37, 47, 49, 54; J Vo IV 8,
13, 19, 39, 90; Out 32, 62, 74; Tale
16; Touch I 3–6, 19–24; Touch III
4–5, 35, 38, 40, 41; Voi I 80, 83,
97, 118, 122; Voi III 83*

OSTRICHES

The Ostrich (Lord Alfred
Douglas)
The ostrich always seems to try
Bat L 129

The Ostrich (Ogden Nash)
The ostrich roams the great Sahara
Zoo 63

OTTERBOURNE

The Battle of Otterbourne (anon)
It fell upon the Lammastide
Fab CV 232

OTTERS

An Otter (Ted Hughes)
Underwater eyes, an eel's
Hug SP 54; Zoo 31; (part) *Dawn 66;
Word 51*

OWEN, WILFRED

*Sleep Now: in Memory of Wilfrid
Owen* (Brian Patten)
Sleep now
Mer 105; Mer R 127; Mer RR 132

OWLS

The Barn Owl (Samuel Butler)
While moonlight, silvering all the
walls
My V 122; PT VI 29; R Nine 62

Once I was a Monarch's Daughter (anon)
Once I was a monarch's daughter
Shad 59

The Owl (Walter de la Mare)
Owl of the wildwood I
Hap 50; Theme II 30

The Owl (John Hewitt)
With quiet step and careful breath
Hap II 47

Owl (George Macbeth)
is my favourite. Who flies
Mod 150

The Owl (Alfred, Lord Tennyson)
When cats run home and light is come
BB 43; Bir 36; Choice 87; Fab CV 87; Fab NV 23; F Feet 160; Merry 307; My R 19; Ox PC 65; Plea 46; P Life III 74; Rain 52; RR 178; Say 28; TD 31; This W 31

The Owl (Edward Thomas)
Downhill I came, hungry and yet not starved
Bat C 66; By 236; Iron II 7; Plea 207; PW 291; Rat 330; RR 182; Theme II 31

The Owl-Critic (James Thomas Fields)
'Who stuffed that white owl?' No one spoke in the shop
Ev 98

Questioning Faces (Robert Frost)
The winter owl banked just in time to pass
Bric 18

A shadow is floating through the Moonlight (Randall Jarrell)
A shadow is floating through the moonlight
BE 55; Drum 53; R Ten 85; Say 59; TD 63; Theme I 25; Voi II 136

Sweet Suffolk Owl (anon)
Sweet Suffolk owl, so trimly dight
Bat A 61; Merry 336; Rat 413

Town Owl (Laurie Lee)
On eves of cold when slow coal fires
Bir 60; ND 65; PT III 27; Theme II 32; Time 114; Touch IV 171

OXEN

The Egyptian Peasant to his Ox 1400 BC (Bertolt Brecht)
O ox, our goodly puller of the plough
Stuf 49

The Oxen (Thomas Hardy)
Christmas Eve, and twelve of the clock
Come 224; DP I 68; F Feet 173; Rat 331; RR 165; Touch III 73; WAS 159

The Ox-Tamer (Walt Whitman)
In a far-away northern county in the placid pastoral region
Rat 332; Voi II 47

PAINTING

Painting the Gate (May Swenson)
I painted the mailbox. That was fun
Stuf 31

PAINTING: POEMS ABOUT PICTURES

Don't let that Horse (Chagall, trans Lawrence Ferlinghetti)
Don't let that horse/eat that violin
Rat 134

In the Land of Cockayne (Ian Crichton Smith)
In the land of Cockayne
Over 39

Landscape with the Fall of Icarus (William Carlos Williams)
According to Brueghel
J Vo III 89

Musee des Beaux Arts (W. H. Auden)
About suffering they were never wrong
DP IV 147; Mod 17; Ten 17; Voi III 135

PAINTING: POEMS FOR PICTURE-MAKING

Animals' Houses (James Reeves)
Of animals' houses
Puf Q 75; Ree C 19

140

The Fly (Walter de la Mare)
How large unto the tiny fly
*By 228; de la M Col 89; Deli 58; DP I
6; DT 76; F Feet 186; Once 38; Plea
42; Poems 28; Touch I 30*

Good Taste (Christopher Logue)
Travelling a man met a tiger, so
*BE 18; Dawn 69; GV V 29; Poems II
109; Prel IV 25; R Eig 95; Say 30;
Tap 13*

Quack! (Walter de la Mare)
The duck is whiter than whey is
*de la M Col 266; Merry 218; Rhyme I
24; R Six 57*

from *The Rime of the Ancient
Mariner* (S. T. Coleridge)
Beyond the shadow of the ship
P Life IV 56

*Stopping by Woods on a Snowy
Evening* (Robert Frost)
Whose woods these are I think I
know
*BE 6; Blow 38; Choice 284; Deli 71;
DP II 27; DT 20; Fab CV 58; Flock
276; GV III 15; Hap 38; Iron I 62;
Like 67; Rat 407; Rhyme IV 15; Tap
44; TD 143; Ten 80; This W 156;
Touch I 155; WAS 154*

PALM SUNDAY

The Donkey (G. K. Chesterton)
When fishes flew and forests
walked
*Bat A 19; By 221; Deli 81; EGV 309;
Fab PR 232; Like 137; ND 76; Rain
53; Rat 133; Rhyme IV 118; Sun 132;
TD 92; WAS 52*

PAN

Pan with Us (Robert Frost)
Pan came out of the woods one day
Puf M 227

PANTHERS

The Panther (R. M. Rilke, trans
W. D. Snodgrass)
Always passing bars has
dulled/His sight so
RR 20
(trans J. B. Leishman)
His gaze, going past these bars, has
got so misted
Flock 61

PANTOMIMES

The Pantomime (Wilma
Horsbrugh)
This is a rhyme
Hor B 37

Pantomime Poem (Roger
McGough)
'He's behind yer!'
*Gang 98; Mer R 63; NV 77; Strict 33;
Third 48*

PARABLES

See also Fables
Dives and Lazarus (anon)
As it fell out upon a day
Fab Bal 153; Flock 165; Sun 163

*The Parable of the Old Man and the
Young* (Wilfred Owen)
And Abram rose, and clove the
wood, and went
*By 275; Flock 250; PW 318; Sun 212;
Voi III 127*

from *The Vision of Piers Plowman*
(Langland, trans Ronald
Tamplin)
The Good Samaritan
I walked the road, deep in
conversation
Sun 162

PARACHUTING

Parachute (Lenrie Peters,
Gambia)
Parachute men say
Ev 229; Theme V 48

PARADOX

The Peacock has a Score of Eyes
(Christina Rossetti)
The peacock has a score of eyes
If 67

A Pin has a Head (Christina
Rossetti)
A pin has a head but has no hair
CTV 71; Fab NV 132

PARASITES

Autobiography of a Lungworm
(Roy Fuller)
My normal dwelling is the lungs of
swine
Ox Con 38

PARKS

Park (Marian Lines)
Asphalt, broad – flat – sweet and
swinging
Lin T 6

The Park (James S. Tippett)
I'm glad that I
Fir 20; Here 125; Hi 40

The Park (Olive Dehn)
In the middle of the city
Deli 96; Full 100

The Park (Leonard Clark)
I often wish when lying in the dark
Puf Y 128

PARODY

See also *Ox LV* throughout;
Touch II 119–125

Ancient Music (Ezra Pound)
(*Original: see* Cuckoos: *Sumer is
icumen in*)
Winter is icummen in
Flock 273; Out 72

Chard Whitlow (Henry Reed)
(*After* T. S. Eliot)
As we get older we do not get any
younger
Ox LV 279

The Cock and the Bull
(C. S. Calverley)
(*After R. Browning*)
You see this pebble-stone? It's a
thing I bought
Fab Non 109

*Fragment in Imitation of
Wordsworth* (Catherine
Fanshawe)
There is a river clear and fair
Fab Non 89

How doth the Little Crocodile
(Lewis Carroll)
(*Original: see* Bees: *How doth the
little busy bee*)
How doth the little crocodile
*Croc 36; CTV 71; Fab Non 113; F
Feet 115; Lolli III 13; Merry 276; My
R 48; Ox LV 125; Ox PC 116*

Leaves (Ted Hughes)
(*Original: see* Robins: *Who killed
Cock Robin?*)
Who killed the leaves?
Third 66

Lewis Carroll (Eleanor Farjeon)
(*Original: see You are Old, Father
William*, below)
'You are wise, Mr Dodgson', the
young child said
OX CV 331

The Lobster (Lewis Carroll)
(*Original: see* Laziness: *The
Sluggard*)
'Tis the voice of the Lobster, I
heard him declare
*Bat C 32; Fab Non 117; Fab NV 146;
If 65; Non 47; Ox CV 241; Ox LV
126; Trad 114*

A London Sparrow's 'If'
(J. A. Lindon)
(*Original: see* Courage: *If*)
If you c'n keep alive when li'l
bleeders
Bill 134; Lon 58

Nutty Nursery Rhymes (Max
Fatchen)
'Jump over the moon?' the cow
declared
Fat S 30–35

*A Quotation from Shakespeare with
Slight Improvements* (Lewis
Carroll)
Warwick: Wilt please your Grace
to go along with us?
Fab Non 96

Ruinous Rhymes (Max Fatchen)
Pussy-cat, pussy-cat, where have
you been?
Fat W 19–21

The Streets of Laredo (Louis
MacNeice)
(*Original: see* Cowboys: *The
Streets of Laredo*)
O early one morning I walked out
like Agag
Bill 172; Mod 36; Peng B 356

Twinkle, twinkle, little bat (Lewis
Carroll)
(*Original: see* Stars: *The Star*)
Twinkle, twinkle, little bat!
Fab Non 114; Ox LV 126

Two Poems (Hugh Kingsmill)
(*Original: see* Hanging: *A
Shropshire Lad*)
What, still alive at twenty-two
Bill 119; Ox LV 221

Variations on . . . Old King Cole
(G. K. Chesterton)
Old King Cole in the manner of
Tennyson, Yeats, Browning, Walt
Whitman, Swinburne
Ox LV 201

You are old, Father William
(Lewis Carroll)
(*Original: see The Old Man's
Comforts*, Robert Southey, *EGV
138; Ox CV 93*)
You are old, Father William
*CBC 149; Fab Non 113; GV IV 32;
Iron I 62; Merry 366; ND 150; OX
CV 239; Ox LV 125; P Life IV 84;
Rhyme IV 77*

PARROTS

I'm a Parrot (Grace Nichols)
I'm a parrot
Stuf 38

Mother Parrot's Advice
(A. K. Nyabongo)
Never get up till the sun gets up
Afr I 7

Parrot (Alan Brownjohn)
Sometimes I sit with both eyes
closed
*ADT 31; Bat L 122; Four 72; R Ten
79*

The Parrot (Thomas Campbell)
The deep affections of the breast
Ev 96; FM 121; Theme I 12
(part) A parrot from the Spanish
Main
Bir 14

The Parrot (Edward
Lucie-Smith)
The parrot is a thief
Stuf 39

Parrot (Stevie Smith)
The old sick parrot
Theme I 13

Parrots (Judith Wright)
Loquats are cold as winter suns
SAS 146

PARTIES

False Security (John Betjeman)
I remember the dread with which
I at a quarter to four
Liv 3

The Party (Reed Whittemore)
They served tea in the sandpile,
together with
Liv 2

PEACE

from *The Garden at Appleton House*
(Andrew Marvell)
See how the flowers, as at parade
Plea 68; RR 45

The Vote (Ralph Knevet)
The helmet now an hive for bees
becomes
Voi II 69

PEDLARS

The Pedlar (Eleanor Farjeon)
There was an old pedlar
Fab NV 39

The Pedlar's Caravan (William
Brighty Rands)
I wish I lived in a caravan
Come 107; Ox CV 233; Ox PC 145

There was an Old Woman (trad)
There was an old woman, as I've
heard tell
*Fab NV 150; Merry 148; My V 78;
Non 195; Ox Dic 427; Ox NR 169; P
Life III 53; Puf NR 142*

PEGASUS

Pegasus (Eleanor Farjeon)
From the blood of Medusa
Poems II 123

Pegasus (Edward Lowbury)
I ask how a horse – for that's what
he is
Low G 33

PELICANS

The Pelican (J. R. Bunting)
With what precision does the
slow-winged pelican
Cari I 36

The Reason for the Pelican (John
Ciardi)
The reason for the pelican
Hi 16

PENGUINS

Enigma Sartorial (Lucy W. Rhu)
Consider the Penguin
Young 18

Peter and Percival (E. V. Rieu)
Peter and Percival lived in a place
Puf Q 125

PESSIMISTS

See also Optimists

The Pessimist (Benjamin
Franklin King)
Nothing to do but work
*Fab Non 226; Imp 84; My V 92; Ox
PC 14; RR 132;* (part) *GV III 34*

*There are Bad Times just around the
Corner* (Noel Coward)
They're out of sorts in Sutherland
Ox LV 237

PETS

See also Theme I 3–18
See also Cats, Dogs, Gerbils

Aunt Ethel (Alastair Sampson)
Aunt Ethel keeps a crocodile
PT V 24

The Dog Lovers (Spike Milligan)
So they bought you
Poems II 72

For a Good Dog (Ogden Nash)
My little dog ten years ago
Dog 14

Mother knows Best (R. C.
Scriven)
I've lots of pets, some small, some
big
R Six 76

My Brother Bert (Ted Hughes)
Pets are the hobby of my brother
Bert
*BBGG 27; Duck 58; Hug F 25; Out
Sc 60; Rhyme III 23; R Six 78; Theme
I 3*

One Day at a Perranworth Pet Shop
(Charles Causley)
One day at a Perranworth pet shop
Cau F 66; Sort 44

Pet Shop (Louis MacNeice)
Cold blood or warm, crawling or
fluttering
Theme I 14

Take One Home for the Kiddies
(Philip Larkin)
On shallow straw, in shadeless
glass
*Bric 48; Poems 29; RR 14; Sort 57;
Theme I 14*

PHEASANTS

Cock-Pheasant (Laurie Lee)
Gilded with leaf-thick paint; a
steady
Time 115

The Pheasant (John
Heath-Stubbs)
Cock-pheasant crows in the
English wood
Hea P 22

The Pheasant (Robert P. Tristam
Coffin)
The pheasant cock sprang into
view
Bite I 48

from *Windsor Forest* (Alexander
Pope)
See! from the brake the whirring
pheasant springs
Bir 31; Flock 127; FM 55

PHOTOGRAPHS

Photograph (Gareth Owen)
Is that you and is that me
Owe S 48

PHOENIXES

The Phoenix (Michael Rosen)
On the banks of the Nile
Drum 154; Ros W 63

The Wicked Fowler (Patric
Dickinson)
The wicked fowler took his gun
TCN 106

PHYSICAL ACTIVITIES

See All-in Wrestling, Bicycling,
Bouncing Balls, Boxing,
Camping, Dancing, Diving,
Flying, Games, Gliding,
Hopping, Mountaineering,
Mowing, Parachuting,

144

Ploughing, Skateboarding,
Skating, Skipping, Sledging,
Surfing, Swimming, Swinging,
Trampolines, Tree Climbing,
Walking

PICNICS

The Delights of a Picnic (J. A.
Lindon)
You are sitting on stones with
rheumaticky bones
Prel I 19

The Picnic (John Logan)
It is the picnic with Ruth in the
spring
*GV V 2; Liv 38; Theme IV 15; Touch
V 39; Voi III 71*

PIGEONS

Mrs Peck-Pigeon (Eleanor
Farjeon)
Mrs Peck-Pigeon
*Far M 10; F Feet 72; Once 32; P Life I
47; R Six 23*

Pigeon (Roy Fuller)
A cropped, grey, too-small, bullet,
Prussian head
Bir 81

Pigeons (Richard Kell)
They paddle with staccato feet
*Drag 47; My V 140; ND 73; Touch II
67*

Pigeons (Alastair Reid)
On the crooked arm of Columbus,
on his cloak
Voi III 150

Pitchfork Department
(D. J. Enright)
It was patent in this ancient city,
paradise of
Theme I 40

PIGS

The Dead Pig (anon)
T'owd pig's got mezzles an' she's
dead, poor thing
Fab Non 76

P (Edward Lear)
P was a pig
P Life I 53

The Pig's Tail (Norman Ault)
A furry coat has the bear to wear
Come 148; P Life III 86

The Poor Man's Pig (Edmund
Blunden)
Already fallen plum-blossom stars
the green
PT VI 15

View of a Pig (Ted Hughes)
The pig lay on a barrow dead
*DP IV 11; Drag 71; Flock 229; Hug
SP 48; Time 75; Touch III 121; View
VII 34*

The Wicked Pig (L. A. G.
Strong)
Merciful powers, will ye look at
this villain
Sun 28

PIKE

The Pike (Edmund Blunden)
From shadows of rich oaks outpeer
Touch V 200

Pike (Ted Hughes)
Pike, three inches long, perfect
*Bat A 82; Drag 18; Fab Mod 387;
Hug SP 59; Mod 79; ND 60; Seven
150; Time 74; Touch V 201; (part)
Zoo 86*

The Pike (Theodore Roethke)
The river turns
Gold IV 51; Theme I 26

PILGRIMS

from *The Canterbury Tales*
(Geoffrey Chaucer)
Whaen that Aprille with his
shoures
Flock 17-33
(trans Nevill Coghill)
When the sweet showers of April
fall and shoot
Flock 16–32

The Passionate Man's Pilgrimage
(Sir Walter Ralegh)
Give me my scallop shell of quiet
Iron IV 13; Rat 334; (part) EGV 17

The Pilgrimage (George
Herbert)
I travell'd on, seeing the hill, where
lay
Touch IV 6

Who would True Valour see (John Bunyan)
Who would true valour see *or* He who would valiant be
Bat C 14; By 94; DP III 113; EGV 87; Fab PR 40; Hymn 41; Merry 349; ND 232; Rain 94; RR 160

PINES

Pines (William Hart-Smith)
Cones exploding sharply in the heat?
Aus 78

PING-PONG

See Table Tennis

PIONEERS

See also USA: Pioneers and the West

Black Harry's Team
(A. B. Paterson, Australia)
No soft-skinned Durham steers are they
Pat A 50

PIPERS

The Pied Piper of Hamelin
(Robert Browning)
Hamelin Town's in Brunswick
Bat L 12; Fab CV 160; ND 101; Ox CV 173
(part) Into the street the piper stept
DT 17
(part) Once more he stepped into the street
Mov 119

A Piper (Seumas O'Sullivan)
A piper in the streets today
GV IV 17; Like 115; Out Sc 66; PT IV 7; Rhyme III 46; TD 24

The Piper o' Dundee (anon)
And wasna he a roguey
Scot 17

Over the Hills and Far Away
(trad)
Tom he was a piper's son
Fab NV 31; Fab PV 99; Merry 76; Ox Dic 408; Ox NR 164; Puf NR 168; Puf SB 56; Rhyme I 13

PIRATES

The Bold 'Princess Royal' (anon)
'Twas the fourteenth of February we sailed from the land
Brit 132

The Coast of High Barbary (anon)
Look ahead, look astern, look the weather and the lee
Ox PV 50; Rain 101; Rhyme IV 57; Wind 63
There were two lofty ships from old England came
Bk Bal 41

The Flying Cloud (anon)
My name is Edward Holland
Iron I 24

Great Black-Backed Gulls (John Heath-Stubbs)
Said Cap'n Morgan to Cap'n Kidd
Hea P 17; Sea 173

Henry Martin (anon)
In merry Scotland, in merry Scotland
Merry 189
There lived in Scotland three Brothers
Brit 131
There were three brothers in merry Scotland
Bk Bal 37

The Inchcape Rock (Robert Southey)
No stir in the air, no stir in the sea
Blow 34; Down 19; DP I 63; EGV 135; Nar 114; Plea 145; Wind 59

The Last Buccaneer (Charles Kinglsey)
Oh, England is a pleasant place for them that's rich and high
EGV 229

The Pirate (Hugh Chesterman)
He walks the deck with swaggering gait
PT V 12

The Pirate Don Durk of Dowdee
(Mildred Meigs)
Ho for the pirate Don Durk of Dowdee
Fab NV 45; Once 99; P Life III 12

Pirates on Funafuti (E. V. Rieu)
Full many a magic island lies within the seas of coral
Hap II 20

The Salcombe Seaman's Flaunt
(anon)
A lofty ship from Salcombe came
Peng B 264

Teach the Rover (anon)
Will you hear of a bloody battle
Peng B 261

The Value of Gold to Sailors
(Brian Patten)
'We've ransacked the town' the
pirates said
Sea 207

PLANE TREES

Pavement Plane Trees (Marian
Lines)
Every seventeenth paving stone, as
far as eye can see
Lin T 28

PLANETS

The Undiscovered Planet (Norman
Nicholson)
Out on the furthest tether let it run
Time 119

PLANTS

See also Nettles

How to treat the House-Plants (Kit
Wright)
All she ever thinks about are
house-plants
Wri H 42

PLATYPUSES

The Diplomatic Platypus (Patrick
Barrington)
I had a duck-billed platypus when
I was up at Trinity
Touch II 113

Old Man Platypus
(A. B. Paterson)
Far from the trouble and toil of
town
Aus 64; Pat A 23; Rain 58

The Platypus (Oliver Herford)
My child, the duck-billed platypus
Rhyme IV 94

PLOUGHING

As the team's head-brass flashed out
(Edward Thomas)
As the team's head-brass flashed
out on the turn
Choice 171; Plea 185; Rat 42

Ploughing on Sunday (Wallace
Stevens)
The white cock's tail
*Deli 122; My V 20; Rat 346; R Eig
100; Say 45; This W 19; Voi I 115*

Sunset Ploughing (Norman
MacCaig)
The ploughhorse leaning through
the red haze
P Scot 26

POACHERS

Dick Daring the Poacher or
A Shining Night (trad)
Honest regular work Dick Daring
gave up
Bk Bal 98; Nar 85

The Poacher (R.S. Thomas)
Turning aside, never meeting
Choice 307; Time 149

Poaching in Excelsis
(G. K. Menzies)
I've poached a pickle pairtricks
when the leaves were turning sere
Ring 51; Scot 60

The Poaching Man (Clive
Sansom)
He knows these parts, they say, like
the back of his hand
San E 25

Poems for Arthur: I (Brian Jones)
Arthur was wicked, but we loved
Arthur
Jon S 14

Sudborough Heroes (anon 1837)
In eighteen hundred and
thirty-seven
Bal 112

POEMS AND POETRY

Advice to Poets (Roy Fuller)
If you lack an inventive brain
Ful S 36

from *An Essay on Criticism*
(Alexander Pope)
But most by numbers judge a
poet's song
Fab UV 151

Even in a Little Thing (anon,
Gilbert Islands)
Even in a little thing
Dis 123

Found Poem (Brian Jones)
These stockings should be lightly
washed, rinsed and dried
Jon S 18

A Good Poem (Roger McGough)
I like a good poem
McRo 11; ND 245

How to Eat a Poem (Eve
Merriam)
Don't be polite/Bite in
Bite I 66

Jordan II (George Herbert)
When first my lines of heavenly
joys made mention
Touch IV 37

Makers and Creatures (Vernon
Scannell)
It is a curious experience
Sca A 19

*On First Looking into Chapman's
Homer* (John Keats)
Much have I travelled in the
realms of gold
EGV 156; Fab CV 34; ND 219

Poetry for Supper (R. S. Thomas)
'Listen, now, verse should be as
natural
Ox Con 48; Time 152; Touch IV 38

Shallow Poem (Gerda Mayer)
I've thought of a poem
May K 27

Unfolding Bud (Naoshi
Koriyama, Japan)
One is amazed
Bite II 58

Verse (Oliver St John Gogarty)
What should we know
Fab CV 29

Write As You Will (Nicanor
Parra)
Write as you will
GV IV 1; Imp 3

POETS

See also Ful S 36–40
See also Auden, Chaucer, Clare,
Hardy, Keats, Lear, Owen,
Shakespeare, Vaughan
The Acrobat (Lawrence
Ferlinghetti)
Constantly risking absurdity
Theme VI 19; Touch IV 36

Lintie in a Cage (Alice V. Stuart)
Yon is the laddie lo'ed to daunder
far
Scot 121

Madly Singing in the Mountains
(Po Chu-I, trans A. Waley)
There is no one among men that
has not a special failing
Voi II 7

A Minor Bird (Robert Frost)
I have wished a bird would fly
away
Bir 87; R Nine 59

Poem for a Dead Poet (Roger
McGough)
He was a poet he was
NV 78; Strict 169

The Poet Inspired (Roger
McGough)
7.30 on a pristine June morning
McG S 29

*To a Poet a Thousand Years Hence
(I)* (James Elroy Flecker)
I who am dead a thousand years
By 246; Gold IV 4

*To a Poet a Thousand Years Hence
(II)* (John Heath-Stubbs)
I who am dead a thousand years
Gold IV 5; Ox Con 106

What the Chairman told Tom
(Basil Bunting)
POETRY? It's a hobby
Strict 172; Theme VI 62

POLAR BEARS

The Polar Bear (Lord Alfred
Douglas)
It's always well to take great care
Dou T 44

POLICEMEN

Brooklyn Cop (Norman
MacCaig)

Built like a gorilla but less timid
Seven 174

PC Plod is on the Beat (Roger McGough)
PC Plod is on the beat
McG S 20

The Suspect (Edwin Morgan)
Asked me for a match
suddenly/with his hand up
Seven 241

POLITICIANS

Epitaph on a Tyrant
(W. H. Auden)
Perfection, of a kind, was what he
was after
Choice 239; GV V 38; Rat 142; Voi III 58

Leader of Men (Norman MacCaig)
When he addressed ten thousand
Voi III 58

On a Dead Statesman (Rudyard Kipling)
I could not dig; I dared not rob
Iron IV 19; RR 168; Touch V 112

POLITICS

Socialist's Song (Roy Fuller)
It was an ex-sailor grown old in the war
Bill 38

POLO

The Geebung Polo Club
(A. B. Paterson)
It was somewhere up the country
in a land of rock and scrub
Aus 35; Theme V 12

PONDS

The Pond (Anthony Thwaite)
With nets and kitchens sieves they
raid the pond
Touch III 81

Our Pond (Daniel Pettiward)
I am fond
PT VI 28

PONIES

Hunter Trails (John Betjeman)
It's awf'lly bad luck on Diana
By 289; CBC 138; Dawn 82; Duck 56; EGV 350; Ev 245; Hor 46; Mod 59; Prel II 27; Theme V 14; Touch II 159

The Runaway (Robert Frost)
Once when the snow of the year
was beginning to fall
Drag 28; Fab CV 79; F Feet 125; Gold I 55; Hap 68; Hor 29; Prel I 44; Touch III 116; World 118; Zoo 36

The Tale of a Pony (Bret Harte)
Name of my heroine, simply 'Rose'
Hor 20

POOLS

The Pool in the Rock (Walter de la Mare)
In this water, clear as air
de la M Col 95; Fan 110; Iron II 29; P Life III 9; PT I 7; World 96

The Rock Pool (Philip Hobsbaum)
My life could have ended then,
crouched over the pool
DP III 2

The Rock Pool (Edward Shanks)
This is the sea. In these uneven
walls
PT I 15

Water Picture (May Swenson)
In the pond in the park
Tap 57

POPLARS

Aspens (Edward Thomas)
All day and night, save winter,
every weather
Choice 176; Ten 129

Binsey Poplars (Gerard Manley Hopkins)
My aspens dear, whose airy cages
quelled
Choice 116; Flock 104; Iron IV 106; Rat 77; Scene 154; Theme VII 54

The Poplar Field (William Cowper)
The poplars are felled; farewell to
the shade
Flock 105

PORCUPINES

The Porcupine (Ogden Nash)
Any hound a porcupine nudges
By 287; Nas C 38

The Porcupine (Jack Prelutsky)
The porcupine is puzzled
Full 38

PORTERS

The Porter (C. J. Dennis)
I'd like to be a porter, and always
on the run
Al III 43

PORTRAITS

See RR 119–134

PORTRAITS: COMIC

See also Nonsense, Nonsense:
Lewis Carroll, Nonsense: Ted
Hughes, Nonsense: Edward
Lear
Cousin Reggie and *Cousin Nell*
(Roger McGough)
Cousin Reggie/who adores the sea
Cousin Nell/married a frogman
McRo 70; Sec 22

from *The Hunting of the Snark*
(Lewis Carroll)
There was one who was famed for
the number of things
Fab NV 209

Sir Smashem Uppe (E. V. Rieu)
Good afternoon, Sir Smashem
Uppe!
*CC 32; DP III 97; P Life IV 88; Puf
Q 115; Rhyme IV 72*

PORTRAITS: FEMALE

Aunt Flo' (John Cotton)
Was like a dumpling on legs, with a
face as gentle
Sec 24

Aunt Julia (Norman MacCaig)
Aunt Julia spoke Gaelic
Mod 178; PT V 22; Rat 51; Seven 180

Aunt Kate: a moral story (Shirley
Toulson)

When Aunt Kate woke each
shining day
Sort 96

Elsie Marley (anon)
Elsie Marley is grown so fine
Ox Dic 159

Mrs McHingy (Diana Harland)
Old Mrs McHingy so drab and so
dingy
Sort 25

Mrs Malone (Eleanor Farjeon)
Mrs Malone
*Far M 90; Ox CV 332; Puf Q 32; Sun
194*

PORTRAITS: MALE

Elegy for Alfred Hubbard (Tony
Connor)
Hubbard is dead, the old plumber
*Ev 114; Mod 98; Theme VI 8; Touch
IV 48; Voi III 52*

Judge Selah Lively (Edgar Lee
Masters)
Suppose you stood just five foot
two
Gold III 8; Theme VI 16

The Love Song of J. Alfred Prufrock
(T. S. Eliot)
Let us go then, you and I
Ten 67

The Man in the Bowler Hat
(A. S. J. Tessimond)
I am the unnoticed, the
unnoticeable man
Burn 135; Poems II 124; Theme III 54

Mr Flood's Party (Edwin
Arlington Robinson)
Old Eben Flood, climbing alone
one night
Theme IV 61

'Old Charley' (Clive Sansom)
'Charley a hundred?
San E 9

Sporus [Lord Hervey] (Alexander
Pope)
Yet let me flap this bug with gilded
wings
Touch IV 112

Who's Who (W. H. Auden)
A shilling life will give you all the
facts
Choice 241

POSTMEN

The Postman (Jon Stallworthy)
Satchel on hip
Drag 38; Full 92; Hap II 44; PT V 15

POTATOES

Giving Potatoes (Adrian Mitchell)
Mashed potatoes cannot hurt you, darling
Rat 178

PRAISES

See also Hymn throughout
Behold (Mary Kawena Pukui, Hawaii)
Above, above/All birds in air
Oral 289

Bless the Lord (Psalm 104, A.V.)
Bless the Lord, O my soul
Dis 114

Bless Ye the Lord (Book of Common Prayer)
O all ye works of the Lord, bless ye the Lord
DP II 98
(part) *O ye whales and all that move in the waters*
Bat A 88

Glory to Thee (T. Ken)
Glory to Thee, my God this night
Hymn 50; Rhyme III 82

God's Grandeur (Gerard Manley Hopkins)
The world is charged with the grandeur of God
Voi III 149

i thank You God (e. e. cummings)
i thank You God
ND 11

Let All the World (George Herbert)
Let all the world in every corner sing
Hymn 31

Ogun, Yoruba God of Iron and War (Obutunde Ijimere)
Ogun is not like pounded yam
RAP 26

The Old Hundreth [Psalm 100] (William Kethe)
All people that on earth do dwell
Fab PR 27
Make a joyful noise unto the Lord, all ye lands
DP I 97

O Worship the King (Sir Robert Grant)
O worship the King
Hymn 82

Paradise (George Herbert)
I blesse thee, Lord, because I GROW
Iron II 21; Voi III 66

Pied Beauty (Gerard Manley Hopkins)
Glory be to God for dappled things
By 195; Choice 116; Deli 70; DP IV 26; EGV 266; Ev 48; Fab Mod 65; Flock 101; Iron II 12; Like 72; My V 182; ND 224; Rat 344; RR 165; Scene 107; Theme VII 40; This W 112; Touch IV 68; (part) F Feet 194

Praise the Lord (John Milton)
Let us with a gladsome mind
Fab CV 352; Hymn 35

Psalm 23 (A.V.)
The Lord is my shepherd. I shall not want
Hymn 18; Puf V 273; Rhyme III 67

Psalm 150 (Book of Common Prayer)
O praise God in his holiness
R Eig 126

The Scribe (Walter de la Mare)
What lovely things
de la M Col 125

from *A Song to David* (Christopher Smart)
Glorious the sun in mid career
Sun 36

Thanksgiving Carol (German, trans Eleanor Farjeon)
Fields of corn give up your ears
Sun 42

PRAYERS

See also CTV 157–161; Hymn throughout
The Body: Final Chant (Adrian Mitchell)

Long live the child
Seven 216

A Child's Evening Prayer
(S. T. Coleridge)
Ere on my bed my limbs I lay
Sun 40

from *Epithalamium* (Edmund
Spenser)
Let no lamenting cries nor doleful
fears
Hist 37

For Sleep or Death (Ruth Pitter)
Cure me with quietness
My V 178

God be in my Head (anon)
God be in my head
*DP I 97; Ev 210; Merry 270; My V
174; Puf V 129*

Matthew, Mark, Luke and John
(anon)
Matthew, Mark, Luke and John
*Merry 134; Ox Dic 303; Ox NR 17;
Puf V 269; Rhyme II 66; TD 84; WAS
119*

Morning Prayer (Ogden Nash)
Now another day is breaking
Ox CV 349; WAS 64

Prayer (Gavin Ewart)
Lord I am not entirely selfish
Ox Con 78; Sun 43

Prayer before Birth (Louis
MacNeice)
I am not yet born: O hear me
*Burn 183; DP III 111; EGV 353;
Look 10; Mod 43*

Recessional (Rudyard Kipling)
God of our Fathers, known of old
EGV 288; Hymn 120

The Robin's Song (anon)
God bless the field and bless the
furrow
Come 219; Rhyme II 65

St Patrick's Hymn (Irish, trans
J. C. Morgan)
Christ as a light
Sun 35

PRIDE

Feigned Courage (Charles and
Mary Lamb)
Horatio, of ideal courage vain
Ox CV 146

The Great Detective (Kit Wright)
Oh, I am the greatest detective
Wri H 55

How I See It (Kit Wright)
Some say the world's
Four 7; Wri H 72

Pride (Violet Jacob)
Did iveer ye see the like o' that?
Ring 37; Scot 118

Pride (Kit Wright)
Two birds sat in a Big White Bra
Wri H 52

The Song of Mr Toad (Kenneth
Grahame)
The world has held great heroes
Ox LV 180

That Man Came Shouting (anon,
Gilbert Islands, trans Arthur
Grimble)
That man came shouting, 'I am a
chief'
J Vo IV 83

PRISONERS

The Commuted Sentence (Stevie
Smith)
Shut me not alive away
Theme III 16

Durham Gaol (Thomas
Armstrong)
You'll all have heard of Durham
Gaol
Voi II 144

En Route (Dennis Brutus, South
Africa)
Sixty packed in a truck
Ima 99

Jailbird (Vernon Scannell)
His plumage is dun
Ox Con 163

The Knight in Prison (William
Morris)
Wearily, drearily
J Vo III 83; PW 255; World 83

from *Letter to Martha* (Dennis
Brutus, South Africa)
Cold/the clammy cement
Att 43
In prison/the clouds assume
importance
Ima 99

152

Letter 2 (Martin Carter, Guyana)
After twenty days and twenty nights in prison
Bite II 49

The Prisoner (Emily Bronte)
I used to weep when winter's snow
Bat C 22

Song (John Keats)
I had a dove and the sweet dove died
Poems II 70

PROFESSIONS

See Occupations

PROGRESS

Inexpensive Progress (John Betjeman)
Encase your legs in nylons
Liv 86

The Village Inn (John Betjeman)
The village inn, the dear old inn
Time 8

PROPERTY

Get off this Estate (Carl Sandburg)
'Get off this estate.'
ADT 64; GV II 24; J Vo IV 43; PT VI 23

Jigsaw II (Louis MacNeice)
Property! Property! let us extend
Conf 99; Touch V 162

A Summer Morning (Richard Wilbur)
Her young employers, having got in late
Fab Mod 365; Scene 70

What I shall need (Chinese)
What I shall need are very few things
GV IV 6

PUB SIGNS

'The General Elliott' (Robert Graves)
He fell in victory's fierce pursuit
Hap 25

PUCK

See Robin Goodfellow

PUDDLES

Watch Your Step – I'm Drenched (Adrian Mitchell)
In Manchester there are a thousand puddles
Rat 457

PUNS

Cautionary Verses to Youth of Both Sexes (Theodore Hook)
My little dears, who learn to read, pray early learn to shun
Fab UV 98; Ox CV 157

Faithless Nellie Gray (Thomas Hood)
Ben Battle was a soldier bold
Bill 27; Ox LV 78
Faithless Sally Brown (Thomas Hood)
Young Ben he was a nice young man
Ox LV 76

The Polar Bear (Edward Lucie-Smith)
A polar bear who could not spell
Four 82; OSF 51

PYTHONS

Hello Mr Python (Spike Milligan)
Hello Mr Python
Deli 83; Mil SV 47; Third 48

The Python (Hilaire Belloc)
A python I should not advise
Bat L 118; Ox CV 311

Python (Yoruba)
Swaggering prince
Oral 163

QUAILS

The Quails (Francis Brett Young)
All through the night
Ev 268

QUEENS

See also Kings and Queens

Lullaby for a Naughty Girl (E. V. Rieu)
O peace, my Penelope, slaps are the fate
Fab NV 271; P Life III 91; Puf V 148

QUESTION AND ANSWER

The Debate between Villon's Heart and Body (Francois Villon, trans Galway Kinnell)
Who's that I hear? *It's me.* Who? *Your heart.*
Voi III 31

Edward, Edward! (anon)
How came this blood on your shirt-sleeve?
Iron II 20
Why does your brand so drip with blood?
Bk Bal 142; EGV 6; Fab PR 21; Peng B 203; P Tale 25; Wind 11
Why dois your brand sae drap wi' bluid?
Bk Bal 189; Fab Bal 119; PW 4; Scot 91

The False Knight upon the Road or *The False Knight and the Wee Boy* (anon)
O whare are ye gaun?
Fab CV 105; Fab PV 288; Peng B 44
O where are you going?
Deli 112; Gold I 9; Merry 122; Ox PC 84; Puf V 205; Shad 18; Tale 71; Wind 41

Heigho! who's above? (anon)
Heigho! who's above?
Ox Dic 201

Intelligence Test (Vernon Scannell)
What do you use your eyes for?
CC 4; Here 30; Sort 76

Lord Randal (anon)
O where have you been, Lord Randal my son?
Bk Bal 164; Blow 52; EGV 9; Fab Bal 34; PW 14; RR 26; Say 73; Tale 18; Voi II 133; Wind 23

Overheard on a Saltmarsh (Harold Monro)
Nymph, nymph, what are your beads?
Bite I 55; Drum 146; J Vo I 16; Like 104; Puf M 207; This W 33

O Where are you going? (W. H. Auden)
'O where are you going?' said reader to rider
Choice 238; Deli 113; Fab CV 294

The Quarry or *O what is that sound?* (W. H. Auden)
O what is that sound which so thrills the ear
Bite I 16; Choice 237; Dawn 42; DP I 61; Flock 254; Ima 101; Mod 15; P Tale 186; Say 77; Theme I 32; Touch II 50; Wind 93

Questions (Wes Magee)
What is . . . a million?
Third 12

Rabbiting on (Kit Wright)
Where did you go?
Wri R 7

QUESTIONS

I Keep Six Honest Serving-Men (Rudyard Kipling)
I keep six honest serving-men
Gold I 2

Inquisitiveness (Colin West)
Please, how does one spell *definite*?
Wes N 91

I Wonder (Jeannie Kirby)
I wonder why the grass is green
Fir 122

Questions (Edward Lowbury)
Which came first – the egg? the chicken?
Low G 20

from *Questions of the Hour* (S. M. B. Piatt)
How old is God? Has he grey hair?
By 191

Tell Me Why (Roger McGough)
Daddy will you tell me why
McG S 16

Why? (John Kitching)
Why are the leaves always green, Dad?
Sec 7

Why (Michael Rosen)
I'm just going out for a moment./Why?
Poems 16; Ros W 46

RABBITS

Myxomatosis (Philip Larkin)
Caught in the centre of a soundless
field
Theme I 41

The Snare (James Stephens)
I hear a sudden cry of pain
Bite I 32; Blow 28; Deli 87; DP I 10;
F Feet 129; My V 129; ND 84; Ox PC
130; P Life II 25; Rhyme III 53

We are going to see the Rabbit
(Alan Brownjohn)
We are going to see the rabbit
DP I 12; Ev 271; Hap 36; Mod 106;
ND 85; Tel 40; Theme VII 60; Touch
II 74; WAS 98

The White Rabbit (E. V. Rieu)
He is white as Helvellyn when
winter is well in
My V 164; Puf Q 136

RACEHORSES

At Grass (Philip Larkin)
The eye can hardly pick them out
Dawn 62; Ev 78; Hor 26; Rat 45

The Start of a Steeplechase (John
Masefield)
The horses sparred as though
drunk with wine
Theme V 10

RACE RELATIONS

See also AP, Att, Blue, Ima, NS,
RAP, Root, Stuf
See also Being Black, Foreigners

Africa's Plea (Roland Tombekai
Dempster)
I am not you
GV III 13; Ima 62; RAP 56; Voi III
24

Alpesh (Mick Gowar)
Come on over here/Paki
Gow S 41

A Baby is a European (trad Ewe)
A baby is a European
RAP 54

The Ballad of Postman William L.
Moore (Wolf Biermann, trans
Steve Gooch)
Sunday meant rest for William L.
Moore
Bat S 90

The Ballad of Rudolph Reed
(Gwendolyn Brooke)
Rudolph Reed was oaken
Rat 62

Colonisation in Reverse (Louise
Bennett)
What a joyful news, Miss Mattie
Bite I 75; NS 60

Even There (Jacob Stanley
Davies, Sierra Leone)
There was a great commotion in
the cemet'ry last night
Ima 57

For Saundra (Nikki Giovanni,
American)
i wanted to write
Att 54

George II and the Chinese Emperor
(Robert Graves)
Prince George of Hanover was
thirty-one
Bat L 42

Hats Off (D. J. Enright)
I once knew a teacher, a tough old
bird
Enr R 10

Hypocrite (Elizabeth Hart)
She spoke of heaven
Conf 69

Incident (Countee Cullen)
Once riding in Old Baltimore
Conf 73; Imp 77; In O II 21

I, Too (Langston Hughes)
I, too, sing America
Att 21; Like 119

The Lament of the Banana Man
(Evan Jones)
Gal, I'm tellin' you, I'm tired fo'
true
Cari I 86; Mod 165; NS 29; PT III 20

Me, coloured (Peter Abrahams,
South Africa)
Aunt Liza/*Yes?*/What am I?
Afr II 46

Meeting of Strangers (Earle
Birney, Canada)
'Nice jacket you got deh, man!'
Bite III 49

The Moon (Soussou)
The moon lights the earth
Tam 63

No Irish Need Apply (anon)
I'm a decent boy just landed
Oral 187

Old Father (Hugh Boatswain, Antigua)
Old Father to England in Winter '59
Blue 34

A Strange Meeting (W. H. Davies)
The moon is full, and so am I
Bill 31; Ox PC 148; PT V 30

Telephone Conversation (Wole Soyinka)
The price seemed reasonable, location
AP 116; Bite III 48; Conf 69; Flock 134; Ima 59; Many 22; Root 32; Touch V 101; Voi III 26

Terminal (D. J. Enright)
A small boy, four years/Or so of age
Liv 16

An Un-African Breakfast (Joe de Graft, Ghana)
So here I am this morning
Many 57

RAILWAY ENGINES

Locomotive (Shigeharu Nakano, trans Takamichi Ninomiya and D. J. Enright)
He has a giant's frame
Mov 50; Rail 74; Rhyme IV 68

The Locomotive (Alexander Anderson, 1845–1909)
Hurrah for the mighty engine
Rail 15

The Locomotive (Thomas Wolfe)
Then the locomotive drew in upon them
P Rail 90

Right of Way (Henry Herbert Knibbs)
Corralled in the sooty roundhouse the steel-ribbed Titan stands
P Rail 20

RAILWAYS

See P Rail, Rail throughout
See Engine Drivers, Railway

Engines, Railway Stations, Trains, Underground Railways

RAILWAY STATIONS

See also P Rail 106–164

Aldestrop (Edward Thomas)
Yes, I remember Adlestrop
Bric 59; Choice 169; Duck 30; EGV 317; F Feet 165; Like 171; Out 42; Ox PC 141; P Rail 122; Puf V 180; Rail 57; RR 86; Theme VII 37; TD 21; Touch I 152

from *The Angel in the House* (Coventry Patmore)
I stood by Honor and the Dean
P Rail 161

At Charing Cross (J. Ashby-Sterry)
A busy scene I must confess
P Rail 150

At the Railway Station, Upway (Thomas Hardy)
There is not much that I can do
Deli 103; Flock 71; Say 72; Voi I 36

In a Waiting Room (Thomas Hardy)
On a morning sick as the day of doom
P Rail 156

I was going to see my Uncle Harry (Michael Rosen)
The train was standing
Third 37

King's Cross Station (G. K. Chesterton)
This circled cosmos whereof man is god
Lon 160; P Rail 108

Liverpool Street Station (John Davidson 1857–1908)
Through crystal roofs the sunlight fell
P Rail 108; Rail 64

The Metropolitan Railway (John Betjeman)
Early Electric! with what radiant hope
Rail 86

On the Departure Platform (Thomas Hardy)

We kissed at the barrier, and passing through
P Rail 159; Rail 85

On the Platform (Brian Lee)
The distance swims in the heat where the rails reach far to the south
Lee L 28

Station (Vivian de Sola Pinto)
Late at night in the station
P Rail 132

Steel Cathedrals: 1943 (D. Van Dan Bogaerde)
It seems to me, I spend my life in stations
TR 90

RAIN

See also Noah, Puddles

After Rain (Arthur Waley)
Peach blossom after rain
BE 22

How Beautiful is the Rain (H. W. Longfellow)
How beautiful is the rain
BE 23; Out Sc 74; TD 36

I Hear Leaves (W. H. Davies)
I hear leaves drinking rain
Bk S 36; Come 102; GV IV 18; P Life I 63

Jardins sous la Pluie (John Redwood Anderson)
Tenderly, gently, the soft rain
Tap 54

Night Rain (John Pepper Clark, Nigeria)
What time of night it is
Att 73; Bite I 23; Prel III 15

A Prayer for Rain (Herbert Palmer)
O God, make it rain!
In O II 23; Prel III 10

Rain (Brian Lee)
The lights are all on, though it's just past midday
Lee L 12; Poems 68; Sort 37

The Rain-man's Praise-song of Himself (trad Aadonga)
No house is ever too thick-built
Rhy 110

Rainy Nights (Irene Thompson)
I like the town on rainy nights
Out 58

Signs of Rain (Dr Edward Jenner)
The hollow winds begin to blow
Fab UV 34

A Soft Day (W. M. Letts)
A soft day, thank God!
Like 113

Spell of the Raingods (Leslie Norris)
We are the Raingods, we are the clouds
Drum 21

Spring Rain (Tu Fu, trans Kenneth Rexroth)
A good rain knows its season
BE 22

Sudden Shower (John Clare)
Black grows the southern sky, betokening rain
Full 74

Weather (Eve Merriam)
Dot a dot dot dot a dot dot
Like 29

Wet Through (Hal Summers)
Being now completely wet through to the skin
Prel III 12; Round 7

RAINBOWS

A Great Time (W. H. Davies)
Sweet Chance, that led my steps abroad
Bk S 32; By 220; F Feet 167; TD 13

The Rainbow (Walter de la Mare)
I saw the lovely arch
CTV 36; de la M Col 21; Fan 82; P Life II 52; TD 16

The Rainbow (William Wordsworth)
My heart leaps up when I behold
CTV 53

RAMS

See also Sheep

The Derby Ram (trad)
As I was going to Derby, sir
Come 194; Fab Non 45; Fab NV 70;

Fab PV 81; Gold I 43; Iron I 2; Merry
173; Non 176; Ox Dic 145; Ox NR
205; Rain 54; Rhyme II 16; R Ten 54;
Voi I 37

RATS

An Advancement of Learning
(Seamus Heaney)
I took the embankment path
Theme I 49; Touch III 126

Bishop Hatto (Robert Southey)
The summer and the autumn had
been so wet
ND 128; Rhy 118

from *The Pied Piper of Hamelin*
(Robert Browning)
Rats!/They fought the dogs and
killed the cats
F Feet 116

What Became of Them? (anon)
He was a rat and she was a rat
*Hi 19; Merry 155; My V 170; Ox PC
38; Plea 43*

RAVENS

The Corbie and the Crow (anon)
The corbie with his roupie throat
Plea 58

The Raven (Edgar Allen Poe)
Once upon a midnight dreary,
while I pondered, weak and weary
EGV 191; Fab CV 190

Ravens (Ted Hughes)
As we came through the gate to
look at the few new lambs
Hug SP 189

The Raven's Nest (John Clare)
Upon the collar of a huge old oak
Voi II 36

The Twa Corbies (anon)
As I was walking all a-lane
*Bk Bal 171 and 192; EGV 5; Fab Bal
38; Fab CV 266; Flock 256; Imp 69;
Merry 241; Plea 256; P Tale 21; Puf V
98; PW 6; Rat 440; RR 170; Scot 49;
Tale 64; Touch I 13; Voi II 159;
Wind 10*

The Two [Three] Ravens (anon)
There were two ravens who sat on
a tree

Bk Bal 170; Ev 158; Fab Bal 37; Fab
PV 245; Peng B 83; P Tale 24; Theme
I 22; Voi II 160

RED INDIANS

See Indians, Red

REFUGEES

*Algerian Refugee Camp,
Ain-Khemouda* (Alan Ross)
You have black eyes
Conf 38; Time 137

The Companion (Yevgeny
Yevtushenko, trans R.
Milner-Gulland and P. Levi)
She was sitting on the rough
embankment
DP III 69; Flock 252; (part) *Bric 31*

The Evacuee (R. S. Thomas)
She woke up under a loose quilt
Choice 303

The Little Cart (Ch'en
Tzu-Sung, trans Arthur Waley)
The little cart jolting and banging
through the yellow haze
*Al III 12; Flock 89; Imp 52; Iron I 47;
Mov 23; Pluc 33; PT V 21; Tel 50;
Touch IV 59; Voi I 28*

Orphan's Airlift (Ian Serraillier)
I never knew my soldier dad
Root 70

Refugee Blues (W. H. Auden)
Say this city has ten million souls
*Conf 39; Gold IV 14; Ima 108; ND
174; Theme III 39; Touch V 102*

The Refugees (Herbert Read)
Mute figures with bowed heads
Theme III 39

Survivors (Valerie Sinason)
When the knock knocking started
Root 27

RELIGIOUS THEMES

See also Hymn, Sun throughout
See also Angels, Baptism,
Churchgoing, Martyrdom,
Spirituals, Superstition

RELIGIOUS THEMES:
NEW TESTAMENT

See Christ, Christmas:
Religious, Crucifixion, Dives
and Lazarus, Easter,
Epiphany, Herod, John the
Baptist, Joseph, Judas Iscariot,
Lazarus, Martha of Bethany,
Mary Magdalene, Palm
Sunday, Transfiguration,
Virgin Mary

RELIGIOUS THEMES:
OLD TESTAMENT

See Abraham and Isaac, Adam,
Babel, Balaam, Belshazzar,
Creation, Daniel, David and
Goliath, Eden, Jonah, Joseph,
Lot's Wife, Moses, Noah,
Samson, Satan, Ten
Commandments

RELIGIOUS THEMES

All but Blind (Walter de la
Mare)
All but blind
*de la M Col 96; DP I 94; Gold II 43;
RR 168; Trad 88*

The Ballad of Father Gilligan
(W. B. Yeats)
The old priest Father Gilligan
Sun 201

The Darky Sunday School (trad)
Jonah was an emigrant, so says the
Bible tale
Voi I 43

The Destruction of Sennacherib
(Lord Byron)
The Assyrian came down like a
wolf on the fold
*By 148; EGV 148; Fab CV 254; Rat
126*

The Elixir (George Herbert)
Teach me, my God and King
Bat C 37; Fab CV 353

The Experiment (Christian
Morgenstern, trans R. F. C.
Hull)
Once for experiment I bought
J Vo III 58

I am the Great Sun (Charles
Causley)

I am the great sun, but you do not
see me
Burn 145; Cau C 69; Seven 43

The Kingdom of God (Francis
Thompson)
O world invisible, we view thee
By 204

The Latest Decalogue (Arthur
Hugh Clough)
Thou shalt have one God only;
who
Voi III 113

Little Gidding (T. S. Eliot)
Midwinter spring is its own season
Fab Mod 138

Lord of the Dance (Sydney
Carter)
I danced in the morning
Liv 67

Love (George Herbert)
Love bade me welcome, yet my
soul drew back
*By 68; Iron IV 101; ND 231; Plea
336; Sun 78; Touch IV 69*

Mrs Malone (Eleanor Farjeon)
Mrs Malone
*Far M 90; Ox CV 332; Puf Q 32; Sun
194*

Peace (Samuel Speed)
I sought for Peace but could not
find
Sun 210

Peace (Henry Vaughan)
My soul there is a country
EGV 85; Fab CV 368; Sun 211

Song About Mary (Adrian
Mitchell)
Mary sat on a long brown bench
Peng B 363

The Spiritual Railway (anon, in
Ely Cathedral)
The line to heaven by Christ was
made
Poems II 44; Voi II 162

Sunday (D. J. Enright)
My mother's strongest religious
feeling
Sun 205

What Tomas said in a Pub (James
Stephens)
I saw God. Do you doubt it?
By 243

REPTILES

See Chameleons, Crocodiles,
Iguanas, Lizards, Pythons,
Snakes, Tortoises, Vipers

REVENGE, THE

A Ballad of the Fleet (Alfred,
Lord Tennyson)
At Flores in the Azores Sir Richard
Grenville lay
*DP II 59; EGV 215; Fab CV 247;
Fab PR 156; ND 38; Puf V 87; Touch
I 137*

RHINOCEROSES

Poaching in Excelsis
(G. K. Menzies)
I've poached a pickle pairtricks
when the leaves were turning sere
Ring 51; Scot 60

The Rhinoceros (Ogden Nash)
The rhino is a homely beast
F Feet 112; Full 16; Zoo 37

RHYME

The Fox Rhyme (Ian Serraillier)
Aunt was on the garden seat
*Al I 27; Lolli III 14; My V 160; Puf Q
168*

*Katharine and Jane's Poem about
Rhyme* (Peter Porter)
Dear girls, the English language
which you speak
Sort 122

Rhyme-Time (Vernon Scannell)
I know that poems do not have to
rhyme
Over 97

RHYMES

See Alphabet Rhymes,
Counting Rhymes,
Counting-Out Rhymes,
Cumulative Rhymes, Ruthless
Rhymes

RICH AND POOR

The Case for the Miners (Siegfried
Sassoon)
Something goes wrong with my
synthetic brain
Gold IV 13; Theme VI 45

The Chancellor's Gravel Drive
(Po Chu-I, trans A. Waley)
A Government-bull yoked to a
Government cart
Pluc 19

Child of the Romans (Carl
Sandburg)
The dago shovelman sits by the
railroad track
Theme VI 40

The Garden (Ezra Pound)
Like a skein of loose silk blown
against a wall
Say 106

The Poore Man Payes for All
(anon 1630)
As I lay musing all alone
Bal 16

We'll Turn Things Upside Down
(John Bruce Glasier)
O the world is overburdened
Bal 158

RIDDLES

See *ADT 51; Afr I 59; Bat C 12;
Come 12; CTV 99–101; Deli
108–9; Drum 25; Fab Non 168–9;
Fab NV 48–54; Fab PV 17–18,
36–7, 39, 58–9, 65, 70–2, 73, 91,
323–4; Ful P 20–1; FV 66–7, 71,
73; GV III 27; Here 42; J Vo II 1,
III 2, IV 19; Lolli IV 8; Merry
135, 235, 254, 296, 329; My V 25;
Ox Dic 57, 81, 87, 137, 161, 190,
196, 212, 213, 268, 326, 346, 355,
363; Ox NR 147–155; Plea 17;
Poems 8; Puf M 183; Puf NR
72–5, 112, 159, 182; Rat 428–9;
Rhy 28, 41, 52, 105; R Six 10; Sea
37, 70, 118, 128, 168; Star 62; Stuf
22; Tale 27, 59, 94; Trad 22;
Young 40–1; Voi I 7–9, 13–14, 15;
Word 122*

RIDDLES (L & D)

Anglo-Saxon Riddles (trans
M. Alexander, G. Bone, K.
Crossley-Holland)
Moon and Sun
I saw a creature sally forth with
booty
PW 27

I saw a strange creature
Puf M 183; Tap 31

Swan
Silent is my dress when I step
across the earth
Drag 23; Word 122
When it is earth I tread
Voi I 8
A curious fair creature came
floating on the waves
Tap 63

See also *Drag 38, 39; Rhyme III
55, IV 19, 109; Tap 9, 13, 46, 66*

Six Riddles (John Fuller)
Mermaids' tears, crusted with time
Ful C 18

RIDDLES (N)

The Devil's Questions (anon)
You must answer me questions
nine
Rhyme IV 27

King John and the Abbot (anon)
An ancient story I'll tell you anon
*Bk Bal 176; Gold I 44; Puf V 103;
Wind 43*

Riddles Wisely Expounded (anon)
There was a knicht riding frae the
east
*Fab Bal 25; Fab PV 277; Merry 310;
Peng B 36*

The Riddling Knight (anon)
There were three sisters fair and
bright
Brit 198; Fab CV 281; Trad 126

There was a lady in the west (anon)
There was a lady in the west
Wind 38

RIVERS

Clear and Cool (Charles
Kingsley)
Clear and cool, clear and cool
Gold II 24; Ox CV 227

The River is a Piece of Sky (John
Ciardi)
From the top of a bridge
Hi 11; Puf Y 63

The River's Tale (Rudyard
Kipling)
Twenty bridges from Tower to
Kew
Lon 133

Tweed and Till (anon)
Tweed said to Till
Fab CV 268; Fab PV 176; Shad 69

ROADMAKERS

The Roadmenders's Song (anon,
Gond)
Hungry and thirsty we break these
stones in the heat of the sun
Oral 35

Song of the Road Builders (Ewan
MacColl)
Come all you gallant drivers
Mov 81; Rhyme IV 67

The Tar-Boiler (Brian Lee)
Black, battered and sticky, and
smoking blue fumes
Full 96; Lee L 45

ROADS

The By-Road (from 'Punch')
The main road swings serenely
PT VI 4

The Old Coach Road (Rachel
Field)
There's hardly a wheel rut left to
show
Mov 15

The Rolling English Road
(G. K. Chesterton)
Before the Roman came to Rye or
out to Severn strode
DP IV 48; Fab CV 292; Ox LV 206

ROBIN GOODFELLOW

Robin Goodfellow (?Ben Jonson)
From Oberon in fairy land
Fab CV 206; Merry 313; Puf M 221

ROBIN HOOD

The Death of Robin Hood (anon)
When Robin Hood and Little John
*Bk Bal 107; Fab Bal 94; Flock 156;
Wind 49*

A Merry Jest of Robin Hood
(Thomas Love Peacock)
Bold Robin has robed him in
ghostly attire
DP I 48; Peng B 289

Robin Hood and Allan-a-Dale
(anon)
Come listen to me, you gallants so
free
*BHL 23; Fab PV 247; Merry 316;
Peng B 221; Tale 21*

*Robin Hood and the Bishop of
Hereford* (anon)
Come gentlemen all and listen a
while
DP I 50
Some will talk of bold Robin Hood
*Brit 110; Nar 31; Ox PC 73; Peng B
229*

Robin Hood and the Curtal Friar
(anon)
In summer time when leaves grow
green
BHL 27

Robin Hood and Little John (anon)
When Robin Hood was about
twenty years old
DP II 84

Robin Hood and the Monk, etc.
(anon)
In somer, when the shawes be
sheyne
Fab Bal 81–93

Robin Hood and the Sheriff (anon)
Robin Hood's to Nottighame gane
Peng B 225

*Robin Hood and the Widow's Three
Sons* (anon)
There are twelve months in all the
year
Bk Bal 102

Song (?Anthony Munday)
Weep, weep, ye woodmen! wail
Ox PC 152; This W 85

ROBINS

Cock Robin (trad)
Who killed Cock Robin?
*Fab NV 114; Merry 9; Non 192; Ox
Dic 131; Ox NR 166; P Life I 28; Puf
NR 76; Puf SB 94; Puf V 38; Trad
159*
Who killed Cocky Robin?
Iron I 60

The Red Robin (John Clare)
Cock Robin, he got a new tippet in
spring
Merry 221

The Robin (Thomas Hardy)
When up aloft
*Bat A 79; R Eig 14; Rhyme IV 108;
Say 31; Tap 37*

Robin (Hal Summers)
With a bonfire throat
Drag 83; Poems 72; PT VI 7

Robin Redbreast (W. H. Davies)
Robin on a leafless bough
Bir 67

ROLLER-COASTERS

Flight of the Roller-Coaster
(Raymond Souster)
Once more around should do it,
the man confided
Deli 30; Mov 106

ROMAN BRITAIN

Logria (David Holloway)
None wept to see the garrisons
depart
Ev 208

A Pict Song (Rudyard Kipling)
Rome never looks where she treads
J Vo IV 35

The Roman Centurion's Song
(Rudyard Kipling)
Legate – I had the news last night –
my cohort ordered home
Scene 66

The Roman Wall (Andrew
Young)
Though moss and lichen crawl
Ten 171

Roman Wall Blues
(W. H. Auden)
Over the heather the wet wind
blows
*Dawn 43; Choice 242; GV IV 29; J Vo
IV 37; My V 79; ND 144; PT V 14;
Say 83; Theme VI 37; Touch II 170*

ROME

See also Horatius

Rome (David R. Slavitt)
Rome is fountains
My R 40

ROOKS

Rookery (Seamus Heaney)
Here they come, freckling the sunset
BE 54; Touch III 119

ROUNDABOUTS

See Merry-Go-Rounds

ROWING

At Putney (R. C. Lehmann)
When eight strong fellows are out to row
Theme V 29

RUGBY LEAGUE

Rugby League Game (James Kirkup)
Sport is absurd, and sad
Theme V 70; Time 99; Touch IV 62

RUINS

The Ruin (Anglo-Saxon, trans K. Crossley-Holland)
Wonderful is this wall of stone, wrecked by fate
Tho 49

RUTHLESS RHYMES

See also Bat C 58, 64; BBGG 94–101; Bill 36, 54, 71; CBC 28, 75, 82, 96, 97; Fat S 44; FV 44, 46, 48, 56, 62, 109, 119; GV 3, 29; Mov 85, 94, 115; My V 166; Plea 312-13; R Nine 50, 59; R Ten 22, 38, 50, 69, 88; Young 33–5

Vicious Verses (Colin West)
In her frock so gaily patterned
Wes N 71–82

SAILORS (L & D)

See also Benbow, Drake, Nelson, Vikings, William Duke of Clarence

Admirals All (Sir Henry Newbolt)
Effingham, Grenville, Raleigh, Drake
Fab PR 209

from *The Canterbury Tales* (Geoffrey Chaucer)
A shipman was ther, wonynge fer by weste
Flock 27
(trans Nevill Coghill)
There was a skipper hailing from far west
Flock 26; Sea 137

Captain Lean (Walter de la Mare)
Out of the East a hurricane
Sea 147

The Press Gang (anon)
Here's the tender coming
Sea 145

Psalm 107 v.23 (A.V.)
They that go down to the sea in ships
DP III 41; P Life IV 57

Sailor (Eleanor Farjeon)
My sweetheart is a sailor
Puf Q 28

The Sailor Boy (Alfred, Lord Tennyson)
He rose at dawn, and, fired with hope
Puf M 193

A Sailor sat on the Watery Shore (Charles Causley)
A sailor sat on the watery shore
Cau F 56

from *The Seafarer* (Anglo-Saxon)
(trans Michael Alexander)
The tale I frame shall be found to tally
Mov 34; Voi I 28
(trans K. Crossley-Holland)
I can sing a true song about myself
Sea 115
(trans Ezra Pound)
May I, for my own self, song's truth reckon
DP III 37; Rat 368

Seamus Beg (James Stephens)
A man was sitting underneath a tree
Ox PC 144; Sea 132

Skipper (of the clipper ship 'Mary Ambrose') (C. Fox Smith)
A rough old nut
PT V 13

SAILORS (N)

Angel Hill (Charles Causley)
A sailor came walking down Angel Hill
Sea 200

Cawsand Bay (anon)
In Cawsand Bay lying, with the Blue Peter flying
Plea 142

The Death of Parker (anon)
Ye gods, above, protect a widow, and with pity look down on me
Bal 82; Sea 151

The Female Sailor (anon)
Good people give attention, that now around me stand
Brit 119

The Old Sailor (A. A. Milne)
There was once an old sailor my grandfather knew
Fab NV 36; Mil NS 36

The Rime of the Ancient Mariner (S. T. Coleridge)
It is an ancient mariner
DP III 42; Fab CV 301; P Tale 36; PW 179; Touch II 79
(part) And now the storm-blast came, and he
Say 66; Sea 216
(part) Beyond the shadow of the ship
P Life IV 56

SAILORS' SONGS

See also Sea Shanties
Come, Cheer up my Lads (David Garrick)
Come cheer up my lads
Sea 108

The Darned Mounseer (W. S. Gilbert)
I shipped, d'ye see, in a Revenue sloop
Ox LV 145

Has Anybody seen our Ship? (Noel Coward)
What shall we do with the Drunken Sailor?
Sea 156

Jack the Guinea Pig (anon)
When the anchor's weigh'd and the ship's unmoored
Sea 107

The Master, the Swabber, the Boatswain and I (William Shakespeare)
The master, the swabber, the boatswain and I
The Tempest II ii 44; Ox LV 1; Plea 156; Sea 192

Rule Britannia (James Thomson)
When Britain first, at heaven's command
Sea 241

The Sailor's Consolation (William Pitt)
One night came on a hurricane
By 99; Ev 140; Plea 142

The Sailor's Wife (W. J. Mickle)
And are you sure the news is true?
Scot 34; Sea 192

The Saucy Sailor Boy (anon)
Come, my only one, come, my fond one
Sea 184

Ship Ahoy! (A. J. Mills)
All the nice girls love a sailor
Sea 185

Song of the Galley-Slaves (Rudyard Kipling)
We pulled for you when the wind was against us and the sails were low
J Vo III 85

Tom Bowling (Charles Dibdin)
Here, a sheer hulk, lies poor Tom Bowling
Sea 143

SAINTS

See also Beckett, Joseph

For all the Saints (Bishop W. W. How)
For all the saints, who from their labours rest
Hymn 108; WAS 131

St Catherine (anon)
Saint Catherine, Saint Catherine, O lend me thine aid
GV III 33

St Christopher: Midstream (D. J. Enright)
Halfway across the racing river
Ox Con 113

Saint Christoper (Eleanor Farjeon)
'Carry me, Ferryman, over the ford'
Four 53; Young 50

Saint Columba and the Flounder (anon, Gaelic)
Columba passing on his way
Dis 77

St Dunstan (anon)
St Dunstan, as the story goes
Ox Dic 155

St Francis and the birds (Seamus Heaney)
When Francis preached love to the birds
Flock 89; WAS 124

St George and the Dragon (anon)
Of Hector's deeds did Homer sing
Bat S 111

from *St Jerome and the Lion* (Rumer Godden)
One February, there came an afternoon
Sun 172

St Jerome (anon)
St Jerome in his study kept a great big cat
Trad 53

St John the Baptist (William Drummond)
The last and greatest herald of heaven's king
Sun 192

St Kevin (anon)
At Glendalough lived a young saint
Oral 192

St Martha and the Dragon (Charles Causley)
In far Provence, where runs the brawny river
Cau C 208; Cau N 65

St Martin and the Beggar (Thom Gunn)
Martin sat young upon his bed
Hap 47; Nar 63; Theme II 22

St Mawes: A Saint of Cornwall (C. Fox Smith)
I don't know who St Mawes was, but he surely can't have been
Sea 134

St Patrick: his Hymn before Tara (Irish, trans J. C. Mangan)
Christ, as a light
Sun 35

Saint Patrick's Breastplate (Irish, trans C. F. Alexander)
I bind unto myself today
Fab CV 366

St Patrick was a Gentleman (anon)
Oh! St Patrick was a gentleman
Sun 176

St Stephen and King Herod (anon)
St Stephen was a clerk
Peng B 19; P Tale 19; Puf V 258; Sun 183

SAMSON

How Samson bore away the Gates of Gaza (Vachell Lindsay)
Once, in a night as black as ink
J Vo III 85

from *Samson Agonistes* (John Milton)
Occasions drew me early to this city
Flock 173; P Tale 202; Sun 67
The building was a spacious theatre
Ev 216

SARDINES

How to Open (John Fuller)
You don't have to grope in a
Ful C 20; Sort 12

Sardines (Spike Milligan)
A baby sardine
Al III 37; Bric 46; Deli 59; Mov 46; Once 27; R Six 47; Sec 50

SATAN

from *Paradise Lost: Satan* (John Milton)
. . . his pride/Had cast him out from Heav'n with all his host
P Tale 191

SCARECROWS

The Lonely Scarecrow (James Kirkup)
My poor old bones – I've only two –

Dawn 19; Full 102; Hap 38; Ox PC
139; PT VI 18; Puf Y 57; R Eig 22;
Say 23; Tel 52; Touch I 100

The Scarecrow (Walter de la
Mare)
All winter through I bow my head
Bk S 17; de la M Col 188

The Scarecrow (Gregory
Harrison)
The farmer carried some bits of
coal
Sec 87

Scarecrow (Clive Sansom)
Dressed in the farmer's ancient
coat
San E 20

Scarecrow Independence (James
Kirkup)
I may look raggy and queer
Fir 102

S is for Scarecrow (Eleanor
Farjeon)
Hi, Mister Scarecrow!
Far M 64

SCHOOL

See also *Touch III 138–146; Touch
IV 138–149*
See also Teachers

Back to School (Allan Ahlberg)
In the last week of the holidays
(Ahl P 12)

The Best of School
(D. H. Lawrence)
The blinds are drawn because of
the sun
*Choice 190; Ima 46; Tam 97; Theme
VI 13*

The Bully Asleep (John Walsh)
This one afternoon, when grassy
*Deli 84; Prel II 9; Touch III 145;
World 14*

Bus Home (John Walsh)
The school bus now
World 17

Bus to School (John Walsh)
Rounding a corner
*Prel II 2; Rhyme IV 69; TD 74; Word
149; World 10*

Children coming from School
(Roger Mais)

I can hear the gospel
Cari I 2

Exercise Book (Jacques Prévert,
trans Paul Dehn)
Two and two four
*Bite I 59; Ev 192; Gang 64; Hap II
75; Touch III 141*

First Day at School (Roger
McGough)
A millionbillionwillion miles from
home
*ADT 35; Deli 79; McRo 66; NV 81;
Poems 66; Strict 15*

Holidays (J. K. Annand)
As I gang up the Castlehill
Scot 16

In the Girls' Playground (Marion
Lines)
Girls' games!
Lin T 22

Last Lesson (Robert Morgan)
The room is silent, desks initialled
and empty
Theme VI 12

Last Lesson of the Afternoon
(D. H. Lawrence)
When will the bell ring and end
this weariness?
*Bite III 52; Choice 189; DP II 5; Ima
45; ND 117; Theme III 51; Touch III
140*

A Medieval Schoolboy's Complaint
(anon)
What availeth it me if I say nay?
PC 72

Morning Break (Wes Magee)
Andrew Flag plays football
ADT 42

Our School (Gareth Owen)
I go to Weld Park Primary)
ADT 37; Owe S 20; Word 74

Out of School or **School's Out** (Hal
Summers)
Four o'clock strikes
*Dawn 28; Drum 106; Gold I 4; Hap
70; ND 118; Out Sc 16; Prel II 15;
TD 78; Theme V 65*

A Question of Faith (Vernon
Scannell)
When I was in the top class in the
school
Prel II 12

The Schoolboy (William Blake)
I love to rise in a summer morn
*DP I 40; Fab CV 102; Flock 136; ND
116; PC 70*

The School Nurse (Allan Ahlberg)
We're lining up to see the nurse
Ahl P 24

Schule in June (Robert Bain)
There's no a clood in the sky
Scot 7

Slow Reader (Vicki Feaver)
He can make sculptures
Strict 51

Thug (Raymond Garlick)
School began it
Strict 29

Truant (Phoebe Hesketh)
They call him dunce and yet he can
discern
Hes S 7; Prel II 4; Touch III 144

Truant (Clive Sansom)
Two days in five young Jeremy's
not in school
San E 12

The Unhappy Schoolboy (anon
c. 1525)
Hey! Hey! By this day!
Ox CV 11

A Wheel called Progress (Cecil
Gray, Trinidad)
When I was sent to school
Bite III 67

SCHOOLMASTERS

See also Teachers

Brainy Teacher (anon, Medieval,
trans Brian Stone)
Brainy teacher, is it your
DP II 42

from *The Deserted Village* (Oliver
Goldsmith)
Beside yon straggling fence that
skirts the way
EGV 105; ND 114; Prel II 15

*Distracted the Mother said to her
Boy* (Gregory Harrison)
Distracted the mother said to her
boy
Third 9

The Man of the Family (Stanley
Cook)

The man of the family, who swears
at his widowed mother
RR 193

Schoolmaster (Yevgeny
Yevtushenko, trans
R. Milner-Gulland and
P. Levi)
The window gives onto the white
trees
Bite II 15; Flock 137; Imp 53

To a Crippled Schoolmaster
(Mervyn Morris)
We hogged the billiard table in
your room
Bite III 8

SCHOOLMISTRESSES

Please Mrs Butler (Allan
Ahlberg)
Please Mrs Butler
Ahl P 10

Schoolmistress: Miss Human
(Clive Sansom)
Straight-backed as a Windsor chair
*Liv 19; Mod 125; Poems II 105; Prel
II 14; PT V 16*

SCORPIONS

Night of the Scorpion (Nissim
Ezekiel, India)
I remember the night my mother
*Att 18; Bite I 21; Ev 112; Ima 34;
Many 65*

SCOTLAND

See also Landscapes, Wilderness

In the Highlands (Robert Louis
Stevenson)
In the highlands, in the country
places
P Scot 83

My Heart's in the Highlands
(Robert Burns)
My heart's in the highlands, my
heart is not here
*Ox PC 141; Plea 106; Rhyme III 43;
Root 47*

On the Massacre of Glencoe (Sir
Walter Scott)
O tell me, Harper, wherefore flow
Poems II 84

Scotland (Sir Alexander Gray)
Here in the uplands
P Scot 19

Scotland Small? (Hugh MacDiarmid)
Scotland small? Our multiform, our infinite Scotland *small?*
Rat 365

Scotland's Winter (Edwin Muir)
Now the ice lays its smooth claws on the sill
Touch III 109

Scots wha hae (Robert Burns)
Scots wha hae wi' Wallace bled
EGV 120

SEA

See also PTI, Sea, throughout; *Tho 19–28*

See also At Sea, Bathing, Beachcombing, Beaches, Coral, Diving, Drowning, Fishermen, Fishes and Sea Creatures Fishing, Lifeboats, Lighthouses, Mermaids and Mermen, Oceans, Pirates, Pools, Sailors, Sailors' Songs, Sea Birds, Sea Anemones, Sea Monsters, Sea Shanties, Seaside, Shells, Ships, Shipwrecks, Smugglers, Surfing, Tides, Waves, Whaling

SEA (L & D)

All Day I Hear (James Joyce)
All day I hear the noise of waters
Fab CV 330; Fan 134

A Beginner's Guide to the Ocean (Ogden Nash)
Let us now consider the ocean
PT I 4

Channel Crossing (Edward Lowbury)
No rougher than a plate of soup
Low G 22

Fog (Crosbie Garstin)
Over the oily swell it heaved, it rolled
RR 38

Harp Song of the Dane Women (Rudyard Kipling)
What is a woman that you forsake her
BE 40; Poems II 79; RR 38; Theme VI 58

I started early, took my dog (Emily Dickinson)
I started early, took my dog
Sea 25

Look, Stranger (W. H. Auden)
Look, stranger, on this island now
Bite III 42; Choice 243; DP IV 26; Gold IV 43; Mod 1; ND 44; Scene 47; Sea 91; Tam 62; Tap 83; Ten 22; Touch II 35

The Main-Deep (James Stephens)
The long-rolling/Steady-pouring
BE 29; Bite I 50; Bric 61; Fan 130; PT I 4; Tap 65; Touch I 132

Old Man Ocean (Russell Hoban)
Old Man Ocean, how do you pound
Hob P 19; Out Sc 49; Tap 63

Once by the Pacific (Robert Frost)
The shattered water made a misty din
Sea 52

Ramhead and Dodman (Charles Causley)
Said Ramhead to Dodman
Cau F 48

The Sea (James Reeves)
The sea is a hungry dog
Fan 122; ND 47; PT I 31; Puf Q 82; Ree C 53; Tam 6; Tap 64

The Sea (Iain Crichton Smith)
Today the sea is playful and
Third 52

The Sea (R. S. Thomas)
They wash their hands in it
Four 30; Sea 23; Tap 66

The Sea and the Skylark (Gerard Manley Hopkins)
On ear and ear two noises too old to end
FM 212; PW 264; Voi I 116

Sea-Wash (Carl Sandburg)
The sea-wash never ends
BE 29; Poems 40

Sound of the Sea on a Still Evening
(Norman MacCaig)
It comes through quietness, softly
crumbling in
ND 47

Tell Me, Tell Me, Sarah Jane
(Charles Causley)
Tell me, tell me, Sarah Jane
Cau F 40; PT I 8; Sea 24; Tap 68

from *Under Milk Wood* (Dylan
Thomas)
What seas did you see
J Vo II 5

Winter Seascape (John Betjeman)
The sea runs back against itself
Out 86

SEA (N)

The Last Chantey (Rudyard
Kipling)
Thus said the Lord in the Vault
above the Cherubim
Fab CV 323; Sea 31

The Rime of the Ancient Mariner
(S. T. Coleridge)
It is an ancient mariner
*DP III 42; Fab CV 301; P Tale 36;
PW 179; Touch II 79*

The Sea eats the Land at Home
(Kofi Awoonor, Ghana)
At home the sea is in the Town
RAP 48

SEA ANEMONES

A is for Anemone (Eleanor
Farjeon)
O what a pleasure by the sea
P Life III 9

The Anemone (John Walsh)
Under this ledge of rock a brown
PT I 19; R Nine 54

Z is for Zoophyte (Eleanor
Farjeon)
Upon the seashore what delight
P Life III 10

SEA BATTLES

See also Armada, Lepanto,

Revenge, Sole Bay, Trafalgar
The Arethusa (Prince Hoare)

Come, all ye jolly sailors bold
Fab PR 60

A Ballad for a Boy (William
Cory)
When George the Third was
reigning a hundred years ago
OX CV 290

A Burnt Ship (John Donne)
Out of a fired ship, which, but no
way
RR 45

from *On the Victory obtained by
Blake, 1657* (Andrew Marvell)
. . . The thundering cannon now
begins the fight
Iron III 62

Stoker Rock's Baby (Charles
Causley)
On a tropical night when the stars
were alight
Cau N 31

Token of All Brave Captains
(Captain Marryat)
The captain stood on the
carronade: 'First Lieutenant' says
he
Puf V 114

*Would you hear of an old-fashioned
sea-fight?* (Walt Whitman)
Would you hear of an
old-fashioned sea-fight?
Rat 471

SEA BIRDS

See also Cormorants, Seagulls

At Porthcothan (Christopher
Middleton)
A speck of dark at low tide on the
tideline
DP IV 7

The Echoing Cliff (Andrew
Young)
White gulls that sit and float
DP IV 9

From the Shore (Carl Sandburg)
A lone grey bird
Full 126

The Oystercatcher (John
Heath-Stubbs)
They say in the Highlands and the
Western Isles
Hea P 20

The Storm (Walter de la Mare)
First there were two of us then
there were three of us
de la M Col 123; Ev 20; Rain 83

The Storm-Petrel (John
Heath-Stubbs)
Far out at sea, a little dark bird
Hea P 16

SEAGULLS

Great Black-backed Gulls (John
Heath-Stubbs)
Said Cap'n Morgan to Cap'n Kidd
Hea P 17; Sea 173

Gulls on a Hill Loch (Norman
MacCaig)
They resent our arrival, they rise
like big snow-flakes
Mus 35

The Seagull (Mary Howitt)
Oh the white seagull, the wild
seagull
Ox CV 161

A Visit from the Sea (Robert
Louis Stevenson)
Far from the loud sea beaches
FM 220; In O II 30

SEALS

*The Great [Grey] Silkie of Sule
Skerrie* (anon)
An earthly nourrice sits and sings
*Bk Bal 13; Fab Bal 69; Fab CV 68;
Fab PV 282; Isle 23; Peng B 249*
I heard a mother baing her bairn
Peng B 251
In Norway there sits a maid
Ring 129; Voi II 115
There lived a maid in the Norway
lands
Brit 56

The Sailor and the Seal (Rumer
Godden)
When the seal saw the sailor
Zoo 88

Seal (William Jay Smith)
See how he dives
Fir 50; Full 26; Young 8

Seal Lullaby (Rudyard Kipling)
Oh! hush, thee, my baby, the night
is behind us
Zoo 82

SEA MONSTERS

See also Kraken, Whales
Just then another event (Virgil,
trans C. Day Lewis)
Just then another event, the most
alarming yet
Sea 57

The Sea-Pig (Gavin Ewart)
Five miles through forest from the
bathyscape
Bat C 49

The Sea-Serpent Chantey (Vachell
Lindsay)
There's a snake on the western
wave
AM 72; J Vo III 24; Touch II 102

SEA SHANTIES

Billy Boy (anon)
Where have you been all the day,
Billy boy, Billy boy?
Bat C 15; Ox Dic 78; Ox NR 189

Blow the Man Down (anon)
Blow the man down, bullies, blow
the man down
DP II 66; Iron IV 5; Touch I 44

Bobby Shaftoe (trad)
Bobby Shaftoe's gone to sea
*Fab PV 104; Lolli II 10; Merry 168;
Ox Dic 90; Ox NR 184 P Life I 25;
Trad 131*

Boney was a Warrior (anon)
Boney was a warrior
PW 21

Fire Down Below (trad)
Fire in the galley, fire down below
*Merry 179; P Life III 65; Puf SB 123;
Rain 19; Rhyme II 6*

Johnny Todd (anon)
Johnny Todd he took a notion
Gold II 20

Leave her, Johnny (anon)
I thought I heard the captain say
My V 56

Lowlands (trad)
I dreamt a dream the other night
Peng B 311; Sea 174

Spanish Ladies (anon)
Farewell and adieu to you, fair
Spanish ladies
Fab CV 300

Stormalong (trad)
O Stormy, he is dead and gone
Merry 333; Sea 146

A Yankee Ship came down the River
(anon)
A Yankee ship came down the river
Merry 362

SEASIDE

See also Bathing, Beaches

The Arrival (John Walsh)
Our train steams slowly in, and we
creep to a stop at last
Theme V 65; World 90

At the Seaside (Robert Louis
Stevenson)
When I was down beside the sea
*Al II 18; Bits p; Croc 65; CTV 108;
DT 39; Ox CV 293; Ste CG 3*

The Beach (Robert Graves)
Louder than gulls the little
children scream
Tam 8; Touch III 82

Cornish Holiday (John
Betjeman)
Then before breakfast down
toward the sea
ND 50

Delectable Duchy (John
Betjeman)
Where yonder villa hogs the sea
Sea 80

Greenaway (John Betjeman)
I know so well this turfy mile
Ten 34

I do like to be beside the Seaside
(J. A. Glover-Kind)
Everyone delights to spend their
summer's holiday
Sea 73

The Lugubrious, Salubrious Seaside
(Louis MacNeice)
The dogs' tails tick like
metronomes
Sea 78

maggie and milly
(e. e. cummings)
Maggie and Milly and Molly and
May
*BE 29; Bits y; Burn 10; Deli 15; Hap
18; ND 53; Out Sc 48; Poems 69; Prel
II 37; PT I 12; Rat 260; R Nine 79*

The Sand Artist (James Kirkup)
On the damp seashore
Sea 77

Sand-between-the-toes (A. A.
Milne)
I went down to the shouting sea
Mil VY 73

Sea Shore (John Kitching)
Sandy shore and seaweed
Hi 26

Seaside Serenade (Ogden Nash)
It begins when you smell a funny
smell
Touch I 135

Work and Play (Ted Hughes)
The swallow of summer, she toils
all summer
Hug S 36; ND 51

SEASONS

See also Bk S, Hug S throughout,
Word 23–42
See also Autumn, Christmas,
Easter, New Year, Spring,
Summer, Weather, Winter
The Calendar (Barbara Euphan
Todd)
I knew when Spring was come
Like 75; Out Sc 68; Puf V 24

Candlemas Eve (Robert Herrick)
Down with the rosemary and bays
Sun 129

Days and Seasons in London, 1715
(John Gay)
Experienced men, inured to city
ways
DP III 30; Iron III 24

Nature (H. D. Carberry,
Jamaica)
We have neither Summer nor
Winter
Bite I 68; Many 78; NS 30

The Seasons in North Cornwall
(Charles Causley)
O spring has set off her green fuses
Cau C 44

SEEDS

Fuelled (Marcia Hans)
Fuelled/by a million
Bite III 27

Seeds (Walter de la Mare)
The seeds I sowed –
Bk S 25; de la M Col 89; Hap II 24

Seeds (James Reeves)
A row of pearls
Tap 49

The Seed Shop (Muriel Stuart)
Here in a quiet and dusty room
they lie
By 283; Ring 23

SENSES

See Noises, Smells

SEPTEMBER

September (Mary Coleridge)
Now every day the bracken
browner grows
Bk S 53; Puf V 25

SHADOWS

I would Run with my Shadow
(Edmund Leo Wright)
I would run with my shadow
Over 20

My Shadow (Robert Louis
Stevenson)
I have a little shadow that goes in
and out with me
*CTV 108; Fab NV 112; Here 108;
Once 92; Ox CV 295; P Life I 61; Ste
CG 19*

Shadow March (Robert Louis
Stevenson)
All round the house is the jet black
night
Ste CG 44

SHAKESPEARE

The Coiner (circa 1611) (Rudyard
Kipling)
Against the Bermudas we foundered,
whereby
Sea 213

SHARKS

Basking Shark (Norman
MacCaig)
To stub an oar on a rock where
none should be
Seven 174

The Flattered Flying-Fish
(E. V. Rieu)
Said the Shark to the Flying-Fish
over the phone
Puf Q 122; Tam 84

The Maldive Shark (Herman
Melville)
About the Shark, phlegmatical one
*Bat A 64; Iron III 1; PW 236; Rat
261; RR 177; Sea 43; Touch IV 156*

The Shark (Lord Alfred
Douglas)
A treacherous monster is the shark
Bat A 37; Like 71; My R 46; Sea 42

SHEARERS

The Banks of the Condamine
(anon)
O hark the dogs are barking, love
*Fab Bal 231; Fab PV 212; Peng B
306; SAS 94*

Shearing at Castlereagh
(A. B. Paterson, Australia)
The bell is set aringing and the
engine gives a toot
Aus 76

SHEEP

See also Lambs, Rams

A Child's Pet (W. H. Davies)
When I sailed out of Baltimore
P Life III 79; Rat 106

Sheep (W. H. Davies)
When I was once in Baltimore
*Blow 49; DP I 10; Merry 322; P Life
III 78; Rat 379; R Eig 29; Rhyme IV
117*

Sheep (Ted Hughes)
The sheep has stopped crying
Hug S 31; Hug SP 193
(part) The mothers have come
back
ND 77

Sheep (K. E. Ingram)
God made sheep in the early
morning
Cari I 98; NS 36

Sheep Dipping (Norman
MacCaig)
The sea goes flick-flack or the light
does. When
Ox Con 22

A Sheep Fair (Thomas Hardy)
The day arrives of the autumn fair
Gold III 39; Iron II 56; Voi I 93; Zoo 40; (part) *TD 134*

Sheep in Winter (John Clare)
The sheep get up and make their many tracks
Ev 64; Flock 280; Rhyme III 58

Sheep Party (John Fuller)
Under thorn and bramble
Sort 54

Spraying Sheep (Norman MacCaig)
Old tufts of wool lie on the grass
Gold II 28

SHEEP-DOGS

'Glen', a Sheep-Dog (Hilton Brown)
I ken there isna a p'int in yer heid
Scot 33

Morgan's Dog (A. B. Paterson, Australia)
Morgan the drover explained
Pat A 54

Old English Sheep-Dog (George MacBeth)
Eyes/drowned in fur
Hap II 30

Praise of a Collie (Norman MacCaig)
She was a small dog, neat and fluid
Rat 351; Strict 138

Sheep-dog Trials in Hyde Park (C. Day Lewis)
A shepherd stands at one end of the arena
Dog 52

SHELLS

The Sea Shell (Amy Lowell)
Sea Shell, Sea Shell
Fan 112; P Life III 10

The Shell (James Stephens)
And then I pressed the shell
Bite II 34; DT 40; Flock 43; ND 49; PT I 11; Rhyme IV 39; Round 16; Sea 65; Theme II 55; Touch I 134; (part) *Bits b*

The Shell (Alfred, Lord Tennyson)

See what a lovely shell
Come 182; PT I 25; Touch I 133

SHEPHERDS

The Shepherd (Mary Gilmore, Australia)
Old Sam Smith
Imp 40; SAS 9

SHIPS

See also Boats, Cutty Sark

SHIPS (L & D)

The Cable Ship
(H. E. Martinson, trans Robert Bly)
We fished up the Atlantic Cable one day
Rat 98

Cargoes (John Masefield)
Quinquireme of Nineveh from distant Ophir
EGV 317; Fab PR 240; Like 42; ND 42; Touch I 132

The Dismantled Ship (Walt Whitman)
In some unused lagoon, some nameless bay
Mov 38; Tel 60; Tho 47

HMS Hero (Michael Roberts)
Pale grey, her guns hooded, decks clear of all impediment
Sea 125

The Old Ships (James Elroy Flecker)
I have seen old ships sail, like swans asleep
ND 42; Plea 164

The Ship (Richard Church)
They have launched the little ship
Drag 35; Fir 37; Mov 33; P Life IV 56

SHIPS (N)

See also Jervis Bay, Nabara, Revenge

Down the Clyde (Wilma Horsbrugh)
Here is a tale told by Grandpa McBride
Hor B 59

The Golden Vanity or *Sailing in the Lowlands* (anon)

A ship have I got in the North
Country
*Brit 108; Down 11; Fab CV 171; Ox
PC 57; Plea 161*
A ship called *The Golden Vanity*
Tale 35
Sir Walter Raleigh has built a ship
Bat L 60
There was a ship that sailed all on
the Lowland Sea
Bk Bal 39; Iron I 54

HMS Glory (Charles Causley)
I was born on an Irish sea of eggs
and porter
Cau C 19

The Yarn of the 'Nancy Bell'
(W. S. Gilbert)
'Twas on the shores that round our
coast
*Bat L 38; Bill 31; CBC 115; DP II
34; EGV 258; Nar 116; Ox LV 148;
Peng B 322; Touch I 70*

SHIPWRECKS

The 'Alice Jean' (Robert Graves)
One moonlight night a ship drove
in
*Drag 56; Hist 64; J Vo I 31; Shad 40;
Theme II 7*

from **The Borough** (George
Crabbe)
Darkness begins to reign; the
louder wind
DP III 63

A Channel Rhyme (C. Fox Smith)
Start Point and Beachy Head
Sea 86

Clarence's Dream (William
Shakespeare)
What was your dream? I long to
hear you tell it.
Richard III I iv 8; Deli 17; Rat 286
Lord, Lord, methought what pain
it was to drown
Richard III I iv 21; Touch I 131
Methought I saw a thousand
fearful wracks
*Richard III I iv 24; PW 65; Sea 160;
Tho 38*

Grace Darling (anon)
'Twas on the Longstone
Lighthouse there dwelt an English
maid
Brit 121

How's My Boy? (Sydney Dobell)
Ho, Sailor of the sea!
Say 87

**In Memory of the Circus Ship
'Euzkera'** (Walker Gibson)
The most stupendous show they
ever gave
Sea 160

The Inchcape Rock (Robert
Southey)
No stir in the air, no stir in the sea
*Blow 34; Down 19; DP I 63; EGV
135; Nar 114; Plea 145; Wind 59*

from **The Odyssey** (Homer, trans
J. W. Mackail)
Even as he spoke a monstrous wave
abaft
Sea 207

**Pat Cloherty's version of 'The
Maisie'** (Richard Murphy)
I've no tooth to sing you the song
Rat 339; Sea 225

Posted (John Masefield)
Dream after dream I see the wrecks
that lie
ND 43; Tel 17

The Rescue (Ted Hughes)
That's what we live on; thinking of
their rescue
Drag 62; Gold IV 61

She is Far from the Land (Thomas
Hood)
Cables entangling her
Fab Non 91

Sir Patrick Spens (anon)
The king sits in Dunfermline town
*BHL 45; Bk Bal 45, 185; Brit 74;
Deli 18; DP III 38; Duck 111; EGV
11; Fab Bal 121; Fab CV 296; Fab
PR 22; Flock 46; ND 33; Ox PC 47;
Peng B 211; P Life IV 61; Puf V 99;
PW 7; Rat 391; Scot 37; Touch I 38;
Wind 54*

The Survivors (R. S. Thomas)
I never told you this?
GV V 14

from **The White Ship**
(D. G. Rossetti)
Swifter and swifter the *White Ship*
sped
Sea 210

174

*The Wreckers' Prayer
(Newfoundland)* (Theodore
G. Roberts)
Give us a wrack or two, Good Lord
Bill 92; J Vo IV 20

The Wreck of the Hesperus
(H. W. Longfellow)
It was the schooner *Hesperus*
*CTV 11; EGV 182; Fab PR 128; Nar
111*

The Yarn of the 'Loch Achray'
(John Masefield)
The *Loch Achray* was a clipper tall
P Tale 156

SHOOTING

First Blood (John Stallworthy)
It was. The breech smelling of oil
Drag 13; Theme VII 58; Touch IV 168

The Fowler (John Clare)
With boots of monstrous leg and
massy strength
Theme VII 29

I saw a jolly hunter (Charles
Causley)
I saw a jolly hunter
*Cau C 225; Cau F 14; CC 50; Liv 58;
Many 76; Once 138; PT VI 26; Strict
141*

The Keeper (anon)
The keeper did a-shooting go
Merry 118; P Life III 50

The Sportsman (Clive Sansom)
Nature he loves, and next to nature
– death
Theme I 65; Theme V 72

The Towerer (John Masefield)
Old Jarge, Hal, Walter and I, the
Rector and Bill
TCN 107

The Wicked Fowler (Patric
Dickinson)
The wicked fowler took his gun
TCN 106

from *Windsor Forest* (Alexander
Pope)
See! from the brake the whirring
pheasant springs
Bir 31

SHOPKEEPERS

My Friend Luigi (John Smith)

My friend Luigi keeps/A
delicatessen store
Full 46; My R 41

*The invisible backward-facing
grocer who rose to fame* (Alasdair
Clayre)
John Green the grocer lived a
hesitant life
Gang 94

Madam (Christopher Logue)
Madam/I have sold you
Gang 42

Welsh Dairy in Our Street
(Marion Lines)
Mrs Jenkins (busy person)
Lin T 31

SHOPPING

Song of the Supermarket (Leslie
Norris)
COME IN! COME IN! COME
IN!
Drum 87

SINGING

See also Love Songs, Sailors'

Songs, Sea Shanties, Soldiers'
Songs, Spirituals
Everyone Sang (Siegfried
Sassoon)
Everyone suddenly burst out
singing
EGV 329; My V 173; TD 17; Tel 83

The Solitary Reaper (William
Wordsworth)
Behold her, single in the field
*Choice 21; DP IV 76; EGV 130; Fab
CV 119; Fab PR 71; Iron III 14; Ox
PC 146; Plea 190; P Scot 70; PW 173;
RR 123; This W 145*

SINS

Madam and the Minister
(Langston Hughes)
Reverend Butler came by
Say 75

Punishment Enough (Norman
Cameron)
They say that women, in a
bombing raid
DP IV 148

SISKINS

The Siskins (Theodore Roethke)
The bank swallows veer and dip
Bir 78

SIZES

The Fly (Walter de la Mare)
How large unto the tiny fly
By 228; de la M Col 89; Deli 58; DP I 6; DT 76; F Feet 186; Once 38; Plea 42; Poems 28; Touch I 30; Trad 83

High on the Hill (Tom Wright)
High on the hill I can see it all
Ev 42; Third 118

It is not Growing like a Tree (Ben Jonson)
It is not growing like a tree
Deli 115; DP IV 145; Ev 155; Puf V 239; Rat 216; RR 157; TD 148

Lines on a Small Potato (Margaret Fishback)
Reflect upon the dinosaur
Dino 35

The Magnifying Glass (Walter de la Mare)
With this round glass
Theme II 47

Small, Smaller (Russell Hoban)
I thought that I knew all there was to know
BE 37; Hob P 9; Poems 28; Sort 57; Third 90

from *Verses on Gulliver's Travels* (Alexander Pope)
From his nose
Drum 75; R Nine 19
See! and believe your Eyes!
Deli 61

SKATEBOARDING

Skateboarder (Charles Connell)
I can soar, I can swoop
CC 30

SKATES

Skate (Alan Brownjohn)
Flitting the sea-bed, wide and flat
Hap II 69

SKATING

The Midnight Skaters (Edmund Blunden)
The hop poles stand in cones
DP IV 121; ND 238; RR 28; Theme V 39; Touch I 157; Voi III 163

from *The Prelude Book I* (William Wordsworth)
And in the frosty season, when the sun
Choice 23; Deli 13; Ev 32; Fab CV 57; ND 93; Prel II 23; PW 173; RR 93; Touch III 111

Skating (Herbert Asquith)
When I try to skate
Out Sc 42; Theme V 38

SKIPPING

Skipping (Thomas Hood)
Little children skip
Out Sc 32; Puf Y 34

from *Skipping Song* (Gareth Owen)
Anne and Belinda
Drum 129

SKUNKS

Skunk (Ted Hughes)
Skunk's footfall plods padded
Hug U 40

SKYLARKS

See Larks

SKYSCRAPERS

See also Tower Blocks
Building a Skyscraper (James S. Tippett)
They're building a skyscraper
Full 80; Hi 21; Once 16; PT III 13

SLAVERY

The Flying Cloud (anon)
My name is Edward Holland
Iron I 24

The Slave Chase (c. 1850) (anon)
Set every stitch of canvas to woo
the fresh'ning wind
Iron IV 46

The Slave in the Dismal Swamp
(H. W. Longfellow)
In the dark fens of the Dismal
Swamp
Theme I 31

SLEDGING

Jingle Bells (anon)
Dashing through the snow
Puf SB 70

Sledging (Laurence Lerner)
Blotches of people in crimson or
lilac or tan
Theme IV 40

SLEEP

Counting Sheep (Wes Magee)
They said/'If you can't get to sleep
ADT 123

Falling Asleep (Siegfried
Sassoon)
Voices moving about in the quiet
house
Theme II 34

Insomniac (Sylvia Plath)
The night sky is only a sort of
carbon paper
Theme II 35

Nod (Walter de la Mare)
Softly along the road of evening
de la M Col 239; Rhyme III 63

Sonnet (John Keats)
O soft embalmer of the still
midnight
Voi III 139

Sweet Dreams (Ogden Nash)
I wonder as into bed I creep
Croc 89; Nas C 80

SLEET

Sleet (Norman MacCaig)
The first snow was sleet. It swished
heavily
Drag 88; Gold II 16; Out 73; TD 49

SLIMMING

Adelaide (Jack Prelutsky)
Adelaide was quite dismayed
Pac 75

Give up slimming, Mum (Kit
Wright)
My mum/is short
Pac 58; Third 18; Wri R 20

SLOTHS

The Sloth (Theodore Roethke)
In moving-slow he has no peer
Hap 73; Mov 123; Touch I 83

SLUGS

Slug (Theodore Roethke)
How I loved one like you when I
was little!
Theme I 42

SLUMS

New Light on Terry Street
(Douglas Dunn)
First sunshine for three weeks, and
the children come out
Theme VII 7

We live in a Rickety House
(Alexander McLachlan)
We live in a rickety house
Theme IV 38

SMELLS

Buying Fuel (Richard Church)
Now I come to the farmer about
some logs
Prel IV 46

Smells (Christopher Morley)
Why is it that the poets tell
P Life IV 53; Prel IV 46; Word 18

The Song of Quoodle
(G. K. Chesterton)
They haven't got no noses
Duck 62; Theme I 11

SMUGGLERS

Rum Lane (James Reeves)
Gusty and chill
Ree C 98

The Smuggler (anon)
O my true love's a smuggler and
sails upon the sea
Mov 45

Smugglers (George Mackay
Brown)
Midnight. Measured musical cold
sea circles
Ox Con 125

A Smuggler's Song (Rudyard
Kipling)
If you wake at midnight and hear a
horse's feet
*DP I 60; Duck 96; Ox CV 322; Ox
PC 52; Plea 168; P Life III 92; Rhyme
IV 54*

SNAILS

Considering the Snail (Thom
Gunn)
The snail pushes through a green
*BE 35; DP III 18; Drag 23; Gold II
45; Say 116; Seven 85; Touch III 136*

The Housekeeper (Charles Lamb)
The frugal snail, with forecast of
repose
Ev 66

The Poor Snail (J. M. Westrup)
The snail says 'Alas!'
Come 134

The Snail (James Reeves)
At sunset when the night-dews fall
*Al III 34; Blow 29; Fan 36; Ox PC
123; Puf Q 74; Ree C 3*

Snail (John Tompkins)
I'm sorry I can't put you up
R Six 58

The Snail (William Cowper)
To grass, or leaf, or fruit, or wall
Come 149; Ev 67; If 68 (part) *Croc 38*

Upon the Snail (John Bunyan)
She goes but softly, but she goeth
sure
*Drum 47; Like 23; ND 59; Ox CV 36;
RR 173; Touch III 135; Voi I 97*

SNAKES

The Apeman who Hated Snakes
(Adrian Mitchell)
Was an apeman lived next door to
me
Gang 13

The Brown Snake (Douglas
Stewart, Australia)
I walked to the green gum-tree
SAS 28

Grass Snake (Olive Dove)
We waited so long to see
Drum 54

In the Snake Park (William
Plomer)
A white-hot midday in the Snake
Park
Bill 125

Leviathan (Douglas Livingstone)
A puff-adder, khaki
Touch IV 157

A Narrow Fellow (Emily
Dickinson)
A narrow fellow in the grass
*Bat A 35; BB 12; F Feet 107; Flock
210; FM 190; PW 249; Rat 307*

Rattlesnake Ceremony Song
(Yokuts Indians, trans
A. L. Kroeber)
The king snake said to the
rattlesnake
J Vo III 9; Puf M 29

*Sensemaya: A Chant for Killing a
Snake* (Nicholas Guillen trans
G. R. Coulthard)
Mayombé – bombé – mayombé!
Bite I 28; NS 37

The Serpent (Theodore Roethke)
There was a serpent who had to
sing
*AM 46; Duck 80; Hap II 40; Touch I
127; Voi I 94; Zoo 80*

The Serpent (Percy Bysshe
Shelley)
Wake the serpent not – lest he
F Feet 65

Snake (George Barker)
I the reptilian
Bar A 'S'

Snake (D. H. Lawrence)
A snake came to my water-trough
*Bite III 33; Deli 24; DP IV 18; EGV
325; Fab Mod 177; Full 18; Gold II
47; Ima 117; ND 62; Rat 395; Tam
81; TCN 110; Touch IV 173*

Snake Moving (Olive Dove)
With undulations
Drum 55

Snakes (A. K. Ramanujan)
A basketful of ritual cobras
Tho 79

The Snake Song (John Mbiti)
Neither legs nor arms have I
Rhy 43; World 126

The Viper (Ruth Pitter)
Barefoot I went and made no
sound
Dawn 68

SNAKES AND LADDERS

The Game of Life (Roy Fuller)
Have you been in sight of heaven?
Ful P 46; Poems 84

Snakes and Ladders (Frank
Collymore)
Up and down the board they run
Bite I 77

SNARES

See Traps

SNEEZES

Sneezing (trad)
Sneeze on Monday, sneeze for
danger
Here 22

SNOW (L & D)

See also Sleet, Thaw

Cat and the Weather (May
Swenson)
Cat takes a look at the weather
Tap 44

The First Snow (Wilfrid Gibson)
From the pit's mouth men pour, a
stream of black
Gold II 16

Frying-Pan's Theology
(A. B. Paterson)
Scene: On Monaro
Aus 16: Iron I 40

London Snow (Robert Bridges)
When men were all asleep the snow
came flying
*EGV 269; Gold III 43; ND 12; Touch
I 96;* (part) *Bk S 68*

Only Snow (Allan Ahlberg)
Outside the sky was almost brown
Ahl P 66

Outdoor Song (A. A. Milne)
The more it/SNOWS – tiddely
pom
Like 14

Snow (Edward Thomas)
In the gloom of whiteness
*Four 112; Out 75; Prel III 40; TD 51;
Voi III 157; WAS 151*

Snow (Walter de la Mare)
No breath of wind
*Blow 48; de la M Col 185; DP II 26;
Gold I 22; Tap 37; WAS 150*

Snow (Andrew Young)
Ridged thickly on black bough
Touch II 134

Snow (Roy Fuller)
Snow falling in November
Sort 31

Snow (Archibald Lampman,
Canada)
White are the far-off plains, and
white
Ev 30

Snow and Ice Poems (Roger
McGough)
Our street is dead lazy
McG S 30

Snow and Snow (Ted Hughes)
Snow is sometimes a she, a soft one
Hug S 73

Snow and Sun (anon)
White bird, featherless
Drum 25

Snow Harvest (Andrew Young)
The moon that now and then last
night
Tap 45

Snow in the Suburbs (Thomas
Hardy)
Every branch big with it
*DP IV 35; EGV 263; Gold II 17; Out
80; P Life IV 29; Prel III 40; RR 67;
Say 95; Tap 43; This W 129; Touch I
96; Word 26*

*Snow on the City Three Days before
Christmas* (Mitchell Goodman)
Out of a snow-/white night sky
Out 90

from *Snow Storm* (John Clare)
What a night! The wind howls,
hisses, and but stops
Flock 275; Prel III 44; TD 50

White Fields (James Stephens)
In winter-time we go
Come 89; P Life II 59; R Six 40; Say 14

Winter (Walter de la Mare)
Clouded with snow
DT 18

Winter (Walter de la Mare)
Green Mistletoe!
de la M Col 194; Out 82; Star 19

Winter Morning (Ogden Nash)
Winter is the king of showmen
Croc 72; Fir 90; Like 58; Nas C 22; Out 76; Puf Y 76; R Six 59

Winter Snowstorm (John Clare)
Winter is come in earnest, and the snow
Iron II 87

SNOW (N)

No Snow (Wilma Horsbrugh)
This is a story/Of Mrs McRory
Hor B 51

The Runaway (Robert Frost)
Once when the snow of the year
was beginning to fall
Drag 28; Fab CV 79; F Feet 125; Gold I 55; Hap 68; Hor 29; Prel I 44; Touch III 116; World 118; Zoo 36

Stopping by Woods on a Snowy Evening (Robert Frost)
Whose woods these are I think I know
BE 6; Blow 38; Choice 284; Deli 71; DP II 27; DT 20; Fab CV 58; Flock 276; GV III 15; Hap 38; Iron I 62; Like 67; Rat 407; Rhyme IV 13; Tap 44; TD 143; Ten 80; This W 156; Touch I 155; WAS 154

SNOWDROPS

The Snowdrop (Mary Webb)
Three softly curved white petals
veined with light
WAS 185

SNOWFLAKES

The Snowflake (Walter de la Mare)
Before I melt
de la M Col 193; P Life IV 30; Prel III 43; R Six 72

Snowflakes (David McCord)
Sometimes this winter if you go
Deli 65; Full 122

To a Snowflake (Francis Thompson)
What heart could have thought you?
Bk S 67; Say 95; This W 113; Touch II 30

SNOWMEN

Boy at the Window (Richard Wilbur)
Seeing the snowman standing all alone
Like 161; Prel II 32; Say 92; Voi I 125

Death of a Snowman (Vernon Scannell)
I was awake all night
Fir 91; Sca A 20; Sort 36

The Snowman (Roger McGough)
Mother, while you were at the shops
McG S 34

Snowman (Shel Silverstein)
'Twas the first day of the springtime
Out 20

SOLDIERS

The Ballad of Mulan (sixth century Chinese, trans Arthur Waley)
Click, click, for ever click, click
Pluc 23

Buckingham Palace (A. A. Milne)
They're changing guard at Buckingham Palace
FV 88; Mil VY 2; Ox CV 340

The Duke of Plaza-Toro (W. S. Gilbert)
In enterprise of martial kind
CBC 136

The Modern Major-General
(W. S. Gilbert)
I am the very pattern of a modern
Major-General
Ox LV 147

Oh Stay at Home
(A. E. Housman)
Oh stay at home, my lad, and
plough
Poems II 85

Old Timers (Carl Sandburg)
I am an ancient reluctant conscript
Theme VI 15

Soldier Freddy (Spike Milligan)
Soldier Freddy/Was never ready
Full 66; Touch I 128

Tommy (Rudyard Kipling)
I went into a public 'ouse to get a
pint of beer
Fab PR 224

SOLDIERS' SONGS

All the Hills and Vales along
(Charles Sorley)
All the hills and vales along
Fab CV 261; Ima 106

Bonny Dundee (Sir Walter Scott)
To the Lords of Convention 'twas
Claver'se who spoke
Fab CV 252

from *Hassan* (James Elroy
Flecker)
We are they who come faster than
fate:
EGV 324

Men Who March Away (Thomas
Hardy)
We be the King's men, hale and
hearty
DT 15

Pibroch of Donuil Dhu (Sir
Walter Scott)
Pibroch of Donuil Dhu
Fab CV 231; Fab PR 73; J Vo III 78

Roman Wall Blues
(W. H. Auden)
Over the heather the wet wind
blows
*Dawn 43; Choice 242; GV IV 29; J Vo
IV 37; My V 79; ND 144; PT V 14;
Say 83; Theme VI 37; Touch II 170*

The War Song of Dinas Vawr
(Thomas Love Peacock)
The mountain sheep are sweeter
*EGV 143; Fab CV 255; Fab PR 88;
Plea 270; Poems II 82; Rain 104*

We be Soldiers Three (anon, 1609)
We be soldiers three
Fab PV 235

*What Did the Soldier's Wife
Receive?* (Bertolt Brecht, trans
H. R. Hays)
And what did the soldier's wife
receive?
DP IV 57; Theme VI 59

The Widow's Party (Rudyard
Kipling)
Where have you been this while
away?
Peng B 326

SOLE BAY

The Battle of Sole Bay (anon,
1672)
One day as I was sitting still
Fab PV 189

SORCERERS

from *The Sorcerer* (W. S. Gilbert)
Oh my name is John Wellington
Wells
CBC 124; Puf M 83

SOUP

Beautiful Soup (Lewis Carroll)
Beautiful soup, so rich and green
*ADT 54; Bat L 93; Croc 26; Fab Non
118; Merry 340; My V 160; Ox PC
12; Pac 31; P Life II 28*

SOUTH AFRICA

Always a Suspect (Oswald
Mtshali)
I get up in the morning
Ima 70

Boy on a Swing (Oswald
Mtshali)
Slowly he moves
Afr II 25; Ima 71

In Memory of Steve Biko
(Elizabeth Bartlett)
Somehow the drains of feeling were
blocked that week
Root 16

Just a Passerby (Oswald
Mtshali)
I saw them clobber him with
kieries
AP 199

Nightfall in Soweto (Oswald
Mtshali)
Nightfall comes like/a dreaded
disease
AP 196

One Exile to Another (David
Evans)
That old sage
Root 34

SOWING

Putting in the Seed (Robert Frost)
You come to fetch me from my
work tonight
Iron IV 70

Seeds (Walter de la Mare)
The seeds I sowed
Bk S 25; de la M Col 89; Hap II 24

Sowing (Edward Thomas)
It was a perfect day
*Choice 175; Iron III 33; PT VI 11;
Tap 51; TD 128; Theme VII 30; Voi I
114*

SPACE TRAVEL

Bombscare (Brian Patten)
Without much effort the piece of
earth I was sitting on
Tel 56

The First Men on Mercury (Edwin
Morgan)
We come in peace from the third
planet
Seven 252

Love in a Space Suit (James
Kirkup)
Dear, when on some distant planet
Mod 116

Missionary (D. M. Thomas)
A harsh entry I had of it, Grasud;
Mod 193

The Moon, February 1973 (Edwin
Morgan)
At the edge of the Sea of Serenity
Seven 253

The Moonrocket (Wilma
Horsbrugh)
Here is a rocket that flew to the
moon
Hor B 65

Spacepoem 3: Off course (Edwin
Morgan)
the golden flood; the weightless
seat
*Gang 93; J Vo IV 56; RR 21; Seven
251*

Space Travellers (James Nimmo)
There was a witch, hump-backed
and hooded
P Life IV 95; PT II 25

Tea in a Space-Ship (James
Kirkup)
In this world a tablecloth need not
be laid
*Bric 12; Mod 115; Time 101; Touch
III 96*

Translunar Space March, 1972
(Edwin Morgan)
The interior of Pioneer-10
Seven 235

SPANIELS

On a Spaniel called Beau (William
Cowper)
A spaniel, Beau, that fares like you
Dog 56

SPARROWS

from *The Boke of Philip Sparrow*
(John Skelton)
It was so pretty a fole
Bir 58
When I remember again
Fab CV 84

The House-Sparrow (John
Heath-Stubbs)
Citizen Philip Sparrow, who likes
Sun 38

Two Sparrows (Humbert Wolfe)
Two sparrows, feeding
My V 141; WAS 42

SPELLING

Hints on Pronunciation for Foreigners (T. S. W.)
I take it you already know/Of tough and bough and cough and dough?
Flock 237

The Kangaroo's Cough (Anthony Thwaite)
The eminent Professor Hoff
Sort 90

SPIDERS

Spider (Alan Brownjohn)
I am a spider spinning down
Zoo 11

The Spider (Kenneth Mackenzie)
Just as my fingers close about the pen
Voi II 53

The Spider and the Fly (anon)
'Will you walk into my parlour?' said the spider to the fly
Blow 33; Ox CV 158

The Spider holds a Silver Ball (Emily Dickinson)
The spider holds a silver ball
Poems II 31

SPIES

My Neighbour, Mr Normanton (Charles Causley)
My neighbour, Mr Normanton
ADT 69; Cau F 75

SPIRITUALS

The Boneyard Shout (anon)
Down in de valley de sperrit spoke
Iron III 23

Go Down, Moses (anon)
When Israel was in Egypt's land
J Vo IV 35

I Got a Robe (anon)
I got a robe, you got a robe
Puf SB 58

Joshua Fit de Battle of Jericho (anon)
Joshua fit de battle of Jericho
J Vo III 96

Nobody knows the Trouble I've seen (anon)
Nobody knows the trouble I've seen
Puf SB 74

Swing Low, Sweet Chariot (anon)
I ain't never been to heaven but I've been told
Fab PV 327
Swing low, sweet chariot
Afr I 49; Puf SB 10

This Train (anon)
This train is bound for glory, this train
Rail 671

SPORTS

See also Theme V throughout
See also Boxing, Deerstalking, Games, Hunting, Physical Activities, Rowing, Shooting

Confessions of a Born Spectator (Ogden Nash)
One infant grows up and becomes a jockey
Tam 18

SPRING

See also Hug S 13–24
See also April, March, May, Weather

Carol for St Valentine's Day (adapted from Chaucer)
St Valentine that art full high aloft
WAS 23

Chanson Innocente (e. e. cummings)
In Just-/spring when the world is mud-
Bric 16; Croc 76; Fab NV 25; Hap 67; This W 69; Touch II 31; Word 30; Young 69

The Coming o' the Spring (Lady John Scott)
There's no a muir in my ain land but's fu' o' sang the day
Scot 27

Deceptions (Ted Hughes)
The oak is a railway station
Hug S 24

The Fight of the Year (Roger McGough)
And there goes the bell for the third month
Drum 28; Duck 25; McRo 60; Mer 79; Out 16

The First Day of Spring (Phoebe Hesketh)
There's strength in the sun, strength in the wind
Hes S 24

from *The Georgics* (Virgil, trans C. Day Lewis)
Then are the trackless copses alive with the trilling of birds
Georgics II 328; Flock 11

from *The Song of Solomon* (A.V.)
For lo the winter is past
Song of Solomon II 11; Bat V 15; Bk S 13; Croc 75; CTV 22; Like 61; P Life IV 36; Puf V 21; TD 116

Spring (Gerard Manley Hopkins)
Nothing is so beautiful as spring
Choice 115; Out 30; Rat 405; Touch IV 70; Word 29; (part) *F Feet 56*

from *The Spring* (Thomas Carew)
Now that the Winter's gone, the earth hath lost
Deli 63; Ev 16; R Nine 70; Round 64

Spring (Henry Howard, Earl of Surrey)
The soote season, that bud and bloom forth brings
Flock 6

Spring goeth all in white (Robert Bridges)
Spring goeth all in white
Fan 92; P Life I 56; Puf V 16

Spring is like (e. e. cummings)
Spring is like a perhaps hand
Flock 7

A Spring Morning (John Clare)
The spring comes in with all her hues and smells
Fab LP 22

Spring Nature Notes (Ted Hughes)
The sun lies mild and still on the yard stones
Hug S 17

Spring, the Sweet Spring (Thomas Nashe)
Spring, the sweet spring, is the year's pleasant king
Bat C 65; By 26; Flock 6; Merry 331; Once 54; Ox PC 102; R Eig 92; (part) *Croc 75*

from *The Throstle* (Alfred, Lord Tennyson)
Summer is coming, summer is coming
Bk S 15; F Feet 202; WAS 41

When daffodils begin to peer (William Shakespeare)
When daffodils begin to peer
Winter's Tale IV iii 1; Bat L 109; Fab CV 52

When daisies pied (William Shakespeare)
When daisies pied and violets blue
Love's Labour's Lost V ii 902; BB 17; Plea 107; P Life II 45; This W 72; (part) *Trad 47*

SQUIDS

Squid Squirt Ink (Max Fatchen)
Squid Squirt ink
Fat S 38

SQUIRRELS

Five Little Squirrels (anon)
Five little squirrels sat up in a tree
CTV 93

Flying Squirrels (A. B. Paterson, Australia)
On the rugged water-shed
Pat A 25

The Grey Squirrel (Humbert Wolfe)
Like a small grey/coffee pot
Bric 37; F Feet 19; Gold III 18; PT VI 19; Touch IV 15; Young 21

The Squirrel (anon)
Whisky, frisky
Al III 33; Croc 39; CTV 64; Drum 53; J Vo I 58; R Six 16

The Squirrel (William Cowper)
The squirrel, flippant, pert, and full of play
Bat A 67

To a Squirrel at Kyle-Na-No (W. B. Yeats)

Come and play with me
*Al II 42; Bric 36; Croc 40; Fan 34;
FM 233; Imp 26; Lolli III 5; Ox PC
131; PT VI 19; Puf Y 108; R Nine 9;
This W 45; Word 49*

STAGS

The Runnable Stag (John
Davidson)
When the pods went pop on the
broom, green broom
EGV 274; Fab PR 195; FM 230

The Stag (Ted Hughes)
While the rain fell on the
November woodland shoulder of
Exmoor
Hug S 56

STANLEY

Stanley meets Mutesa (David
Rubadiri)
Such a time of it they had
AP 93; Att 14; Ima 82; RAP 52

STARLINGS

The Starling (John
Heath-Stubbs)
The starling is my darling,
although
Flock 91; Mod 111

Starlings (Marion Lines)
When summer evenings die
Lin T 11

Starlings (Clive Sansom)
Out of the sky, with their wild,
shrill, chattering
San E 26

Starlings (David Sutton)
My father got up determinedly that
Sunday
Drag 15

The Starlings in George Square
(Edwin Morgan)
Sundown on the high stonefields!
J Vo IV 10; PT III 16

STARS

Astronomer (David O'Neil)
On a lone hillside
Bric 25

Blue Stars and Gold (James
Stephens)
While walking through the trams
and cars
R Nine 63

*Dibby Dubby Dhu rose one
Midnight* (George Barker)
Dibby Dubby Dhu rose one
midnight
Drum 16

Escape at Bedtime (Robert Louis
Stevenson)
The lights from the parlour and
kitchen shone out
*ADT 115; CTV 129; Drum 15; P Life
II 80; Rain 118; Ste CG 22*

I never see the stars at night
(George Barker)
I never see the stars at night
TD 66

I Stood and Stared (Ralph
Hodgson)
I stood and stared; the sky was lit
TD 25

On Looking Up by Chance (Robert
Frost)
You'll wait a long, long time for
anything much
RR 116

The Star (Ann and Jane Taylor)
Twinkle, twinkle, little star
*Blow 60; Croc 87; CTV 147; DT 37;
Here 126; My V 146; Ox CV 122; Ox
Dic 397; Puf V 217; Trad 52*

Star and dead leaves (Tsuboi
Shigiji)
A star was talking with the
withered leaves
Al III 30

The Starlight Night (Gerard
Manley Hopkins)
Look at the stars! look, look up at
the skies!
*Choice 117; Plea 222; This W 105;
(part) DT 38*

The Stars (Andrew Young)
The stars rushed forth tonight
By 251

Summer Stars (Carl Sandburg)
Bend low again, night of summer
stars
Drum 19

When I heard the Learn'd Astronomer (Walt Whitman)
When I heard the learn'd astronomer
Like 141; PW 232; RR 72

STATUES

The Stone Gentleman (James Reeves)
Let us move the stone gentleman to the toadstool wood
Dawn 48

STEAM SHOVELS

Steam Shovel (Charles Malam)
The dinosaurs are not all dead
Bite I 42; Drum 84; Duck 85; Full 76; J Vo IV 93; Poems 36; R Nine 43; Tap 76

STEEPLE-JACKS

Steeple-jack (Michael Baldwin)
I saw the jack lean outward into space
Theme VI 66

STORMS

See also Thunder and Lightning

from *The Ancient Mariner* (S. T. Coleridge)
And now the storm-blast came, and he
Say 66

The Hailstorm in June 1831 (John Clare)
Darkness came o'er like chaos; and the sun
Prel III 5

He gets up in dark dawn (Ted Hughes)
To misted stillness
Hug M 24

The Leech Gatherer (William Wordsworth)
There was a roaring in the wind all night
Puf V 111; (part) Fan 46; Flock 36; GV III 17; Imp 66; Iron II 72; P Life IV 34; Prel III 32; Rain 86; Rhyme IV 9; TD 57; WAS 92

The Storm (Theodore Roethke)
Against the stone breakwater
Touch II 131

The Storm (Edward Lowbury)
The garden looks like its own photograph
Low G 36

Storm (Roger McGough)
They're at it again
Out 56

from *Storm in the Black Forest* (D. H. Lawrence)
Now it is almost night, from the bronzey soft sky
DP III 27; Iron IV 39; Out 57; Prel III 32; RR 85; Say 63; Touch II 130; Word 38

Storm on the Island (Seamus Heaney)
We are prepared; we build our houses squat
Touch IV 92

A Sudden Storm (Pious Oleghe)
The wind howls, the trees sway
Afr I 41; Rhy 51

Tropic Storm (W. Adolphe Roberts)
The scent of jasmines in the sultry air
NS 32

The wind begun to rock the grass (Emily Dickinson)
The wind begun to rock the grass
Poems II 32

STREET CRIES

See also Fab NV 36; Pac 8–10; Ox NR 72–3

The Cries of London (trad)
Cherries: Here's round and sound
Pac 8; World 35

Old Chairs to Mend! (anon)
Old chairs to mend! Old chairs to mend!
Ox Dic 114; Ox NR 72

The Trader's Medley (trad)
Holly and Ivy or Mistletoe
World 32

SUBURBS

Earl's Court (Gavin Ewart)
Earl's Court – a bourgeois slum
Lon 154

Housing Scheme (Richard Church)
All summer through
Tel 39

Little Boxes (Malvina Reynolds)
Little boxes on the hillside
PT III 14

Suburbs (Charles Martin, aged 12)
The drizzle slants down over the grey suburbs
Tho 52

SUMMER

See also Hug S 27–39
See also June, July, Weather

Cut Grass (Philip Larkin)
Cut grass lies frail
Mus 74; Ox Con 158

Heatwave (Phoebe Hesketh)
Heat over all, not a lark can rise
Hes S 24

High Summer on the Mountains (Idris Davies)
High summer on the mountains
Out 39

A Hot Day (A. S. J. Tessimond)
Cottonwool clouds loiter
Fan 50; Out 41; Prel III 7; Round 11; Tap 60; TD 34; Touch II 133; (part) *Bits g*

from *The Muses' Elysium* (Michael Drayton)
Clear had the day been from the dawn
DP IV 30; Duck 117

The Obby Oss (Charles Causley)
Early one morning
Cau N 45

Poem about the Sun Slinking Off and Pinning Up a Notice (Roger McGough)
the sun/hasn't got me fooled
Out 36

Summer (Christina Rossetti)
Winter is cold-hearted
CTV 26; F Feet 137; Iron I 59; Plea 122; P Life II 50; PW 251; TD 121; Voi I 118; (part) *Say 64*

Summer Farm (Norman MacCaig)

Straws like tame lightnings lie about the grass
Out 34

Summer Moods (John Clare)
I love at eventide to walk alone
Out 38

The Waking (Theodore Roethke)
I strolled across
Deli 64

SUN

from *Jazz for Five* (John Smith)
Have you ever heard the sun in the sky
Drum 19

Moon and Sun (Anglo-Saxon riddles, trans G. Bone, K. Crossley-Holland)
I saw a creature sally forth with booty
PW 27
I saw a strange creature
Puf M 183; Tap 31

Rising Sun (anon, trans Fon)
Softly, softly, Lisa-O
Afr II 2

SUPERMARKETS

The Fate of the Supermarket Manager (Kit Wright)
There was once a supermarket manager
Gang 109; Pac 17; Wri R 70

Jones the Grocer (Herbert Williams)
Jones the Grocer, we called him
Theme VI 6

Superman (John Updike)
I drive my car to supermarket
Imp 83; Liv 85

Supermarket (Felice Holman)
I'm/lost/among a/maze of cans
Pac 6; Sort 70

SUPERNATURAL

See also Theme II 3–24
See also Dwarfs, Fairies Ghosts, Giants, Goblins, Ogres, Trolls, Werewolves, Will o' the Wisps, Witches, Wizards

The House on the Hill (Wes Magee)
It was built years ago
ADT 106

A January Night (Thomas Hardy)
The rain smites more and more
Voi III 164

SUPERSTITION

The Evil Eye (John Ciardi)
Nona poured oil on the water and saw the eye
Sun 225

Superstition (Minji Karibo)
I know/that when a grumbling old woman
Rhy 74

The Rowan (Violet Jacob)
When the days were still as deith
Ring 126; Scot 97

Unlucky Boat (George Mackay Brown)
That boat has killed three people. Building her
Ring 121

The Well (John Loveday)
You'll never bring him up, my dear
Over 28

Yule Log (Robert Herrick)
Kindle the Christmas brand, and then
Star 73

SURFING

The Surfer (Judith Wright)
He thrust his joy against the weight of the sea
Mov 113; SAS 38; Tam 7; Tap 64

The Surf-Rider (Zulfikar Ghose)
Out in the Golfe de Gascogne, on the far
Theme V 38

SURGERY

A Correct Compassion (James Kirkup)
Cleanly, sir, you went to the core of the matter
Conf 111

SWAGMEN

The Dead Swagman (Nancy Cato)
His rusted billy left beside the tree
Bill 102; Voi II 122

Independence (Nancy Cato)
How the red road stretched before us, mile on mile
Mov 89

Mad Jack's Cockatoo (anon)
There's a man that went out in the flood-time and drought
Bat S 27

The Swagman (Roland Robinson)
Transfixed by stars, he lay upon the bed
SAS 149

The Swagman's Rest (A. B. Paterson)
We buried old Bob where the bloodwoods wave
Iron III 70

Waltzing Matilda (anon)
Once a jolly swagman camped by a billabong
Aus 29; Fab PV 259; Gold II 21; Merry 344; Peng B 353; SAS 97

SWALLOWS

The Swallow (Lucy Aitken)
Swallow, that on rapid wing
Ox CV 110

The Swallows (Andrew Young)
All day – when early morning shone
Touch I 77

Swallows over the South Downs (Mary Holden)
England, we're here again
F Feet 39; WAS 40

Work and Play (Ted Hughes)
The swallow of summer, she toils all summer
Hug S 36; ND 51

SWANS

A Riddle (Anglo-Saxon)
(trans K. Crossley-Holland)

Silent is my dress when I step
across the earth
Drag 23; Word 122
(trans Michael Alexander)
When it is earth I tread
Voi I 8

The Silver Swan (anon)
The silver swan, who living had no
note
Fab CV 89; Rat 389; Zoo 65

The Swans (Clifford Dyment)
Midstream they met. Challenger
and champion
Time 55

The Wild Swans at Coole
(W. B. Yeats)
The trees are in their autumn
beauty
*Bir 54; F Feet 197; Flock 260; FM
232; Touch V 170*

SWEET PEAS

Sweet Peas (John Keats)
Here are sweet-peas, on tiptoe for a
flight
P Life II 48

SWEETS

Sweet Song (Vernon Scannell)
This is the sweet song
Fir 35; Pac 106

SWIFTS

Swifts (Ted Hughes)
Fifteenth of May. Cherry-blossom.
The swifts
Hug S 27; Hug SP 146; Mus 109

SWIMMING

Down at the swimming-pool
(Gerda Mayer)
Down at the swimming-pool
May K 15

One Tuesday when I was about ten
(Michael Rosen)
One Tuesday when I was about
ten
Sec 44

The Swimmers (Edward Shanks)
The cove's a shining plate of blue
and green
Ev 240; Theme V 35

Swimming Pool (Marion Lines)
Splash! Echo!
Lin T 7

With a Swimmer's Stroke (Lord
Byron)
How many a time have I
Ev 239

SWINGING

The Swing (Robert Louis
Stevenson)
How do you like to go up in a
swing
CTV 116; Ste CG 34

Swing Song (A. A. Milne)
Here I go up in my swing
Mil NS 77

A Swing Song (William
Allingham)
Swing, swing/Sing, sing
CTV 127

SWORD-FISHES

The Sword-Fish (Lord Alfred
Douglas)
The sword-fish is an awful brute
Dou T 9

Xiphias or Swordfish (George
Barker)
Xiphias is the swordfish. He
Bar A 'X'

TABLE MANNERS

See also BBGG 45–62
See also Greed

The Boy Serving at Table (John
Lydgate ?1370–1450)
My dear child, first thyself enable
Ox CV 4

Dave Dirt came to Dinner (Kit
Wright)
Dave Dirt came to dinner
Pac 55; Wri H 61

Manners at Table when away from Home (anon c. 1480)
Little children, here ye may lere [learn]
Ox CV 7

Table Manners (Gelett Burgess)
The Goops they lick their fingers
BBGG 45; CTV 57

Table Rules for Little Folks (anon c. 1858)
In silence I must take my seat
Ox CV 226

The Visitor (Katherine Pyle)
John's manners at the table
BBGG 50; Once 74

With his Mouth full of Food (Shel Silverstein)
Milford Dupree, though he knew it was rude
Pac 89

TABLE TENNIS

Ping-Pong (Gareth Owen)
Swatted between bats
ADT 90; Owe S 51; Word 120

TAILORS

Tailor (Eleanor Farjeon)
I saw a little tailor sitting stitch, stitch, stitching
Ox CV 331; Puf Q 24

TALES: CAUTIONARY

The Boy who Laughed at Santa Claus (Ogden Nash)
In Baltimore there lived a boy
BBGG 16; Nas C 50

The Chewing-Gum Song (Roald Dahl)
Dear friends, we surely all agree
Gang 120

The Hoyden (anon 1811)
Miss Agnes had two or three dolls and a box
PC 48

Ice-Cream Poem (Gerda Mayer)
The chiefest of young Ethel's vices
May K 26; Poems 19

Inhuman Henry (A. E. Housman)
O would you know why Henry sleeps
BBGG 25

Meddlesome Matty (Ann Taylor)
One naughty trick has often spoiled
Ox CV 115

Winifred Waters (William Brighty Rands)
Winifred Waters sat and sighed
Ox CV 237

TALES: CAUTIONARY (BELLOC)

Charles Augustus Fortescue (Hilaire Belloc)
The nicest child I ever knew
Bel CV 48; Puf V 138

George (Hilaire Belloc)
When George's Grandmamma was told
Fab NV 159; FV 122; Rhyme III 22

Henry King (Hilaire Belloc)
The chief defect of Henry King
Bat L 139; BBGG 48; Bel CV 22; Fab Non 246; Fab UV 101; FV 113; GV V 28; P Life II 16

Jack and his pony Tom (Hilaire Belloc)
Jack had a little pony, Tom
Bel CV 62; F Feet 178; Hor 72

Jim, who ran away from his Nurse and was eaten by a Lion (Hilaire Belloc)
There was a boy whose name was Jim
Bat L 25; BBGG 70; Bel CV 15; Fab NV 161; Merry 284; ND 109; Ox CV 312; Young 62

Lord Lundy (Hilaire Belloc)
Lord Lundy, from his earliest years
P Tale 162

Matilda (Hilaire Belloc)
Matilda told such dreadful lies
BE 48; Bel CV 26; CBC 102; DP I 24; EGV 304; Fab CV 96; Ox CV 314; Ox PC 30; P Life IV 90; Puf V 152; Rhyme IV 79

Rebecca (Hilaire Belloc)
A Trick that everyone abhors
Bel CV 42; DP II 33; Fab NV 156; FV 116; Ox LV 195

TALES: CAUTIONARY (HOFFMAN)

Augustus (Dr Heinrich Hoffman)
Augustus was a chubby lad
ADT 52; BBGG 48; Fab NV 101; Fab UV 95; Non 164; Ox CV 205; Pac 71; Young 57

Harriet and the Matches (Dr Heinrich Hoffman)
It's really almost past belief
Fab NV 157; Non 152

Johnny Head-in-Air (Dr Heinrich Hoffman)
As he trudged along to school
ADT 62; BBGG 78; Fab NV 162; Non 168; Ox CV 206

Little Suck-a-Thumb (Dr Heinrich Hoffman)
One day Mamma said, 'Conrad dear
Fab NV 95; Non 162

The Story of Fidgety Philip (Dr Heinrich Hoffman)
One evening Philip's Father said
FV 118; Non 166; Ox CV 208

The Story of Flying Robert (Dr Heinrich Hoffman)
When the rain comes tumbling down
Mov 97; Non 172

TALES: TALL

Adventures of Isabel (Ogden Nash)
Isobel met an enormous bear
Croc 22; Fab NV 105; My R 33; Nas C 88; Once 143; P Life II 10; Young 72
Once on a night as black as pitch (part) *PT II 12*

The Lum Hat wantin' the Croon (Dr David Rorie)
The burn was big wi' spate
Scot 18

Mickety Mulga (T. Ranken)
He worked wid us at Wantigong
SAS 104

Once there was a Sailor (D. J. Enright)

Once there was a sailor and he sailed off to sea
Enr R 7

Yarns (Carl Sandburg)
They have yarns
Str 18

TALKERS

Chocolates (Louis Simpson)
Once some people were visiting Chekhov
Mus 88; Ox Con 188

The Huntsman (Edward Lowbury)
Kagwa hunted the lion
Many 86; Nar 36

Reflections at Dawn (Phyllis McGinley)
I wish I owned a Dior dress
Ox LV 244

The Silent Shearer (A. B. Paterson)
Weary and listless, sad and slow
Pat A 68

Talk (D. H. Lawrence)
I wish people, when you sit near them
Imp 15; PW 299; Touch I 25

They Walked and Talked (C. Uche Okeke, Nigeria)
They talked and walked
Bite I 8; RAP 76; Rhy 62

The Two Old Women of Mumbling Hill (James Reeves)
The two old trees on Mumbling Hill
Ree C 47

A Word in Edgeways (Charles Tomlinson)
Tell me about yourself they
OX LV 318

TATTOOISTS

'Blackie, the Electric Rembrandt' (Thom Gunn)
We watch through the shop-front while
Flock 130; Seven 86

from *Tattooed* (William Plomer)
On his arm he wears
Touch II 166

Chocolates (Guy Boas)
Here the seats are; George, old man
CBC 140

THIEVES

The Burglary (Tony Connor)
It's two o'clock now; somebody's pausing in the street
Theme III 6

The Conscientious Deacon (Vachell Lindsay)
Black cats, grey cats, green cats miau
By 237

The Great Train Robbery 1963 (Barbara Wilson)
Come listen to my tale of the southbound Royal Mail
Bal 180

He was a Strong but Simple Man (Gregory Harrison)
He was a strong but simple man
Four 91

The Man who finds his Son has become a Thief (Raymond Souster)
Coming into the store at first angry
Gold III 26; Theme III 5

THISTLES

The Fear of Flowers (John Clare)
The nodding oxeye bends before the wind
Poems II 52

Thistle (Laurie Lee)
Thistle, blue bunch of daggers
Poems II 54

Thistledown (Andrew Young)
Silver against blue sky
Poems II 53

Thistles (Ted Hughes)
Against the rubber tongues of cows and the hoeing hands of men
Drag 68; Gold II 35; Hug SP 63; Mod 173; Poems II 56; Touch V 163; Voi III 171

Thistles (Jon Stallworthy)
Half grown before half seen
Poems II 57

THRUSHES

See also Missel Thrushes

Come In (Robert Frost)
As I came to the edge of the woods
By 231; F Feet 151

The Darkling Thrush (Thomas Hardy)
I leant upon a coppice gate
Choice 134; Rat 120; RR 89; Ten 93

The Throstle (Alfred, Lord Tennyson)
Summer is coming, summer is coming
Bk S 16; F Feet 202; WAS 41

Thrush (Phoebe Hesketh)
Timorously I write about the thrush
Hes S 20

Thrushes (Ted Hughes)
Terrifying are the attent sleek thrushes on the lawn
Seven 149; Time 73

The Thrush's Nest (John Clare)
Within a thick and spreading hawthorn bush
Bir 23; By 153; Ev 90; F Feet 42; Flock 12; My V 118; Ox PC 67; This W 117

THUNDER AND LIGHTNING

An African Thunderstorm (David Rubadiri)
From the west
AP 91; Att 70; Bite I 52; Prel III 19; RAP 42; Rhy 112

Description of a Thunderstorm (John Clare)
Slow boiling up, on the horizon's brim
Bat R 91; Iron II 47

Giant Thunder (James Reeves)
Giant Thunder, striding home
Al III 19; Drum 77; My V 120; Pac 105; Ree C 105; TD 39

from *Summer Storm* (James Russell Lowell)
Look! look! that livid flash!
TD 38

Thunder (Walter de la Mare)
Call the cows home!
de la M Col 29; Iron I 6

Thunder and Lightning (James Kirkup)
Blood punches through every vein
Out 59; TD 37; Touch II 38

What could be lovelier
(Elizabeth Coatsworth)
What could be lovelier than to hear
TD 124

TIDES

The Tide in the River (Eleanor Farjeon)
The tide in the river
Al II 22; Bits b; Far M 21; My V 10; Ox PC 136; Poems 40; PT I 7; Puf Q 29; Tap 56

The Tide rises, the Tide falls (H. W. Longfellow)
The tide rises, the tide falls
Fan 126; PT I 20; Rain 86; R Eig 75; Say 64; Sea 54

The Tides to me, the Tides to me (George Barker)
The tides to me, the tides to me
Sea 73

TIGERS

India (W. J. Turner)
They hunt, the velvet tigers in the jungle
Drum 63; OX PC 112; Round 25; Word 56

Tiger (Leslie Norris)
He stalks in his vivid stripes
Four 70

The Tiger Caged (John Cotton)
The tiger treads his cage
Tel 23

Tigress (Ted Hughes)
She grins-lifts
Hug M 14

The Tyger (William Blake)
Tyger! Tyger! burning bright
Bat A 55; Bat C 62; BB 10; By 109; Choice 43; Come 153; Deli 82; DP IV 85; EGV 112; Fab CV 64; Fab PR 61; FM 89; Gold I 58; ND 80; Ox PC 111; Plea 53; P Life IV 15; Puf V 52; PW 154; Rat 444; Theme I 21; Touch II 66

TIME

Blue Girls (John Crowe Ransom)
Twirling your blue skirts, travelling the sward
Conf 91; Fab LP 56; Gold IV 16

Cities and Thrones (Rudyard Kipling)
Cities and thrones and powers
By 210; Theme VII 64

Do not I, Time (Stephen Hawes)
Do not I, Time, cause Nature to augment
Trad 71

Even such is Time (Sir Walter Ralegh)
Even such is time, which takes in trust
Burn 167; Iron III 24; ND 239; Plea 288; Rat 143; RR 100; TD 148

His Poetrie His Pillar (Robert Herrick)
Onely a little more
Say 99

Late Home (Brian Lee)
I looked up – the sun had gone down
Lee L 7; Poems 90

Lines on a clock in Chester Cathedral (anon)
When as a child I laughed and wept
Puf V 214

Past. Present, Future (Emily Bronte)
Tell me, tell me, smiling child
Bat C 13

The Slow Starter (Louis MacNeice)
A watched clock never moves, they said
Look 81; Mod 76

Sonnet 60 (William Shakespeare)
Like as the waves make towards the pebbled shore
Bat C 35

The Sunlight on the Garden (Louis MacNeice)
The sunlight on the garden
By 292

Time, you Old Gypsy-man (Ralph Hodgson)
Time, you old gypsy-man
By 223; This W 133; TD 154

Times and Seasons (A.V.)
To everything there is a season
Ecclesiastes III 1–8; GV IV 14

What does the Clock say? (George Barker)
What does the clock say?
Bar R 52; Hap II 20

TIMES PAST

The Past (R. W. Emerson)
The debt is paid
Like 143

Then (Walter de la Mare)
Twenty, forty, sixty, eighty
de la M Col 37; P Life I 69; R Eig 114

TOADS

A Friend in the Garden (Juliana Horatia Ewing)
He is not John the gardener
Come 139; Ox CV 256

Speckle-black Toad (George Darley)
Speckle-black toad and freckle-green frog
FM 134

The Toads' Chorus (Rumer Godden)
The Toads' choir will never tire
Zoo 48

warty bliggens the toad (Don Marquis)
i met a toad
In O II 44

TONGUE-TWISTERS

See Bat L 75

TOOTHACHE

Address to Toothache (Robert Burns)
My curse upon your venom'd stang
Iron IV 32; Touch III 65

A Charm against the Toothache (John Heath-Stubbs)
Venerable Mother Toothache
Dawn 53; Flock 231; My V 159; Poems 58

TORTOISES

Baby Tortoise (D. H. Lawrence)
You know what it is to be born alone
Choice 194; Gold IV 65; World 66

Living Tenderly (May Swenson)
My body a rounded stone
J Vo II 57

Tortoise (David Speechley)
Lumbering carefully over stone and earth
Fan 28; Word 48

TOUCANS

Toucannery (Jack Prelutsky)
whatever one toucan can do
Lolli I 14

TOWER BLOCKS

Apartment House (Gerald Rafferty)
A filing-cabinet of human lives
Bite I 46

Half Term (Mick Gowar)
Up and down/Up and down
Gow S 33

Looking Down on Roofs (Marion Lines)
When I lived in a basement
Lin T 46; Sec 108

New Block (Patric Dickinson)
Three hundred fillings high
Liv 90; Tel 37

The Planster's Vision (John Betjeman)
Cut down that timber! Bells, too many and strong
RR 69

Think of this Tower-Block (Michael Rosen)
Think of this tower-block
Poems II 59; Ros W 67; World 38

Tower Block (Marion Lines)
How did I come to be here in the sky?
Lin T 12

TOWN AND COUNTRY

See also Theme VII throughout
See also Cities and Towns

Clancy of the Overflow
(A. B. Paterson)
I had written him a letter which I
had, for want of better
SAS 89

*The Country Mouse and the City
Mouse* (R. S. Sharpe)
In a snug little cot lived a fat little
mouse
Ox CV 139

The Day we moved to Greenford
(Brian Jones)
The day we moved to Greenford all
Theme VII 21

Housing Scheme (Richard
Church)
All summer through
Conf 107; Touch I 108

Mamie (Carl Sandburg)
Mamie beat her head against the
bars of a little Indiana town
Theme VII 9

Northern Nigerian Chiefs (John
Press)
A dozen visiting Nigerian Chiefs
Root 39

Of Evening in the Wintertime
(George Barker)
Of evening in the wintertime
Bar R 17

Spring in Tothill Street (Virginia
Graham)
Spring comes slowly to Tothill
Street
Lon 46

*To Miss Blount on her leaving the
Town* (Alexander Pope)
As some fond virgin, whom her
mother's care
PW 137

The Visit (Queenie Scott-
Hopper)
Amy Elizabeth Ermyntrude Annie
Rhyme II 7

What's wrong with towns?
(Marion Lines)
I've got this aunt who comes to
stay
Lin T 44

TRACTORS

Cynddylan on a Tractor
(R. S. Thomas)
Ah, you should see Cynddylan on a
tractor
*Bite III 9; Choice 307; Dawn 78; DP
IV 79; Gold III 22; Hap 26; Liv 49;
Mod 54; Mov 88; ND 135; PT VI 27;
Theme VII 53; Touch I 8*

Tractor (Ted Hughes)
The tractor stands frozen – an
agony
Hug SP 182

TRAFALGAR

See also Nelson, Lord

The Night of Trafalgar (Thomas
Hardy)
In the wild October night-time
when the wind raved round the
land
Fab CV 258

TRAFFIC JAMS

I Went to the Doctor (Michael
Rosen)
I went to the doctor, yes
Poems II 10; Ros W 59

TRAINS

See Rail and P Rail throughout
See also Accidents: Railway,
Engine Drivers and Firemen,
Porters, Railway Engines,
Railway Stations, Travelling,
Underground, USA: Railroads

TRAINS (L & D)

The Arriving Train (1844)
(Charles Mackay)
Behold, smoke-panoplied, the
wondrous car!
Rail 59

from *The Bridge* (J. Redwood
Anderson)
Out of the silence grows
*DP II 69; P Life IV 38; Tho 15;
Touch II 165*
Here with one leap
Mov 62

Train in Ireland (Kenneth Hopkins)
The train has stopped – it was going only slowly
DP II 74; P Rail 183

The Train now Standing (Michael Rosen)
The train now standing
Ros W 51

Travel (Edna St Vincent Millay)
The railway track is miles away
Rail 38

Waving at Trains (Roger McGough)
Do people who wave at trains
NV 105

TRAINS (N)

'Are ye right there, Michael?' (Percy French)
You may talk of Columbus's sailing
Oral 196

Night Mail (W. H. Auden)
This is the night mail crossing the border
DP II 71; Ev 226; Gold I 34; Like 53; ND 17; P Life IV 40; P Scot 23; Rail 53; Touch II 18; Young 86

Oh! Mr Porter (Thomas le Brunn)
Lately I just spent a week with my old Aunt Brown
Rail 84

Opening the Oxford Railway (anon 1852)
If you will listen to my song
Bal 134

The Railway Historical Steam Weekend (Max Fatchen)
'Will you come,' says the letter, 'and join our outing'
Fat W 15

Skimbleshanks the Railway Cat (T. S. Eliot)
There's a whisper down the line at 11.49
DP II 21; Eli OP 40; Fab CV 285; Ox LV 218; P Rail 67; Rail 32; Touch II 53; Young 14

The Train to Glasgow (Wilma Horsbrugh)
Here is the train to Glasgow
CBC 40; Fab NV 251; Hor B 32; Once 11; Young 90

TRAMPOLINES

The Trampoline (John Pudney)
You can weigh what you like for a trampoline
Ev 246; Theme V 64

TRAMPS

See also Hoboes, Swagmen
Ballad (Henry Treece)
Oh come, my joy, my soldier boy
Dawn 40; Hap 59; Tel 28

Lousy Peter (Osbert Sitwell)
Lousy Peter's terror was the workhouse
Conf 56

Move On (William Plomer)
They made love under bridges, lacking beds
Theme III 8

Tramp (R. S. Thomas)
A knock at the door
Choice 301; Theme III 33

The Vagabond (John Drinkwater)
I know the pools where the grayling lies
P Life IV 21

The Vagabond (Robert Louis Stevenson)
Give to me the life I love
ND 137; P Life IV 20; Puf V 175; (part) DT 61

TRANSFIGURATION

The Transfiguration (Edwin Muir)
So from the ground we felt that virtue branch
Ring 26

TRANSPLANTING

Transplanting (Theodore Roethke)
Watching hands transplanting
Deli 91; Full 86; J Vo IV 84; Tel 81; World 76

TRANSPORT

See also Bicycling, Buses,
Lorries, Motor Cars, Motor-
Cycles, Railways, Traffic Jams,
Travel, Travelling

Transport (Marion Lines)
London Bus! Fun for us!
Lin T 16

Transportation Problem (Richard
Armour)
Kiddy cars of little tykes
Mov 118

TRANSPORTATION

Jim Jones at Botany Bay (anon)
O listen for a moment, lads
*Bat S 81; Fab PV 257; Peng B 302;
Root 63; Theme III 11*

Old Botany Bay (Mary Gilmore)
I'm old/Botany Bay
Imp 75; SAS 74

Van Diemen's Land (anon)
Come all you gallant poachers that
ramble void of care
Fab Bal 224; Iron III 21
You rambling lads of Liverpool
Gold II 23; Rhyme IV 59

TRAPS

The Rabbit (W. H. Davies)
Not even when the early birds
Theme I 60

The Snare (James Stephens)
I hear a sudden cry of pain!
*Bite I 32; Blow 28; Deli 87; DP I 10;
F Feet 129; My V 129; ND 84; Ox PC
130; P Life II 25; Rhyme III 53*

TRAVEL

See Air Travel, Explorers,
Railways, Roads, Space Travel,
Trains, Travelling

TRAVEL: IMAGINARY

Hay's Wharf (Richard Church)
Who hasn't heard of London
Bridge?
Lon 140

The Ice-Cart (Wilfrid Gibson)
Pe.:ched on my city office-stool
DP IV 45; Touch II 144

Roundabout (James Reeves)
At midsummer fair on a galloping
pony
Puf Q 70; Ree C 11; Say 39

Travel (Robert Louis
Stevenson)
I should like to rise and go
*CTC 10; Deli 128; DP I 46; Ev 138;
Fab CV 100; Out Sc 86; R Nine 37; Ste
CG 10*

The Traveller (Brian Lee)
The world is vast in the light of my
torch
Lee L 32

TRAVELLING

The Boy in the Train
(M. C. Smith)
Whit wey does the engine say *Toot-
toot?*
Ring 9; Scot 22

Dawn (Rupert Brooke)
Opposite me two Germans snore
and sweat
P Rail 179; Rail 56

The End of the Road (Hilaire
Belloc)
In these boots and with this staff
*Ev 221; Mov 16; Puf V 179; Rhyme
III 36; Word 110*

Johnny Fife and Johnny's Wife
(anon)
Oh, Johnny Fife and Johnny's wife
Puf Y 19

Midnight on the Great Western
(Thomas Hardy)
In the third-class seat sat the
journeying boy
*Poems II 50; P Rail 193; Prel I 45;
Rail 13*

TREACHERY

The Castle (Edwin Muir)
All through that summer at ease
we lay
Ev 211; TCN 18

TREE CLIMBING

Birches (Robert Frost)
When I see birches bend to left and right
Choice 281; DP IV 28; Gold II 33; Hap 55; Rat 78; Tam 25; Ten 81; Touch V 155 (part) *Out Sc 80*

The Climb and the Dream (Vernon Scannell)
The boy had never seen the tree before
Sca A 12

The Rescue (Hal Summers)
The boy climbed up into the tree
Dawn 58; DP I 42; Gold I 18; Poems 88; Prel I 16; Tap 29

Windy Boy in a Windswept Tree (Geoffrey Summerfield)
The branch swayed, swerved
Liv 6; Out Sc 22; PT V 15; Theme V 51; Word 142

TREES

See also Beeches, Birches, Cherry Trees, Chestnuts, Elms, Holly Trees, Oaks, Pines, Plane Trees, Poplars, Willows Weeping, Woodmen, Woods

Child's Song in Spring (E. Nesbit)
The silver birch is a dainty lady
Come 93; Ox CV 308; Puf V 18; Rhyme I 42

The Hollow Tree (John Clare)
How oft a summer shower hath started me
Gold I 7; Out Sc 71

Pruning Trees (Po Chu-I, trans Arthur Waley)
Trees growing – right in front of my window
Flock 107; Gold III 49; Pluc 82; PT VI 24; Theme VII 55

Sweeney praises the Trees (Seamus Heaney)
The branchy leafy oak-tree
Rat 411

Tree at my Window (Robert Frost)
Tree at my window, window tree
Choice 286

Trees (Sara Coleridge)

The oak is called the king of trees
Come 96; Croc 80; Ox CV 170; Rhyme II 53

TROJAN WAR

Sthenelus' Daughter (John Masefield)
King Sthenelus, my father, has often told me
TCN 13

TROLLS

Gunderstridge (R. C. Scriven)
The troll's daughter
Drum 146

Perry-the-Winkle (J. R. R. Tolkien)
The lonely Troll he sat on a stone
Tol T 41

The Stone Troll (J. R. R. Tolkien)
Troll sat alone on his seat of stone
Str 13; Tol T 39

The Troll (Jack Prelutsky)
Be wary of the loathsome troll
Night 20; Third 47

The Troll (Thomas Blackburn)
A troll once lived in a high pasture
Bla D 26

TROUT

Brooktrout (Ted Hughes)
The Brooktrout, superb as a matador
Hug U 32

Trout (Mary Innes)
In mountain lake and stream the trout
Inn B 'T'

Trout (Seamus Heaney)
Hangs, a fat gun-barrel
Drag 17; Four 48; RR 188; Tho 64; Touch V 184

The Trout (John Montague)
Flat on the bank I parted
Theme I 29

TUGS

Tugs (Sir George R. Hamilton)
At noon three English dowagers ride
Lon 138

TURKEYS

A Black November Turkey
(Richard Wilbur)
Nine white chickens come
Voi I 91

A Melancholy Lay (Marjorie
Fleming, aged 8, 1811)
Three Turkeys fair their last have
breathed
Fab CV 66; This W 29

The Turkey (Ogden Nash)
There is nothing more perky
Nas C 75

Turkeys Observed (Seamus
Heaney)
One observes them; one expects
them
Many 71; Touch IV 170

TURPIN, DICK

The Ballad of Dick Turpin (Alfred
Noyes)
The daylight moon looked quietly
down
DP II 89; Gold I 49

My Bonny Black Bess (anon)
Dick Turpin bold! Dick, hie away
BHL 39; Poems 80

Turpin's Valour (anon 1739)
On Hounslow Heath, as I rode o'er
Bal 51

TURTLE DOVES

The Turtle Dove (John Heath-
Stubbs)
One day, one day
Hea P 32; Sun 212

TURTLES

The Little Turtle (Vachell
Lindsay)
There was a little turtle
Croc 37; CTV 13; Hi 11; J Vo I 59

Tony the Turtle (E. V. Rieu)
Tony was a turtle
*DP I 23; Fab NV 85; P Life III 75;
Puf Q 124*

TWINS

The Twins (H. S. Leigh)
In form and feature, face and limb
*CBC 80; CTV 93; DP I 34; Prel I 9;
R Nine 53*

ULSTER

Belfast Linen or *The Ballad of
William Bloat* (anon)
In a mean abode on the Shankill
Road
Oral 200; Ox LV 182

Derry (Robert Greacen)
As a child in Derry I heard the
shots
Root 40

The ould Orange Flute (Nugent
Bohem)
In the County Tyrone, near the
town of Dungannon
Fab Bal 216; Fab PV 192; Oral 198

ULYSSES

The Return (Edwin Muir)
The doors flapped open in Ulysses'
house
PW 305

Ulysses (Alfred, Lord
Tennyson)
It little profits that an idle king
*Choice 92; Fab PR 153; Plea 338; PW
221; Scene 167*
Come, my friends
P Life IV 93

UNCLES

My Wicked Uncle (Derek
Mahon)
His was the first corpse I had ever
seen
Ox Con 273

The Spitfire on the Northern Line
(Brian Jones)
Harry was an uncle. I saw him
twice
Jon S 10

Uncle Albert (Vernon Scannell)
When I was almost eight years old
Prel I 37

UNDERGROUND RAILWAYS

In the Tube (Richard Aldington)
The electric car jerks
P Rail 175; Theme VII 11

Subway (Etsuro Sakamoto)
Every day I step into a coffin
Imp 83

The Subway in New York
(Tsutomu Fukuda)
Here forests of skyscrapers
Mov 59

From *Summoned by Bells* (John Betjeman)
. . . There was no station, north to Finsbury Park
Rail 55

The Underground (Guy Boas)
The Underground
Mov 60

Underground (Mary Kendall 1861 – ?)
A quarter of an hour to wait
Rail 43

UNHAPPINESS

To the Terrestial Globe
(W. S. Gilbert)
Roll on, thou ball, roll on!
Fab Non 165

UNICORNS

The Late Passenger (C. S. Lewis)
The sky was low, the sounding rain was falling dense and dark
Str 81

Unicorn (Zoë Bailey)
Where shall we find him?
Drum 156

Unicorn (George Barker)
When the unicorn descends from the Hartz Mountains
Bar A 'U'

Unicorn (Mary Innes)
The unicorn/With its single horn
Inn B 'U'

The Unicorn (Edward Lowbury)
Look hard enough and you will find
Low G 25

The Unicorn (E. V. Rieu)
The Unicorn stood, like a king in a dream
AM 78

Unicorn (William Jay Smith)
The unicorn with the long white horn
Puf Y 111

UNITED STATES OF AMERICA

See USA

UNKNOWN CITIZENS

The Man in the Bowler Hat
(A. S. J. Tessimond)
I am the unnoticed, the unnoticeable man
Burn 135; Poems II 124; Theme III 54

The Unknown Citizen
(W. H. Auden)
He was found by the Bureau of Statistics to be
Burn 133; Choice 244; Liv 84; Ox LV 259; RR 130; Touch V 30

UNPOPULARITY

Fat Boy (Mick Gowar)
I know it
Gow S 20

Words (Brian Lee)
Sticks and stones
Lee L 83

USA

Hot Night on Water Street (Louis Simpson)
A hot midsummer night on Water Street
DP IV 47

My Country (Samuel Francis Smith)
My country, 'tis of thee
EGV 190

The Pampered (Marya Mannes)
Junior needs the car tonight
RR 17

The Star-Spangled Banner
(Francis Scott Key)
O say, can you see, by the dawn's
early light
EGV 141

Stately Verse (anon)
If Mary goes far out to sea
FV 39

USA: BLACKS

See also Being Black, Race
Relations
America (Claude McKay,
Jamaican)
Although she feeds me bread of
bitterness
Att 20

I, too, sing America (Langston
Hughes)
I, too, sing America
Att 21; Like 119

USA: CIVIL WAR

See also Lincoln
Barbara Frietchie (John
Greenleaf Whittier)
Up from the meadows rich with
corn
DP I 65; Fab PR 141

Battle Hymn of the Republic (Julia
Ward Howe)
Mine eyes have seen the glory of
the coming of the Lord
EGV 233; Fab PR 173

Marching through Georgia
(H. C. Work)
Bring the good old bugle, boys,
we'll sing another song
Fab PR 186

Old John Brown's Body (anon)
Old John Brown's body lies
a-mould'ring in the grave
Iron II 39

USA: PIONEERS AND
THE WEST

See also James, Jesse
The Ballad of William Sycamore
(Stephen Vincent Benét)
My father, he was a mountaineer
Wind 87

Idaho (anon)
They say there is a land
Deli 132; Fab PV 178

Pretty Boy Floyd (Woody
Guthrie)
Come and gather 'round me,
children
J Vo IV 37

The Sioux Indians (anon)
I'll sing you a song and it'll be a
sad one
Bk Bal 88; Voi I 51

Sweet Betsy from Pike (anon)
Did you ever hear tell of sweet
Betsy from Pike
Fab Bal 239; Iron IV 107; Peng B 340

Tying a Knot in the Devil's Tail
(anon)
Way up high in the Syree peaks
Bill 78

USA: RAILROADS

See also P Rail, Rail
Boy on a Train (Steven Allen)
In the night, the clackety night,
quiv'ring in the Pullman
P Rail 193

Casey Jones (anon)
Come all you rounders, listen here
*Bat C 46; Bite I 14; Bk Bal 93; DP II
75; Duck 91; Gold I 33; Iron IV 6; Ox
PC 76; P Rail 58; Rail 66; Touch II
106; Wind 85*

Coal for Mike (Bertolt Brecht,
trans H. R. Hays)
I have heard how in Ohio
DP II 77

John Henry (anon)
John Henry was a very small boy *or*
Well, every Monday morning
*Afr II 49; BHL 13; Bk Bal 94; Fab
Bal 243; Imp 42; Iron IV 27; Peng B
322; P Tale 29; Touch IV 60*

The Railroad (Ebenezer Jones
1820–60)
Why! why to your arch do the
people drift
Rail 28

*Railroad-Coach Seating-
Arrangements I cannot but deplore
you* (Morris Bishop)

What a BOON to literature railway
carriages are!
P Rail 31

Song of the Freight Car
(Strickland W. Gillilan)
I'm a bumped and battered
freight-car on a side-track in the
yard
P Rail 25

*What the Engines Said: Opening of
the Pacific Railroad* (Bret Harte)
What was it the engines said?
P Rail 184

Workin' on the Railway (anon)
In eighteen hundred and forty-one
[eighty-one]
Rail 16; Rhyme III 37

The Wreck of the Six-Wheel Driver
(anon)
Joseph Mickel was a good engineer
Rail 50

USA: WAR OF INDEPENDENCE

Paul Revere's Ride (Henry
Wadsworth Longfellow)
Listen, my children, and you shall
hear
*DP II 44; EGV 178; Fab PR 136;
Nar 167; Str 71*

VAUGHAN, HENRY

At the Grave of Henry Vaughan
(Siegfried Sassoon)
Above the voiceful windings of a
river
Sun 233

VEGETARIANS

Vegetarians (Roger McGough)
Vegetarians are cruel, unthinking
people
NV 90

VENICE

On the Lido (Arthur Hugh
Clough)
On her still lake the city sits
Sea 76

VICUNAS

Vicuna (Mary Innes)
The vicuna's a creature with long
silky hair
Inn B 'V'

VIKINGS

Abbey Tomb (Patricia Beer)
I told them not to ring the bells
Poems II 80

The Danes (George Walter
Thornbury)
Their sails, black as a starless night
P Life IV 50

Harp Song of the Dane Women
(Rudyard Kipling)
What is a woman, that you forsake
her
*BE 40; Poems II 79; RR 38; Theme VI
58*

O'er the wild gannet's bath
(George Darley)
O'er the wild gannet's bath
Sea 234

The Raiders (Alastair Cameron)
The raiders came out o'er the land
this morn
BE 41

Thorkild's Song (Rudyard
Kipling)
There's no wind along these seas
Sea 235

VIOLINS

See also Fiddlers
At the Railway Station, Upway
(Thomas Hardy)
There is not much that I can do
Deli 103; Flock 71; Say 72; Voi I 36

Carol (T. W. Shapcott)
On Friday in the shopping crowd
Sun 39

VIPERS

The Viper (Lord Alfred Douglas)
The viper is a sickening snake
Dou T 28

VIRGIN MARY

Diptych: An Annunciation
(Suzanne Knowles)
She was alone
Mus 37

I sing of a Maiden (anon)
I sing of a maiden
*By 13; Croc 110; Puf V 256; PW 18;
RR 155; TD 105; This W 97; Touch I
43*

Lady Day (G. James)
Where did Gabriel get a lily
Puf V 20; WAS 39

Magnificat (Book of Common
Prayer)
My soul doth magnify the Lord
DP III 116

The May Magnificat (Gerard
Manley Hopkins)
May is Mary's month, and I
Iron III 33; Sun 154; WAS 72

This Maiden called Mary (anon
fifteenth century)
This maiden called Mary, she was
full mild
RR 153

Welcome, O great Mary (Alice
O'Gallagher)
Welcome thou of high estate
Oral 178

VISIONS

In Midwinter a Wood was (Peter
Levi)
In midwinter a wood was
Sun 82; WAS 167; Word 27

Lowery Cot (L. A. G. Strong)
This is the house where Jesse
White
Sun 90

VISITORS

Domestic Asides (Thomas Hood)
'I really take it very kind
*Bat L 152; CBC 87; DP III 98; Touch
II 111*

Silence (Marianne Moore)
My father used to say
Fab Mod 163

Sir Smasham Uppe (E. V. Rieu)
Good afternoon, Sir Smasham
Uppe!
*CC 32; DP III 97; P Life IV 88; Puf
Q 115; Rhyme IV 72*

VOWELS

The Consonants and Vowels (Mary
O'Neill)
Our vocal chords are harpstrings
ONe W 13

The Five (Jonathan Swift)
We are little airy creatures
*Fab NV 53; Fab UV 139; FV 67;
Merry 252; Ox PC 21; Poems 23; Rain
16; Rhyme II 2*

VULTURES

The Black Vulture (George
Sterling)
Aloof upon the day's immeasured
dome
Bir 71

The Vulture (Hilaire Belloc)
The vulture eats between his meals
*Bits p; Fab NV 77; Fir 33; FV 21; GV
III 25; Ox CV 312; Pac 95; P Life III
74; Young 23*

Vulture (X. J. Kennedy)
The vulture's very like a sack
Sort 43

Vulture (Douglas Livingstone)
On ragged black sails
Touch V 171

Vultures (Simon Pederek)
Bald pate/scrawny neck
Afr II 61

WAGTAILS

Little Trotty Wagtail (John
Clare)
Little Trotty Wagtail, he went in
the rain
*Bir 80; Come 52; Fab NV 32; If 34;
Merry 202; My R 72; Once 43; Ox PC
65; P Life II 26; Puf V 43; Rat 248;
Rhyme III 49* (part) *Lolli I 7*

Wagtail and Baby (Thomas
Hardy)
A baby watched a ford, whereto
Voi I 75

WALES

Welsh Landscape (R. S. Thomas)
To live in Wales is to be conscious
Fab Mod 316; Liv 92; Scene 34

A Welsh Testament
(R. S. Thomas)
All right, I was Welsh. Does it
matter?
Like 133

WALKING

The End of the Road (Hilaire
Belloc)
In these boots and with this staff
*Ev 221; Mov 16; Puf V 179; Rhyme
III 36; Word 110*

WAR

*See also Touch III 148–163; IV
119–134; V 55–76*
See also Air Raids, Battles,
Dirges and Laments, Nuclear
War, Refugees, Sailors, Sea
Battles, Soldiers, Soldiers'
Songs, Spies, Treachery,
Trojan War

As The Team's Head-brass
(Edward Thomas)
As the team's head-brass flashed
out on the turn
Choice 171; Plea 185; Rat 42

The Battle (Edward Lowbury)
Not Alamein or Waterloo
Low G 31

Carentan O Carentan (Louis
Simpson)
Trees in the old days used to stand
Mod 40; Rat 101

Channel Firing (Thomas Hardy)
That night your great guns,
unawares
Rat 103

Conquerors (Henry Treece)
By sundown, we came to a hidden
village
Mod 42; Tel 32

Desperados (David Wevill)
These four lie on a blanket
Tel 33

The Fly (Miroslav Holub, trans
I. Milner and G. Theiner)
She sat on the willow-trunk
Touch III 163

For the Record (R. S. Thomas)
What was your war record,
Prytherch?
Liv 99

Geography Lesson (Zulfikar
Ghose)
When the jet sprang into the sky
Liv 97; Mod 155; Tel 56

*In Time of 'The Breaking of
Nations'* (Thomas Hardy)
Only a man harrowing clods
EGV 262; Rat 211; Ten 95

James Honeyman (W. H. Auden)
James Honeyman was a silent
child
My V 94; Nar 142

The Man He Killed (Thomas
Hardy)
Had he and I but met
Gold IV 59; Rat 267; Touch III 150

The Minstrel Boy (Thomas
Moore)
The minstrel boy to the war is gone
By 148; Prel II 41

*A Protest in the Sixth Year of Ch'ien
Fu (AD 879)* (Ts'ao Sung, trans
Arthur Waley)
The hills and rivers of the lowland
country
Pluc 92; Touch V 112; Voi II 75

The Shield of Achilles
(W. H. Auden)
She looked over his shoulder
Fab Mod 267; Say 155

The Unconcerned (Thomas
Flatman)
Now that the world is all in a maze
Fab CV 263

War (Li Po)
Last year the war was in the north-
east
Imp 87

Where have all the flowers gone?
(Pete Seeger)
Where have all the flowers gone?
Conf 30

The White Horse (Tu Fu, trans
Rewi Alley)

Out of the North-east
Mov 22

WAR: AFTERMATH

The Casualties (John Pepper
Clark, Nigeria)
The casualties are not only those
who are dead
AP 136

Disabled (Wilfred Owen)
He sat in a wheeled chair, waiting
for dark
Touch V 58

Does it Matter? (Siegfried
Sassoon)
Does it matter? – losing your leg?
Conf 30

The Dream (Mungo
B. MacCallum)
Floating in file across a glassy
waste of sand
Bill 141

*Fighting South of the Ramparts
[Castle]* (Chinese, trans Arthur
Waley)
They fought south of the ramparts
[castle]
*Flock 249; Gold III 9; PW 314; Voi II
69*

Grass (Carl Sandburg)
Pile high the bodies at Austerlitz
and Waterloo
Gold III 11; Touch III 162

Gunpowder Plot (Vernon
Scannell)
For days these curious cardboard
buds have lain
*Flock 267; Mod 64; Theme II 58;
Touch III 61; Voi II 17*

*Hearing that his Friend was
Coming Back from the War*
(Wang-Chien, trans Arthur
Waley)
In old days those who went to fight
Voi II 74

The Horses (Edwin Muir)
Barely a twelvemonth after
*Conf 21; Ima 114; Rat 191; Ring 115;
RR 185; Ten 120; Touch V 74*

In Kensington Gardens (Humbert
Wolfe)

Between the oak-tree and the elm
Lon 55

Johnny, I hardly knew Ye (anon)
While going down the road to
sweet Athy
Fab Bal 212; Fab PV 241; Peng B 297

Memorial Tablet (Siegfried
Sassoon)
Squire nagged and bullied till I
went to fight
Bill 155; RR 50; Theme III 63

Mrs McGrath (anon)
'Oh Mrs McGrath!' the sergeant
said
Fab Bal 211

The Return (Francis Newbold)
Who are these silent strangers?
Root 91

'They' (Siegfried Sassoon)
The Bishop tells us: 'When the
boys come back
Bill 141; Touch V 111

Vergiesmeinicht [Forget me not]
(Keith Douglas)
Three weeks gone and the
combatants gone
*Bill 139; Fab Mod 361; Mod 31; TR
107*

Victory (Francis King)
Tempest and flood
TR 189

Will it be so again? (C. Day
Lewis)
Will it be so again?
Conf 33; Look 82

WAR: CHEMICAL

See also War: Vietnam
Open Day at Porton (Adrian
Mitchell)
These bottles are being filled with
madness
Seven 213

WAR: CONSCIENTIOUS
OBJECTORS

The Conscientious Objector (Karl
Shapiro)
The gates clanged and they walked
you into jail
Theme III 66

Dooley is a Traitor (James Michie)
So then you won't fight?
DP IV 60; Theme III 67; Touch IV 107

WARS: BOER

Boots (Rudyard Kipling)
We're foot-slog-slog-slog-sloggin'
over Africa
Fab PR 226

Drummer Hodge (Thomas Hardy)
They throw in Drummer Hodge, to rest
RR 46; Ten 93

WARS: CRIMEA

See also Balaclava
The Kerry Recruit (anon)
One fine morning in May I was tilling the land
PW 22

WARS: SPANISH CIVIL

Bombing Casualties in Spain (Herbert Read)
Doll's faces are rosier, but these were children
Bill 170; Conf 39; Iron IV 79

My Brother was a Pilot (Bertolt Brecht, trans Michael Hamburger)
My brother was a pilot
DP III 65

To the Wife of a Non-interventionist Statesman: March 1938 (Edgell Rickword)
Permit me, madam, to invade
Iron III 46

WARS: VIETNAM

Cease-Fire (Adrian Mitchell)
The outside of my body was half-eaten
Seven 218

Norman Morrison (Adrian Mitchell)
On November 2nd 1965
Seven 221

What Were They Like? (Denise Levertov)
Did the people of Viet Nam
Voi III 108

WARS: 1914–18 (AIR)

The Airman (R. C. Trevelyan)
I do not know – would that I knew!
Conf 27

An Irish Airman foresees his Death (W. B. Yeats)
I know that I shall meet my fate
DP IV 60; EGV 296; Fab CV 270; Fab Mod 74; PW 276; RR 48; Ten 148

When the Plane Dived (Wilfrid Gibson)
When the plane dived and the machine gun spattered
Mov 105; Tel 29

WARS: 1914–18 (GAS)

Dulce et Decorum Est (Wilfred Owen)
Bent double, like old beggars under sacks
Bill 155; Choice 156; ND 180; RR 47; Theme III 64; Touch IV 124

WARS 1914–18 (GENERAL)

Anthem for Doomed Youth (Wilfred Owen)
What passing-bells for those that die as cattle?
Burn 106; Choice 158; Fab Mod 192; Flock 250; Like 169; ND 183; PW 319; Voi III 125

Base Details (Siegfried Sassoon)
If I were fierce, and bald, and short of breath
By 257; ND 173; Touch V 111

The Chances (Wilfred Owen)
I mind as 'ow the night afore that show
Gold IV 34

Counter-Attack (Siegfried Sassoon)
We'd gained our first objective hours before
Bill 152; Touch III 154

The Effect (Siegfried Sassoon)
'He'd never seen so many dead before.'
Burn 107

Futility (Wilfred Owen)
Move him into the sun
Burn 112; Choice 161; Fab Mod 191; PW 317; Rat 170; Touch V 55; Voi III 127

The General (Siegfried Sassoon)
'Good morning; good morning!' the general said
ND 176; Touch V 61

Goliath and David (Robert Graves)
Once an earlier David took
Bat S 48

The Hero (Siegfried Sassoon)
'Jack fell as he'd have wished', the Mother said
Bill 169; Touch IV 122

Home Thoughts from Abroad (John Buchan)
After the war, says the papers, they'll no be content at hame
Scot 71

In Flanders Fields (John McCrea)
In Flanders fields the poppies blow
Fab PR 232

Into Battle (Julian Grenfell)
The naked earth is warm with spring
DP IV 65; Fab PR 243

I saw a Film one Sunday (John Kitching)
I saw a film one Sunday
Sec 116

next to of course god america i (e. e. cummings)
next to of course god america i
Iron III 35; Touch IV 110

The Parable of the Old Man and the Young (Wilfred Owen)
So Abram rose, and clave the wood, and went
By 275; Flock 250; PW 318; Sun 212; Voi III 127

The Send-Off (Wilfred Owen)
Down the close, darkening lanes they sang their way
Choice 155; ND 160; P Rail 138; Rat 374; Touch III 148

Six Young Men (Ted Hughes)
The celluloid of a photograph holds them well
Hug SP 31; Seven 144; Theme VI 75; Time 67

The Soldier (Rupert Brooke)
If I should die, think only this of me
EGV 333; Fab PR 242; ND 163; Touch IV 123

WARS: 1914–18 (TRENCHES)

Attack (Siegfried Sassoon)
At dawn the ridge emerges massed and dun
Gold IV 32; Tel 32; Theme VI 39; Touch III 151

Bayonet Charge (Ted Hughes)
Suddenly he awoke and was running – raw
Conf 28; Hug SP 30; Theme III 62; Touch V 64

Break of Day in the Trenches (Isaac Rosenberg)
The darkness crumbles away
Fab Mod 185; Iron IV 122

Exposure (Wilfred Owen)
Our brains ache, in the merciless iced east winds that knive us
DP IV 54; Fab Mod 188; Rat 145; Theme VI 38

The Rear-Guard (Siegfried Sassoon)
Groping along the tunnel, step by step
Gold IV 32; Touch IV 119

The Sentry (Wilfred Owen)
We'd found an old Boche dug-out, and he knew
Conf 29

A Square Dance (Roger McGough)
In Flanders fields in Northern France
Mer R 72; Mer RR 76

Strange Meeting (Wilfred Owen)
It seemed that out of battle I escaped
Choice 160; EGV 342; Fab Mod 192; Rat 407; TCN 60; Theme II 20; Voi III 129

Suicide in the Trenches (Siegfried Sassoon)
I knew a simple soldier boy
DP IV 59; Theme II 59

What I never saw (Timothy Corsellis, killed in action 1941)
I was ready for death
TR 70

WARS: 1939–45 (AIR)

The Casualty (Ted Hughes)
Farmers in the fields, housewives behind steamed windows
Drag 60

Combat Report (John Pudney)
Just then I saw the bloody Hun
TR 76

Death of an Aircraft: Crete 1941 (Charles Causley)
One day on our village in the month of July
Bill 166; Cau C 81; DP III 76; Nar 133; Seven 50; Time 25

The Death of the Ball Turret Gunner (Randall Jarrell)
From my mother's sleep I fell into the State
Bill 162; Rat 125

For Johnny (John Pudney)
Do not despair
TR 77

The Heart to Carry On (Bertram Warr, killed in action 1943)
Every morning from this home
Bill 160

Night Bombers (anon)
Eastward they climb, black shapes against the grey
Ev 230

'Operations Calling' (David Bourne, killed in action 1941)
'Clearing Black Section
TR 73

Reported Missing (John Bayliss)
With broken wing they limped across the sky
TR 78

Swing Song (Louis MacNeice)
I'm only a wartime working girl
Bill 168

Unseen Fire (R. N. Curry)
This is a damned inhuman sort of war
Mod 26; TR 50

WARS: 1939–45 (BLITZ)

Ballad of the Safe Area (Francis Scarfe)
A little reading and a little loving
TR 55

The Entertainment of War (Roy Fisher)
I saw the garden where my aunt had died
Fab Mod 393

Five Minutes after the Air Raid (Miroslav Holub trans Ian Milner and George Theiner)
In Pilsen
Burn 104; DP III 66

Night Raid (Desmond Hawkins)
The sleepers humped down on the benches
TR 57

Rural Raid (Denton Welch)
Earth opens where the squandered bombs fall wide
TR 59

The Streets of Laredo (Louis MacNeice)
O early one morning I walked out like Agag
Bill 172; Mod 36; Peng B 356

These are Facts (Ruthven Todd)
These are facts: observe them how you will
TR 65

WARS: 1939–45 (GENERAL)

See also TR throughout
See also Churchill, El Alamein

from *Autumn Journal* (Louis MacNeice)
Today was a beautiful day, the sky was a brilliant
TR 13

Bournemouth: September 3rd 1939 (Anthony Thwaite)
My summer ends, and term begins next week
Over 23

In Westminster Abbey (John Betjeman)
Let me take this other glove off
Ox LV 249; Touch IV 105

The Light of Day (David Geraint Jones, died of wounds 1944)
The light of day is cold and grey and there is no more peace
TR 154

Now as Then (Anne Ridler)
When under Edward or Henry the English armies
TR 19

St Aubin D'Aubigné: August 1944 (Paul Dehn)
It was only a small place and they had cheered us too much
TR 180

Snipers (Roger McGough)
When I was kneehigh to a tabletop
Mer R 74; Mer RR 78

War Dead: La Spezia: April 1945 (Gavin Ewart)
With grey arm twisted over a green face
TR 178

WARS: 1939–45 (LOCAL DEFENCE VOLUNTEERS)

The Stand-To (C. Day Lewis)
Autumn met me today as I walked over Castle Hill
TR 48

WARS: 1939–45 (SEA)

Action Stations (John Wedge)
'Action Stations'. Tin hats and apprehension
TR 117

A Day in Early Summer (Charles Causley)
A day in early summer
Cau F 85

The Night Patrol (Alan Ross)
We sail at dusk. The red moon
Mov 36; Tel 31; Time 131; Touch III 160

Song of the Dying Gunner AA1 (Charles Causley)

Oh mother my mouth is full of stars
Cau C 18; Seven 49; Touch IV 132; TR 119

Survivors (Alan Ross)
With the ship burning in their eyes
Drag 62; Touch IV

War Service (Thomas Blackburn)
In the war I first served in the 'bunkers'
Bla D 23

WARS: 1939–45 (TRAINING)

All Day it has Rained (Alun Lewis)
All day it has rained, and we on the edge of the moors
TR 36

Judging Distances (Henry Reed)
Not only how far away, but the way that you say it
Touch IV 127; TR 33

Naming of Parts (Henry Reed)
Today we have naming of parts
Bite III 53; EGV 361; Mod 24; ND 159; RR 53; Touch V 63; TR 35

Squadding (Jack Lindsay)
The sergeant's roar, interpreted aright
TR 32

Unarmed Combat (Henry Reed)
In due course of course you will all be issued with
Ev 264

WARTS

Warts (Jeni Couzyn)
You can sell them for a penny to
Deli 111; Puf M 26

WASHING: CLOTHES

Bendix (John Updike)
This porthole overlooks a sea
Touch IV 100

Dashing away with a Smoothing Iron (trad)
'Twas on a Monday morning
Merry 93; P Life III 66

They that Wash on Monday (trad)
They that wash on Monday
Fab NV 228; Merry 78; Ox PC 145;
Puf NR 90; Voi I 55

Washing Day (D. H. Thomas)
The chalk-lined tub, like a coral
basin, is choked with soap and
water
Theme VI 10

The Washing Machine (Jeffrey
Davies)
It goes fwunkety
World 104

WASHING UP

Chip the Glasses and Crack the
Plates (J. R. R. Tolkein)
Chip the glasses and crack the
plates
Like 41; Poems 42

Sink Song (J. A. Lindon)
Scouring out the porridge pot
J Vo III 36; Pac 101; Poems 42; Rhyme
III 31; Word 12

WASPS

I am a Wasp (Michael Rosen)
I am a wasp
Ros W 53

The Wasp (William Sharp)
When the ripe pears droop heavily
FM 223; TD 126

The Wasp's Nest (George
MacBeth)
All day to the loose tile behind the
parapet
Drag 15; Touch IV 157

WATCHES

The Watch (May Swenson)
When I/took my
J Vo IV 61

WATCHMEN

Dan the Watchman (John
D. Sheridan)
Dan the watchman
Here 112; R Six 94

No Thoroughfare (Ruth Holmes)
In a dear little home of tarpaulin
and boards
Come 173

WATERFALLS

The Cataract at Lodore (Robert
Southey)
How does the water
DP I 27; Ox CV 94
The cataract strong
Mov 116; Poems 44
Dividing and gliding and sliding
Word 112

Waterfall (Seamus Heaney)
The burn drowns steadily in its
own downpour
Touch IV 89

WATER LILIES

The Water Lilies (John Clare)
The water lilies, white and yellow
flowers
R Ten 19

WATERLOO

from *Childe Harold: The Eve of*
Waterloo (Lord Byron)
There was a sound of revelry by
night
EGV 145; Fab CV 259; ND 157

The Field of Waterloo (Thomas
Hardy)
Yea, the coneys are scared by the
thud of hoofs
Fab CV 260

WAVES

The Horses of the Sea (Christina
Rossetti)
The horses of the sea
Bat A 30; Rain 48; Rhyme II 42

There are Big Waves (Eleanor
Farjeon)
There are big waves and little
waves
Bits p; Come 42; Once 61; P Life I 59;
PT I 6; Puf Y 66

Upon this Beach (Louis
MacNeice)
Upon this beach the falling wall of
the sea
Gold III 4

The Waves of the Sea (Eleanor
Farjeon)
Don't you go too near the sea
Fan 108; Rhyme III 61

WEASELS

The Weasel (Iain Crichton Smith)
The weasel eels out from the walls
Four 76

The Weasel (Lord Alfred Douglas)
The weasel is a perfect dear
Bat A 51; Bat L 130; Dou T 35

WEATHER

See also Bk S, Out, Prel III throughout; *Fab NV 230–1; Fab UV 31–5; Ox NR 117*
See also Drought, Fog, Frost and Ice, Mist, Months, Rain Rainbows, Seasons, Sleet, Snow, Storms, Thaw, Thunder and Lightning, Wind

Glass Falling (Louis MacNeice)
The glass is going down. The sun
Dawn 37; Duck 41; Gold I 21; Hap II 86; Out 49; R Eig 45; R Ten 32; Say 62; TD 32

It's Never Fair Weather (Ogden Nash)
I do not like the winter wind
Nas C 14; Out 12

Mad Dogs and Englishmen (Noel Coward)
In tropical climes there are certain times of day
Ox LV 235

The Weather (Gavin Ewart)
What's the weather on about?
Bat L 146; Sort 31

Weather Ear (Norman Nicholson)
Lying in bed in the dark I hear the bray
DP III 18; PT III 30; Tap 45; TD 42

The Weather Prophet (A. B. Paterson, Australia)
"Ow can it rain,' the old man said, 'with things the way they are?'
Pat A 67

Weather Rhymes (anon)
Rain, rain go away, etc.
Deli 62

Weathers (Thomas Hardy)
This is the weather the cuckoo likes
BB 36; By 194; Choice 133; Deli 63; EGV 262; Fab CV 69; Gold II 15; Merry 347; My V 121; Out 8; Ox PC 96; Plea 118; Prel III 2; Puf V 165; Rat 458; TD 29; Touch I 103
This is the weather the shepherd shuns
Bk S 58

WEATHER VANES

The Pedalling Man (Russell Hoban)
We put him on the roof and we painted him blue
Hob P 6; Out 10

WEDDINGS

The Blythsome Bridal (Sir Francis Sempill)
Fy, let us all to the briddel
Ring 3

The Whitsun Weddings (Philip Larkin)
That Whitsun, I was late getting away
Mod 72

WEEKDAYS

Finger Nails (anon)
Cut them on Monday, cut them for health
Ox NR 16; Voi II 101

Monday's Child (anon)
Monday's child is fair of face
Croc 108; CTV 79; Fab CV 93; Fab NV 226; Ox Dic 309; Ox NR 1; P Life I 17; Rain 10; TD 70; Trad 32; Young 44

Sneeze on Monday (trad)
Sneeze on Monday, sneeze for danger
BE 4; Fab NV 228; Young 45

They that Wash on Monday (trad)
They that wash on Monday
Fab NV 228; Merry 78; Ox PC 145; Puf NR 90; Voi I 55

WENDIGOS

The Wendigo (Ted Hughes)
The Wendigo's tread
Hug U 33

213

The Wendigo (Ogden Nash)
The Wendigo
AM 29; Fab NV 80; Nas C 36

WEREWOLVES

The Farmer's Wife (Thomas Blackburn)
Spring is the time for a wedding
Bla D 16; Nar 42

WHALES

Fastitocalon (J. R. R. Tolkien)
Look: there is Fastitocalon
Hap 90; Tol T 49

The Littleton Whale (Charles Tomlinson)
What you wrote to know
Over 73

The Song of the Whale (Kit Wright)
Heaving mountain in the sea
Four 31; Wri H 17

The Whale (John Donne)
At every stroke his brazen fins to take
DT 74

The Whale: Fastitocolon (Anglo-Saxon, trans Gavin Bone)
To explain the nature of fishes in craft of verse
PW 27

The Whale (Erasmus Darwin)
Warm and buoyant in his oily mail
Bat A 71

Whale (Geoffrey Dearmer)
Wouldn't you like to be a whale
Come 152; Young 12

The Whale (Lord Alfred Douglas)
When you are swimming do not fail
Dou T 36

The Whale (Middle English, trans Brian Stone)
The whale's a fish of all that be
Sea 40

Whale (D. M. Thomas)
A whale lay cast up on the island's shore
Gang 83

Whale Hunt (Jacques Prevert, trans Stanley Chapman)
Off to catch a whale, we're off to catch a whale
Hap 84

WHALING

Paddy and the Whale (anon)
Well, Paddy O'Brien left Ireland with speed
Brit 32

The [Greenland] Whale (anon)
It was in the year of forty-four
Bk Bal 43
O' 'twas in the year of ninety-four
Sea 223
'Twas in the year of forty-nine
Fab PV 217; Peng B 270
We can no longer stay on shore
Iron III 72

WHEAT

The Golden Boy (Ted Hughes)
(cf. Barley, *John Barleycorn*)
In March he was buried
Bat S 18; Hug S 39; Out 46; Third 64; WAS 116

WILDERNESS

Inversnaid (Gerard Manley Hopkins)
This darksome burn, horseback brown
Choice 113; Fab Mod 67; Iron II 76; ND 10; P Scot 62; Rat 215; Theme VII 40; Touch II 50

Rannoch, by Glencoe (T. S. Eliot)
Here the crow starves, here the patient stag
Choice 221; P Scot 74; PW 307

Rocky Acres (Robert Graves)
This is a wild land, country of my choice
Choice 258; DP IV 49; Theme VII 39

The Tame and the Wild (Dennis Hall)
The fields of Farmer Hiram Brown
Sort 115

The Wilderness (John Cotton)
This is the wilderness my uncle said
RR 14

WILL O' THE WISP

The Will o' the Wisp (Jack Prelutsky)
You are lost in the desolate forest
Night 10

Will O' Wisp (John Clare)
I've seen the midnight morris-dance of hell
Ev 170; Hist 45; Theme II 13

WIND (L and D)

Address to a Child during a Boisterous Winter Evening (Dorothy Wordsworth)
What way does the wind come? What way does he go?
Come 113; Ev 22; Merry 355; Ox CV 128; Ox PC 100; Prel III 23; Puf V 226; (part) *Rhyme III 58*

And it was windy weather (James Stephens)
Now are the winds are riding by
Drum 122

from *The Hobbit*
(J. R. R. Tolkien)
The Wind was on the Withered Heath
Duck 83

Like Rain it sounded (Emily Dickinson)
Like rain it sounded till it curved
Rat 243

Mid-Country Blow (Theodore Roethke)
All night and all day the wind roared in the trees
Gold III 2; TD 43; Touch I 102

The North Wind doth blow (trad)
The north wind doth blow
Blow 15; Croc 70; Fab NV 29; Merry 54; Ox Dic 426; Ox NR 50; Ox PC 97; P Life I 72; Prel III 37; Puf NR 178; Puf V 28; (part) *DT 19; My V 2; Trad 161*

from *Ode to the North-East Wind* (Charles Kinglsey)
Welcome, wild North-Easter
Bk S 56

O Western Wind (anon)
O western wind, when wilt thou blow
Plea 104

The Pedalling Man (Russell Hoban)
We put him on the roof and we painted him blue
Hob P 6; Out 10

Praise Song of the Wind (Siberian, trans W. Redloff and W. R. Trask)
Trees with weak roots
J Vo II 21

A Song to the Wind (Welsh, Taliessin, trans A. P. Graves)
Guess who is this creature
Fab CV 59

The Sound of the Wind (Christina Rossetti)
The Wind has such a rainy sound
Hi 38; Lolli IV 12; Once 65; Ox PC 58; P Life I 71; Rhyme I 39

The Villain (W. H. Davies)
While joy gave clouds the light of stars
PW 280; Rat 449

Wenlock Edge (A. E. Housman)
On Wenlock Edge the wood's in trouble
By 202; ND 14; PW 269; Rat 326; TD 160

What the Wind Said (Russell Hoban)
'Far away is where I've come from', said the wind
Out 63

When the wind is in the East (trad)
When the wind is in the east
Come 16; Fab NV 230; Fab UV 31; P Life II 52; Puf V 166; TD 44

Who has seen the Wind? (Christina Rossetti)
Who has seen the wind?
Croc 81; CTV 146; Merry 242; Ox CV 278; Ox PC 96; P Life I 71; Prel III

Wind (Ted Hughes)
This house has been far out at sea all night
DP III 26; Drag 36; Flock 37; Gold III 1; Hug Sp 28; J Vo IV 69; Liv 50; Mod 78; ND 13; Out 64; Prel III 24; Seven 142; Touch III 24

The Wind (James Reeves)
I can get through a doorway without any key
Fir 84; Puf Q 91; Puf Y 59; Ree C 24; R Six 73; WAS 77

The Wind (Robert Louis
Stevenson)
I saw you toss the kites on high
CTV 146; Ste CG 25

The Wind (Sherry Ward, written
at school)
Blow, wind, blow today!
Fan 48

Wind (Ted Hughes)
This house has been far out at sea
all night
*DP III 26; Drag 36; Flock 37; Gold
III 1; Hug SP 28; J Vo IV 69; Liv 50;
Mod 78; ND 13; Out 64; Prel III 24;
Seven 142; Touch III 24*

The Wind and the Moon (George
Macdonald)
Said the Wind to the Moon
Bits b

The Wind at Night (David
Shavreen)
The dustbin lids clang on the
ground
Out Sc 24

A Windy Day (Andrew Young)
This wind brings all dead things to
life
*Bite I 51; Drag 37; Fan 62; Gold II
38; Prel III 25; This W 116; Word 42*

Windy Nights (Robert Louis
Stevenson)
Whenever the moon and stars are
set
*Croc 82; Deli 120; Fab NV 241; Fir
86; Like 13; Ox CV 294; P Life I 70;
Puf M 185; Puf V 218; Shad 49; Ste
CG 9; Tap 63*

WIND (N)

Aunt Jessie's Hat (Wilma
Horsbrugh)
Here is Aunt Jessie. Today she is
dressed
Hor B 21

The Wind in a Frolic (William
Howitt)
The wind one morning sprang up
from sleep
Merry 243; Ox CV 162

Winds Light to Disastrous (Spike
Milligan)
As I sipped morning tea
Out 66

WINDOW BOXES

Window Boxes (Eleanor Farjeon)
A window-box of pansies
P Life II 48

WINTER

See also Hug S 65–74
See also Frost and Ice, Months,
Sleet, Snow, Snowflakes, Thaw

The Coming of the Cold
(Theodore Roethke)
The ribs of leaves lie in the dust
J Vo III 100

Cultivators (Susan Taylor)
We
Strict 134

In midwinter a wood was (Peter
Levi)
In midwinter a wood was
Sun 82; WAS 167; Word 27

In the bleak mid-winter (Christina
Rossetti)
In the bleak mid-winter
*Hymn 110; Puf V 257; Rhyme IV 119;
WAS 163* (part) *DT 19; Rain 71*

In the Wood (Eileen Mathias)
Cold winter's in the wood
Come 90

The Last Word of a Bluebird
(Robert Frost)
As I went out a Crow
Fab NV 33; Puf Y 79; R Eig 58

Morning (John Clare)
The morning wakens with the
lumping flails
R Ten 26

Up in the Morning's no' for Me
(Robert Burns)
Up in the morning's no' for me
*DP I 15; Ev 27; Iron I 7; Ox PC 98;
P Life IV 34; Prel III 38; RR 92; TD
73*

Week of Winter Weather (Wes
Magee)
On Monday icy rain poured down
Third 82

When Icicles Hang by the Wall
(William Shakespeare)
When icicles hang by the wall
*DP I 19; Fab CV 56; Gold I 22; Iron I
57; Merry 348; ND 66; Ox PC 98; P
Life II 58; Puf V 128; Rain 32; Say*

93; Tap 46; TD 142; Theme VII 36; This W 72; Trad 43; WAS 155

Winter (John Clare)
Old January clad in crispy rime
Voi I 131

Winter (Alfred, Lord Tennyson)
The frost is here
Merry 357; TD 141; WAS 147

Winter Days (Gareth Owen)
Biting air/Winds blow
Out 77; Word 28

Winter Ducks (Russell Hoban)
Small in the shrink of winter, dark of the frost and chill
Out 84

Winter in the Fens (John Clare)
So moping flat and low our valleys lie
Flock 4

Winter Morning (Ogden Nash)
Winter is the king of showmen
Croc 72; Fir 90; Like 58; Nas C 22; Out 76; Puf Y 76; R Six 59

Winter Time (Robert Louis Stevenson)
Late lies the wintry sun abed
Ox CV 298

WITCHES

See also PT II, Wit throughout; *Hist 11–28; Puf M 71–85; Shad 91–105*

See also Charms and Spells, Halloween, Magicians, Sorcerers

WITCHES (L AND D)

Dame, dame! the watch is set (Ben Jonson)
Dame, dame! the watch is set
Hist 16; Merry 360; PT II 7; Shad 94

hist whist (e. e. cummings)
hist whist/little ghostthings
Fan 17; Merry 113; PT II 28; Tap 25; Wit 30

from *The Lady's not for Burning* (Christopher Fry)
Why do they call me a witch?
Bric 51

The Little Creature (Walter de la Mare)

Twinkum, twankun, twirlum and twitch
de la M Col 176; DP I 88; In O I 27

Look Out, Boys! (Oliver Wendell Holmes)
Look out! Look out, boys! Clear the track!
ADT 103; Fan 15

from *Macbeth* (William Shakespeare)
Thrice the brindled cat hath mewed
Macbeth IV i 1; Hist 18; ND 193; Puf M 79; Rat 429; Touch I 163
When shall we three meet again?
Macbeth I i 1; Puf M 77

from *The Masque of Queens: the Hag's Song* (Ben Jonson)
I have been all day looking after
Hist 70; Puf M 80; Shad 96

Mother Maudlin the Witch (Ben Jonson)
Within a gloomy dimble she doth dwell
Hist 13

My Cats: a witch speaks (Stevie Smith)
I like to toss him up and down
BE 11; Fab Non 300; R Nine 3

Old Moll (James Reeves)
The moon is up
Wit 25

The Ride-by-Nights (Walter de la Mare)
Up on their brooms the witches stream
de la M Col 174; Merry 312; Mov 94; P Life III 96; PT II 24; R Nine 84

Space Travellers (James Nimmo)
There was a witch, humpbacked and hooded
P Life IV 95; PT II 25

Two Witches (Alexander Resnikoff)
There was a witch/The witch had an itch
Third 71

Wild Witches' Ball (Jack Prelutsky)
late last night at wildwitchhall
Wit 17

217

The Witch (John Hewitt)
A bunch of wrack was hung inside
the porch
Hap II 87

The Witch (Jack Prelutsky)
She comes by night in fearsome
flight
Night 22

The Witches' Ride (Karla
Kuskin)
Over the hills
Wit 9

The Witch's Work Song
(T. H. White)
Two spoons of sherry
Fab Non 300

WITCHES (N)

Alison Gross (anon)
O Alison Gross that lives in yon
tower
*Bk Bal 24; Fab CV 222; Nar 12; Peng
B 51; Ring 128; Shad 101; Wind 35*

The Allansford Pursuit (Robert
Graves)
Cunning and art he did not lack
Rat 26

As Lucy went a-walking (Walter
de la Mare)
As Lucy went a-walking one
morning cold and fine
de la M Col 175; My V 40

A Country Witch (William
Barnes)
There's that old hag Moll Brown,
look, see, just past
Hist 22; PT II 22

The Hag (Robert Herrick)
The hag is astride
*Ev 175; Fab CV 221; Hist 14; My V
38; Ox PC 85; Poems 57; PT II 24;
Shad 91; TD 82; Theme II 12; Voi I 68*

I Saw Three Witches (Walter de
la Mare)
I saw three witches
de la M Col 172; Hist 20; Isle 47

Mixed Brews (Clive Sansom)
There once was a witch
Fir 110

A Moon-Witch (Ted Hughes)
A moon-witch is no joke
Hug M 12

from *Tam o' Shanter* (Robert
Burns)
Inspiring bold John Barleycorn!
PT II 9

The Two Witches (Robert
Graves)
O sixteen hundred and ninety-one
*Dawn 51; DP I 87; Hap 41; Hist 78;
PT II 11; Shad 103; Voi I 51*

The Witch (Mary Coleridge)
I have walked a great while over
the snow
GV V 41; Hist 21

The Witch (Walter de la Mare)
Weary went the old witch
Hist 80

Witchcraft (anon 1618)
Of damned deeds and deadly dole
Bal 14

Witch goes Shopping (Lilian
Moore)
Witch rides off
Four 44; Wit 21

Witch Spawn (Beth Cross)
It's true I knew her mother
burned;
Strict 55

The Witch's Cat (Ian Serraillier)
'My magic is dead', said the witch,
'I'm astounded
Hap 28; PT II 19

WIZARDS

The Cunjah Man (James Edwin
Campbell)
O children run, the cunjah man
Afr I 51

The Wizard (Jack Prelutsky)
The wizard, watchful, waits alone
Night 28

WOLVES

Wolf (Ted Hughes)
The Iron Wolf, the Iron Wolf
Hug U 42

*The 'word' of a wolf encircled by the
hunt* (Sandag, Mongolian)
I, a blue wolf/Born on the steppes
Oral 70

WOMBATS

The Diggers (A. B. Paterson)
Bristling Billy the porcupine
Pat A 20

Weary Will (A. B. Paterson)
The strongest creature for his size
Deli 51; Ev 69; Pat A 19

WOODMEN

See also Loggers

from *The Task* (William Cowper)
Forth goes the woodman, leaving unconcerned
Dog 79; DP III 23; R Ten 53

Throwing a Tree (Thomas Hardy)
The two executioners stalk along over the knolls
Drag 75; Gold II 32; Iron III 63; Touch II 178; Word 156

WOODPECKERS

Green Woodpecker (Reginald Arkell)
When I were a-coming
WAS 84

Woodpecker (Ted Hughes)
Woodpecker is rubber-necked
Hug U 26

WOODS

See also Trees, Woodmen

The Way through the Woods (Rudyard Kipling)
They shut the road through the woods
DP IV 38; EGV 289; Fab CV 377; Gold I 25; Hist 67; Isle 81; Like 96; ND 18; Ox CV 323; Plea 240; P Life IV 26; Rain 80; Rhyme IV 16; Theme II 6; This W 163; Touch I 156

WOOD-SWALLOWS

The Wood-Swallows (William Sharp, Australia)
The lightning-stricken giant gum
FM 225

WORK

Toads (Philip Larkin)
Why should I let the toad *work*
DP IV 86; Ox LV 308; Theme VI 28; Touch V 132

Toads Revisited (Philip Larkin)
Walking around in the park
Theme VI 29; Touch V 142

Work (D. H. Lawrence)
There is no point in work/unless
. . .
DP IV 72; Theme VI 27; Touch V 135

WORMS

Worms and the Wind (Carl Sandburg)
Worms would rather be worms
Deli 57; Imp 24; Word 43; World 127; Zoo 85

WRENS

Jenny Wren (W. H. Davies)
Her sight is short. She comes quite near
F Feet 83

Jenny Wren (Walter de la Mare)
Of all the birds that rove and sing
de la M Col 118

WRESTLING

See All-in Wrestling

YAKS

The Mad Yak (Gregory Corso)
I am watching them churn the last milk
Imp 26; Theme I 61; Zoo 51

The Yak (Hilaire Belloc)
As a friend to the children commend me the yak
Fab NV 166; Mov 23; Ox CV 310; Ox LV 194; Ox PC 117; Zoo 50

Yak (William Jay Smith)
The long-haired yak has long black hair
FV 32

YETIS

Yeti (Mary Innes)
Up among the mountain snows
Inn B 'Y'

Yeti, the Abominable Snowman
(George Barker)
High in the Himalayan west,
between Kanchenjunga and
Everest
Bar A 'Y'

YORK

York, York for my Money (William
Elderton)
As I went through the north
country
Merry 364

ZEBRAS

Zebra (Mary Innes)
Not only in the zoo
Inn B 'Z'

The Zebra (James Kirkup)
Zany
R Ten 10

The Zebra (Lord Alfred
Douglas)
The zebra is a perfect jewel
Bat A 51

The Zebras (Roy Campbell)
From the dark woods that breathe
of fallen showers
Plea 45

ZODIAC

The Signs of the Zodiac (Ebenezer
Cobham Brewer)

Our vernal signs the RAM begins
Fab UV 29

Zodiac (Eleanor Farjeon)
What are the signs of Zodiac
R Nine 90

The Zodiac Rhyme (anon)
The Ram, the Bull, the Heavenly
Twins
Fab PV 35

ZOOS

Au Jardin des Plantes (John
Wain)
The gorilla lay on his back
*Deli 50; Ev 81; Flock 220; Full 12;
Tel 23; Theme I 70*

Our Local Zoo (Geoffrey
Johnson)
Expert officials at our zoo
Hap 40; Word 62

Our Visit to the Zoo (Jessie Pope)
When we went to the Zoo
Plea 28

Riverdale Lion (John Robert
Colombo)
Bound lion, almost blind from
meeting their gaze and popcorn
Liv 56

The Zoo (Boris Pasternak, trans
Lydia Pasternak)
The zoo lies in the parkland
thickets
Flock 221
A lionness the people facing
Drum 64

Books to Which Reference is Made

Explanations of the symbols used for books

The abbreviation used for a book of poems by a single author begins with the first three letters of the poet's name: e.g. *Hug S*, Ted Hughes' *Season Songs*; *Ros Y*, Michael Rosen's *You Can't Catch Me*.

Anthologies are coded by title: e.g. *Hap, Happenings*; *Say, First I Say This*; *Touch, Touchstones*. When a series of volumes is graded for classroom use, the volumes are indicated by Roman figures, the pages by Arabic numbers: for example *Voi III 16* is *Voices*, volume III, page 16.

The abbreviations used for publishers such as *Bat*, Batsford; *Fab*, Faber; *Ox*, Oxford are easily recognisable.

A very brief description of each book gives some indication of its type, and the age-range for which it is designed.

ADT

All the Day Through (coll. Wes Magee)
Evans Bros 1982   128pp
Goes through the child's day: 'Me and my family', 'The School Day', etc. Mainly contemporary verse plus some tried favourites.

Afr I – II

African Poetry for Schools (ed. Noel Machin)
Longman Group   Afr I 1978   87pp; Afr II 1978, 3rd ed 1981   101pp
Includes Afro-American poetry. Intended for junior-secondary pupils, with ample notes and suggestions for increasing understanding, appreciation and participation in writing.

Ahl P

Please Mrs Butler (Allan Ahlberg)
Kestrel Books 1983   94pp
Very light but pointed verses, covering episodes from a boy's point of view. Children can find themselves and their teachers reflected here.

Al I – III

Poetry Allsorts I – III (comp. Roger Mansfield)
Edward Arnold 1981   32, 48, 48pp
Bright colours attract young children to explore these carefully-graded books, with much writing by their contemporaries, and many verses so short that even poor readers will not be exhausted. Some unusual Japanese poems.

AM

Amazing Monsters (ed. Robert Fisher)
Faber and Faber 1982   96pp
Monsters both traditional and newly invented, described by poets from Tennyson and Lear to Ogden Nash and Michael Rosen.

AP

A Selection of African Poetry (intro. K. E. Senanu and T. Vincent)
Longman 1976 12th imp. 1981   224pp
Adult poems, many of them difficult, by Africans of many nationalities. Heavily annotated and explained with 'exercises', e.g. 'In what way is the river symbolic?'

Att

Attachments to the Sun (ed. D. Blackburn, A. Horsfall and C. L. Wanjale)
Edward Arnold 1978   100pp
A sensitive introduction and brief notes make these poems, by black poets of many nationalities, more accessible. Many poems on cultural conflict and tension.

Aus

Land of the Rainbow Gold: Poetry for young Australians (ed. Mildred M. Fowler)
Thomas Nelson 1967   109pp
Poems, with notes and striking illustrations, give a vivid picture of Australian life, particularly of the heat and drought of 'the bush'.

Bal

A Ballad History of England (ed. Roy Palmer)
Batsford 1979   192pp
Unique compilation of over 80 ballads (1588–1973) on e.g. the Armada, the
Fire of London, the Great Train Robbery. Notes, contemporary illustrations
and tunes are included. Invaluable to historians.

Bar A

The Alphabetical Zoo (George Barker)
Faber 1972 Unnumbered
26 poems about animals from Ape to Yeti with 'Zong, not Zebra' as a final
jeu d'esprit. New and different 'animal poems', and illustrations.

Bar R

Runes and Rhymes and Tunes and Chimes (George Barker)
Faber 1969   62pp
George Barker's first book of verses for (young) children; enticing jingles to
read aloud.

Bat A

The Batsford Book of Animal Verse for Children (ed. Francis Maxwell)
Batsford 1977   88pp
Bewick's woodcuts, and excellent colour photographs, enhance this collec-
tion of well-chosen poems on an ever-popular theme.

Bat C

The Batsford Book of Children's Verse (ed. Gavin Ewart)
Batsford 1976   87pp
Personal choices of a poet, from Milton to Harry Graham, Ralegh to
T. S. Eliot, each good of its kind. Directed to ages 10–12 years but far wider
in appeal.

Bat L

The Batsford Book of Light Verse for Children (ed. Gavin Ewart)
Batsford 1978   160pp
Chosen by a master of light verse, a brilliant collection, ranging from
Shakespeare to Noel Coward, illustrated by Nicholas Bentley. Something for
all ages.

Bat R

The Batsford Book of Romantic Poetry (ed. Samuel Carr)
Batsford 1982   124pp
See *Bir*. Excellent introduction to Romantic Period, in poetry and painting,
for top forms. Lavish and appropriate illustrations.

Bat S

The Batsford Book of Stories in Verse for Children (ed. Charles Causley)
Batsford 1979   133pp
Collection of most unusual narrative verse, from many periods and countries,
wide variety from ribald to tragic.

BB

Bird, Beast and Flower (chosen Ian Parsons)
Chatto and Windus 1980   64pp
Poems of nature, combined with exquisite water colours by Marie Angel to make a remarkably fine book.

BBGG

Beastly Boys and Ghastly Girls (sel. William Cole)
Methuen 1970 repr. '71, '73, '75, '79   125pp
Self-explanatory title: appropriate spidery drawings by Tom Ungerer. Useful for children who think poetry is solemn and goody-goody, but the humour is sometimes strained.

BE

Bulls Eyes (chosen Brian Thompson)
Penguin Kestrel 1977   66pp
Unusual poems strikingly presented. Great variety, long and short, new and old, comic and serious.

Bel CV

Selected Caustionary Verses (Hilaire Belloc)
Puffin 1940 repr. many times   185pp
The immortal Jim, Matilda, and others of Belloc's children, beasts and peers. Enjoyable, easily-memorised light verse. Available in many editions.

BHL

Ballads High and Low (presented by W. A. Gatherer)
Heinemann Educational 1975   72pp
A few good ballads with many 'reading aids' and 'study aids' which might dampen pupils' response, but could help the inexperienced teacher.

Bill

Billy the Kid: An Anthology of Tough Verse (ed. Michael Baldwin)
Hutchinson 1963 9th repr. 1980   176pp
Battle, murder and sudden death in a variety of unpleasant forms; many war poems. Just what it says: tough.

Bir

The Poetry of Birds (ed. Samuel Carr)
Batsford 1976   88pp
One of a high quality series (see *Bat R, Cat, Dog, Hor, Hymn, Rail*) of collections on a single theme, imaginatively compiled, superbly produced, each with four colour plates and some 30 in monochrome, by artists as diverse as Dürer, Tiepolo and Picasso. Attractive in appearance and content.

Bite I – III

Bite In I – III (ed. Cecil Gray)
Nelson Caribbean 1972 revised and repr. many times by 1983   104, 101, 111 pages
'A three year secondary course in reading poems', with ample notes on points for discussion. About half the poets are Caribbean, the others from Britain,

New Zealand, Japan, Pakistan, etc. For teachers who want something out of the ordinary.

Bits

Bits and Pieces (chosen P. Blakely)
A. & C. Black 1970 repr. 3 times by 1973   64pp
Very short poems and fragments of poems, printed in large type on coloured, unnumbered pages (y, yellow; p, pink; b, blue; g, grey). Meant for the youngest, but much appeals to any age. Available as four booklets.

Bk Bal

A Book of Ballads (comp. Alan Bird)
Longmans Heritage of Literature 1967   200pp
Seventy ballads from many lands, and in many moods, including some music hall ditties. Very useful collection.

Bk S

A Book of the Seasons (made by Eve Garnett)
Frederick Muller 1968 repr. 1969   80pp
Beautifully produced book of drawings of children in the country, matched with appropriate snatches of little-known poetry. Unique in plan, style and effect.

Bla D

The Devil's Kitchen (Thomas Blackburn)
Chatto Poets for the Young 1975   32pp
Mixture of precisely-observed poems about natural scenes and mountaineering, with tales of trolls and werewolves.

Blow

The Way the Wind Blows (comp. Leonard Clark)
Evans Bros 1979   64pp
Conventional popular poems attractively presented for children's reading.

Blue

Bluefoot Traveller (ed. James Berry)
Harrap 1976 revised 1981   64pp
Poetry by nineteen 'West-Indians in Britain', many written in Creole. Themes vary from Caribbean villages to the black people's struggle to find their place in British society while retaining their identity.

Bod L

Let's Marry, said the Cherry (N. M. Bodecker)
Faber 1977   79pp
Short American nonsense verses, with lilting movement, clever rhyming and appropriate illustrations. A book for children to dip into.

Bric

Bric-a-Brac (chosen Peggy Blakeley)
Adam and Charles Black 1973 repr. 74   64pp

Attractive selection: format and coloured paper suggest young children, but much splendid material for top juniors.
Unnumbered pages: see *Bits*.

Brit

Everyman's Book of British Ballads (ed. Roy Palmer)
Dent 1980   256pp
Over 120 ballads, from medieval to music hall, with tunes. Useful as narrative poems and songs. Notes on recordings, sources and authenticity.

Burn

The Burning Thorn (sel. Griselda Greaves)
Hamish Hamilton 1971   202pp
Adult poems in style and content, for senior pupils. Basic themes – love, marriage, nuclear war – and many poems not anthologised elsewhere.

By

By Heart (chosen Francis Meynell)
Nonesuch Press 1965   338pp
Poems chosen because easily memorised and worth remembering. All rhythmic, shapely and direct – from all periods. Beautifully produced book, ideal for browsing.

Cari I

Caribbean Voices (sel. John Figueroa)
Evans Bros 1966   119pp
An early collection of Caribbean poets, accessible to middle school (and older) readers.

Cat

The Poetry of Cats (ed. Samuel Carr)
Batsford 1974 2nd ed 1980   96pp
See *Bir*. This volume has particularly apt illustrations of the highest quality.

Cau C

Collected Poems 1951–75 (Charles Causley)
Macmillan 1975   289pp
Assembled from his seven separate books, an attractive collection by one of the very best modern poets for children.

Cau F

Figgie Hobbin (Charles Causley)
Macmillan 1970   96pp
New poems for juniors by the ever-popular Cornish schoolmaster-poet.

Cau N

Figure of Eight: Narrative Poems (Charles Causley)
Macmillan 1969   86pp
Varied stories in verse; useful to have *new* narrative poems for children.

Cau T

The Tail of the Trinosaur (Charles Causley)
Brockhampton Press 1973   121pp
Nonsense story 'told in 24 shakes'. Rollicking verses admirable for reading as a serial story.

CBC

The Children's Book of Comic Verse (chosen Christopher Logue)
Batsford 1979   162pp
A collection of unusual pieces, with a long bibliography of anthologies. But what seems comic to one class may not raise a smile in another.

CC

Comic and Curious Verse (chosen Zenka and Ian Woodward)
Ladybird Books 1983   51pp
Favourite recent comic verses in a tiny, very brightly-coloured book. Comic-strip style illustrations.

Choice

A Choice of Poets (comp. R. P. Hewett)
George Harrap 1968 repr. 9 times by 1975   318pp
Fourteen poets from Wordsworth to R. S. Thomas, for readers of 14 upwards. Rather heavily annotated, perhaps because used widely overseas as a set book, but the reader is invited to use only what is needed for elucidation and appreciation.

Come

Come Follow Me (no author given)
Evans Bros 1956 11th printing 1976   254pp
All-embracing collection from nursery rhymes to poems for top juniors. Slightly old-fashioned choices, e.g. fairy poems, but good action rhymes and a wide variety of themes, styles and moods.

Conf

Conflict and Compassion (ed, John Skull)
Hutchinson Educational 1969   122pp
Poems on current social problems, including race relations, the atomic bomb, poverty and homelessness.

Croc

If you should meet a Crocodile (comp. Margaret Mayo)
Kaye and Ward 1974   112pp
Verses and snatches of memorable verse, bright illustrations, admirable for the youngest children. [Not *If*]

CTV

A Child's Treasury of Verse (ed. Eleanor Doan)
Hodder and Stoughton 1980   188pp
Big American anthology, printed in double columns, with many old-fashioned favourites, and a leaning towards improving rather than entertaining.

Dah R

Revolting Rhymes (Roald Dahl)
Jonathan Cape 1982 repr. 1982   32pp
Perversions of standard fairy tales, told in slangy quick-moving verse, illustrated by Quentin Blake, these are immensely popular. Unnumbered pages.

Dawn

Dawn and Dusk (ed. Charles Causley)
Brockhampton Press, Leicester 1962   128pp
Still an excellent anthology, 91 poems by 50 twentieth-century poets, cunningly arranged to be read, if you wish, in meaningful sequence. For older children.

de la M Col

Collected Rhymes and Verses (Walter de la Mare)
Faber 1944, continually revised, enlarged, repr. 1975   320pp
The poet *par excellence* for imaginative children. This enlarged edition contains all his verse for children, and some adult poems children have appreciated. Other selections are available.

Deli

Delights and Warnings (sel. John and Gillian Beer)
Macdonald Educational 1979   141pp
A rich and balanced collection with useful brief notes. For all ages.

Dino

Dinosaurs and Beasts of Yore (sel. William Cole)
Collins 1979   62pp
Rather facetious verses by a variety of British and American authors, about a variety of dinosaurs.

Dis

Distant Voices: Poetry of the Preliterate (ed. Denys Thompson)
Heinemann Educational 1978   143pp
Translations of poems from every continent and period, useful material connected with particular nations or tribes. But how many literal translations are poems?

Dog

The Poetry of Dogs (ed. Samuel Carr)
Batsford 1975   87pp
See *Bir*. Dogs inspire superb illustrations by Bewick, Picasso, Jan van Eyck and many more. Perhaps the poetry is less distinguished, but this is an interesting and amusing anthology for dog-lovers especially.

DP I – IV

Discovering Poetry I– IV (sel. E. W. Parker, revised M. Marland)
Longmans 1953 (16 impressions) 2nd ed. 1971   100, 102, 122, 160pp
Collection of the most popular poems for schoolchildren, still useful, well-presented and attractively revised by an expert.

Dou T

Tails with a Twist: Animal Nonsense Verse (Lord Alfred Douglas)
Batsford 1979   64pp
Allegedly the inspiration for Belloc's *Bad Child's Book of Beasts*, these 'nineties jingles have their own brand of nonsense, perhaps a little monotonous.

Down

All Along Down Along (comp. Leonard Clark)
Longmans 1971   64pp
Ten popular stories in verse, gaily and lavishly illustrated.

Drag

Dragonsteeth (ed. Eric Williams)
Edward Arnold 1972   96pp
Primarily for ages 13–15. A vital and well-organised collection strikingly presented, with many photographs. See also *Look, Tap, Tel.*

Drum

Drumming in the Sky (ed. Paddy Bechely)
BBC 1981   160pp
Poems from BBC's 'Stories and Rhymes', including children's writing and specially commissioned poems. Very accessible.

DT

Drums and Trumpets (sel. Leonard Clark)
The Bodley Head 1962 4th repr. 1971   96pp
Skilfully chosen and tellingly-arranged poetry for the youngest groups, including nursery rhymes and Elizabethan verse.

Duck

Ducks and Dragons (ed. Gene Kemp)
Faber 1980   124pp
Delightfully fresh anthology, with much for both upper juniors and older pupils.

EGV

Everyman's Book of Evergreen Verse (ed. David Herbert)
J. M. Dent 1981   387pp
Old – and old-fashioned – favourites which the author regards as 'evergreen', from Chaucer to the 1950s. Many do still appeal and there is much for all ages.

Eli OP

Old Possum's Book of Practical Cats (T. S. Eliot)
Faber 1939 continually reprinted   45pp
A classic written by a distinguished modern poet for his friends' children. Source of the popular musical, *Cats.*

Enr R

Rhyme Times Rhyme (D. J. Enright)
Chatto Poets for the Young 1974   32pp
This attractive series encourages children interested in a poem to read

further in the same writer's work. Enright writes amusing light verse specifically for children. See also *Bla D, Hea P, Hes S, Jon S, Low G*, etc.

Ev

Evans Book of Children's Verse (ed. Howard Sergeant)
Evans Bros 1972   286pp
Admirable large collection for the secondary teacher, covering many centuries and countries and many moods. Useful juxtapositions.

Fab Bal

The Faber Book of Ballads (coll. Matthew Hodgart)
Faber 1965 reissued 1982   267pp
Comprehensive collection of ballads and broadsides, for secondary children. Some Australian ballads for tough boys, and verses too from Ireland and America.

Fab CV

Faber Book of Children's Verse (ed. Janet Adam Smith)
Faber 1953 repr. 1968   412pp
Admirably wide-ranging selection for children already interested in poetry, including many classic poets. Grouped under imaginative headings, for example, Marvels and Riddles, History and Time. Top juniors to adults.

Fab LP

Faber Book of Love Poetry (ed. Geoffrey Grigson)
Faber 1973   407pp
An editor who shuns translation – 'that thin line by line prose which now passes too easily for poems' – includes some French poems in this cornucopia of strongly-felt love poems. Only a small sample can be included in this book.

Fab Mod

Faber Book of Modern Verse (ed. Michael Roberts, revised Peter Porter)
Faber 1936 4th edn. 1982   432pp
Comprehensive collection from what was 'modern' in 1936 to what was 'modern' in 1982. Sixth-form material.

Fab Non

Faber Book of Nonsense Verse (ed. Geoffrey Grigson)
Faber 1979   352pp
Four centuries of nonsense verse (with notes of sources and dates) from which each teacher can draw material for a particular group. Many unusual poems as well as tried favourites.

Fab NV

Faber Book of Nursery Verse (ed. Barbara Ireson)
Faber 1958 repr. 1975 pback 1983   286pp
Splendid perennial collection for younger children, including those well beyond the nursery. Emphasis on rhythmic verse easy to speak aloud and remember.

Fab PR

Faber Popular Reciter (ed. Kingsley Amis)
Faber 1978   256pp
Pieces from the 17th century to 1915, which were, say 50 years ago, the best known and most recited poems. Still good to read aloud, as 'graceful monuments to the obvious'; rhythmical, clear and appealing to the ear. A real 'period' collection.

Fab PV

Faber Book of Popular Verse (ed. Geoffrey Grigson)
Faber 1971   376pp
Folksongs, carols, ballads, odd snatches of verse, grouped by theme, and relating to man's basic needs and emotions.

Fab UV

Faber Book of Useful Verse (ed. Simon Brett)
Faber 1981   254pp
'Useful' poems from Hesiod (8th century BC) to Tom Lehrer, telling how to grow cucumbers, to predict the weather, to bring up children, to pronounce English, to cook trout, etc. etc. Unusual and amusing, but mainly 18th century verse requiring literate readers.

Fan

Fancy Free (sel. Dennis Saunders)
Evans Bros 1974   136pp
Poems and admirable photographs enhance each other and are designed to inspire children's writing. See also *Full*. (*Fan* and *Full* are also available divided into attractive booklets on various themes.)

Far M

Invitation to a Mouse (Eleanor Farjeon, chosen Annabel Farjeon)
Pelham Books 1981   95pp
Easy-moving verses mainly for young children. Perhaps the assumptions are dated, but there are many favourites, for instance '*Cat! Scat!*'

Fat S

Songs for my Dog and other People (Max Fatchen)
Kestrel Books 1980   64pp
Witty, ingeniously-rhymed verses of everyday life, plus limericks and nonsense poems. Shows that it is possible to be colloquial without writing free verse.

Fat W

Wry Rhymes for Troublesome Times (Max Fatchen)
Kestrel 1983   79pp
Lively and amusing; a few narratives and many short nonsensical pieces, a pleasant mixture for young readers.

F Feet

Four Feet and Two (comp. Leila Berg)
Puffin 1960 repr. 4 times by 1970   220pp
Still one of the best collections of nature poems for juniors; some unusual and stimulating choices, and short relevant extracts from long poems on other subjects.

Fir

A First Poetry Book (comp. John Foster)
OUP 1979 repr. 1980   128pp
See also *Sec, Third, Four*. A cleverly graded series which attempts to give a child's-eye view, and is very popular with children. Much recent material by, for example, Michael Rosen, Kit Wright, Wes Magee.

Flock

A Flock of Words (coll. David Mackay)
Bodley Head 1969 repr. 1973, 79   323pp
An expert and sympathetic teacher's commonplace book, wide-ranging in every way. Surprising juxtapositions; a book to return to again and again.

FM

Fellow Mortals (chosen Roy Fuller)
Macdonald and Evans 1981   274pp
Serious verse about animals; published in aid of the World Wildlife Fund. Illustrates, incidentally, man's changing attitude to animals over the last 400 years.

Four

A Fourth Poetry Book (comp. John Foster)
OUP 1982   128pp
See *Fir*. Chosen, like its predecessors, to express vividly both everyday and fantastic aspects of a child's life and thought.

Ful C

Squeaking Crust (John Fuller)
Chatto Poets for the Young 1974   32pp
Longer poems commissioned by a Schools' Festival to be set to music, and skilful riddles, all light-hearted and ingeniously rhymed.

Full

Full Swing (sel. Dennis Saunders)
Evans Bros 1974   136pp
Poems closely matched with richly-coloured evocative photographs, to inspire children's writing. See also *Fan*.

Ful P

Poor Roy (Roy Fuller)
Andre Deutsch Ltd 1977   64pp
Successor to *Ful S*, enhanced by Nicholas Bentley's illustrations. Literate children could enjoy many of the poems.

Ful S

Seen Grandpa Lately? (Roy Fuller)
Andre Deutsch Ltd 1972   64pp
A Professor of Poetry writes slightly highbrow poems for children, often funny, sometimes sinister. They include a quatrain on the uselessness of slapping babies, limericks on famous British poets and twisted 'tails on fairy tales'.

FV

The Children's Book of Funny Verse (comp. Julia Watson)
Faber 1979   128pp
Such variety that everyone will find something funny – many *very* short; limericks, 'ruthless rhymes', etc.

Gang

Gangsters, Ghosts and Dragonflies (chosen Brian Patten)
George Allen and Unwin 1981   159pp
Nearly 80 modern poems, many unfamiliar, each telling a story. Curious mixture of sensitive poetry and coarse 'ruthless rhymes'.

Gi

Giant Poems (ed. Daisy Wallace)
Pepper Press 1980   32pp
17 poems on giants with elegant lay-out and splendid illustrations.

Gold I – IV

The Golden Bird I – IV (ed. Frank Whitehead)
Oliver and Boyd 1969   69, 54, 54, 75pp
Beautifully produced. Poems of real quality, chosen to be spoken and sung. Very well arranged, one poem leading to the next. Secondary.

Gow S

Swings and Roundabouts (Mick Gowar)
Collins 1981   80pp
Boy's-eye view of family life in a city, many comic moments as well as serious insights.

GP

Ghost Poems (ed. Daisy Wallace)
Pepper Press 1981   32pp
Slim picture book of not-too-frightening poems of the supernatural.

GV I – V

Evans Graded Verse I – V (ed. Michael Knight and Ronald Ridout)
Evans Bros 1977, '77, '77, '78, '79   30, 30, 46, 46, 44pp
Slim brightly-bound booklets, pleasantly unpretentious and skilfully graded, with lots of interesting material at all levels. Teacher's books and cassette of spoken and sung poems available.

Hap

Happenings (ed. M. Wollman and D. Grugeon)
Harrap 1964 7th repr. 1976   93pp
Popular middle school anthology; many poems good for any age. Unrelated photographs to encourage children's writing.

Hap II

Happenings II (ed. M. Wollman and Alice Austin)
George G Harrap and Co 1972   96pp
Has the virtues of its predecessor, *Hap*. Poems of quality.

Hea P

A Parliament of Birds (John Heath-Stubbs)
Chatto Poets for the Young 1975   32pp
44 different birds keenly observed; poems often witty, short evocations of the distinctive features of each species, and their real or fabled history.

Here

Here We Go (sel. Shona McKellar)
Evans Bros 1982   135pp
Specially taken photographs exactly match the very short verses. A book for young children to explore themselves.

Hes S

A Song of Sunlight (Phoebe Hesketh)
Chatto Poets for the Young 1974   32pp
Unpretentious and accessible poems on subjects of interest to children: animals, weather, truancy and motor bikes.

Hi

Hi-Ran-Ho (comp. Aiden and Nancy Chambers)
Longmans 1971   48pp
Attractive clearly-printed picture book to tempt the child to read on after teacher has finished. Unusual American poems.

Hist

Hist Whist (coll. Dennis Saunders)
Evans Bros 1975   91pp
Ample selection of witches, ghosts, magic and mystery.

Hob P

The Pedalling Man (Russell Hoban)
World's Work Ltd 1969   33pp
American poems for children by well-known story writer. Fresh flavour and quiet humour.

Hor

The Poetry of Horses (ed. Samuel Carr)
Batsford 1980   88pp
See *Bir*. The painters are better than the poets in this volume, but splendid for horsy children.

Hor B

The Bold Bad Bus (Wilma Horsbrugh)
BBC 1973 new edn. 1977   72pp
Her classic 'Train to Glasgow', with ten other stories in verse. Perfect for reading aloud with children joining in.

Hug F

Meet my Folks (by Ted Hughes)
Faber 1961 now Puffin   42pp
High-spirited nonsense poems about an extraordinary family which nevertheless has affinities with one's own.

Hug M

Moon-Bells and other Poems (Ted Hughes)
Chatto 1978   32pp
Recent poems, slightly fey, perhaps, but very attractive to the right child.

Hug S

Season Songs (Ted Hughes)
Faber 1976   75pp
New material for teachers who have explored too often the stock poems about the weather.

Hug SP

Selected Poems 1957–1981 (Ted Hughes)
Faber 1982   238pp
A storehouse for the teacher which contains Ted Hughes' own selection from his work of the last 24 years.

Hug U

Under the North Star (Ted Hughes)
Faber 1981   47pp
An extra-large grandly produced book in which poems and pictures combine to evoke the Arctic Circle and the animals that inhabit it.

Hymn

Hymns as Poetry (ed. Samuel Carr)
Batsford 1980   125pp
See *Bir*. The reader is asked, for once, to forget the hymn tunes and consider the verses as poetry.

If

If You should meet a Crocodile (sel. Diane Elson)
World's Work Ltd 1979   105pp
Jingles and nonsense verses presented with brightly coloured illustrations to attract reluctant readers. [Not *Croc*]

Ima

Images and Impressions (ed. Kolawole Ogungbesan and David Woolger)
OUP 1978   153pp
Follows *Rhy*. Many interesting and unusual poems for the teacher seeking

new material. The notes may overweigh the books for children's own enjoyable reading.

Imp

improving on the blank page (sel. deborah cook and keith gallasch)
Rigby Ltd (Australia) 1972   114pp
Two Australian teachers chose a wide variety of verses to help children to write. A teacher's book outlines their methods and gives samples of the resulting work.

Inn B

A Book of Creatures (Mary Innes)
Franklin Watts 1975   48pp
A light-hearted animal bestiary from Armadillo to Zebra.

In O I – II

Inside, Outside: If I had a Hammer and *Inside, Outside: Sky with Diamonds* (comp. Frank Plimmer)
MacMillan 1972   48pp each
Strikingly unusual presentation of varied verses.

Iron I – IV

Iron, Honey, Gold I-IV (ed. David Holbrook)
CUP 1961 repr. 1967   73, 100, 99, 160pp
Interestingly original anthologies. Adolescents quickly appreciate much, and can be helped to enjoy those poems that are more difficult.

Isle

The Isle of Gramarye (ed. Jenifer Westwood)
Rupert Hart-Davies 1970   93pp
Poetry of magic – enchanters, fairies, elfs, ghosts – lavishly illustrated in black and white.

Jon S

The Spitfire on the Northern Line (Brian Jones)
Chatto Poets for the Young 1975   32pp
Direct accounts of experiences and reminiscences of childhood.

J Vo I – IV

Junior Voices I – IV (ed. Geoffrey Summerfield)
Penguin 1970 repr. 1976   88, 88, 116, 109pp
These were refreshingly different from earlier anthologies, with their exciting illustrations, and wealth of songs, riddles, jingles *and* poems, and have been much imitated in style and content, but hold their own.

Lee L

Late Home (Brian Lee)
Kestrel Books 1976   55pp
Events and emotions in a boy's daily life – particularly moments of alarm – are evocatively expressed.

236

Like

I Like this Poem (ed. Kaye Webb)
Puffin 1979 repr. 3 times by 1980   192pp
Unique; the only book of poems chosen by children as their own favourites
(with reasons for the choice). Skilfully arranged and edited; good for all ages.

Lin T

Tower Blocks: Poems of the City (Marian Lines)
Franklin Watts 1975   47pp
Short rhythmic poems echoing the experiences of the city child. Vividly
illustrated by Charles Keeping.

Liv

Living Poets (comp. Michael Morpurgo and Clifford Simmons)
John Murray 1974   115pp
Modern poems from many countries, about childhood, adolescence, and
adult life. Remarkable because the poems have substantial content, but are
yet accessible to others than 'A' stream.

Lolli I – IV

Lollipops I–IV (chosen Brian Thompson)
Longman Young Books 1971, 73   64pp
Unique book, where carefully-chosen poems, enjoyed by both junior children
and adults, are richly illustrated. In four parts – Birds, People, Animals,
Weather.

Lon

London between the Lines (comp. John Bishop and Virginia Broadbent)
Simon Publications 1973   176pp
Poems and verses about London life and landmarks over the last 300 years.
Useful mainly as social history.

Look

Looking Glass (ed. Eric Williams)
Edward Arnold 1973   96pp
Successor to *Drag* and predecessor of *Tap* and *Tel*, sophisticated contempor-
ary poems for older students, mainly about people and relationships.
Admirably produced, with appropriate photographs.

Low G

Green Magic (Edward Lowbury)
Chatto Poets for the Young 1972   42pp
Delightful poems, both realistic and nonsensical, attractively illustrated.

Many

Many People, Many Voices (ed. Norman Hidden and Amy Hollins)
Hutchinson of London 1978   159pp
Poetry from all the English-speaking world – a much wider choice than
usual, though there are several well-known pieces.

May K

The Knockabout Show (Gerda Mayer)
Chatto Poets for the Young 1978   32pp
Very short poems, often nostalgic, of the exiled poet's personal experience.

McG S

Sky in the Pie (Roger McGough)
Kestrel Books 1983   88pp
Roger McGough's latest collection; snatches of verse with more than 'a grain or two of truth among the chaff'.

McRo

You Tell Me (Roger McGough and Michael Rosen)
Kestrel Books 1979   72pp
Typical work by each poet; everyday events seen through boys' eyes; often ending with a comic twist.

Mer, Mer R, Mer RR

The Mersey Sound (Adrian Henri, Roger McGough, Brian Patten)
Penguin Modern Poets 10: *Mer* 1967 repr 7 times by 1973; *Mer R* revised 1974 repr. 5 times by 1982; *Mer RR* revised 1983.
The 'first blast of the Trumpet' which established the Liverpool poets and their new sound. Still very popular; mainly adult themes; much love-making. Over 250,000 copies sold. See *NV*.

Merry

The Merry-Go-Round (chosen James Reeves)
Heinemann 1955 repr. 6 times by 1969 Puffin 1967 repr. 1969   384pp
A poet's choice; excellent anthology for all juniors. Many traditional rhymes, jingles and nursery ballads.

Mil NS

Now We Are Six (A. A. Milne)
Methuen 1927 repr. 45 times by 1971   101pp
See *Mil VY*. And all ages can enjoy the wit and technical accomplishment in, for example, 'The Old Sailor', *Mil NS 36*.

Mil SV

Silly Verse for Kids (Spike Milligan)
Puffin 1959 7th imp. 1975   61pp
Accurately titled. Snatches of attractive nonsense verse for Milligan fans. Children who won't touch 'poetry' will read these.

Mil VY

When we were very young (A. A. Milne)
Methuen 1924 repr. 78 times by 1977   100pp
If chosen with discrimination, many of Milne's verses still delight young children.

Mod

Modern Poetry (sel. John Rowe Townsend)
OUP 1971 repr. 1973, 1979   222pp
Nearly 150 varied poems, adult in tone, arranged to picture aspects of life in the last 50 years. Relevant modern works of art increase the reader's pleasure.

Mov

Moving Along: Poems of Travel and Transport (coll. Barbara Ireson)
Evans Bros 1977   123pp
A skilled anthologist's choice of everything to do with transport, real and fantastic, on land, sea, air and space.

Mus

The Music of What Happens (ed. Derwent May)
BBC 1981   151pp
75 poems from *The Listener* 1965–80, by 48 poets, chosen from the 750 published in that period. For senior pupils who wish to tackle modern poetry seriously.

My R

My Kind of Rhymes (comp. John Smith)
Burke Publishing Co 1972   96pp
A successor, for younger children, to the very popular *My V*. Pleasant, rather conventional verses, easy to read and learn

My V

My Kind of Verse (comp. John Smith)
Burke 1965   204pp
Poems selected by the English Speaking Board for Junior Examinations, and therefore particularly good for speaking aloud. Gentle in general tone, but varied and with some unfamiliar pieces.

Nar

Narrative Poems (ed. Michael Harrison and Christopher Stuart-Clark)
OUP 1981   188pp
Outstanding collection of interesting narrative poems for the middle years of the senior school, ranging from fanciful legend to factual history.

Nas C

Custard and Company (Ogden Nash)
Kestrel Books 1979   128pp
Light verse in his inimitable style – children particularly enjoy his animals.

ND

The New Dragon Book of Verse (ed. Michael Harrison and Christopher Stuart-Clark)
OUP 1977 repr. 1978   267pp
Poems old and a few new, of high quality, arranged by theme. Chosen for ages 9–15, but clearly for academic children, and even adults.

Night

Nightmare: Poems to Trouble your Sleep (Jack Prelutsky)
Adam and Charles Black 1978   40pp
Scary pictures heighten the blood-curdling effect of verses on such creatures as the vampire, the ogre and the ghoul.

Non

The Book of Nonsense (chosen Roger Lancelyn Green)
J. M. Dent and Sons Ltd 1956 repr. 1973   260pp
Useful compendium for the teacher, lots of Carroll, Lear, Hoffman and many other older writers of light verse.

NS

New Ships (ed. D. G. Wilson)
OUP 1975 repr. 1980   96pp
West Indian poems, opening windows on another world, compiled by nine 'teachers and educationists' for the 7th, 8th and 9th grades of Jamaican Secondary Schools. Many attractive poems.

NV

New Volume (Adrian Henri, Roger McGough, Brian Patten)
Penguin 1983   144pp
Successor to *Mer, Mer R, Mer RR*, the latest poems of the Liverpool poets. Adult manner and themes.

Once

Once Upon a Rhyme (ed. Sara and Stephen Corrin)
Faber 1982   157pp
101 poems chosen for young children, attractively printed, and useful for all juniors.

ONe W

Words Words Words (Mary O'Neill)
World's Work 1967   63pp
Verses, many useful mnemonics, about words, language, parts of speech and punctuation marks – a painless way to learn grammar!

Oral

The Penguin Book of Oral Poetry (ed. Ruth Finnegan)
Penguin Books 1978   548pp
Unique collection in translation from 13 different cultures – Gond, Eskimo, Malay, etc. – with helpful introductions to each section.

OSF

Oh, Such Foolishness (sel. William Cole)
Methuen 1980   96pp
50 nonsense verses by contemporary writers, exactly as title.

Out

Out of the Blue (chosen Fiona Waters)
Fontana Lions 1982   96pp
Weather poems by poets old and new; children can find poems to match each day's weather.

Out Sc

Out of School (comp. Dennis Saunders)
Evans Bros 1972 3rd repr. 1973   94pp
Out of school activities for juniors celebrated in lively verses, some of them by children.

Over

Over the Bridge (ed. John Loveday)
Kestrel Books 1981 also Puffin   110pp
Unique. Original poems written for children at Whitchurch School by leading contemporary poets.

Owe S

Salford Road (Gareth Owen)
Kestrel Books 1979   79pp
Vivid accounts of childhood experience, a boy's view of home, school, football *et al.*

Ox Con

The Oxford Book of Contemporary Verse 1945–80 (chosen D. J. Enright)
OUP 1980   299pp
Substantial selections from the works of 40 moderen poets. Very little overlap with, for example, *Fab Mod*. Often difficult.

Ox CV

The Oxford Book of Children's Verse (chosen Iona and Peter Opie)
Oxford 1973   407pp
A comprehensive classic collection for teachers, of 332 poems specifically written for children, from Chaucer to Ogden Nash. Notes on authors and sources. Many early poems still appeal.

Ox Dic

The Oxford Dictionary of Nursery Rhymes (ed. Iona and Peter Opie)
OUP 1951 revised 1952 repr. 1966   467pp
Gives the history and sources of the best 500 rhymes and songs for the youngest children. Children reading for themselves should have *Ox NR* or *Puf NR*; this is the teacher's book.

Ox LV

The New Oxford Book of Light Verse (chosen Kingsley Amis)
OUP 1978 repr. 1979
250 poems exemplifying the description of 'light verse' as 'true humour expressing itself in perfectly-controlled rhyme and rhythm'. Much parody.

Ox NR

The Oxford Nursery Rhyme Book (ed. Iona and Peter Opie)
OUP 1955 repr. 4 times by 1966   224pp
The most complete collection available: 800 rhymes and songs. Invaluable for teachers of the youngest children.

Ox PC

The Oxford Book of Poetry for Children (ed. E. Blishen)
OUP 1963   168pp
Excellent choice of real poems, designed for younger children but appropriate at many ages. Should be in every class library. Attractive illustrations by Brian Wildsmith.

Pac

A Packet of Poems (picked by Jill Bennett)
OUP 1982   112pp
Very brightly illustrated collection of very light verse about food in its many aspects.

Pat A

The Animals Noah Forgot (A. B. Paterson)
Arlington Book with Lee Cooper 1982   71pp
'Banjo' Paterson (1864–1941), singer of the people, scenery and animals of Australia, provides verses refreshingly different about dingo, wombat, etc.

PC

The Poetry of Childhood (ed. Samuel Carr)
Batsford 1981   93pp
Poems covering four centuries; illustrations from early brasses to Rembrandt, Mary Cassatt, Lucien Freud. Modern youngsters may be amused by the romanticising of childhood.

Peng B

The Penguin Book of Ballads (ed. Geoffrey Grigson)
Penguin 1975   374pp
Comprehensive collection of all the favourite ballads plus some unusual poems.

Plea

Poetry for Pleasure (made by Ian Parsons)
Chatto 1977   352pp
Ranges from memorable jingles and rhymes to profound adult poetry. A storehouse of great variety, written during 400 years.

P Life I – IV

Poetry and Life I – IV (ed. N. Grisenthwaite)
Schofield and Sons Ltd 1961 repr. 1969   76, 80, 80, 96pp
Poems both attractive to children and of real quality. One of the best and most popular sets for juniors, expertly graded.

Pluc

Plucking the Rushes (comp. D. Holbrook)
Heinemann 1968   118pp
Something different: translations of Chinese poems, amazingly relevant
though sometimes 1000 years old.

Poems and **Poems II**

Poems and *Poems II* (ed. Michael Harrison and Christopher Stuart-Clark)
OUP 1979, 1980, 1981 twice   96, 128pp
Specifically for ages 10–12, but much for older readers. Excellent choices;
some awkward to read because printed (fashionably) on top of photographs.
Teacher's book available, and a cassette for *Poems II*.

P Rail

The Poetry of Railways (sel. Kenneth Hopkins)
Leslie Frewin 1966   271pp
Not as grandly produced as *Rail*, but contains an immense amount of railway
verse by poets including William Wordsworth, D. H. Lawrence, Dannie
Abse, Wilfred Owen, Robert Frost.

Prel I – IV

Preludes I – IV (ed. Rhodri Jones)
Heinemann Educational 1971   56, 56, 49, 54pp
Well-chosen groups of poems (I Families, II Work and Play, III Weathers,
IV Five Senses) for middle schools. Good relevant photographs. Helpful
teacher's book available.

P Scot

Poetry of Scotland (ed. Douglas Dunn)
Batsford 1979   127pp
Superbly produced and illustrated collection of little-known poems, mainly
on landscapes.

PT I – VI

Poetry Themes (comp. C. G. Stokes)
Collins 1973 repr 1976   32pp
Available in packs of six slim booklets each containing a variety of poems,
some unusual, on a theme. Booklets – I In a Seashell, II Witches and
Charms, III Streets Ahead, IV Airs and Graces, V Everyone is Somebody,
VI Stray or Stop.

P Tale

The Poet's Tale (chosen A. A. Evans)
University of London Press 1957 10th impr. 1975   224pp
A standard collection of narrative poems, from ballads through Chaucer and
Crabbe to Auden, much used as a set book.

Puf M

The Puffin Book of Magic Verse (chosen Charles Causley)
Penguin 1974   239pp
The familiar and the new, ranging over 900 years and including Polish, Red
Indian and Anglo-Saxon verses on an ever-fascinating theme.

Puf NR

Puffin Book of Nursery Rhymes (ed. Iona and Peter Opie)
Puffin 1963 often repr.   219pp
Selected from *Ox NR* some 150 rhymes, plus 200 more. Admirable for young
children to read for themselves.

Puf Q

A Puffin Quartet of Poets (E. Farjeon, J. Reeves, E. V. Rieu, I. Serraillier)
Puffin 1958 often repr.   190pp
Delightful poems by poets who excel in writing for young children.

Puf SB

The Puffin Song Book (comp. Leslie Woodgate)
Puffin 1956 repr. 5 times by 1970   194pp
Traditional songs grave and gay, and familiar carols. (For unfamiliar carols
see the two Penguin Books of Christmas Carols.)

Puf V

Puffin Book of Verse (ed. E. Graham)
Puffin 1953 repr. 16 times by 1975   96pp
A conventional but wide selection; a standby for the teacher to draw on.

Puf Y

The Young Puffin Book of Verse (comp. Barbara Ireson)
Puffin 1970 often repr.   206pp
Enjoyable, memorable verses for younger children, arranged in helpful
sequence.

PW

The Poet's World (ed. James Reeves)
Heinemann 1948 15 reprints 2nd edn. 1972   392pp
A poet's selection of adult poetry for upper forms, including some well-
chosen passages from the Old Testament.

Rail

The Poetry of Railways (ed. Samuel Carr)
Batsford 1978   88pp
See *Bir*. 'And all unseen. Romance brought up the 9.15'. Railway poems and
pictures, British and American, in great variety. (see also *P Rail*)

Rain

The Swinging Rainbow (sel. Howard Sergeant)
Evans Bros 1969   128pp
Varied verses grouped by subject; attractive book for juniors to explore by
themselves.

244

RAP

Reading African Poetry (ed. Robert Fraser)
Collins 1975   96pp
Designed for African secondary schools, but much for the teacher interested in race relations in Britain.

Rat

The Rattle Bag (sel. Seamus Heaney and Ted Hughes)
Faber 1982   498pp
Some 500 poems in alphabetical order, mainly modern, chosen by two distinguished poets. A storehouse for the teacher of older academic pupils.

Ree C

Complete Poems for Children (James Reeves)
Heinemann 1973   195pp
Handy to have in one volume, illustrated by Ardizzone, these poems by a favourite writer.

R Eig, R Nine, R Ten

Round about Eight; Round about Nine; Round about Ten (sel. Geoffrey Palmer and Noel Lloyd)
Frederick Warne 1972, 1976, 1979   128, 102, 104pp
Verses varying in difficulty and quality; simple rather prosaic illustrations.

Rhy

Rhymes and Rhythms (David Woolger and Kolawole Ogunbesan)
OUP 1978   155pp
Primarily a poetry course for the first three years in African secondary schools, with many African oral poems in English translation. Interesting choice of English poems for the purpose. Its successor is *Ima*.

Rhyme I –IV

Rhyme and Rhythm I – IV (comp J. Gibson and R. Wilson)
Macmillan 1965 repr. 1967   54, 70, 86, 131pp
Four lively, well-graded and well-produced collections of poems and songs to delight juniors. Attractive illustrations.

Ring

The Ring of Words (ed. A. MacGillivray and J. Rankin)
Oliver and Boyd 1970   150pp
Scottish poetry, many unfamiliar pieces, some in Lowland Scots. Refreshingly different in language and style.

R Nine

See *R Eig*

Root

How Strong the Roots (col. Howard Sergeant)
Evans Bros 1981   96pp
Multi-national! Adult poems of exile, emigration, homesickness, pilgrimage, return home. Many very moving.

Ros M

Mind your own business (Michael Rosen)
Andre Deutsch 1974   95pp
The first of three very successful collections of Michael Rosen's verses. A child's-eye view of daily life, in a child's language.

Ros W

Wouldn't You Like to Know (Michael Rosen)
Andre Deutsch 1977   95pp
Ingenious chatty pieces, some only two lines long. Family life and fantasy. Aptly illustrated by Quentin Blake. Very popular with upper junior boys.

Ros Y

You Can't Catch Me (Michael Rosen)
Andre Deutsch 1981
More popular idiosyncratic pieces spoken by various members of the family. Many too short to itemise. Pages unnumbered.

RR

Rhyme and Reason (chosen R. O'Malley and Denys Thompson)
Chatto and Windus 1957 18th impr. 1976   224pp
For the oldest pupils, a particularly good selection of some 200 sensitively-chosen poems of many periods and styles, grouped by subject.

R Six

Round about Six (sel. Margaret G. Rawlins)
Frederick Warne 1973   96pp
Attractive miscellany graded in three sections, many choices excellent for saying aloud together. Pleasant proportion of comic verses. Large print for youngest readers.

R Ten

See *R Eig*

SAS

Songs for all Seasons (chosen Rosemary Dobson)
Angus and Robertson 1967   177pp
Australian poems for ages 9–14, giving a strong impression of life in the outback, its trials and triumphs, its drovers, bell-birds and swagmen.

San E

An English Year (Clive Sansom)
Chatto Poets for the Young 1975   32pp
Straightforward verses about country experiences and people.

Say

First I Say This (ed. Alan Brownjohn)
Hutchinson 1969   160pp
Over 150 poems, many unusual, chosen by a poet to give special pleasure when read aloud.

Sca A

The Apple-Raid (Vernon Scannell)
Chatto Poets for the Young 1974   32pp
Vivid re-creation of physical experiences (boxing, tree-climbing, eating apples) as well as evocation of feeling and thought.

Scene

The Scene (ed. Fred Inglis)
CUP 1972   200pp
Prose passages and (mostly long) poems about landscape and townscape; often difficult but rewarding to the able reader.

Scot

A Scots Kist (pub. Burns Association)
Oliver and Boyd 1979   154pp
Anthology of Scots passages and poems, refreshingly unusual and robust. A little help from the teacher, and the ample glossary, should reduce the language barrier.

Sea

The Puffin Book of Salt-Sea Verse (comp. Charles Causley)
Kestrel Books 1978   272pp
Ample, varied and comprehensive collection about every aspect of the sea and seamen. Virgil to present day.

Sec

A Second Poetry Book (comp. John Foster)
OUP 1980   128pp
See *Fir*. Fresh lively verse, all twentieth century, with references to tower blocks, T.V., helicopters. Illustrations rather garish for some tastes.

Seven

Worlds: Seven Modern Poets (ed. Geoffrey Summerfield)
Penguin 1974   288pp
Well-chosen poems by Causley, Gunn, Heaney, Hughes, MacCaig, Mitchell and Morgan. Illuminating biographies and photographs.

Shad

Shadows and Spells (ed. Barbara Ireson)
Faber 1969   111pp
Eerie poems for all ages, but primarily for readers of 8–12. Ghosts, witches and charms during 350 years.

Sort

All Sorts of Poems (ed. Ann Thwaite)
Angus and Robertson 1978   128pp
Methuen 1980
Many poems specially written by well-known poets for the compiler's annual *Allsorts* (1968–76) with others written recently. Much that younger children can enjoy with their elders; many good verses too short to list.

Star

A Single Star (comp. David Davis)
The Bodley Head 1973   94pp
An unhackneyed collection of Christmas poems, arranged from just before Christmas Eve to Epiphany.

Ste CG

A Child's Garden of Verses (Robert Louis Stevenson)
J. M. Dent 1960 repr. 3 times by 1973   128pp
A classic: the genuine voice of a child. Available in many editions. This edition also contains Stevenson's 'Moral Emblems', with his own woodcuts.

Str

Strange to Tell (comp. Dennis Saunders)
Evan Bros 1974   96pp
Varied narrative poems; mainly easy to read and enjoy.

Strict

Strictly Private (chosen Roger McGough)
Kestrel Books 1981   185pp
A bold modern collection for unconventional teachers of older pupils.

Stuf

I Like that Stuff (sel. Morag Styles)
CUP 1984   95pp
Unique anthology of poems which do not appear elsewhere, and come from many cultures. Selected by an experienced and inspiring teacher. Many verses by children.

Sun

The Sun Dancing: Christian Verse (comp. Charles Causley)
Kestrel Books 1982   248pp
Invaluable collection of unusual poems on religious themes for older children.

Tale

I'll Tell You a Tale (Ian Serraillier)
Kestrel Books 1973 revised 1976   120pp
Poems by Seraillier and traditional ballads, an attractive mixture.

Tam

Talk of the Tamarinds (ed. A. N. Forde)
Edward Arnold 1971 repr. 1974, 80, 81   104pp
Mixture of new, unanthologised poems, many from the Caribbean, with some tried favourites. For secondary schools.

Tap

Tapestry (ed. Eric Williams)
Edward Arnold 1974   96pp
Varied selection from haiku to contemporary Australian verse; primarily for

10–12s but something for all ages. Brilliant photographs. See also *Drag, Look, Tel.*

TCN

Twentieth Century Narrative Poems (comp. M. Wollman)
Harrap 1954 repr. 12 times by 1976   176pp
Widely-used collection of 35 longer poems, written 1900–1950; for secondary schools. Helpful notes.

TD

Time's Delights (chosen Raymond Wilson)
Hamlyn 1977   176pp
Beautifully produced and illustrated, poems connected with aspects of Time, arranged in interesting groups.

Tel

Telescope (ed. Eric Williams)
Edward Arnold 1974   96pp
Equally interesting successor to *Drag*, for ages 14–16, designed to encourage 'vigorous discussion and sensitive writing'. Suggestions for teaching. See also *Look, Tap.*

Ten

Ten Twentieth Century Poets (ed. Maurice Wollman)
Harrap 1957 repr. 13 times by 1969   222pp
Very popular selection for top forms, with helpful notes on each poet.

Theme

Themes I – VII (ed. Rhodri Jones)
Heinemann Educational 1969 often repr. 70pp each
I *Men and Beasts*, II *Imagination*, III *Conflict*, IV *Generations*, V *Sport and Leisure*, VI *Men at Work**, VII *Town and Country*. Excellent slim booklets with (mainly recent) poems grouped by subject. Much unusual material, relevant to modern living. Teacher's book provides ideas for teaching and supplementary book-lists. (*ed. John Skull)

Third

A Third Poetry Book (comp. John Foster)
OUP 1982   128pp
See *Fir.* Slightly more complicated verses than in *Sec.* Amazingly varied styles of layout and illustration. Liked by children.

This W

This Way Delight (ed. Herbert Read)
Faber 1957 repr. 1970   192pp
Poems mainly lyrical and fantastical, many impossible to classify. Much 17th century material. A delightful collection.

Tho

Thoughtshapes (coll. Barry Maybury)
OUP 1972 repr. 1974, 76   157pp
Successor to the popular and useful *Wordscapes* (*Word*) on the same lines.

Time

Poets of Our Time (ed. F. E. S. Finn)
John Murray 1965 repr. 4 times by 1974   160pp
About a dozen early poems by each of Betjeman, Causley, P. Dickinson, Dyment, Hughes, Kirkup, Laurie Lee, Norman Nicholson, Alan Ross, R. S. Thomas.

Tol T

The Adventures of Tom Bombadil (J. R. R. Tolkien)
George Allen and Unwin 1962   64pp
Poems by and for Hobbits, supplementing *Lord of the Rings* but also worth reading for themselves.

Touch I – V

Touchstones I – V (ed. Michael and Peter Benton)
English Universities Press 1968, 69, 69, 71, 71   176, 192, 176, 180, 212pp
Five handsome, substantial volumes of well-chosen and ingeniously arranged poems and pictures, with suggestions for teaching. In *Book V* many poems too complex to classify, some on painful subjects, and interesting pairs for comparison in sixth forms.

TR

The Terrible Rain (sel. Brian Gardner)
Eyre Methuen 1966 3rd repr. 1978   227pp
Poems written 1939–45, by 119 poets, of whom nearly one-sixth were killed. A re-creation of war years at home and abroad. Much found nowhere else.

Trad

Traditional Nursery Rhymes and Children's Verse (coll. Michael Foss)
Michael Joseph 1976   184pp
Most useful collection for the teacher, mingling traditional rhymes with songs by Shakespeare, Blake and modern writers, most of them quite possible for young children.

Voi I – III

Voices I – III (ed. Geoffrey Summerfield)
Penguin 1968 still in print   160, 192, 190pp
Like *Junior Voices*, (*J Vo*), set a new fashion when it appeared. Extremely varied poems, lavishly and strikingly illustrated. Vol. III is virtually adult. Still an excellent series.

WAS

Words for All Seasons (chosen Malcolm Saville)
Lutterworth Press 1979   192pp
Popular author's choice of favourite passages, going round the year. A cheerful, wholesome book.

250

Wes N

Not to be Taken Seriously (Colin West)
Hutchinson 1982   96pp
As the title says! Nonsense verse with some witty and ingeniously rhymed accounts of 'hysterical' characters and impossible animals.

Wind

Words on the Winds: a book of ballads (comp. Dennis Saunders)
Evans Bros 1974   94pp
Well-known popular ballads, usually anonymous. Useful collection.

Wit

Witch Poems (ed. Daisy Wallace)
Pepper Press 1980   32pp
Like *Gi*, a well-produced and suitably-eerily illustrated collection which fulfils its title and is manageable for a child put off by big books. Some little-known American verses.

Word

Wordscapes (coll. Barry Maybury)
OUP 1970 repr. 1972, 74, 76   157pp
Unusual combination of prose, poems and pictures; includes much remarkably good children's writing, and is intended to encourage more.

World

My World: Poems from 'Living Language' (ed. Joan Griffiths)
BBC 1976   144pp
Verses from the popular Radio 4 programme, closely concerned with a child's world, poems about school, family life, friends.

Wri H

Hot Dog and other Poems (Kit Wright)
Kestrel Books 1981   72pp
Irreverent casual verses, often very short, about family life. Often very funny. Juniors find themselves reflected.

Wri R

Rabbiting On and other Poems (Kit Wright)
Fontana Lions 1978   95pp
Slight, amusing and ingenious verses, catching a boy's view of family, friends and pets, with some fantastical pieces also. Very popular. Posy Simmons illustrates fittingly.

Young

Fontana Lions Book of Young Verse (chosen Julia Watson)
Fontana 1973 10th impr. 1983   96pp
Splendid anthology for the youngest, to succeed nursery rhymes and give a foretaste of grown-up poetry. Quentin Blake's illustrations.

Zoo

A Children's Zoo (chosen Julia Watson)
Fontana Lions 1978   96pp
Animal poems and jingles of quality, divided under such headings as 'Six Feet and More', 'Four Feet'. Appropriate and attractive illustrations.

Index of poets